Advance Praise for

The Pentagon's Wars

"In unflinching detail, Mark Perry takes us behind the scenes of America's often tense civil-military relationship. The public and the national security community will want to ponder carefully the implications of this fascinating and engaging narrative."

—Richard H. Kohn, professor emeritus of history and peace, war, and defense, University of North Carolina at Chapel Hill, and former chief of Air Force history, US Air Force

"This is a hard-hitting insider's walk through the corridors of American power. Mark Perry marshals decades of interviews and applies his keen journalistic insight to grapple with a question that all citizens need to ask: Why can't the most powerful nation in the world achieve its strategic policy aims when it goes to war? He does a great service by explaining in clear, human terms the failures and the limits of American military power. A must-read."

—David E. Johnson, author of *Fast Tanks Heavy Bombers: Innovation in the U.S. Army, 1917–1945*

THE

PENTAGON'S

WARS

THE MILITARY'S UNDECLARED WAR
AGAINST AMERICA'S PRESIDENTS

MARK PERRY

BASIC BOOKS
New York

Basic Books
Hachette Book Group
1290 Avenue of the Americas, New York, NY 10104
http://www.basicbooks.com
@BasicBooks

Printed in the United States of America

First Edition: October 2017

Published by Basic Books, an imprint of Perseus Books, LLC, a subsidiary of Hachette Book Group, Inc.

The Hachette Speakers Bureau provides a wide range of authors for speaking events. To find out more, go to www.hachettespeakersbureau.com or call (866) 376-6591.

The publisher is not responsible for websites (or their content) that are not owned by the publisher.

Print book interior design by Amy Quinn

Library of Congress Cataloging-in-Publication Data has been applied for.

ISBN: 978-0-465-07971-1 (hardcover)

ISBN: 978-0-465-09310-6 (e-book)

LSC-C

10 9 8 7 6 5 4 3 2 1

For Amaya, Nayel, and Wilder

"What I fear is not the enemy's strategy, but our own mistakes."

— Thucydides,
The History of the Peloponnesian War

Contents

Bill Crowe's Warning

*"That's the ultimate. You know,
to win without fighting."*

Soon after the end of the Cold War, in 1991, it occurred to senior military officers that the demise of the Soviet Union was actually a military victory. Among this group was Admiral William Crowe, the eleventh chairman of the Joint Chiefs of Staff, who'd served during the Reagan and George H. W. Bush presidencies and was acknowledged as one of the most influential officers of his generation. An outspoken iconoclast and hulking figure, Crowe was celebrated in Washington for dishing out pithy homilies, or issuing homespun lessons to disbelieving senators. "Your mind is like a parachute," he once told a Senate committee. "If it won't open when you need it, it isn't much good." He added: "I have an open mind." When he was JCS chairman, Crowe cracked jokes with his military colleagues, especially during tense budget sessions or international crises. "He saved my sleep, my hair, my digestion and my sanity," Army chief of staff Edward C. Meyer, who served with him, said.[1]

But during an interview in Washington, DC, several years after retiring, Crowe turned suddenly serious, commenting on the Cold War's end in an interview that focused on the history he'd observed. "It's the ultimate irony, really," he said in his patented Oklahoma drawl, "but it's true: we not only won the Cold War, we did it without firing a shot. We did it without waging World War III." For a moment, Crowe seemed surprised by his own conclusion and then was lost in his own thoughts. "That's the ultimate," he added, wistfully. "You know, to win without fighting. Think of it. No military has ever done that."[2]

Born in Kentucky, Crowe grew up in Oklahoma during the Great Depression, the son of a hardworking lawyer. But Crowe was bored by Oklahoma and vowed that, if given the chance, he'd travel the world. He graduated from the US Naval Academy in 1947, but he wasn't a seagoing warfighter. He'd once commanded a diesel submarine, and that for only two years, and had actually turned down seagoing assignments with senior officers whose support he needed for promotion. He preferred to pursue his academic studies, notching a master's degree from Stanford and a doctorate, in politics, from Princeton.

But Crowe was much in demand by the Navy's senior officers, primarily for his ability to think creatively. It often got him into trouble. "For Chrissake," one of his Pentagon supervisors told him, "we didn't send you to Princeton so you could come back and tell us how to run the Navy." In fact, Crowe was more of a diplomat and Washington insider than a naval officer; he served as a naval assistant to President Dwight Eisenhower, was a naval adviser to the South Vietnamese during the Vietnam War, then became commander of US forces in the Pacific.[3]

Crowe got his big break in 1984 when he briefed President Ronald Reagan and his secretary of state, George Schultz, in Honolulu. As head of the US Pacific Command, Crowe provided a thumbnail sketch of the forces challenging the United States in the region, and what he recommended the US could do to counter them. Crowe's no-frills style impressed Reagan, with Schultz telling a colleague that Crowe's presentation "was the most comprehensive briefing" he'd ever heard during his time in government. The next year, Reagan appointed Crowe as JCS chairman, surprising nearly everyone in his service, who thought Admiral James Watkins, the chief of naval operations, would get the job.[4]

"Crowe's appointment is unprecedented," one of his colleagues, Admiral Eugene Carroll, noted at the time. "He is a political scientist, not a warfighter. He knows the limits of military power." In fact, while Crowe and Secretary of Defense Caspar Weinberger often disagreed on major budget and military service issues (Weinberger seemed intimidated by the more expressive Crowe, observers noted), they saw eye to eye on the issue of war and peace. Weinberger had once scoffed at a reporter who said he thought the Reagan defense build-up was dangerous and cost too much money. "Good lord," Weinberger explained. "We're not building up our military in order to use it, we're building up our military so that we don't have to." Crowe agreed.[5]

NOTHING IN CROWE'S official biography speaks to his enormous influence. During his tenure, Crowe presided over two events that would indelibly shape the American military over the next three decades. The first was the Revolution in Military Affairs (RMA), a technical revolution spurred by engineers, computer scientists, aerospace experts, military policymakers, and weapons developers in the early 1970s to "offset" the Soviet conventional threat in Europe. The United States could never match the numerical advantage the Soviets enjoyed in troops, tanks, and aircraft, but it could offset those numbers by fielding more lethal and more precise weapons and developing stealth technologies that would shield them from detection. The Soviet Union had more, but the US would have better. Much better.[6]

By the early 1980s the RMA was a reality, with the United States developing precision-guided munitions that eliminated the requirement of using dozens of bombs to destroy a single target, and perfecting stealth innovations that made fighter-bombers safe from enemy radar. The RMA transformed the nature of conflict, taking advantage of the advances in "network-centric warfare" that fielded laser target identification systems, remote-controlled drones, enhanced digital information assets, predator and surveillance weapons, and satellite-based positioning systems. The innovations spread through every service. The Soviets could not hope to compete, knowing that it would drive them to bankruptcy to even try. That is, in fact, what happened: the RMA won the Cold War, to use Crowe's phrase, "without firing a shot."

The second event was the passage of the 1986 Goldwater-Nichols Department of Defense Reorganization Act. Named for Arizona senator Barry Goldwater and Oklahoma congressman William Nichols, the law overhauled the US military command structure. While the legislation was intended to end the crippling interservice competition that hobbled military operations after World War II, it also reflected the RMA: the military's new weapons, RMA evangelists preached, placed a premium on lighter and more mobile forces, while requiring the Army, Navy, Air Force, and Marines to plan and fight together, or "jointly."[7]

Goldwater-Nichols also recast the responsibilities of the nation's military hierarchy by taking the heads of the Army, Navy, Air Force, and Marines out of the chain of command. The four service chiefs' sole responsibility now was to "organize, train and equip" the military. Under the new arrangement, the military chain of command went "from the President to the Secretary of Defense" to the unified combatant commanders—in Europe, North America, Africa, Latin and Central America, the Pacific, and Middle East, and to the three "functional" commands—for special operations, strategic nuclear weapons, and global force projection. That is, the US chain of command now bypassed the JCS altogether. They commanded no one.

But while Goldwater-Nichols took the JCS out of the command chain, it named its chairman "the principle military adviser to the President of the United States, National Security Council and Secretary of Defense," and established the position of vice chairman of the Joint Chiefs of Staff. At first, it was thought that the new law weakened the JCS chairman's influence, but that didn't happen, in large part because of William Crowe. Crowe strengthened the role of the Joint Staff (the JCS chairman's in-house think tank and policy implementer) and was a constant and persistent presence in the Reagan White House. Crowe understood the power that Goldwater-Nichols gave him as the one senior military officer with direct access to the Oval Office.

In many respects, Reagan's appointment of Crowe could not have come at a better time, despite the admiral's inherent conservatism. At first, Crowe was an RMA skeptic, doubting that its adherents could overcome service fears that their "big platforms" (aircraft carriers, bombers, and masses of tanks) would be sacrificed in the name of smaller and better. The precision weapons promoted by RMA enthusiasts were simply too expensive to purchase in large numbers, Crowe added. But eventually, Crowe endorsed the deployment of smaller and lighter units and the new technologies that the RMA made possible, as well as the concept of jointness—a reform he thought long overdue. In truth, Crowe was the first chairman to have spent most of his career as a joint officer. In military parlance, Crowe was "purple," a word that signaled the blending of Army and Marine green with Air Force and Navy blue. "I suppose I am more purple than anyone," he said. Finally, as Crowe later ruefully admitted, his early opposition to both the RMA and Goldwater-Nichols had turned out to be wrong. America's 1991 war to deliver Kuwait from Saddam Hussein's clutches had redeemed both. During Operation Desert Storm, the US military's new RMA-developed weapons and the streamlined leadership made possible by Goldwater-Nichols performed superbly.

The US military's expulsion of Saddam's forces from Kuwait, it turned out, was a kind of showcase for the RMA. In Desert Storm's first hours, the United States and its allies deployed stealth F-117 fighter-bombers and a fleet of radar-jamming aircraft, drones, and air-launched cruise missiles in an onslaught that demolished Iraq's military infrastructure. But it wasn't only the Air Force and Navy that benefited from this high-tech revolution. The Army's "Big Five"—the M1 Abrams main battle tank, the M2 Bradley infantry fighting vehicle, the AH-64A Apache attack helicopter, the sleek UH-60A Black Hawk transport helicopter, and the Army's Patriot Air Defense System—were all RMA products. In fact, the Iraqi army never had a chance: US ground formations saw the enemy sooner than the enemy saw them, had more sophisticated communications systems, used lasers to spot and destroy enemy tanks, navigated over the vast desert with the help of satellites, fired high-tech shells that easily pierced enemy tanks, and sported thermal mounts that lit up the battlefield.

Additionally, in Desert Storm, General Colin Powell (Crowe's successor as JCS chairman) had proven to be a strong commander, using his Goldwater-Nichols mandate to exert his influence with civilian leaders at the same time that he carefully managed the war's overly sensitive and sometimes volcanic ground commander, Army general Norman Schwarzkopf. Which is exactly what Goldwater-Nichols had intended. Powell was not in the nation's chain of command, which now went from George H. W. Bush to Defense Secretary Dick Cheney and then to Schwarzkopf, but that didn't matter. Powell exerted enormous influence, and all without issuing a single order. So it was that the RMA and Goldwater-Nichols triumphed.

Had they? Seated in his Washington office, his celebrated military career behind him, William Crowe praised both the RMA and Goldwater-Nichols. But then he shook his head and offered a corrective. What nagged at him, he said, was "the central question" of war and peace, and he worried that America would squander its opportunity as the world's lone superpower. There were two problems, he said. The first was that a professional, and inbred, military establishment would not be able to find in the future the same kind of leaders who had led it to victory in two world wars and a four-decade nuclear standoff. The second was "over-reach," the idea that America, now unchallenged, would somehow be able to shape the world as it saw fit. "Bending another culture to your will can't be done on the cheap," he said, "and very often it can't be done at all. It's fated to fail."[8]

The term *nation building* hovered on his lips, but instead he reprised his judgment on the end of the Cold War. The ideal, the "ultimate," as he said, "is to win without fighting." In the new world, where America was the unchallenged military power, that was the thing to do. Unfortunately, for the thirty years from Crowe's retirement to the end of Barack Obama's second term, the US military ignored Crowe's warning, engaging in a series of military adventures that cost it thousands of lives and trillions of dollars. What had happened, and why?

THE PENTAGON'S WARS is an attempt to answer that question by giving an account of the internal battles between America's highest-ranking military commanders and the nation's most powerful and senior civilian officials over the nearly thirty years since the end of the Cold War. The story begins with the military's internal squabbling over Operation Desert Storm, a victory ensured by the RMA and the passage of the sweeping Goldwater-Nichols reforms, but ultimately squandered, as key senior military officers believed, by an uncertain civilian leadership that failed to provide an answer to the most fundamental of questions: What next?

That question, and the attempt to answer it, plagued our nation's elected officials and military commanders for the next three decades, as America engaged in a series of interventions that saw US soldiers, sailors, and airmen (and women) fighting conflicts in Kuwait, Somalia, Haiti, Bosnia, Serbia, Kosovo, Sudan, Iraq (three times), Afghanistan (twice), and Libya. At the heart of these costly and controversial interventions are the virtually unknown behind-the-scenes battles pitting the nation's often recalcitrant, and quietly dissenting, military establishment against political leaders whose vision of a world made safe by American arms, with nations rebuilt according to our ideals, ignored Bill Crowe's warning: that such an effort was "fated to fail."

Fated to fail? How is that possible? The United States had emerged from the Cold War as the world's unchallenged military power and the globe's most productive economy, an event unprecedented in world history. Such power should have triumphed. Why didn't it? The answer lies, in part, in Bill Crowe's worry that the nation's military would not be able to find the kinds of leaders that had led it in its previous conflicts. It wasn't simply a matter of finding warfighters, for the US military provided the best combat and advanced leadership training of any military in the world, but rather of finding warfighters who understood Washington— and the value of politics and diplomacy. Even in World War II, the most effective of the nation's highest-ranking military commanders proved to be sophisticated political thinkers and adept diplomats, while in Crowe's era (and during the Cold War), visionary policymaking was most often the result of a strong partnership between the Pentagon's ranking civilian leader and the JCS chairman—the kind of partnership solidified between Crowe and Caspar Weinberger and later between Crowe and Weinberger's successor, Frank Carlucci.

But Goldwater-Nichols, for all its intentions, could not legislate visionary military leadership, enforce cooperative partnerships, or mandate reasoned dissent. So it was that, at key points in the thirty years from William Crowe's retirement to the end of Barack Obama's second term, the nation's top civilian officials purposely named military officers they believed they could control to head the JCS or lead the military services. The promotion of top military officers to influential policy positions rewarded agreement, and so stifled dissent. The result was that, at key points in America's wars, the heads of America's military services found themselves in a series of bitter conflicts with the chairman of the Joint Chiefs of Staff—and the president of the United States.

As crucially, while the 1986 defense reorganization law effectively and successfully streamlined the US chain of command, it opened a chasm between the JCS—those who organized, trained, and equipped the US military—and the nation's combatant commanders, who fought the nation's wars. The result was that while Goldwater-Nichols successfully dampened parochial interservice battles over defense dollars, it replaced that crippling conflict with another, pitting Pentagon officers who were focused on readiness against field commanders focused on winning battles. Additionally, while the military's combat capabilities were enhanced by the revolution in military affairs, the weapons developed to fight the Soviet Union in Europe were nearly useless when it came to fighting a dedicated, lightly armed, and hidden enemy, or to rebuilding a nation destroyed by American arms. For thirty years, America's elected officials have recoiled from any suggestion that the US military should be required to engage in nation building—and for thirty years America's elected officials have required the military to do exactly that. It never worked. Nation building has been and remains an ideal that, in Crowe's phrase, is "fated to fail."

And so the answer to the question of why it is that the RMA and the sweeping reforms of the 1980s were squandered in a series of seemingly endless interventions seems almost rhetorical, though the answer to the question of what happened and why lies not on the battlefields of southeastern Europe, East Africa, or the Middle East, but in the offices of the Pentagon. At the heart of this account are the generals and admirals who recruited, trained, equipped, and led the American military through two and a half decades of conflict, and the nation's most senior civilian leaders, who directed them. The debates waged inside the Pentagon and the White House, and between America's senior military leadership and our nation's policymakers, proved the difference between victory and defeat.

The Pentagon's Wars is not a recounting of America's recent wars, but a narrative account of the politics of war—the story of civil-military relations from Operation Desert Storm to the rise of the Islamic State. At its center is what one officer called "that great chasm" between American elected officials and those they command. Ironically, this nearly three-decade account starts with a victory—and a parade.

CHAPTER ONE

John Warden's War

"Why are we stopping? Doug?
Why are we stopping?"

O N JUNE 8, 1991, four months and twenty-two days after the beginning of Operation Desert Storm, General Norman Schwarzkopf led
a parade celebrating the victory down Pennsylvania Avenue. Dressed in
combat fatigues, Schwarzkopf marched at the head of a contingent of soldiers from the US Central Command (CENTCOM), while a squadron
of helicopters roared overhead. By prior arrangement, Schwarzkopf broke
ranks to salute President George H. W. Bush, who'd left the reviewing
stand to greet him. Schwarzkopf introduced Bush to his staff and then,
feigning surprise that he would even be asked, he joined the president
and other dignitaries to watch his troops march in review.

"And the friendly bear has made a lot of friends not just here, but all
over the world," celebrity announcer Willard Scott intoned to a national
television audience as Schwarzkopf greeted Bush. "A great American ambassador, a great American. We luv ya, we luv ya, General."[1] The description of Schwarzkopf seemed oddly over-the-top, but it fit the parade's
intent, which was elaborately choreographed not only to celebrate the

Desert Storm triumph, but to expiate the ghosts of the nation's defeat in Vietnam, then less than twenty years in the past.[2]

The chagrin over the parade's triumphalism was keen among senior military officers who'd served with Schwarzkopf during the war, for while nearly all of them admired the six foot four New Jersey combat veteran, none of them would have described him as a "friendly bear." Stormin' Norman, a nickname he wore with pride, was impatient, petulant, and volcanic. At one point during the war, Schwarzkopf's temper tantrums became so intense that Secretary of Defense Dick Cheney considered firing him, while Joint Chiefs of Staff (JCS) chairman Colin Powell repeatedly counseled him to control his rage. Finally, desperately, Powell assigned Lieutenant General Calvin Waller, who'd served with Schwarzkopf on and off for twenty years, to serve as Schwarzkopf's deputy while providing an essential damper for his notorious expletive-laced tirades.[3]

Waller arrived at Schwarzkopf's headquarters in Saudi Arabia in December 1990 to find the general's staff walking around with "a stunned mullet look." Schwarzkopf's explosions had rubbed everyone raw. Waller's solution was to suggest he be the buffer between the staff and Schwarzkopf, or as Schwarzkopf phrased it, the American triumvirate of Powell, Schwarzkopf, and Waller could replicate World War II's command arrangement of George Marshall, Dwight Eisenhower, and Omar Bradley, with Schwarzkopf slotted into Eisenhower's role. The more he thought about it, the more Schwarzkopf liked the sound of that: he always wanted to be like Eisenhower. Accordingly, Powell would be Marshall and Waller would be Bradley, the beloved World War II ground commander in Europe. That suited Norman just fine.[4]

Waller reluctantly agreed to Schwarzkopf's model, serving as a buffer between Schwarzkopf and his staff, and between Schwarzkopf and his two most important command subordinates: Lieutenant General Fred Franks (who headed up the Army's VII Corps) and Lieutenant General Gary Luck, the commander of the US XVIII Airborne Corps. This decided, Waller went to work, mediating Schwarzkopf's tantrums while soothing the traumas he left in his wake. Waller had seen all of this before: "I certainly understood what was required in working with Norman Schwarzkopf," he later noted. Schwarzkopf's staff officers might have been walking around with "a stunned mullet look," but Waller empathized with Schwarzkopf, who'd been the target of unrelenting pressure to accelerate the flow of US and coalition troops into the Persian Gulf and then plan a response should Saddam's army vault across the Kuwaiti border into Saudi Arabia. Back then, in August 1990, at US Central Command headquarters in Tampa, Schwarzkopf had directed his staff to develop options for retaliating against Saddam, but the options he was given proved starkly inadequate. Schwarzkopf was disgusted: "Not good enough," he shouted at his staff. "Terrible."[5]

The questions preyed on him: what should he do if Saddam began executing the hundreds of foreign nationals, including large numbers of Americans, he'd swept up—and then detained—in Iraq and Kuwait after his invasion? How should the United States respond to increasing Iraqi air incursions along the Kuwait-Saudi border? What should he do if Saddam began using chemical weapons? And if Schwarzkopf was ordered to lead a US offensive to expel Saddam's military from Kuwait, just how would he go about doing it? One of his staff officers suggested that, while waiting for reinforcements, Schwarzkopf could bomb Iraq's dams; another suggested that he take hostages of his own as bargaining chips ("Norm nearly exploded," a now retired staff officer remembers); while a third suggested the US threaten the use of tactical nuclear weapons. This left Schwarzkopf sputtering in disbelief: "Are you out of your fucking mind? God damn it, I want options, real options, not some fairy tale," he screamed.[6]

THE PROBLEM SCHWARZKOPF faced was that his Tampa staff was filled with intelligence and supply officers ("eggheads and bean counters," as Schwarzkopf described them), and hobbled by its devotion to implementing the AirLand Battle doctrine—the counterpunch, tank-heavy warfighting strategy the US military had adopted to defend Western Europe should the Red Army come pouring into West Germany. In many respects, as Schwarzkopf knew, the doctrine was outdated: the Red Army was not only not the threat it had once been, but the capabilities of the US military reflected the result of the far-reaching technological advances made possible by the Revolution in Military Affairs (RMA) during the 1980s. What Schwarzkopf wanted was a strategy that would take advantage of this technological dominance by projecting US military power into the heartland of an aggressor engaged in an attack-and-hold operation, like the one that Saddam had used to seize Kuwait. Additionally, while Schwarzkopf knew that the use of US airpower was his best option for deterring Saddam, General Albert "Chuck" Horner, his primary air commander, was spending eighteen-hour days overseeing Air Force deployments to the Gulf region.[7] He had little time for anything else, and certainly not for planning a war.

"It was about a week into the war," Schwarzkopf later remembered. "They [the Iraqis] had all the hostages and guests. There was a lot of rhetoric on how they better not hurt our guys or else. I am thinking retaliation. I want a list of options, minimal up to full-scale attack. If the president comes to me and says 'I have to retaliate,' I have got a platter to pick from."[8]

On August 8, six days after Saddam's legions swept into Kuwait, Schwarzkopf called JCS chairman Colin Powell to tell him that he wanted to speak with "whoever was in charge" of the air staff at the Pentagon. Schwarzkopf told Powell that he needed a team that could come up with air options to strike at the center of Saddam's power. Powell, in keeping with his "anything you want, Norm" practice, said that Schwarzkopf should call the Air Force vice chief of staff. He would know what to do, Powell said. So it was that, on that very afternoon, while seated at his desk in the Pentagon, Air Force general John M. "Mike" Loh picked up his telephone and heard the voice of Norman Schwarzkopf on the other end.[9]

Schwarzkopf was polite, but brusque. "We are doing a good job on AirLand Battle—on tactical application," he told Loh, "but I need a broader set of targets, a broader air campaign, and I need it fast, because if he [Saddam] attacks with chemicals or nuclear, I have got to be able to hit him where it hurts right away, and that is a strategic air campaign." Schwarzkopf paused for a moment, then continued. "All I'm getting out of my air team at MacDill [Air Force Base in Tampa] is this standard AirLand Battle stuff, you know, close air support, battlefield air interdiction, but nothing of a strategic nature. We can't go out piecemeal with an AirLand Battle plan. I have got to hit Saddam at his heart. I need it kind of fast, because I may have to attack those kinds of targets deep, that have value to him as a leader."[10]

"I could hardly believe what I was hearing," Loh remembers. "Here was an army commander talking like an airpower advocate." Loh told Schwarzkopf he could help. "I will take the lead in fleshing it out as best we can and bring it to you," he promised. "I need a day or two to make sure it works your problem, and I will bring it to you ASAP." Schwarzkopf was relieved. "Thanks," he said, "please hurry." In the years that followed, Schwarzkopf's call would be cited as evidence that, after years of bickering, the Army and Air Force had finally learned how to cooperate. In fact, however, Schwarzkopf's request sparked one of the most divisive controversies in US Air Force history. And it all started with Loh.

A 1960 Air Force Academy graduate, Loh was trained as an engineer and fighter pilot and had come up through his service with a reputation for never straying from Air Force orthodoxy. Brainy, with wavy jet-black hair, Loh was politically savvy, touching all the right bases as he ascended the Air Force promotions ladder. He had taught pilots, and been one, flying 204 missions in Vietnam while piloting an F-4 Phantom fighter. He had engaged in air-to-air duels with Soviet-made fighters over Vietnam and had landed with his jet riddled with shell holes, but somehow he'd survived. Loh had earned the Distinguished Flying Cross and then gone on to command fighter wings before becoming a graduate student in aeronautical engineering at MIT. In June 1990, two months before Schwarzkopf's call, he was named vice chief of staff of the Air Force, his service's second most powerful position.[11]

Loh's career was brilliant, but predictable—until Schwarzkopf called. After that conversation, Loh did what he'd never done before: he broke ranks with his fellow Air Force officers over how to fight a war. Loh's first call after talking with Schwarzkopf should have been to Lieutenant General Jimmie V. Adams, the Air Force's powerful deputy chief of staff for plans and operations. But, since Adams was on a scheduled leave, Loh made sure Schwarzkopf's request made its way to Colonel John A. Warden, a controversial airpower thinker whose views didn't fit with Air Force orthodoxy. Warden had a reputation for going outside of channels, a habit that made him known as "right turn Warden": when his ideas were rejected he simply made a right turn and circumvented the chain of command. Nor was Warden a member of any of his service's three power centers: the "fighter mafia" (who believed that tactical air assets should be used to destroy an enemy's forward units), the "bomber mafia" (who gained prominence for developing strategic nuclear plans during the Cold War), or the "Missileers" (the Air Force's self-styled nuclear elite). Warden viewed the power centers with disdain, convinced they erected artificial barriers inside the service. Moreover, the Air Force's fixation on AirLand Battle's close air support of Army formations, Warden believed, should be replaced by a more flexible doctrine that focused on strategic airpower and the war-fighting technologies of the RMA.[12]

By 1988, Warden's views had landed him in the Pentagon's basement, as head of a strategic planning office called Checkmate, an out-of-the-way group of logisticians, weapons specialists, and intelligence officers. Checkmate was in the Pentagon basement for a reason: the move sidelined Warden and his crew, with the real plans for future wars coming from the mafia staffs, the tactical and strategic offices headed up by the traditionalists. Adams was one of these, as were General Robert Dale "Bob" Russ, the head of the Tactical Air Command; General Michael E. Ryan, Russ's deputy (and the son of a former, and celebrated, Air Force chief of staff); and John T. "Jack" Chain, the head of the US Strategic Air Command. Mike Loh assumed that Adams, Russ, Ryan, and Chain would oppose anything Warden thought of, but he was confident he could circumvent them. Additionally, as Loh calculated, Warden had friends in high places, including Air Force chief of staff Michael Dugan, wunderkind policy analyst Lieutenant Colonel David Deptula, and the Air Force's influential civilian secretary, Donald Rice. "Get together with your intel people and get this done," Loh told Warden, adding that he should be prepared with a briefing within twenty-four hours.[13]

Warden went to work and the morning after his talk with Loh, he briefed the Checkmate team on his thinking, drawing five concentric circles, or "rings," as he called them, on a blackboard in his team's briefing room. The first and smallest circle represented Iraq's leadership, the second represented Iraq's war-fighting resources, the third Iraq's infrastructure, the fourth its population, and the fifth ring Saddam's military force. Warden then rolled out a map of Baghdad and used pushpins to designate actual targets inside the first ring. There were forty-five pins in all, which Warden compared to forty-five similar targets in Washington, DC—including the White House, Capitol, Pentagon, CIA, and FBI headquarters. Destroy the Baghdad targets, Warden told his staff, and you destroy Saddam's capacity to wage war. Finally, Warden announced that he'd decided to call his plan "Instant Thunder," to distinguish it from the ineffective Rolling Thunder air campaign the United States had used in Vietnam. Rolling Thunder had lasted three and a half years and failed. Instant Thunder would take just six days, and would succeed. It would win the war.[14]

* * *

WARDEN'S INSTANT THUNDER idea didn't surprise Checkmate's planners, who were as dedicated to their boss as any group of true believers. Hidden away in the Pentagon's catacombs, behind a vaulted door numbered BF 922, they kept Warden's gospel alive, while overhead (as they might have it) the Air Force empire they served lurched ineffectively along, unaware that a revolution in airpower was brewing just beneath it. Their catechism was Warden's 1988 book *The Air Campaign*, in which Checkmate's director argued that "command is the true center of gravity" in war, a concept so revolutionary that it overturned two hundred years of military thinking.[15]

For decades, the US military's view of war had mimicked the ideas contained in Prussian colonel Carl von Clausewitz's 1832 treatise *On War*, which argued that to defeat an enemy you must attack his strength, what Clausewitz called his "center of gravity." For Clausewitz, and for US commanders, an enemy's center of gravity was invariably his military. So it was that, during the American Civil War, General Ulysses S. Grant had told Abraham Lincoln that so long as General Robert E. Lee's army remained in the field, the Confederacy would survive. Defeat Lee's army, Grant said, and you defeat the Confederacy. The same held true in both world wars, where the defeat of Germany and Japan was predicated on the destruction of their military strength. Germany's center of gravity wasn't Berlin or Hitler, any more than Japan's was Tokyo or the Emperor—it was the German Wehrmacht and the Imperial Japanese Navy.

Warden turned Clausewitz on his head.[16]

For Warden, the center of gravity in the Gulf War was not Saddam's army, but Saddam's elaborate network of Baghdad-based command, control, and intelligence centers—Iraq's leadership ring. This inner ring was surrounded by four others: a system ring (of oil and other resources), an infrastructure ring (transportation), a population ring, and a ring that protected the other four—a military ring. But the inner ring, the leadership ring, was the key; destroy it and the Iraqi military would be leaderless, demoralized, unsupplied, and, inevitably, unable to fight. Warden's five rings theory was revolutionary. For nearly two hundred years, the United States had attacked its enemies from the outside-in, defeating their armies and navies in order to destroy their command centers. The RMA of the 1980s changed all of that, and it was just what Norm Schwarzkopf needed: it was now possible to destroy an enemy from the inside-out, discarding costly step-by-step ground offensives in favor of direct attacks on an enemy by using precision weapons that would strike over the horizon from a war's opening moments. Warden's approach was a new and unique approach to the conduct of war—"an air- and leadership-centric paradigm diametrically opposed to the AirLand Battle doctrine," as a later commenter phrased it. Airpower was no longer relegated to a supporting role: it was a war's centerpiece.[17]

Warden presented his five rings plan to Loh on August 9, then flew to Tampa with a group of officers to brief Schwarzkopf on August 10. Warden knew that in order to sell his plan, he needed to speak to Schwarzkopf in terms that would appeal to an Army officer, so during the flight he sketched out two historical analogies. The first was a reference to Germany's plan to conquer France in the opening days of World War I, in which the German army had launched a powerful right hook through Belgium. The goal of the Schlieffen Plan, named for German count Alfred von Schlieffen, was not to destroy the French army, but to bypass it. And the plan would have worked, if only the German high command had not weakened its punch. Warden's second analogy cited General Douglas MacArthur's surprise landing in Inchon, well in the rear of the North Korean army, during the Korean War. The landing unhinged the North Koreans, sending them retreating, pell-mell, back up the Korean peninsula. Warden's plan would have the same effect. "You have a chance," Warden told Schwarzkopf, "to achieve a victory equivalent to or greater than MacArthur's Inchon landing—by executing an air Inchon in Iraq."[18]

Surrounded by his bleary-eyed staff, Schwarzkopf harrumphed his way through Warden's briefing, but he liked what he heard. Warden punctuated his presentation with a right hand that swooped in on Baghdad, while his immobile left hand shook ever-so-slightly with each dropped bomb. He was a true believer, an officer who was actually excited about what he was saying. As Mike Loh later described it, while the Warden briefing was "heavy on theology, but short on application," it was laced with battlefield metaphors that had Schwarzkopf and his staff visualizing Saddam and his minions cowering under a rain of bombs. The air campaign would be decisive, Warden said, and it would only take six days to complete. That's fine, Schwarzkopf told Warden. Come back in a week with more details.

Mike Loh was relieved. The first obstacle standing in the way of Warden's plan had been overcome. But Loh also knew that opposition to Instant Thunder was growing among the Air Force's three mafias, whose complaints had reached into Colin Powell's office. Predictably, Warden's most outspoken critic was General Bob Russ, his sidekick Michael Ryan, and the group of planners they headed at the Tactical Air Command at Virginia's Langley Air Force Base. At Loh's direction, Russ had provided three officers to help Warden, but since reporting to him they'd done nothing but snipe at his efforts. Why are we here? they asked Warden. We're the ones who should be doing the planning, not you. Additionally, Russ had directed his staff to write a plan to counter Warden's. The problem with Instant Thunder, Russ told his staff, was that it ignored the threat to Saudi Arabia from Saddam's army. It lacked "tactical perspective." Saddam's army needed to be hit hard, Russ said, in Kuwait—not in Baghdad. His staff followed Russ's lead, calling Instant Thunder "Distant Blunder."[19]

When Warden returned to the Pentagon on the night of August 10, he was told of Russ's criticism and was handed an outline of his counterproposal. He shrugged it off. What Russ was proposing, he concluded, was a replay of what had happened in Vietnam, complete with bombing pauses. It was AirLand Battle writ large: it was almost as if the RMA hadn't happened. That hadn't appealed to Norman Schwarzkopf and it wouldn't appeal to JCS chairman Colin Powell, whom he was scheduled to brief the next morning. "Don't get bogged down in the tactical details," Warden told his staff, and don't worry about Adams, Russ, Ryan, or Chain. After all, Schwarzkopf had already approved the plan.[20]

BUT INSTANT THUNDER took a hit the next morning when Warden briefed Powell and a room full of senior officers who were the most influential leaders of the US military. Warden's audience included Admiral David E. Jeremiah, the vice chairman of the JCS; General Michael P. C. Carns, the director of the Joint Staff; Lieutenant General George L. Butler, the head of the JCS's plans division; and Lieutenant General Thomas Kelly, Powell's acerbic J-3, head of the JCS's powerful Operations Directorate. Powell's office was too small for a briefing, but everyone squeezed in tight, with Powell motioning them to their chairs. Warden had a right to be nervous.

This was a constellation of stars, with Powell, Jeremiah, Carns, Butler, and Kelly arrayed in chairs in front of him, while their aides stood in a line along the walls. Mike Loh, who accompanied Warden along with Lieutenant General Robert M. Alexander, the Air Force's planning director, thought the room stifling. The crowd was intimidating. While Warden's presentation had been tweaked since he'd briefed Schwarzkopf, he remained convinced the historical analogies he'd used with the CENTCOM commander would appeal to Powell, an Army officer rubbed raw by the incrementalist approach used to fight in Vietnam. As Warden had predicted, Powell was pleased by Instant Thunder. It was everything that Rolling Thunder wasn't. Immediate, overpowering, relentless. "Good plan, very fine piece of work," Powell said when Warden was finished.[21]

If the briefing had ended then, Instant Thunder would have been adopted and Warden would have been dispatched to Saudi Arabia to implement it. But Powell had some questions. Could Warden have the plan finalized by August 22? Warden answered that he could. Powell then focused on deployment flows, wondering aloud whether the United States could have the air assets in place in Saudi Arabia by September 1. Warden had an answer ready for every question. Powell nodded approvingly, looked down at his notes, and then up at Warden. "Okay, it is day six and the strategic campaign is finished. Now what?" Warden was puzzled. There was no "now what." If the plan was put into effect, it was likely the Iraqi military would be in full retreat. "This plan may win the war," he said. "You may not need a ground attack. I think the Iraqis will withdraw from Kuwait as a result of the strategic air campaign."[22]

Warden's response was a blunder. A good military planner never assumes anything, and while Warden had been careful to say that his air campaign "may win the war," there was no assurance of that. Which is what Powell wanted: certainty, or something as close to it as he could get. He bored in on Warden. Powell said he was confident that Warden's Instant Thunder would cut out "the guts and heart" of Saddam's military, but he wanted a plan that would also destroy "Saddam's hands," his elite Republican Guard armored divisions, on the ground in Kuwait. "I won't be happy until I see those tanks destroyed," Powell told Warden. "I do not want them to go home. I want to leave smoking tanks as kilometer posts all the way to Baghdad."[23]

Warden summoned all the courage he could muster. It would be a mistake to rewrite Instant Thunder to target the Iraqi military in Kuwait, he warned. The United States should instead mount a psychological operations campaign to get the Republican Guard to turn on Iraq's leader. Leaving Saddam's army intact was the key, because then it could be used to overthrow him.

Unease spread through the room as Warden faced Powell. Here was an Air Force officer, a colonel no less, shaping a political campaign. Warden, as his Air Force detractors had often complained, was "out of his lane." Warden, sensing he was losing his audience, tried to explain himself. He looked right at Powell. "General," he said, "one of the things we really need to be careful about is that if there is some action on the ground, we cannot re-role the strategic air campaign. We made that mistake in World War II, and we do not want to do that again."

A sudden chill descended on the room. Mike Loh shifted uncomfortably in his seat. "This man has a talent for trouble," Jimmie Adams had told Loh, and now here it was. Big trouble. "Oh, shit," Loh thought. Warden had not only touched a nerve, he had slurred an officer whose reputation was so hallowed that it ranked just below that of Washington in the Army's pantheon of leaders. No one in the room, not even Navy admiral David Jeremiah, missed Warden's meaning. In 1944, Supreme Allied Commander Dwight Eisenhower, whose portrait hung in the hallway leading to Powell's office, had directed that the then US Army Air Forces "re-role" its priorities from the strategic bombing of Germany to the destruction of transport lines in France in advance of the Normandy landings. The Air Force leadership had bitterly fought the directive, until Eisenhower threatened to resign. The Air Force lost that battle, but the claim that the sainted Eisenhower had botched the European air campaign was a part of Air Force lore, which held that Germany might have collapsed months sooner if only Ike, that dolt, had listened to them. For Army leaders such a view was blasphemy. Powell stared at Warden and said nothing, letting him off the hook. But Lieutenant General Thomas Kelly, the Joint Staff's powerful operations director, was much less forgiving.[24]

"Air power has never worked in the past by itself," he said, dismissing Warden's analogy. "This is not going to work. Air power cannot be decisive." Kelly bit off each word as he said them: "this . . . is . . . not . . . going . . . to . . . work." Loh, fearing that Warden's plan was suddenly in danger, changed the subject, refocusing the discussion on Warden's strategic concept. This was an integrated plan, he said, and had been used before. He cited Israel's successful air campaign in the Bekaa Valley in 1982, adding that Instant Thunder was more extensive than the US Linebacker II campaign, which had targeted Hanoi for eleven days in 1972. Powell responded that he knew that Instant Thunder was an integrated plan, but he was opposed to "just sitting around" waiting for Saddam to surrender. "I cannot only recommend a strategic air campaign to the president," he added. Loh was now seriously worried, fearing that Powell would insist that hitting Iraq's inner ring be accompanied by a tactical air offensive in Kuwait.[25]

Ironically, Loh was saved by Admiral Jeremiah, an unlikely ally, who suggested the United States focus on the strategic campaign first, then follow it by hitting the Republican Guard in Kuwait. The two operations would be sequential, satisfying the Air Force while meeting Powell's requirements. Warden saw his opening, and he took it. Instant Thunder, he said, would target Iraq's leadership and its command and control centers, while Instant Thunder II would torch Saddam's tanks. Powell nodded and had the final word. There would be two plans, he said, and (as he insisted) both would be joint plans, involving all the services. Then, to make it clear, he repeated his major requirement: Instant Thunder II would turn Saddam's tanks into smoking hulks. Powell then directed Warden to provide a more detailed briefing to Schwarzkopf before heading to Saudi Arabia to brief Chuck Horner, the air commander in Saudi Arabia. Powell also told Warden that he wanted a shorter presentation of Instant Thunder that he could provide to the president. None of this was a request. "Yes sir," Warden responded.

Warden was pleased by the meeting, though not completely. He agreed with Loh that in spite of Powell's endorsement, the JCS chairman didn't really believe that Instant Thunder would be decisive enough to pry Saddam's army from Kuwait. Powell had humored Warden ("Very good. Fine piece of work."), then set out to subtly undermine his basic premise. This was Powell at his best, agreeable, but always getting his way, so that at the end everyone went away happy. Warden and his team were praised, their plan was endorsed, the Army had been allowed to slam the Air Force, the Navy had played the role of the reasonable mediator—and Powell had arranged it all. Or, as Warden concluded, Powell had shaped an air campaign that was precisely the opposite of what Warden actually intended. For while Instant Thunder would go forward, the real test for Warden's Checkmate team was to shape a strategic campaign knowing that, after six days of bombing, they would be forced to implement Powell's plan, not theirs. In the end, Warden's vision of Instant Thunder was of burning buildings in downtown Baghdad, while Powell's was of burning tanks in the deserts of Kuwait and southern Iraq.

Warden's greatest fear was that conceding Powell's "now what" question would force him to draw the sting from Checkmate's strategic offensive, re-rolling air assets to focus on Kuwait, the fifth and least important of Warden's five rings. So when he returned to his offices in the basement of the Pentagon, he turned the planning of Instant Thunder II over to Colonel Emery Kiraly, his assistant, with the admonition that any plan to destroy Saddam's tanks in Kuwait ("the operational campaign," as it was called) not take assets away from Warden's strategic campaign in the skies over Iraq. That should have been enough, but Instant Thunder II nagged at him, even after he'd iced his victory by waving off Russ and Ryan's "Tac spies," who presented their plan to him after his return from Powell's office. It was a sweet victory. He looked at the Russ and Ryan plan and threw it on his desk. "It's been decided not to use that," he said.

Warden could have allowed Powell's "now what" question to nag at him, and under any other circumstance he might have. But Powell was the boss, and that was that. So he swallowed his pride and decided to bask in Powell's approval. Then too, convincing Powell was a unique triumph, for Air Force officers had spent years being slighted by the Army, whose leaders would always remind them that, until 1948, they had actually been in the Army. While Warden and his team would never say so explicitly, there was a redemptive quality to the Checkmate triumph. Back in 1944, Carl Spaatz, the head of the US Army Air Forces in Europe, had been forced to cede to Eisenhower's wishes, curbing his strategic vision to the Supreme Commander's wishes. Now, as a result of Warden's work, the Air Force could prove what it always knew to be true—that airpower could win a war all by itself. This was Warden's vision: that after six days of Instant Thunder, Saddam's dictatorship would unravel, with the Republican Guard forces throwing down their weapons and surrendering. And the US Army would have sat through the whole thing in Kuwait, and not have fired a shot. The war would be over, won.

JOHN WARDEN EXPECTED disagreement from his own service, and he got it. Two days after his briefing of Powell, General Jimmie Adams, the Air

Force's powerful deputy chief for plans and operations, returned from leave and lit into him. Adams believed that Warden had engineered the whole thing: he'd hypnotized the gullible Loh, set up the briefing for Schwarzkopf, and then wheedled a meeting with Powell; he'd made another one of his legendary right turns, circumventing Adams and the chain of command. Adams made his views known when Warden gave him the same briefing that he'd given the JCS, showing open disdain and picking away at his conclusions. Adams insisted that Warden reverse the order of his air sequencing; the attack on the "inner ring" should follow the air attack on Saddam's army. Adams made the suggestion as close to a direct order as he could. Warden shook his head. That wasn't what Powell or Schwarzkopf wanted, he said, and he wouldn't do it. "We don't want a half-assed air campaign," he told Adams. Adams could hardly believe what he was hearing. "Right," he said, "but [we] also don't want to leave those Iraqi forces in place to kill 200,000 soldiers."[26]

While Adams outranked him, and had been designated by General Thomas Kelly as the liaison between Checkmate and the JCS, Warden went on with his work as if Adams didn't exist. But that wasn't so easy for Warden's supporters, including Air Force lieutenant general Robert Alexander, the JCS's deputy chief for plans and operations. This was interservice arm wrestling at its finest: Adams needed to sideline as many of Warden's supporters as he could, so he simply cut Alexander out of the planning process, what Alexander called "putting me in the penalty box." Despite this, the Adams-Warden fight was less personal than it looked. While Adams disliked Warden, his views reflected the concerns of a large number of officers who worried that the reason Warden hadn't answered Colin Powell's "now what" question was because he couldn't. So quietly, Warden sketched out the details of hitting the Iraqi army to his deputy planner, Colonel Emery Kiraly—first, gain control of the air over Kuwait, then hit any chemical weapons depots in Iraq, then destroy Iraqi command and control centers, and, finally, destroy the armored forces of the Iraqi Republican Guard. Warden then conceded to Adams that he would include Instant Thunder II in his briefing if Schwarzkopf asked for it.

By August 14, when Warden briefed Air Force chief of staff Michael Dugan, his plan had become far more detailed. While Warden retained Instant Thunder's essential character, his briefing slides now included the JCS logo, a signal that this had been approved at the top. Additionally, the plan's initial tasking order included assets from all the services: this was now a "joint plan," as Colin Powell had directed. The JCS imprimatur made a difference. In the days following the Powell briefing, Warden's staff gained access to dozens of experts on Iraq and harvested invaluable intelligence on the Iraqi military from White House national security experts, as well as senior officials from the CIA, National Security Agency, and National Intelligence Council. The Checkmate staff grew, from dozens of people to over two hundred, as planners from the Army, Navy, and Marines flowed in.

Michael Dugan liked Instant Thunder, and he liked Warden. More easygoing than Adams or Russ, Dugan was an unusual Air Force officer. Unlike many of his colleagues, he didn't have a background as a scientist (his advanced degree was in business administration), he'd graduated from West Point (and not the Air Force Academy), he wasn't a part of an Air Force mafia, and, most importantly, he maintained strong working relations with his service's innovators—those who were on the cutting edge of the RMA. But Dugan's personal qualities also included a sophisticated sense of the politically possible. He'd purposely stayed away from the Adams-Warden brawl, calculating that the sheer force of Warden's arguments would carry the day. That was apparent when Warden finished his briefing. But Dugan had ideas of his own that reflected his finely tuned political sense. Attacking the inner ring might be enough, Dugan speculated, but he was concerned with Saddam's chemical weapons stockpile and directed Warden to set aside a team to study the issue. "Be bold and imaginative," he told Warden, a comment that hardly seemed necessary. And he issued a warning. Schwarzkopf might support the plan, he said, but Warden was bound to have problems selling it to Chuck Horner, the Air Force's commander on the ground in Saudi Arabia.[27]

The next day, August 15, Warden briefed Air Force secretary Rice on the plan and then, on the night of August 16, went back over the briefing with Major General James Meier, the Joint Staff's deputy director. Meier was a heavyweight, the JCS's eyes and ears, so when Meier suggested changes in his briefing, Warden and his team complied. But it was tough going. "There is not enough detail here," Meier railed after Warden briefed him. "You cannot expect to take this to the CINC [Schwarzkopf, the commander in chief]. I mean, the CINC wants a war plan. He wants to know what the details are. This just is not adequate for a four star."[28] Warden tried to comply, but in the end he and Meier even argued about who would present the briefing. Meier wanted to take center stage, but Warden dug in his heals. Meier could introduce him, but he was giving the briefing, Warden insisted. The next day, in the CENTCOM amphitheater at headquarters in Tampa, Schwarzkopf agreed. As Meier appeared at the podium to introduce Warden, Schwarzkopf glowered. "I want to hear the Colonel," he announced.[29]

A military briefing is an art form, a dramatic narrative that sets a hook, then reels in the listener. Warden was a master, and began his talk with a zinger. "Instant Thunder is an intense, focused air campaign, that will incapacitate the Iraqi leadership and destroy Iraq's military capabilities," he began, then showed his first slide. "What it is not, is a graduated long-term campaign plan designed to provide escalation options to counter Iraqi moves." Schwarzkopf leaned forward. No one needed to translate: this would not be Vietnam.

Thirty slides later, Warden called on Colonel James Blackburn, the director of targeting at the Air Force Intelligence, Surveillance and Reconnaissance Agency. Blackburn's style contrasted nicely with Warden's, as he presented Checkmate's ten target sets in a flat, businesslike monotone. But his payoff nearly brought Schwarzkopf out of his seat. He took an aerial photo of an Iraqi command and control center out of an envelope and handed it to the CINC. He explained what the target was and how the Air Force would destroy it. When Blackburn was finished, Warden summed up the plan. There would be two attacks on the first day, he said. The first would start one hour after sunset, the second would start at two hours before sunrise. Saddam faced a wave of destruction. There would be 1,200 air sorties against Iraq's inner ring involving thirty fighter-bomber squadrons, four bomber squadrons, and one special squadron of stealth F-117s. US pilots would fly 700 sorties in each of the next five days following the initial attacks. By day six, Warden said, Saddam's capacity to wage war would be eliminated.[30]

Schwarzkopf posed some questions: How did the plan deal with Iraq's lethal, surface-to-surface Scud missiles? How did Warden plan to "deconflict" aircraft in the skies over Iraq? And finally: "How many men will we lose?" Warden answered each question, and then the final one: "We do not have any precise figures as yet," he said, "but in my professional judgment, we are looking at ten to twenty aircraft the first night." When one of Schwarzkopf's aides speculated that the number would be higher, Warden responded: "I am a volunteer to fly the lead aircraft in the lead raid." Warden then waited for the inevitable query—how would Instant Thunder deal with the Iraqi military? The question came from Schwarzkopf's deputy. "You've ignored the Iraqi Army in Kuwait," Lieutenant General Craven C. "Buck" Rogers announced. Warden started to answer, but was interrupted. "I am not worried about the ground forces in Kuwait," Schwarzkopf said. "This," and his right index finger thumped the plan, "this is what makes the United States a superpower. This uses our strengths against their weakness, not our small army against their large army. Our airpower against theirs is the way to go. That is why I called you guys in the first place."[31]

And after a moment, he stabbed his index finger at Warden. "You guys have got me so excited about this."[32]

AIR FORCE GENERAL Chuck Horner, Schwarzkopf's air commander in Saudi Arabia, didn't like John Warden and he didn't like his plan, which was obvious from the moment that the Air Force colonel showed up at his office in Riyadh on August 20. Despite its name, Horner thought that Instant Thunder was just another idea cooked up in Washington by the "airpower airheads." Horner had first seen the plan a week before Warden's arrival, and he'd thrown it against the wall. He wanted to do that same thing now, but now he also wanted to throw Warden against the wall. He raised his voice, his finger stabbed the air, his body leaned forward. Warden didn't seem to understand that Saudi Arabia could be overwhelmed at any minute. Saddam's military was right there, just across the border. What did he plan to do about them? It was just fine for Warden to ignore Saddam's tanks, but the colonel had the luxury of sitting at a desk in Washington, while Horner had to think about them every day. Horner was barely civil. "It sounds like a decapitate the snake plan," he told Warden.[33]

A minute later, while Warden attempted to mount a defense, Horner lit into him. "We could be looking out the window right now and see the Iraqi tanks coming into Riyadh," he shouted. Warden responded that Horner was being overly pessimistic. There was no way that Saddam would survive in the face of America's power. Horner flashed, but remained silent—and Warden apologized. It was wrong of him to question the judgment of the commander on the ground. Horner eased off, but just barely. "If folks in Washington want to fight this war, tell them to come to [Saudi Arabia]," Horner said, then turned the knife, citing Warden's biggest critic. "Jimmy Adams knows that you don't fight from Washington," he concluded.[34]

And with that, Warden was ushered unceremoniously from Horner's presence, his plan shattered. Or not quite. While Warden was ordered back to Washington, he was told to leave the three aides who'd accompanied him—Dave Deptula of Rice's staff, Ben Harvey of the Air Force strategy division, and Ron Stanfill, a Checkmate planner—behind in Riyadh. Deptula, who'd put flesh on Instant Thunder's operational annex, was the key. Brilliant, tough-minded, and savvy in the ways of the Air Force hierarchy, Deptula was as opinionated as Warden, but never couched his views as pronouncements. That made all the difference. The day after Warden's departure, Deptula gave the Instant Thunder briefing to Air Force general Buster Glosson (Horner's trusted in-house planner), a deceptively brilliant and profane ("He would never say, 'report to my office,'" one of his aides notes, "it was always 'get your ass in here.'") North Carolinian who knew anyone who was anyone. Glosson told Deptula that he liked Warden's plan, liked the idea of raining bombs on Saddam's inner ring, but it needed more work. "84 targets is too few," Glosson wrote in his diary that night.[35]

After the briefing, Glosson ordered Deptula to stay at "the Black Hole" in Riyadh, where Glosson's staffers made their plans, and work with him to meet Horner's objections. On August 26, Glosson and Deptula presented their revised briefing to Horner, paying special attention to Horner's air options if Saddam's tanks came across the border. Horner grudgingly approved the plan and told them to make it a part of the air tasking order for the war's first twenty-four hours. There was one other minor change, and Horner raised his voice: "I never want to hear the words Instant Thunder again," he said. And so it was that Instant Thunder lost its political sheen, becoming "Offensive Campaign, Phase I."

The Navy and Marines were even harder to sell than Horner. Glosson and Deptula traveled to Bahrain to brief Vice Admiral Henry Mauz. Mauz wasn't impressed. The Navy's air arm, based around aircraft carrier task forces, had traditionally targeted an enemy's air defense system first. What was the point of an attack on Baghdad if Saddam could shoot back? Marine Corps major general Royal Moore was also skeptical. The F-117 was overrated, he said. Precision weapons? The Air Force had used the F-117 against two targets in Panama back in 1989, and it had failed to hit either. Precision weapons my ass, he said. But because neither service's air arm was strategic, the Air Force had the last say, and Glosson overruled their objections. Glosson's enthusiasm for the air plan also didn't help in selling it, as naval officers were schooled in their service's tradition of understated professionalism. Sometimes you had to lean forward to hear a Navy officer speak. They seemed never in a hurry, never used the words "fast" or "quickly." It was always, "with alacrity." It was their way, their culture, the way they commanded. But it wasn't Glosson's. Soon enough, Navy officers were calling him "Bluster Glosson."[36]

In mid-September, the fight over the air campaign shifted back to Washington, where Warden's ideas were debated during a series of contentious meetings in the tank, the understated rectangular conference room in the Pentagon where the JCS meet. With Deptula and Glosson in Saudi Arabia, and Warden in semi-exile in the Pentagon basement, Air Force deputy chief of staff Mike Loh became the air campaign's primary defender. "I vigorously defended our leadership role in the Tank during September and October, when the other chiefs realized the Air Force was dominating the plan," Loh recalls. "The Navy wanted to divide the airspace into route packages the way it was done in Vietnam. . . . The Navy wanted to control all air action in the east from carriers in the Persian Gulf, and in the west from carriers in the Red Sea. . . . The Marine Commandant argued forcibly to take the lead with an amphibious landing from the Persian Gulf through Kuwait. The Army Chief did not like the idea of the Air Force operating independently."[37]

Loh's confrontations in the tank brought him eyeball to eyeball with the most influential and powerful senior officers in the military, including Powell's colleagues on the JCS. Loh was able to stand up to them because of his familiarity with what had happened in the 1980s, during the RMA. Two technical advances would make the difference, Loh told them: the arrival of stealth technology, which shielded fighter-bombers from radar detection, and the development of precision-guided munitions. "Airpower had to fight its way into the lead," Loh says. "We had to convince our critics that a rebirth of airpower took place in Vietnam emphasizing the asymmetric application of stealth, precision weapons, and night attacks."

Even after the JCS and the Joint Staff had had their cut at it, the Warden-Glosson-Deptula plan was a target for skeptics. The Navy and Marines called it "a prescription for disaster"; Horner thought the F-117 wouldn't work (and called its spit and polish pilots "a bunch of prima donnas"); the Navy lobbied for the inclusion of its ship-launched cruise missiles; while the Army insisted the plan include a special operations raid to destroy Saddam's early warning radar system in southern Iraq. Glosson agreed with all of this, but the avalanche of requests drove him to distraction. While Glosson went out of his way to ensure that everyone felt a part of the planning process, by mid-September, the plan's target list had ballooned to 12 sets of nearly 200 targets each. Additionally, at Schwarzkopf's insistence, the air campaign was now divided into four phases: over Baghdad (the "Strategic Air Campaign"), in Kuwait ("Air Supremacy in the Kuwaiti Theater of Operations"), in the lead-up to the ground campaign ("Battlefield Preparation"), and against the Iraqi Republican Guard (the "Ground Offensive Campaign").[38]

Along the way, Glosson in Saudi Arabia and Warden in Washington worked through a series of difficult technical problems: how to mount a tactical and strategic deception program, how to destroy Iraqi air-jamming radars, how to determine aircraft payloads, how to measure the effectiveness of stealth technology, which aircraft would be used to target Saddam's chemical weapons stockpiles (and whether the intelligence identifying them was any good), how to neutralize Iraq's Scud missile launchers, how to acclimatize air crews to desert conditions, shaping an identification system for downed pilots, how to best map Iraq's air defense system, how to deploy air rescue crews, whether to use the Marines Corps A-6E Intruder fighter to destroy Iraqi air defense systems, the most effective way to destroy Iraq's Soviet-made surface to air missiles (SA7s, 9s, 13s, and 16s), the proper use of drones and decoys, whether to use the Air Force's F-111 electronic jamming aircraft in advance of attacks by the F-117—and dozens of others.

But the work was paying off. In mid-September, Horner told Schwarzkopf that he had enough air assets in Saudi Arabia to conduct a seven-day war while, in Washington, Glosson reported to Powell that the air plan he had put in place could be executed the next day. Schwarzkopf and Powell were pleased and endorsed Glosson's plan, and Chuck Horner was relieved: he no longer imagined Saddam's tanks rumbling through the streets of Riyadh.

Then the unexpected happened. On a return flight to Washington after a briefing by Glosson in Saudi Arabia, Air Force chief of staff Michael Dugan told reporters that the US air campaign would target Iraq's command and control facilities as well as Saddam and his family. "If push comes to shove," he said, "the cutting edge will be in downtown Baghdad," and then added that the Air Force would strike "centers of gravity where airpower can make a difference early on."[39] When Secretary of Defense Cheney read Dugan's comments he was furious. Dugan made it sound like what was happening in Saudi Arabia was an Air Force show. Powell called Dugan at home on Sunday, September 16, and accused him of leaking the campaign plan. Dugan was summoned to Cheney's office the next morning. "I want your resignation by noon," he said.

THERE WAS ONE final test. Having gained the confidence of Horner, Schwarzkopf, and Powell, Glosson now had to sell the plan to the president. On October 11, Glosson appeared before Bush and his top national security aides at the White House: Vice President Dan Quayle; Secretary of State James Baker; national security adviser Brent Scowcroft and his deputy, Robert Gates; Undersecretary of Defense Paul Wolfowitz; and Bush's chief of staff, John Sununu. Powell and Cheney, who'd signed off on the plan, joined the group. Glosson was accompanied by Marine major general Robert Johnston, Schwarzkopf's chief of staff; Army lieutenant colonel Joseph Purvis, the ground campaign planner; and Richard Francona, from the Defense Intelligence Agency.[40]

Francona went first, providing a noncontroversial summary of Saddam's military deployments. Glosson followed, detailing the air packages for the war's first day and brandishing photos of Saddam's command centers. He then ticked off a list of Baghdad targets, saying that Iraq's leadership would be decapitated. At the end of the briefing, Secretary of State Baker said he didn't like the word "decapitate." It would raise uncomfortable questions among America's Arab allies, he explained. Glosson agreed: Saddam's regime would be "incapacitated." Bush commented that a successful air campaign might make an invasion of Kuwait unnecessary. This was not what Colin Powell wanted to hear. "I have to tell you, Mr. President," he interjected, "that it will not meet your objectives. I cannot assure you that Iraqi ground forces will be out of Kuwait, just because we do an air campaign." The group then focused on technical issues—the position of Navy assets, the likely success of the new stealth technology, the use of Turkish air bases. This was good news for Glosson: the president was sold.

But while that was true for the air campaign plan, it was not for the Army's ground campaign plan. Lieutenant Colonel Purvis, a war planner who'd graduated from the Army's prestigious School of Advanced Military Studies (whose graduates anointed themselves "Jedi Knights"), was only halfway through his briefing when Brent Scowcroft (who'd served thirty years in the Air Force and retired as a lieutenant general) began to shift in his seat. "Why straight up the middle?" he asked. He gestured at Purvis's map of Iraq's Kuwait defenses. "Why don't we go around?" Powell provided the answer: "Logistics," he said. "We don't have enough force to go around." Scowcroft didn't answer, but Cheney could read his mind: if we need more troops, then let's get them. Scowcroft corralled Cheney after the briefing. "This is a bad plan," he said. He used other words: unimaginative, predictable, foolhardy. Cheney agreed.[41]

In Riyadh, Schwarzkopf blew a gasket, but was most upset by Powell's report that one of the White House participants had compared him to General George McClellan, whom Abraham Lincoln had once complained had "the slows." Schwarzkopf was enraged. "Tell me who said that?" Schwarzkopf, who much preferred being Eisenhower than McClellan, demanded. "I'll call the son-of-a-bitch on the phone right now and explain the difference between me and McClellan if they're so stupid."[42] He slammed his desk, then slammed it again. Powell flew to Saudi Arabia on October 21 to hold Schwarzkopf's hand and to review his campaign plan. Powell argued that the VII Corps, from Europe, should be a part of the attack. Schwarzkopf agreed, saying that such a massive force could cut straight into the Republican Guard. "No," Powell said, "they go out here." Standing before a map of the region, he put his index finger on Saudi Arabia's far western desert. He stabbed at the map. "Here. They go right here," he said.

By mid-December, the "left hook" was in place, with US troops pouring into Saudi Arabia from Europe and moving west, into the desert. When the ground campaign began, the US VII Corps (four American divisions, the 1st British Division, plus the Army's strike force, the 2nd Armored Cavalry Regiment) would be the key, sprinting north and then pivoting to take on Iraq's elite Republican Guard units. They would be guarded on their left by the XVIII Airborne Corps, which would add weight to the VII Corps attack and pivot with it. The deployments were massive. The VII Corps alone fielded "forty-eight thousand five hundred vehicles and aircraft, including 1,587 tanks, 1,502 Bradley Fight Vehicles

and armored personnel carriers, 669 artillery pieces, and 223 attack helicopters."[43] In all, the VII Corps' total strength was 142,000 soldiers,
while the XVIII Airborne Corps deployed 116,000. The two corps would
act as a pincer, trapping the Republican Guard between them. Then the
VII Corps would kill it.

And that is exactly how it worked, or nearly so.

During the early morning hours of January 17, 1991, the battleship
USS *Missouri* opened Operation Desert Storm by firing four Tomahawk
cruise missiles from its station in the Persian Gulf into downtown Baghdad. At the same moment, US aircraft flooded the skies over Iraq, focusing on destroying the targets in John Warden's first concentric ring,
including Saddam's all-important air defense system. In Riyadh, meanwhile, Norman Schwarzkopf manned the telephones in his command
bunker, receiving reports on US air strikes while punching the air with
his fist, his voice booming with elation. "God damn it that's great," he'd
exclaim. Across town, Chuck Horner sifted through the air reports, giving Schwarzkopf hourly updates. At sunrise, Horner cataloged the air
campaign's first day: nearly seven hundred coalition aircraft had been
sent over Iraq and almost all of them returned home. Schwarzkopf was
elated. In Washington, John Warden sat at his desk, imagining Saddam
and his commanders hunkered down in a Baghdad bunker while their
nation collapsed around them.[44]

By the second day of the air campaign, Saddam's air defense system
had been shattered. By Day 6, the United States and its coalition partners
had flown eight thousand sorties against targets in Baghdad and southern
Iraq. By February 3, the allies had flown forty thousand missions, and by
Day 40 the US Air Force had flown more missions in Iraq than had been
flown by the Eighth Air Force in Europe in a two-year period in World
War II. The destruction of Iraq's armor in Kuwait (what was called "tank
plinking") began two days after the attacks on Baghdad. By February 14,
nearly one month into the war, US and coalition aircraft had destroyed
over 4,000 tanks, over 2,800 other armored vehicles, and one-third of
Iraq's artillery pieces. But not everything had gone as planned.

One day before the start of the air war, Schwarzkopf had suffered
an emotional meltdown, turning on Buster Glosson as Glosson was describing the first hours of the coming attack. Schwarzkopf, his jaw set,
noted that there weren't any attacks on the Republican Guard by B-52
bombers in the war's first hours. Instead, Saddam's tanks were going to

be targeted by F-117s. Schwarzkopf was livid, saying he'd been lied to. Glosson assured the commander that Saddam's tanks were a vital part of the plan. Schwarzkopf didn't believe him, and exploded. "You're going to do this my way, or I'll find officers who will," he screamed. Later, calmer, Schwarzkopf explained himself. "You have to understand. I'm under enormous pressure," he said. He was almost whimpering. "You don't know the kind of pressure I'm under." Glosson wasn't buying it. They were all under pressure. Schwarzkopf was acting like a baby. Did Eisenhower act like this?[45]

Schwarzkopf passed on the pressures he felt to his ground commanders. Days before the ground offensive, the CENTCOM commander told his chief combat officers what he wanted. "We need to destroy—not attack, not damage, not surround—I want you to destroy the Republican Guard," he told VII Corps commander lieutenant general Frederick M. Franks. "When you're done with them, I don't want them to be an effective fighting force anymore. I don't want them to exist as a military organization." Schwarzkopf used the same language with Lieutenant General Gary Luck, the XVIII Airborne Corps commander, and with Franks and Luck's commander, Lieutenant General John Yeosock, the head of the Third Army. "I want VII Corps to slam into the Republican Guard," Schwarzkopf told Yeosock in mid-February. "The enemy is not worth a shit. Go after them with audacity, shock, action and surprise. . . . Let me make it clear John. You cannot have VII Corps stopping for anything."[46]

That's not what happened. VII Corps commander Fred Franks was a fine officer, a Vietnam combat veteran, but he was cautious and overly worried about casualties, which intelligence reports estimated at more than five thousand US soldiers in the first five days of fighting. So Franks planned a deliberate advance into Iraq, stopping his units from time to time to ensure they maintained the "clenched fist" when they "slammed" into the Republican Guard. "Traffic control and density of force dominated his thinking," Douglas Macgregor, the gifted tank commander and leader of the 2nd Armored Cavalry Regiment's "Cougar Squadron," later wrote.[47]

At the start of the war, in the early morning hours of February 24, Macgregor's squadron had vaulted forward, its tanks churning through the desert. Two days later, the squadron fought the Battle of 73 Easting, named for the longitudinal "phase linc" its commanders used to get their bearings in Iraq's featureless southern desert. The Battle of 73 Easting was the last, and most decisive, tank battle of the twentieth century. Macgregor's squadron made history, destroying dozens of armored vehicles of Iraq's vaunted Tawakalna Division, while suffering a single US casualty. But then, with the desert afire with burning Iraqi tanks, Macgregor's unit was ordered to halt. He couldn't believe it, and neither could his subordinates. "Why are we stopping?" Joe Sartiano, the commander of Macgregor's Iron Troop, asked. Macgregor remained silent, so Sartiano repeated the question. "Doug? Why are we stopping?" But it was a captured Iraqi officer, standing at the back of Macgregor's tank, who expressed the most frustration. "Why do you not go to Baghdad now?" he asked in disbelief. "You have the power. Your army rules the heavens and the earth. Do you think we love Saddam?"[48]

In Riyadh, Schwarzkopf railed at Franks. Just one day after the attack began, Schwarzkopf wondered why he wasn't moving as quickly as Gary Luck, to his west. Studying a map of the battlefield, he noticed that the arrows representing VII Corps movement had slowed. "What the hell's going on with VII Corps?" he asked. "This map is wrong." When he was told the map was right, he turned on an aide. "Get me Yeosock," he bellowed. When Yeosock defended Franks, Schwarzkopf issued a blistering critique. "God damn it, I don't care what the problems are. I told you I wanted you to keep pace and you're not doing it. If Franks can't handle the job, I'll get someone who can." Over the next two days, the problem only got worse. At one point, Colin Powell called from Washington. He was plotting the progress of the ground war on his own map. "Tell Franks to get moving," he told Schwarzkopf. "We can't let the Republican Guard escape." That was all Schwarzkopf needed to hear, and he erupted. "The Chairman is on the ceiling about this," he told Yeosock. "You've got to keep pushing." So Yeosock pushed, calling Franks and telling him to "move, move, move." Franks got the message, but his directive to his units was still tentative. "I want you to push on through. Find the enemy and fix him," Franks told Second Armored Cavalry commander Don Holder. Franks put his fist down on Holder's map of the battlefield for emphasis. "Keep in contact," he said, "but don't become decisively engaged." Holder, one of the original Jedi Knights, nodded his agreement and snapped off a "yes, sir."[49]

LATE ON THE night of February 26, Saddam's Republican Guard divisions began to flee Kuwait north along Highway 80. The line of vehicles was spotted by A-6E Intruders from the 3rd Marine Aircraft Wing, which spread clustered munitions to block their exit. Over the next six hours, Marine, Air Force, and Navy aircraft (from the aircraft carrier USS *Ranger*) systematically destroyed the convoy. The number of Iraqi soldiers killed remains uncertain, but the attack was a slaughter. Reports of the massacre, what one participant called "a turkey shoot," made it into the press, sending shivers through official Washington, where the president and his aides began to consider ways to end the carnage.

The next afternoon, the VII Corps began its battle against the Republican Guard, with the 1st Armored Division's 2nd Brigade engaging the Medina Division outside of Basra. In what became known as the Battle of Medina Ridge, the 2nd Brigade destroyed nearly 200 Iraqi tanks and over 125 other armored vehicles. The Iraqis had no support aircraft, while the Americans deployed A-10 tank killers that streamed over the battlefield, cutting through the Iraqi formations. The Iraqis were tenacious, but they didn't stand a chance. After the war, brigade commander Montgomery Meigs paid tribute to the overmatched enemy. "These guys stayed and fought," he said.

Just hours later, George Bush called his aides into the Oval Office. The president was worried that the United States would be accused of "butchering the Iraqis." This was a war fought by the military, he added, so it was up to them to determine when it would end. "We'll talk to Norm," Cheney said. Colin Powell interjected: "I did talk to him," he said. "He said we are at most twenty-four hours away. There are three thousand destroyed tanks. We are in the home stretch. Today or tomorrow by close of business." Bush nodded. "The issue is how to find a clear end," he said. Bush was subdued. "Why do I not feel elated?" he asked.[50]

Later that night, Norman Schwarzkopf faced the press at the Hyatt Regency Hotel in Riyadh. This was "the mother of all briefings" (as reporters dubbed it) with the imposing Schwarzkopf reeling off a Pattonesque narrative while, behind him, a senior staff aide flipped through a series of graphs and maps. Schwarzkopf described his left hook in sweeping terms. A wall of American tanks had closed in on the Republican Guard in a series of "classic tank battles," he said. The Iraqi military was now trapped. "The gates are closed," he said. Watching Schwarzkopf on television from the Black Hole command center, Buster Glosson was enraged. Schwarzkopf made it sound like he was facing a hardened enemy. He wasn't: most of Saddam's formations had been destroyed by air attacks before the first American soldier had entered Iraq. Glosson was disgusted. "This is dishonest," he told his staff.[51]

Two hours later, Powell called Schwarzkopf. The president was prepared to call a cease-fire at 5:00 am the next morning, he said. Schwarzkopf agreed, but said that US troops would continue their attack should they be fired on, then called his field commanders with the news. In far western Iraq, 24th Division commander Barry McCaffrey couldn't believe it. He was, just then, planning an assault on what was left of Saddam's forces deployed beyond the Jalibah airfield, which he'd taken that afternoon.

At VII Corps headquarters, Fred Franks was confused. He'd been battered by Schwarzkopf for three days but now, just as he was about to launch his clenched fist at Saddam, he was being told to stand down. The planned double envelopment, with McCaffrey wheeling on his left, wouldn't happen. Back in Riyadh, Schwarzkopf heard again from Powell: the announcement of the cease-fire would be made by the president at midnight in Washington, exactly one hundred hours since the ground war began. That has a nice ring to it, Powell said. Schwarzkopf harrumphed: fine with me, he said. When he emerged from his room to tell his subordinates, Schwarzkopf bumped into his deputy, Cal Waller, and told him the news. Waller was incredulous: "You've got to be shitting me," he said.

"Too soon," Chuck Horner announced to his staff. "Too soon." The American high command scrambled to complete what was not yet done. McCaffrey urged his men forward, racing the clock, while VII Corps lurched hesitantly into action, reflecting the uncertainty of its commander. In the Black Hole, Buster Glosson ordered his pilots into the air for a desperate attack on the sole remaining Iraqi causeway over the Euphrates River, but they failed to destroy it. The gates were not closed. The Republican Guard still had a way out of Kuwait.

THE CEASE-FIRE ENDING Operation Desert Storm was sealed by a cessation of hostilities agreement signed by Schwarzkopf and Iraqi military commanders at an air base at Safwan, in southern Iraq, on March 3. "We are well on our way to a lasting peace," Schwarzkopf announced afterward. But that same morning, an Iraqi tank commander fired a shell into a portrait of Saddam hanging in Basra's main square, sparking a Shia uprising in southern Iraq. Bush, who'd urged Iraqis to overthrow the dictator, was slow to react. Worse yet, as became increasingly clear, Norman Schwarzkopf had erred at Safwan by permitting the Iraqi army to fly its helicopters in humanitarian missions. Those same helicopters were used to slaughter Shia rebels. "Schwarzkopf mishandled the meeting," Chuck Horner later claimed. "He was unprepared."

A part of the problem was that the US commander hadn't received clear instructions from the White House. Horner remembers sitting in Schwarzkopf's office when he got the call from Washington. You're in charge of the cease-fire, he was told. Horner shook his head. "We're not peace people, we're kill people," Horner later said. "But they told Schwarzkopf, 'go out there and make the peace.' We sat in his office and he got a sheet of paper out and said, 'what the hell am I going to talk to them about?' So he put a few ideas down." Charles "Chas" Freeman, the US ambassador to Saudi Arabia, remembers that Washington tried to get instructions to Schwarzkopf, but was unable to provide them "because they didn't have a vision of what sort of peace they wanted." Or whether, in fact, Washington wanted peace at all. The move was political, calculated, cynical. "Why do you not go to Baghdad now?" an Iraqi officer had asked Doug Macgregor—and Macgregor didn't have an answer. Now, after Safwan, he did: the White House wanted Saddam to survive. He would be a counter to neighboring Iran.

"What really turned out to be the strategic center, the center of gravity for the Iraqis was the Republican Guards," Horner later explained. "Saddam didn't care about the country, he didn't care about the soldiers, he didn't care about the army, he cared about the Republican Guards because that was the only way he could stay in power. . . . And so when we stopped hostilities, which we did, Saddam Hussein became euphoric. He'd won. He went on the air and talked to people about 'we won, we won, we won.' So anyway, we flew supersonic missions over Baghdad for about two weeks just to remind him that if he won, he didn't win very big. But, you know, by then, it was too late."[52]

DESERT STORM WAS a victory, but it left an uneasy feeling, a sense that just when the US military had had Saddam on the ropes, it was ordered to pull its punch, to draw back from the decisive knockout blow. Once again, it was thought, the politicians had weighed in, carefully excising the word "decisive" from the war's description. Yet no one at the top of the Bush administration ever believed that Schwarzkopf's legions hadn't gone far enough. The war's goal was to expel Saddam Hussein from Kuwait, and that is what happened. Anything more and the fragile international coalition put together by Bush, Cheney, and Secretary of State Baker would have shattered. Then too, the national security staff of the Bush White House included some of the best foreign policy thinkers in modern US history. They knew what they were doing. Certainly, that is what the Air Force's Mike Loh believed.

Twenty-five years later, during the Air Force's commemoration of Desert Storm, Loh reflected on the war, Warden's genius, and Chuck Horner's dedication. And he reflected on the Bush years and the political leadership the White House provided. He'd met them all. He had rubbed shoulders with ambassadors, prime ministers, and presidents, and knew George Bush, and Dick Cheney, and James Baker. He'd had conversations with Brent Scowcroft, sharing an easy Air Force camaraderie. Who, he was asked, was the best politician he'd ever met? He shook his head, smiled. "The best politician I ever met," he said, "was Colin Powell."[53]

CHAPTER TWO

Colin Powell's Other Doctrine

"You can get the Joint Chiefs
off my ass."

COLIN POWELL LOVED to tinker. In 1983, when he served as senior military assistant to Defense Secretary Caspar Weinberger, Powell and his family took up residence at Fort Myer, the Army base just across the Potomac River from the Capitol. The redbrick residence confirmed his status as one of the nation's most important military officers and came with parking spaces reserved especially for him. On his day off, Powell could be found flat on his back in these spaces, elbow-deep in grease, tinkering with a broken-down car.[1]

Officially known as Quarters 23A, the residence was located across from the Fort Myer Officers' Club, where the nation's most influential commanders gathered to rub shoulders. And very often, as the panoply of stars gathered at the end of the day, there would be Powell, toiling underneath some reclaimed car. "The MPs [military police] always took a dim view of me disassembling cars," Powell later observed. "I was surprised I got away with it because it was not the most elegant presentation to have before the officers club."[2]

Tinkering with cars was an imperfect reflection of Powell's approach. One of his colleagues later reported that he was "the smartest of the chiefs, but rarely worked at the margins. He was a conservative in the classic sense of the word. He never tinkered as an officer, ever, but went straight at things." Powell was blunt but without being overbearing, serious but not pretentious. He commanded respect, smiled easily at life's ironies, and viewed officers who upbraided their subordinates as undignified. Powell knew how to get things done, a reputation he'd earned while working for "Cap" Weinberger, a stooped and chiseled figure with a rapier wit who, it was said, ended every conversation with the word "no." "Whenever I really needed something out of Cap, I'd go to Powell," former assistant secretary of defense Lawrence Korb says. "He had the right touch." Which is why, in the wake of Desert Storm, it was Colin Powell, not Norman Schwarzkopf, who emerged as the most influential officer of his generation.[3]

Known for his political acumen, Powell emulated Lieutenant General Henry Emerson, one of the most storied combat generals in the Army's long history. Nicknamed "the gunfighter," Emerson toted a six-shot revolver during his time in Vietnam, when he used it to kill a team of Vietcong fighters headed down a trench at him. Emerson was a gifted battlefield commander, understood war, and reveled in it. No one would ever say that of Powell. But Powell admired Emerson because Emerson cared for his soldiers, a quality Powell revered.[4]

Then too, Emerson was a graduate of West Point, while Powell most decidedly was not. But not being a "ring knocker," which gives an officer an advantage when it comes to promotions, never bothered Powell, who was the Harlem-born son of Jamaican parents who'd discovered the Army after joining the Reserve Officers' Training Corps (ROTC) at the City College of New York. He liked being in the ROTC, and was good at it. But Powell was also thin-skinned. While he was not subject to rages, like Schwarzkopf, he could be abrupt. He complained about press articles that showed him in a bad light, and when a fellow officer made a political gaffe, he became visibly angry. He was not above shouting his displeasure. Michael Dugan told one reporter that when Powell called him after he told the media about the air plan for Desert Storm, he was "out of control, apoplectic and screaming at me on the phone."[5]

Like many of his generation, Powell's experience as an officer in Vietnam haunted him, just as it marked him for higher command. During his second tour he rescued four soldiers from a burning helicopter, an act of bravery that jump-started his career. While he described his leadership skills in Vietnam as "just average," that wasn't the view of his commanders, who gave him glowing reports. After serving as a White House fellow during the Nixon years, Powell was selected to attend the Army War College, then served as a battalion commander of the 101st Airborne Division. Weinberger remembered Powell from his time at the White House and brought him onto his staff in 1983. In the wake of the Iran-Contra scandal (when it came to light that the Reagan administration was secretly shipping arms to Iran and using the proceeds to support the Contras in Nicaragua), he served as Ronald Reagan's national security adviser, then commanded the V Corps in Europe. In April 1989, Powell was named the twelfth chairman of the Joint Chiefs of Staff.

Powell was the first African-American JCS chairman, but the whispering campaign that sometimes accompanies such success was noticeably absent among his colleagues. No one could ignore his military experience, which included a Purple Heart, a Bronze Star, and nine other decorations. But most officers who met him rarely cited his battlefield bravery as the reason for his promotion. Rather, it was his service off the battlefield that is most remembered. He provided steady leadership in Weinberger's office, stabilized White House decision-making during the dark days of the Reagan presidency, and never courted public attention. He was modest, well spoken, and prized punctuality. For him, the glass was always half full. Veteran diplomat Richard Holbrooke called him "a towering figure."[6]

MIKE LOH HAD called Colin Powell the best politician he'd ever met. But for many other Americans of Powell's generation, the best politician they'd ever met wasn't the JCS chairman, it was the forty-second president of the United States, Bill Clinton. Of course, Clinton wasn't supposed to be president—that job was reserved for George H. W. Bush, the president who'd fought in World War II, served in the US Congress, headed the CIA, been Ronald Reagan's vice president, then scored a surprising 1988 election victory as Reagan's successor. And he'd presided over the American victory in Operation Desert Storm, exorcising the ghost of Vietnam. Bush wasn't charismatic, but no one doubted his competence; he was steady, experienced, tested by war.

Clinton, on the other hand, was unpredictable, inexperienced, and a draft dodger. Dogged by a history of extramarital affairs, slippery deals with land developers, and a winking relationship with the truth, the Yale Law School graduate developed his political skills as governor of Arkansas, putting them to good use in the 1988 Democratic Party primaries, where he admitted that he'd smoked marijuana but "never actually inhaled" and sat beside his wife on television to deny rumors of marital infidelities. Clinton won his party's nomination, then chose Senator Al Gore as his running mate, making a bet that an Arkansas governor could team with a Tennessee senator to carry the nation's most important electoral prizes. It was an all-southern team.

In the wake of his surprisingly easy triumph over Bush, in November 1992, political pundits cited Clinton's focus on the economy as the reason for his victory. Americans applauded Schwarzkopf when he marched down Pennsylvania Avenue, but then went home to worry about their future. A sign that read "It's the economy, stupid," held a prominent place in Clinton's campaign headquarters. Even so, Clinton's election was propelled as much by the public's discomfort with the aftermath of Bush's Desert Storm victory as it was by the economy. Saddam's 1991 slaughter of Shia rebels in southern Iraq stained America's victory and fueled claims that the Bush White House had botched the Safwan cease-fire negotiations. Reports of the fighting in Iraq's southern cities were accompanied by ghastly films of mass executions. Bush refused to help the rebels, though he'd urged Iraqis to "take matters into their own hands and force Saddam Hussein to step aside."[7]

Bush was regularly forced to defend himself against claims that US military commanders were upset by the premature end to the fighting, that Saddam's forces were retreating even as Schwarzkopf ordered his left hook, that the bodies that littered the "highway of death" were civilians, not soldiers, and that the US high command used unnecessary force in the war's last hours—that, knowing the war would soon end, they killed as many Iraqis as they could. *Newsweek* published an article quoting Schwarzkopf saying that his only worry was "how long the world would stand by and watch the United States pound the living hell out of Iraq without saying, 'Wait a minute—enough is enough.'"[8]

Among the news stories that gained the widest circulation was a report that, in the war's last hours, air strikes against retreating Iraqi troops were so feverish that naval air crews loaded aircraft with "whatever bombs happened to be closest to the flight deck." On one carrier, the aircrews, "working to the strains of the Lone Ranger theme, often passed up the projectile of choice because it took too long to load."[9] Then there were the intangibles: the sense that Saddam was not Hitler (as Bush had implied), but a two-bit tyrant; that the Iraqi military was not a worthy opponent, but a flock of cowering conscripts; and that Desert Storm wasn't a true test of American military prowess. That seemed to be Schwarzkopf's view: "This is a lousy outfit," he'd told reporters in describing the Iraqi military. "Lousy."[10]

"Americans love a good fight," George Patton had once famously said, but the nation's most astute political leaders know that Americans have never really believed that. What Americans love is a good, clean, and certain victory. Desert Storm was none of these. At its end, Saddam Hussein remained in Baghdad, while Bush promised eternal vigilance. Bill Clinton promised a peace dividend—a cut in military spending that would mean more jobs and higher wages.

It is not a surprise, then, that a large segment of the nation's military leaders viewed Bill Clinton's election as distinctly unfair—not a repudiation of the kind the military had suffered in the wake of Vietnam, but certainly a slap at the victory they'd won. So often in the past, the American people had rewarded military success by conferring elective office on its architects, which had been true for George Washington, Ulysses S. Grant, and Dwight Eisenhower. But they were different: each of them had been a commander in the field, and each of them, from the moment of victory, had worked to send the soldiers they'd commanded home. Bush didn't.

With all of that, Bill Clinton's election might have passed without comment at the Pentagon were it not for his decision to allow gays to serve in the military. The pledge came in the wake of a Veterans Day speech the president-elect gave in Little Rock. Clinton knew he faced a challenge with the military, so in his speech he went out of his way to reassure them that while he would "continue the build-down of our military forces consistent with the end of the Cold War," he would "keep this country the strongest in the world." He said he would maintain "two of the things that were responsible for our victory in Desert Storm, a superbly trained

force of men and women and the best possible technology in our weaponry." But while talking to reporters later, he announced he would "re-
instate members of the military who have been removed from service
because they are homosexual." He viewed his pledge as noncontroversial.
"Should people who have served their country with distinction—many
of them with battlefield ribbons—and who have never had any kind of
question about their conduct raised, be booted out of the military?" he
asked.[11]

In Washington, all of the members of the JCS were aghast and,
within days, the press was filled with reports that they would fight the
policy. Of course, it was not simply Clinton's views on gays that bothered
the JCS. For them, Clinton was a symbol of all that his generation had
gotten away with: he'd dodged the draft, committed adultery, and used
drugs. He'd chosen the soft life at home over a wet foxhole in Vietnam,
then engaged in behavior that would have brought a military officer a
dishonorable discharge. Now, he was overturning a prerogative they'd
always exercised: of deciding who could serve in uniform.

The opposition to Clinton's pledge was clear to anyone walking the
halls of the Pentagon. This wasn't simply a question of gays in the military: the debate was about whether a "smooth-talking, gay-loving, draft
dodging, pot-smoking" (as one general prominently described him) governor from Arkansas was fit to be commander in chief.[12] Members of the
Washington press corps circled in anticipation, knowing they were about
to witness a titanic fight pitting the most respected military officer of his
generation against a draft-dodging upstart. This was Powell vs. Clinton,
and it was going to be a donnybrook.

WHILE THE ISSUE of gays in the military was an early test for Bill Clinton, it was also a test for Colin Powell. The 1986 Goldwater-Nichols
Department of Defense Reorganization Act removed the JCS chairman
from the chain of command, which now ran from the president through
the secretary of defense to the nation's geographic combatant commanders. But while Goldwater-Nichols sheered away the chairman's power, it
stipulated that the chairman would now serve as "the principal military
adviser" to the president, National Security Council, and secretary of defense. Powell's predecessor, Admiral William Crowe, set the standard for
what this meant. Crowe diligently built consensus among the chiefs on

controversial issues, reported dissenting views to the president, and expanded the power of the Joint Staff, the large and powerful executive arm of the chairman.

Powell followed Crowe's precedent, looping his JCS colleagues into his thinking during Desert Storm and soliciting their opinions prior to crucial White House meetings. And that's what Powell did now in the aftermath of Clinton's Little Rock statement. Not surprisingly, what Powell found was that while his JCS colleagues (Army general Gordon Sullivan, Chief of Naval Operations Frank Kelso II, Air Force general Merrill McPeak, Marine commandant Carl Mundy Jr., and the vice chairman, Admiral David Jeremiah) disagreed with Clinton's policy shift, they were more angered that he would make his proposal without asking their opinion. Powell agreed: the issue of gays in the military was far less important than Clinton's belief that he could simply dictate military policy. While the commander in chief could order the military to do what he wanted on issues affecting recruiting, training, and equipping, most presidents conferred with military leaders at length and then made a decision. Clinton hadn't done that, apparently because he didn't think it necessary. "This is a rookie mistake," Powell told a colleague.[13]

News of Clinton's announcement reached Powell while he was traveling in Argentina, along with word that his colleagues were up in arms. Their views were unanimous, Powell learned. Not surprisingly, the most outspoken anti-Clinton voice belonged to Commandant Mundy, who was livid.

Mundy enlisted in the Marine Corps Reserve as a student at Auburn University, then climbed his way up the command ladder while serving in Vietnam. Mundy was a perfect Marine: he thought being shot at was "exhilarating." But Mundy was a traditionalist. Of all of the chiefs, it was Mundy who was most likely to have used the phrase "gay-loving" to describe Clinton. Mundy wasn't simply conservative, he was from another era. Women not only didn't belong in combat, he told colleagues, it wasn't clear to him they should be in uniform. He thought that Marines with families might prove soft in combat and believed African Americans couldn't swim, were poor shots, and had trouble finding their way with a compass.[14]

Despite these views, Mundy liked and respected Powell, though one of Powell's closest colleagues sensed a "low grade sense of bemusement" the chairman harbored whenever he spoke with the Marine. Then too, as

Powell knew, Mundy's opinions couldn't be ignored: he was not only the Marine Corps' highest ranking officer, his journey from Alabama to the Pentagon by way of Vietnam gave him a special authority.[15]

Mundy's views were reflected in a front-page article in the *New York Times* two days after Clinton's speech, which cited an unnamed senior Marine as saying that the president-elect's announcement would "upset the good order and discipline" of the military. The phrase invoked the legal basis the military used to dismiss homosexuals. The officer gave a graphic example of what he meant. "We were standing in this shower tent, naked, waiting in line for 35 minutes for a 5-minute shower. Would I be comfortable knowing gays were there standing in line with us? No. It just introduced a tension we do not need." If this was Mundy, the reporter cleaned up his language, as he would almost certainly not have used "gays" to describe homosexuals.[16]

"This is a political decision," Powell told reporters when he returned to Washington. For Powell, this was the most damning of criticisms. The military was supposed to be above politics, but Clinton was using it to pay off a campaign pledge. Powell echoed what the unnamed Marine had told the *Times*. "The JCS and the nation's senior commanders" believed that allowing gays to serve would be "prejudicial to good order and discipline," he said. "And we continue to hold that view." In private, Powell went further. "The military isn't some kind of social experiment," he told a colleague, "that can be used to score political points."[17]

Powell had the chance to tell Clinton that when the president-elect visited Washington on November 19. The JCS chairman met Clinton at the Hay-Adams hotel for what was billed as a get-acquainted session. "I'm not going to answer any questions," Powell told reporters before the meeting. "I just want to have a nice conversation with the president-elect." In truth, Powell was impressed by Clinton's command of foreign policy issues. "Clinton was self-assured, smart, curious, likable, and passionate about his ideas," Powell later recalled. "He also seemed to be a good listener." The two got on well, but Clinton squirmed when Powell mentioned the controversy over his statement on gays. Powell was blunt. "There are strong objections to this," he told Clinton. "It's a bad idea." Powell added that future controversies could be avoided if only Clinton would confer with the JCS before deciding military policy. "I will do that," Clinton said. Powell then suggested a solution he thought would satisfy everyone. "Give yourself some breathing space," he said. "Get [the issue] out of the Oval Office. Don't make the gay issue the first horse out of the gate with the armed forces." Clinton shook his head. He was committed to his policy.[18]

Powell was also disturbed that Clinton was considering appointing Wisconsin congressman Les Aspin as defense secretary. Powell didn't think Aspin would be a good fit. The two had clashed repeatedly on foreign policy and budget issues; and Powell found Aspin glib and dismissive. And Powell thought that Aspin, who stalked the halls of Congress in a rumpled suit, was a slob. On those occasions when the two had lunch, which was not very often, Aspin was more focused on wolfing down his food than listening to the JCS chair. Powell would reiterate his points, while watching oil and vinegar drip in spicules from Aspin's chin.[19]

The next month, at Clinton's direction, John Holum began a series of consultations with the JCS over the gay issue. But appointing Holum as his emissary was a mistake. The former adviser to liberal South Dakota senator George McGovern was viewed by JCS members as antimilitary. Holum, they thought, wasn't seeking a compromise as much as he was attempting to cajole them into accepting Clinton's views. They didn't trust him. Just before Christmas, the JCS clashed with Holum during a meeting in the tank, after which Mundy gave Holum a copy of a videotape entitled *The Gay Agenda*, a nineteen-minute film produced by right-wing Christian activist Bill Horn; it portrayed gays and lesbians as perverts and pedophiles. After the meeting, Mundy sent the video to his commanders. Holum didn't need to see the film to understand where the JCS stood, and the danger that an open break with them posed for Clinton. By the end of December he'd shaped a compromise: Clinton would issue a "memorandum of instruction" ordering the services to stop asking recruits their sexual orientation and cease discharging them for being gay. The JCS was noncommittal on the proposal, but Clinton wasn't. He opposed Holum's compromise; it didn't go far enough.[20]

Nine days before the inauguration, on January 11, 1993, Powell gave an address at the US Naval Academy that, at first glance, seemed designed to dampen the controversy. But that's not what happened. During his remarks, Powell regaled the midshipmen by referring to the Navy's tradition of producing "virtuous sailors" with an ability to "charm the young ladies," a not so subtle reference to the gay issue. Powell understood his audience, who had followed newspaper articles reporting that Admiral Kelso had been greeted with angry questions about the Clinton policy during his recent tour of naval installations. Even more recently, Commander Craig Quigly, the Navy's press spokesman, had set off a firestorm when he described "homosexuals" as "notoriously promiscuous." It wasn't a surprise, then, that when taking questions, Powell was asked what sailors should do if they disagreed with a White House policy. "If after those decisions are made you still find it completely unacceptable and it strikes at the heart of your moral belief, then I think you have to resign," he said.[21]

Powell's answer hung in the air. Even as he took more questions, it began to dawn on his audience what he'd said. The statement sounded like a threat. If Clinton allowed gays in the military, Powell was implying, the JCS would consider resigning.

On January 21, Les Aspin met with the joint chiefs in the tank. It was less than twenty-four hours since Clinton had been sworn in as president, with much of Washington still recovering from the round of parties the night before. Aspin had asked for the meeting in order to present a second, post-Holum compromise on the gay issue. He told the chiefs that Clinton had agreed to postpone his executive order for six months, during which it would be a subject of internal debate and extensive consultations with the JCS. After six months, Aspin said, he'd draft the order himself. But Aspin mishandled the meeting. Rather than listening, Aspin talked. The president, he announced, was determined to lift the ban on gays. The chiefs were puzzled, then angered. Where was the compromise? they asked. What followed was one of the stormiest meetings in JCS history, with the military's most senior officers in a face-off with a new secretary of defense. The most outspoken JCS officer was Carl Mundy. We're not going to have this shoved down our throats, he announced. Aspin looked around the table. Each of the service heads issued a denunciation, their disagreement obvious. Powell intervened, hoping to lower the temperature, but Aspin had never heard such anger. After the meeting, Aspin told his aides that his hope that the military would "grit their teeth" and accept a compromise wasn't possible. "That was a disaster," he said of the meeting.[22]

When Georgia senator Sam Nunn, the powerful Democratic conservative with close military ties, heard about the Aspin-JCS confrontation, he blanched. The gay controversy had hung in the air since November, but Nunn had always believed a break could be averted. Clinton could kick the issue into some commission and forget about it. Now both sides were digging in. On the one side was a new president surrounded by a staff of political neophytes supported by a rumpled Wisconsin congressman of questionable hygiene. On the other was an uncompromising group of military leaders led by the most widely respected uniformed officer of his generation—"the Black Eisenhower," as one columnist called him. Nunn could hardly believe what he was seeing. He could understand if the military and Clinton had disagreed on issues of war and peace, or the budget, but gay rights? It sounded to him like the president didn't understand how Washington worked. And he didn't need to speculate on what would happen to Clinton if there was a mass resignation at the Pentagon. It would destroy his presidency.[23]

SAM NUNN WAS hardly a disinterested party. Proponents of gay rights viewed him as homophobic, Les Aspin thought he was miffed he'd not been named defense secretary, and Clinton was convinced he was interested in flexing his political muscle. Sam Nunn was a force in Washington, and he wanted to make sure it stayed that way.

Gay lobbying groups made their opposition to Nunn clear when reports surfaced that Clinton was considering naming him to the Pentagon's top spot. The gay and lesbian lobby, high-profile Clinton supporters during his campaign, told Clinton's transition team that Nunn had fired two of his aides for being gay, saying they were a security risk. Then too, it was becoming obvious that Aspin's appointment to head the Pentagon had irritated the Georgia conservative. "Nunn's basic problem with this issue was not the issue," one gay-rights advocate announced, "but that he was passed over for a job, and he turned his fury on the administration as a way of punishing them."[24]

That's not the way Nunn would have phrased it. For him, Clinton's decision on gay rights meant the new president would satisfy gays even if it meant sacrificing a competently run defense department. This was Nunn at his political best, taking an above-it-all pose while quietly working to undermine Aspin's standing with the military. None of this was a secret on Capitol Hill, where the Nunn-Aspin face-off was as talked about as the gay issue. Or, as one senior Pentagon civilian said, the gay issue was actually "a mano a mano struggle to determine who really runs defense policy." Privately, Nunn actually agreed with this, telling aides it was time to "bring [Aspin] down a peg or two." This didn't surprise Clinton, for while he'd depended on Nunn for advice on the military during the campaign, he'd found him thin-skinned, "brittle." Then too, Aspin agreed with Clinton on the gay issue and was easier to get along with than Nunn. Aspin might not be a good fit at the Pentagon, but he was a good fit for Clinton.[25]

On Monday, January 25, Clinton and Vice President Al Gore met with the JCS at the White House. "We were on one side of the table, all of the JCS, including the vice chairman, and Clinton and his team marched in and sat across from us," Air Force chief of staff Merrill McPeak remembers. "Later, it was said that we also discussed military issues. But that wasn't true. It was gays in the military. That was the whole thing. That's all we talked about." Clinton went out of his way to make the chiefs feel at home, nodding from time to time as if in agreement with what they were saying. For Carl Mundy, this was the first time he'd gotten to see Clinton close up. As he later told aides, he could see why Clinton had been elected: he was personable, relaxed, even sympathetic. Which did not mean that the joint chiefs were going to retreat from their decision, or that Clinton was going to adopt their views. The meeting was not a confrontation, but its tone was frank and Clinton was blunt.[26]

At one point, Al Gore looked squarely at Powell and compared the civil rights movement to Clinton's advocacy for gays. Powell got testy. He'd heard this from high-profile Colorado congresswoman Patricia Schroeder, who'd written him comparing the plight of gays and lesbians to that of African Americans. Powell could hardly believe it. "I can assure you," he'd responded to Schroeder, "I need no reminders concerning the history of African-Americans in the defense of their nation and the tribulations they faced. I am a part of that history." In private, Powell described Schroeder's argument as "idiotic." He was more civil when Gore made the same point, but just barely. "That's off base," he said. Race was a "benign characteristic," while sexuality was a lifestyle. Gore pressed him. "What is your underlying theory of homosexuality?" he asked. Powell said he didn't have an "underlying theory." For him, the question was what impact the proposed policy shift would have on those who served. Gore pressed him. Did he think homosexuality was a choice? "For me the answer makes a big difference," Gore said. Powell was exasperated. "I'm not making a moral judgment," he said.[27]

When it was his turn to talk, Mundy chimed in with his own, pre-dictably outlandish views. Citing remarks made by a participant in a "Gay Nation" parade, he described gays as "promiscuous," then added that saying you were gay "was the same" as saying you were a part of the KKK, or a Nazi. Clinton disagreed, though carefully. The comparison wasn't good, he said, and concluded by noting that those he would al-low in the military "wouldn't show up at a Queer Nation parade." Gore didn't respond, but he was shocked by Mundy's views, describing them privately as "borderline." Mundy attempted to dampen their impact. "We do not have witch hunts in the military," he assured Clinton. Years later, McPeak would defend Mundy, while admitting that his views were unorthodox. "You know, Carl was just a heck of a guy and I really liked him. But my sense was that he was very religious. That's the way he was," he says.[28]

Clinton ended the meeting by telling the chiefs that he valued their views, would continue to consult with them, and then talked about how the controversy affected him personally. This was classic Clinton. "The whole thing on both sides causes me great discomfort," he said. "These are men and women who are patriotic and have served with distinction and are otherwise highly conformist personally in the best sense. I believe some are born gay and others not. The job of society is not to discrimi-nate on the basis of a moral judgment. It is my belief gays should be able to serve." The meeting ended, but the issue had not been resolved. No one had changed his mind. "The president is sticking by his commitment to ending discrimination against homosexuals in the military," White House aide George Stephanopoulos told the press.[29]

TWO DAYS LATER, on January 27, Nunn, Aspin, and Clinton met at the White House to search for a way to resolve the issue. The late-night meet-ing followed a speech Nunn had made on the Senate floor that targeted Clinton. Nunn had had a series of conversations with Colin Powell on the issue, and his remarks reflected some of what the JCS chairman had told him. "Too many times," he said, "we in the political world send down edicts and don't think about the implications of the things that have to follow." Nunn then reeled off a list of forty questions that the presi-dent had failed to think about. What would be the impact of the presi-dent's edict on recruitment, retention, morale, and discipline? Would gay couples receive the same benefits as others? Should members of the armed forces have sensitivity training? How would the administration handle the issues of back pay, reinstatement, and promotions? Nunn admitted that he didn't know how to answer these questions, but at least he'd asked them, and then he announced the Senate Armed Services Committee would hold hearings on the issue. Nunn wanted to kick the can down the road: "I'd like to have no decisive, final action by the president," he said, "and no final decisive legislation by the Congress."[30]

But even as Clinton was meeting with Nunn and Aspin, White House spokesperson Dee Dee Myers was telling the press that Clinton wouldn't yield. "The president has decided he is going to take action to rescind the ban," she said. "The president is not willing to compromise on that principle. He's willing to pay the price." Nunn was blindsided by the Myers statement, but soft-pedaled his reaction. "Let's don't legislate on something and, in exchange, let's have the executive show some restraint," he said. It was a modest proposal: Nunn would hold hearings on the issue and in exchange Clinton would postpone his announcement. The problem was that, while this sounded reasonable, Nunn knew it wouldn't work. Clinton had already said "no."

Into this morass stepped Charles Moskos, a Northwestern University sociologist and close friend of Nunn. The previous year, Moskos had sent a memo on gay military service to Nunn and then, after the election, forwarded the memo to Aspin. The problem wasn't whether gays were actually in the military, Moskos argued (because that, clearly, was already known); the problem was whether to openly acknowledge them. Moskos, a brilliant if glib policy wonk who'd written extensively about military integration, suggested that gays be allowed to serve so long as they kept their sexual orientation a secret. The military would condone homosexuality, or ignore it, but retain the right to punish it under military law. That such a policy made military officers hypocrites didn't bother Moskos in the least, he wrote, since "a little hypocrisy may be the only thing that allows imperfect institutions to function in an imperfect world." In fact, Moskos seemed to confirm Powell's view that while being black was a "benign characteristic," being gay was a lifestyle. Put another way, the military had to adopt a policy on race, because a person's race was obvious. That wasn't true for gays, so why ask someone who was in the military or wanted to be whether they were? If you don't ask, Moskos said, they won't tell.

At first, Moskos's proposal sounded wacky to Nunn, but the more he thought about it, the more practical it sounded. It offered a way out. The proposal also made sense to Aspin, who was desperately trying to bridge the gulf between Clinton and the JCS. Aspin and Nunn pressed Clinton to accept the idea, with Nunn arguing that the Moskos concept didn't mean Clinton had to give up his views. He suggested that the president appoint a military commission to look into the issue and report back to him. In the meantime, Nunn proposed, the Senate could hold its hearings while Aspin worked on the JCS. Clinton could even claim the postponement was a victory, as new recruits would no longer be asked whether they were gay. The three worked on the language of an executive order on the night of January 27, just two weeks after Clinton's inauguration, then sent their draft on to Powell and the JCS the next morning.[31]

Nunn met with Clinton again on the night of the twenty-eighth, finalizing the language the president would use in announcing the policy. The next day, speaking to the press, Clinton directed Aspin to provide a draft executive order to the White House by July 15, vowed to work with Congress to draft legislation on the issue, and appointed a military commission to study it. "This compromise is not everything I would have hoped for or everything I have stood for," he said, "but it is plainly a substantial step in the right direction." The adoption of "Don't Ask, Don't Tell" was touted by Clinton as a victory for gay rights, "but few observers were fooled. The policy was a concession to the JCS, set a marker for civilian-military relations during the Clinton presidency, and reasserted Colin Powell's influence on military policy. Powell had won, setting in stone his firm belief that this wasn't a matter of war and peace; if a president wanted to impose a social policy on the military that had to do with recruiting, training, and equipping the force, the least he could do was confer with them.

Powell's triumph added to his luster in the military and his standing inside the administration. In fact, after Don't Ask, Don't Tell was put in place, Powell's influence on military policy was nearly unprecedented. For the first time in history, the head of the military had a veto: Clinton believed he couldn't successfully promote a military policy decision without his concurrence.

Within weeks of his inauguration, the new president appointed openly gay members to sensitive posts in his administration, but he never again crossed the JCS. During a particularly chilly meeting between

Clinton and Powell in the Oval Office in the midst of the debate, Powell had told Clinton that if he insisted on issuing an executive order on the issue, he'd go to Congress to get it overturned. "I don't want that," Powell said, "but I'll do it. And if I lose, I'll resign." The threat was clear: Powell had the votes, Clinton didn't. In the wake of that meeting, Nunn intervened to head off an ugly public confrontation. "You're going to have to figure out a way to get along with this guy," Nunn warned Clinton. "He can beat you."[32]

"Clinton was apoplectic on the subject of Colin Powell, terrified of Colin Powell," former secretary of labor and Clinton insider Robert Reich later observed. Clinton solicited Powell's views on the military budget, cleared command nominations with him, and promoted senior officers on his recommendation. On military issues, Powell didn't have the final word, but nearly so. Clinton didn't dare cross him. Even on seemingly minor issues, and well after Powell's departure as JCS chairman, Clinton looked over his shoulder at the military, seeing the ghost of Colin Powell in every corner. When a group of nongovernmental organizations lobbied the White House to ban land mines, a weapon the military rarely used but that remained in the ground and continued to take lives long after a war was ended, Clinton was paralyzed. The argument was made during a White House dinner by former JCS chairman David Jones, who noted that fifteen senior retired military officers had endorsed a land mine ban. Clinton agreed, but he couldn't do it—not so long as the joint chiefs disagreed. "What can we do to help you?" Jones asked. Clinton shook his head, clipping off his bitter instruction. "You can get the joint chiefs off my ass," he responded. "I can't afford a breach with the joint chiefs."[33]

ON THE MORNING of April 4, 1993, Bill Clinton went jogging with General Barry McCaffrey, the commander of the 24th Division during Desert Storm and the special assistant to Colin Powell. Clinton was making it up to McCaffrey, who'd been insulted by a White House aide in the early days of his presidency. While walking across the White House lawn, McCaffrey greeted the aide with an airy "good morning." The young woman barely looked at him. "I don't talk to the military," she said. McCaffrey related the incident to his colleagues and it made the rounds, evidence, it was said, of Clinton's hatred of the uniformed services. Clinton called the story an "abject lie," but it was true, even if there was more to it than what was reported. In fact, Clinton was so upset by his deteriorating relations with those in uniform that his message to his staff made sense: don't talk to the military, he'd instructed them, that's my job.[34]

But there was good reason to believe the worst. In the early days of the administration, senior military officers were kept waiting to meet the president, even as Clinton's staff struggled to remember who they were. "General who?" his staff would ask. "When we met on the gay issue," Merrill McPeak remembers, "we sat there for ninety minutes. This guy was never on time." The problem was worsened by Clinton's uncomfortable salute, an embarrassing three-fingered jab that looked like something a boy scout would use. Clinton first practiced the salute when Ronald Reagan made him repeat it during a meeting the two had had when Clinton was president-elect, but it was still sloppy until an adviser took Clinton in hand and watched as he tried to perfect it. Bring your arm up slow, fingers together, then snap it off. Clinton practiced and practiced, but never seemed to get it right. But the problem wasn't just Clinton.

Anthony Lake, Brent Scowcroft's successor as head of the NSC, ran White House meetings like they were college seminars. Aides filled the room, sitting along the walls. Young, fresh-faced, just-out-of-college gofers, back-benchers from various agencies, even interns were included. Clattering coffee cups and briefing papers were spread everywhere. Everyone seemed to be talking at once, and everyone's views were solicited. For Colin Powell, this was a far cry from the days when the room contained a handful of officials, all of them foreign policy experts with decades of experience. Powell looked around and reported back to his colleagues. Why the hell would Lake even listen to the views of someone under forty? he asked. What did they know? Who the hell are these people?

But there is another side to this story. Clinton detractors criticized the new president for being a foreign policy amateur, but he wasn't elected to fix foreign policy. He was elected to fix the economy. The sign in his campaign headquarters didn't read, "It's the military, stupid." Nor was Clinton's decision not to consult the military on a policy affecting them unprecedented.

The same had happened under Bush, whose "this will not stand" statement after Saddam's invasion of Kuwait surprised Powell, who thought he was being stampeded. And while Powell was irritated by Lake's endless policy meetings, he was as irritated by the backslapping atmosphere of the Bush White House. It struck him as a bunch of Ivy League elitists deciding who would live and die. He thought it was too chummy.

There was also a growing sense among retired officers that Powell's disagreements with Clinton were undermining the Clinton presidency— and the Office of the President. "I wouldn't say this in public," former JCS chairman William Crowe said at the time, "but I think there's a limit to this kind of thing, and Colin has probably reached it."[35] Crowe passed his views on to Powell. Crowe, who'd prominently supported Clinton's election and served as a kind of dean of the retired set, wasn't alone. Air Force chief of staff Merrill McPeak worried about the effect of the controversy on the services. McPeak admired Powell, lived next door to him at Fort Myer, and would grab a handful of wrenches to take to him on his off days—finding him in his garage "working on a Volkswagen." The two would chat, talking politics. "Gen. Powell had definite opinions, and wasn't afraid to voice them," he noted, "and he knew more about Washington than anyone on the JCS. He was very political. He just knew the city and had it over the rest of us, he really did." But McPeak worried that Powell's confrontation with Clinton reinforced the open disdain for the president being shown by service members.[36]

Some of this disdain came close to insubordination, including statements made by sailors during Clinton's visit to the aircraft carrier *Theodore Roosevelt* in March 1993. One sailor said that a protestor had thrown a draft beer at Clinton, "but he dodged it," while a senior commander said that the president's three-hour visit should count as his time in the military, as it was more than he'd ever served before. "I owe a personal apology on this matter to the American people," McPeak told reporters when these remarks appeared in the press, then circulated a warning to Air Force personnel against criticizing Clinton. In his own offices, McPeak silenced talk about Clinton with a steely stare. "Remember, you're talking about the President of the United States," he'd say.[37]

Clinton was embittered by the controversy over gays in the military, viewing Powell's criticisms as purposely aimed at weakening him. He later pointed out that more than one hundred self-avowed gays had served during Desert Storm, but were dismissed after the conflict "when they were no longer needed." Then too, it was Powell's job to support the president, and he hadn't done it. Richard Kohn, a military scholar, viewed the military's opposition to Clinton as "out of control." Powell might have been "the most powerful JCS chairman since George C. Marshall headed the military," Kohn said, "but he was also the most political since Douglas MacArthur," who was dismissed by Harry Truman for insubordination.[38]

The ever-sensitive Powell was wounded by the criticism, telling his colleagues that he'd simply been expressing the opinions of the services. He was responsibly reflecting their views. That wasn't political, that was his job, he said. Then too, he'd been the one to suggest how to resolve the issue, telling the president during the JCS's meeting on January 25 that "we should stop asking people about their sexual orientation when they enlist." But Powell's role in the debate left a lot of policymakers convinced that while Clinton was out of step with the military, the debate showed that the military, and Powell, were out of step with the American people.

During an Air Force awards banquet in the Netherlands on May 24, General Harold Campbell referred to Clinton as a "womanizing, pot-smoking, gay-loving draft dodger." The remark brought guffaws from his audience, but also a smattering of boos. Campbell later said he was joking, but McPeak was appalled. "God damn it, that's enough," he shouted at his staff. McPeak ordered an investigation of the incident, directed Campbell to apologize, wrote a letter reprimanding him, fined him two months pay, then had him forcibly retired from the service.

The *New York Times* called it "the political equivalent of a public execution." Clinton, astutely, allowed the military to bathe in the public condemnation, leaving Campbell's punishment in their hands. McPeak was merciless. "I want him drummed out of the service," he'd told Powell.[39]

Powell scrambled to undo the damage. He urged the president to visit the Pentagon, suggested he give a speech at West Point, and told him to rub shoulders with the troops at the Quantico, Virginia, Marine base. On May 31, Powell escorted Clinton to the Vietnam Veterans Memorial, where he was scheduled to introduce him to a Memorial Day gathering of veterans. When Clinton was greeted by a smattering of jeers ("draft dodger," "liar"), Powell reminded them that Clinton outranked them all. "We all here know that the Vietnam War caused deep wounds within American society," he said, "but now the passage of time, a growing spirit of understanding of different views, a pressing need to move forward together as a nation allow us now to complete our reconciliation and to heal those wounds." He paused, then continued. "And therefore, my dear friends, at this wall of honor, as the senior Vietnam veteran on active duty as chairman of the Joint Chiefs of Staff, I want to welcome, I want to welcome and introduce you to the commander in chief of the armed forces of the United States, our president, President Bill Clinton."[40]

POWELL'S INTRODUCTION OF Clinton was a deft attempt to smooth over their relationship, but it was also good politics. Powell needed Clinton to help him shape a defense budget that would retain important weapons programs. The military had faced steep funding cuts during the last two years of the Bush administration, but since no one in Congress wanted the cuts to cost defense jobs, they were less than the military expected, or than Clinton wanted. In March, Aspin had announced that the administration planned to cut $131.7 billion beyond what Bush had proposed. "This budget begins to use resources freed by the end of the Cold War to help at home," Aspin said. But Powell thought that Aspin's numbers didn't make sense. No one knew what programs Aspin wanted to cut or why, and, as it turned out, neither did Aspin. He said the final numbers would result from a soon-to-be-launched "Bottom Up Review." But if the review would determine the cuts, where did Aspin get his $131.7 billion figure?[41]

Nunn pounced. "We have been dealing with numbers grabbed out of thin air," he said. "No one knows where these cuts are going to come from." This was a two-front war; while Powell was fighting Clinton on gays, he was fighting Aspin on the budget. It was a head-spinning debate: the standard way to determine what the military needs is to assess national threats and then build a military to counter them. The threats drive the numbers. Aspin turned this upside down. Aspin's budget numbers would have made it difficult for the United States to respond to simultaneous regional threats, so he rejiggered the threats. If faced with two crises, he proposed, the US would engage in "a holding action" on one front "until the other was secured." His reasoning incensed the JCS ("just what exactly is a holding action?" Carl Mundy asked one of his colleagues), shattered the unanimity they'd shown during the debate over gays, and spurred a series of internal spats over who would get what.[42]

The biggest argument centered on the Air Force and its chief of staff, Merrill McPeak, who said he understood the administration's views and the significance of the Revolution in Military Affairs. Why expend money on recruiting and training soldiers when Desert Storm showed that the Air Force could do the job by itself? What McPeak wanted was a "wall-to-wall review" that would cut personnel while retaining funding for new defense technologies that favored his service. It would double down on the RMA. In fact, the strategy that John Warden had advocated for bringing down Saddam was mimicked by McPeak to undercut Army, Navy, and Marine budget numbers. The three other services, McPeak argued, should make greater budget sacrifices, since their job in a future war would be to mop up after the Air Force victory. Iraq had shown that the Air Force could put more bombs on target more accurately while using fewer aircraft than at any time in history. Sure, the Air Force would lose personnel to the budget cutters, but it wasn't the number of aircraft the Air Force could deploy that mattered, but the accuracy of the bomb loads they carried. McPeak didn't like the cuts any more than anyone else, but the Air Force could ride them out.[43]

That wasn't true for the Navy, whose budget position was weak and under attack. Ronald Reagan had envisioned building a six-hundred-ship navy, but Aspin believed the Navy could do with three hundred ships. As crucially, as the budget debate escalated the Navy's leadership was undercut by revelations that its pilots had been involved in sexually assaulting women at an annual Tailhook Association Symposium held in Las Vegas in 1991. The investigation alleged that eighty-three women and seven men were assaulted while senior Navy officers stood by and did nothing (Navy women were made to run a gauntlet of inebriated aviators on the third floor of the Las Vegas Hilton who grabbed at them as they ran past). Nor, as it turned out, was this the first time it had happened. Navy women had been assaulted at other conventions, as if it was accepted practice among the service. The revelations about "Tailhook" stunned the public and embarrassed Admiral Frank Kelso, chief of naval operations, who'd been in Las Vegas but claimed he'd been standing in the hotel parking lot during the incident. Few believed him.[44]

Kelso was also under fire when an initial report cleared senior Navy officers of any wrongdoing. The report was written by an admiral appointed by Kelso, who explained to Navy assistant secretary Barbara S. Pope that "a lot of female pilots are go-go dancers, topless dancers or hookers." Navy women were enraged.[45] What followed was a bloodletting unrivaled in the Navy's history, accompanied by reports that Kelso had covered up the scandal, what Pope called "one of the largest abrogations of leadership in Navy history." In fact, the scandal had been a long time in coming, with senior Navy officers arguing that their alcohol-fueled pilots had been out of control since at least the mid-1980s. The scandal was embarrassing for other reasons: it was the Navy that had announced that it opposed gays in the military because, as its spokesman said, homosexuals were "notoriously promiscuous." Now the tables were turned, with the public treated to lurid headlines that made it seem that sexual promiscuity was a service-wide stain. Then too, the scandal touched nearly anyone of consequence in the service. Navy secretary John Lehman attended some of the Navy's more riotous parties, brazenly beckoning prostitutes to sit on his lap while Navy officers hooted their support. The Navy's most influential officers believed the Navy's leadership was derelict, with Kelso their target. With morale slipping, Kelso spent most of his time defending himself while trying to stanch his service's wounds. For him, the Navy budget was a secondary issue.[46]

JCS vice chairman David Jeremiah, an influential Navy admiral, stepped into the breach, working to calm concerns among senior Navy officers. Jeremiah's seagoing background made him an odd fit on the JCS, but he was an effective manager and Powell's most important adviser. At key points during the Clinton years, Jeremiah defused JCS tensions by suggesting that meetings of the chiefs be held in Powell's office kitchen, where the informal setting dampened disagreements. He did this often in the summer of 1993, when senior Navy officers began what came to be known as the "Kelso death watch."[47] The question for them wasn't whether Kelso would be fired, but when. Kelso was alternately angered and morose. He'd always been willing to give people a second chance, he told Jeremiah, but now when he needed one no one was listening. At a key point in the scandal, Jeremiah, who'd served under Kelso in a senior command slot in the Reagan years, reassured him that he was a good officer and doing a good job. He would lightly touch his elbow, nodding: "You'll get through this, Frank," he said, "You'll get through this."[48] Jeremiah took the same stance on the fight over the defense budget, cajoling the chiefs to adopt common positions. "Admiral J was incredibly effective," a retired senior officer now remembers. "He didn't always get full agreement on specific budget issues, but he kept the JCS members from tearing each other apart."[49]

The budget issue took months to resolve, but in the end Aspin and Powell came to an uneasy agreement. Clinton's chosen instrument for forcing this was Frank Wisner, the then designate undersecretary of defense for policy. Wisner delivered Clinton's message in a memo to Aspin that was circulated to senior defense officials in early March 1993. The president, Wisner wrote, was committed to reaching "a broad political consensus" on the military's size and strategy. "To reach this goal we will need you and the chairman standing shoulder to shoulder on the basic positions." Referred to by Aspin's colleagues as Clinton's "or else" message, the memo forced Aspin to hear out the chiefs on the issue of readiness, while Powell and his colleagues reciprocated by adopting a budget in which every service would face cuts. The idea was to shed personnel but keep weapons programs, to maintain quality while "shredding bulk." It was the kind of compromise that had worked to defuse the gay issue: there would be cuts, but the military would have the most influence in determining them.

In May, the chiefs aired their budget grievances during congressional hearings. Army chief Gordon Sullivan sniffed that Clinton's cuts left his service at the "razor's edge" of readiness, Carl Mundy argued that Marine Corps funding was at its lowest point since the "hollow force" of the late 1970s, while Frank Kelso described the Navy as being "on the ragged edge." McPeak joined this chorus, saying Aspin's budget numbers would cause the Air Force to make "major adjustments."[50] The description was not what McPeak's colleagues expected. In fact, McPeak's colleagues viewed him skeptically, finding him eccentric and detached. He regularly scoffed at their commitment to interservice cooperation ("jointness," as it is called), told Carl Mundy that the Marines didn't need fighter jets because the Air Force already had them, talked endlessly about the reorganization he'd imposed on his service, and extolled his controversial decision to remake the Air Force uniform, free from frills. "Good God, Merrill McPeak. He talks and talks," Sullivan said to Kelso during one session in the tank. McPeak knew his JCS support was thin, telling reporters that he'd likely be outvoted 5–1 by the other chiefs on any important issue. "Yeah," he later commented, "there were a lot of times when I was in there all alone."[51]

But for many Air Force officers, the budget controversy was McPeak's finest moment. While they were skeptical of his reorganization plan and critical of his eccentricities, McPeak had shown he could stand up to the other services when it came to crunching budget numbers. Then too, McPeak was one of them: he'd grown up poor in Oregon, made extra cash by slinging hash, and flew 269 combat missions in Vietnam. When Michael Dugan was fired for talking about the Air Force's Desert Storm plan for Saddam, Dick Cheney had asked Powell who should replace him, and Powell recommended McPeak. McPeak remembered this, so while he'd pointedly criticized other JCS members during the budget debate, he never openly criticized Powell. But in the late spring and early summer of 1993, that began to change. The disagreement was never made public, but for McPeak it was crucial. McPeak's break with Powell was not over budget numbers, it was about war and peace.

IN THE WINTER 1992 edition of *Foreign Affairs*, Powell detailed what became known as the Powell Doctrine. Heavily influenced by his experiences in Vietnam and by the thinking of Reagan defense secretary Caspar Weinberger, Powell argued that the United States should only go to war as a last resort, only when its vital interests were threatened, only when there were clearly defined objectives, only with a full commitment of US resources applied through overwhelming force—and, most crucially, only with the support of the American people.[52]

The beauty of the Powell Doctrine was its alluring simplicity: it was elegantly stated, easy to understand, and made perfect sense. When it wasn't invoked, disaster followed, as in Vietnam. But the problem for Powell was that key members of the Clinton administration didn't agree with it. The doctrine provided a good guide during the Cold War, they said, but it didn't apply in a world where the United States was the lone superpower. In some situations, they argued, the right mix of diplomacy and force could protect the defenseless or stop genocide. As the lone superpower, the US was under a moral obligation to defend the innocent. That had happened in the wake of Desert Storm, in 1991, when the US deployed the military to northern Iraq in Operation Provide Comfort to protect Kurdish refugees fleeing Saddam's army. Then, in 1992, the Bush administration launched Operation Restore Hope to provide emergency aid to starving Somalis victimized by their country's civil war. Neither crisis involved vital American interests, and each had inserted American forces in limited conflicts. Then too, and despite his doctrine, Powell had supported both interventions. For many, Powell's actions smacked of hypocrisy: he supported a doctrine of nonintervention, except when it suited his own purposes.[53]

Powell dismissed the criticism. Sure, he'd supported the Kurdish and Somali interventions, he said, but Provide Comfort was a natural follow-on from the Desert Storm victory, while Restore Hope highlighted America's global reach. Then too, Powell believed, the US military could be a force for good, but only so long as it was capable of projecting the power that robust defense budgets ensured. His message was clear: if Clinton wanted to use the American military, he'd have to pay for it. Clinton heard this, but was skeptical. Powell was going to use the budget issue as leverage to keep the administration from intervening in Bosnia, where well-armed Serb militias were slaughtering unarmed Bosnian Muslims. The fighting had been going on since the breakup of Yugoslavia, in 1991, but Powell opposed using the military to end it, or to protect the innocent. "We don't have a dog in this fight," Secretary of State James Baker had argued in the last years of Bush's term. Powell agreed.

The pressure to do something in Bosnia had escalated from the moment Clinton was inaugurated as president. Clinton had criticized Bush's inaction on the crisis during the campaign, and said that as president he would use air strikes against the Serbs if the war continued. But when Clinton took office he was faced with the same doubts that had paralyzed Bush. Bosnia was a morass, and it wasn't clear to Clinton that actually using force would work to end the killing. By the summer of 1993, the administration was split, with pro-interventionist hawks facing off against those urging caution. The most outspoken hawk was Madeleine Albright, the US ambassador to the UN. Albright had consistently argued for US military intervention and had written a memo in favor of it to Clinton in early August 1993. "Why America Must Take the Lead" argued that the administration's failure to act on Bosnia was undermining its international credibility, especially with its NATO allies. The president should opt for air strikes, she said, as force was the only thing that would deter the Serbs.

The debate over Bosnia came to a head in a meeting at the White House just weeks after Albright had circulated her memo. Powell was at his best, playing on the Clinton team's uncertainty. Armed with flip charts, maps, and budget projections, Powell aimed his arguments at Anthony Lake.

Bosnia had all the makings of a disaster, Powell said. Serb targets would be hard to find, the terrain was difficult, and the outcome uncertain. The United States could launch air strikes against Serb military positions, but it might take months for them to have an impact. And the operation would cost billions. Seated near Lake, Albright seethed.

When Powell was finished, she turned on him. "What's the point of having this superb military you're always talking about if we can't use it?" she asked. Powell was stunned, writing later that "I thought I would have an aneurysm."[54]

For Powell, Albright's statement symbolized everything wrong with the Clinton administration's foreign policy team. They just didn't get it. Back in 1985, Caspar Weinberger had scoffed at criticism of Reagan's defense spending by enunciating the philosophy behind the Reagan buildup. "We're not spending money on weapons in order to use them," he'd told a reporter. "We're spending money on them so we don't have to." For Powell, Weinberger's statement was a quintessential expression of what worked. The whole point of having a strong military was to deter war, not invite it. America was at its most vulnerable when it deployed its troops incrementally, while overwhelming force signaled true commitment. "American GIs are not toy soldiers to be moved around on some kind of global game board," he'd told Albright.

For the majority of his colleagues on the JCS, Powell's opposition to Albright, and to intervening in Bosnia, was viewed as heroic. Like Vietnam, Bosnia would be the wrong war at the wrong time and in the wrong place. For them, Powell's arguments provided a fitting cap to his four-year tenure as JCS chairman. Slated to retire on the last day of September 1993, Powell would leave the military with his reputation intact, his influence unimpaired, and his record as a self-described "reluctant warrior" enhanced. And Powell would retire with his stamp on American foreign policy, as author of an influential doctrine that was, many believed, the perfect distillation of their views. The only dissenter was McPeak. McPeak admired Powell and considered him a friend. But over the last year of Powell's term, he'd quietly made his doubts about Powell's beliefs, and his doctrine, clear to a handful of friends and colleagues. Don't say this in public, McPeak would warn them, and don't repeat it to the press. But McPeak's opinions inevitably circulated among the Pentagon's most senior military commanders, where they provided an alternative narrative on Powell's tenure.

McPeak started with the controversy over gays in the military. He'd stood with his colleagues in facing down Clinton. The chiefs were unanimous. But as time went on, McPeak doubted that the JCS or Powell had handled the issue well. Since when does a president have to confer with the JCS when shaping a military policy? he asked. As for Clinton's salute, well, the job of the military was to salute him, not the other way around. So too, McPeak found himself lining up with critics of the Powell Doctrine. "I never thought too much of it," he says. "The real smart doctrine was the Weinberger Doctrine, because it talked about American interests. That wasn't true for Powell. His doctrine boiled down to one thing: massive numbers. You bring a knife, I'll bring a gun." More crucially, as McPeak told Powell, it wasn't what the doctrine said that bothered him, it's that it was said at all. The proper role of a military officer wasn't to determine if America should fight, but how. "I told him it's not our job to issue doctrines," McPeak says. "That's the job of elected officials. That simple." Powell was out of his lane.[55]

McPeak wasn't alone in his criticism. His views were shared by many airpower advocates, foreign policy experts, and senior defense officials. If Desert Storm had showed anything, it proved the United States could intervene successfully and with overwhelming force to shape the international environment. If done right, the interventions could save lives. Operation Provide Comfort was proof of that.

As the Bosnia crisis was heating up, McPeak went there on a fact-finding mission. When he returned, he met with Powell. "I told him, 'Listen, we need to do something. It's just awful. They're killing women and children. We could end that.' And he turned to me and looked down at his desk, 'Thanks for your interest in national security,' he said. And that was that." Or not quite: in one JCS session on Bosnia, McPeak turned on Powell, reminding him that it was the job of the joint chiefs to provide the president with options. "That's with an 's,'" he pointedly told Powell. "That means more than one option. And it means more than just yours." McPeak also remembers that Powell would bring politicians into his office, where he'd show them aerial photographs of camouflaged Serb mortar positions. "You think we're going to bomb that and destroy it?" he'd ask. "No way." McPeak didn't say anything, but he disagreed. Bomb that target? "Yeah, sure," he thought. "I could do that. The Air Force could do that."[56]

Surprisingly, McPeak's views were shared not only by his Air Force colleagues, but by a small number of senior officers in Powell's own service. One of these was General John Shalikashvili (or "General Shali," for those who had trouble pronouncing his name), who'd commanded Operation Provide Comfort. Provide Comfort had made Shalikashvili's reputation, brought him to Powell's attention, and vaulted him into the

JCS chairmanship as one of the most unlikely dark-horse appointments to that office in JCS history. Ironically, however, General Shali, as he was affectionately called, used his office to promote the career of Army general Wesley Clark, an officer whose personality and actions would cast a cloud on his tenure. Clark would be remembered as one of the most learned and experienced officers of his generation—and the one officer who was as loathed as John Shalikashvili was loved.

CHAPTER THREE

Wes Clark: Water Walker

"You know who Courtney
Massengale is? Well, Clark
is Massengale."

I N THE MIDDLE of the afternoon of Sunday, October 3, 1993, two days after Colin Powell retired, Major General William F. Garrison ordered a contingent from Task Force Ranger into central Mogadishu to arrest two of Somali warlord Mohamed Farrah Aidid's lieutenants. The force, comprising 19 aircraft, 12 vehicles, and 160 men, was ordered to storm a house near the Olympic Hotel, arrest the two commanders, and return to their compound, located near the airport.

The United States had gotten involved in Somalia in July 1992 when, responding to international pressure, it mounted an airlift to feed the country's starving population. Somalia was in chaos, victimized by a clan-based civil war that followed a 1991 coup that overthrew Siad Barre, a brutal dictator. Over the next year, 300,000 Somalis were killed and another 4.5 million displaced. On December 3, 1992, the UN Security Council passed Resolution 794, authorizing the US to lead a military intervention to enforce a shaky cease-fire. The Joint Chiefs of Staff was hesitant to support the deployment, but shifted their position as public pressure mounted. "If you think US forces are needed," JCS vice chairman admiral David Jeremiah told administration officials, "we can do that job." Operation Restore Hope began in early December 1992, and Clinton inherited it when he took office.[1]

The October 3 mission was the seventh for Task Force Ranger, and no one thought it would be different than any of the half dozen that had preceded it, which had all gone smoothly. The sole exception came on September 25, when the United States lost a helicopter and three soldiers. That said, Aidid had shown a willingness to fight the Americans, despite their overpowering advantage in heavy weapons. That proved true during the October 3 operation, which went wrong from the very beginning. While Aidid's two commanders were quickly captured, Army private Todd Blackburn missed the rope dangling from his helicopter and fell seventy feet to the street. A US soldier was then killed by a Somali. A little more than one hour later, a Black Hawk helicopter was downed by a rocket-propelled grenade. Early in the evening a second helicopter was downed; eventually its crew members were killed along with a sniper who volunteered to rescue them. A second sniper was taken prisoner.

By now thousands of Somalis had descended on the central Mogadishu battleground. Americans sent to rescue the crew of the first downed copter were surrounded by Somali fighters, so Garrison dispatched a rescue convoy consisting of soldiers from the US 10th Mountain Division, who broke through the Somali lines. By the time the convoy returned to the US compound the next morning, eighteen Americans were dead and dozens wounded. Somalis cheered as the body of an American soldier was dragged through the streets. Upward of a thousand Somalis were killed. It was the fiercest urban battle involving US soldiers since Vietnam.[2]

Writing about the incident in *Black Hawk Down*, reporter Mark Bowden noted that "at least in strictly military terms" the operation was a success. But the victory was Pyrrhic. The US prisoner was held for eleven days, while "images of gleeful Somalis abusing American corpses prompted revulsion at home, embarrassment at the White House, and such vehement objections in Congress" that the mission to help provide relief to starving Somalis was called off. That decision was made by Clinton two days after the debacle in a meeting he had with Al Gore, Tony Lake, Madeleine Albright, and members of the JCS. In the end, Clinton offered the American people a deftly worded sleight of hand, saying he would dispatch 1,700 soldiers to Somalia along with 104 tanks and other armored vehicles to reinforce the US mission. Then, he said, the United States would get out.

The Somali disaster didn't surprise Marine general Joe Hoar, Garrison's boss. A lanky Bostonian, Hoar had doubts about the Somali deployment from the moment it was announced at the end of the Bush administration. For Hoar, whose combat experience included facing off against Iranian gunboats in the 1980s, Bush's decision was "a classic example of good intentions getting the better of good thinking." Unlike many Marines, Hoar's most important Vietnam experience took place not in Vietnam, but in Toulon, in the mid-1960s, where he shared a drink with a French naval commando. After Hoar predicted victory in Southeast Asia citing US "air power, mobility and superior numbers," the French officer shook his head. "The look he gave me—a mixture of disbelief and pity—remains with me to this day," Hoar subsequently wrote.[3]

Hoar had said some of this to Bill Clinton back in August, when the president talked to him about being Powell's successor. The meeting followed a White House dinner in which Clinton invited fifteen senior military officers, including David Jeremiah, Air Force general George L. Butler, Admiral Paul Miller (the head of the Atlantic Command), Army general John Shalikashvili, and Hoar. In the wake of that event, the press anointed Hoar the front-runner for Powell's job because, as one reporter noted, he was viewed as "an iron man, a guns-and-missiles kind of guy, and right now there are no real gunfighters at the top levels in the Clinton administration."[4]

Clinton liked Hoar and thought it would be a nice touch to appoint him as the first Marine JCS chairman, but he settled on Shalikashvili, a low-key, open-faced, grandfatherly officer who would be the first draftee to serve in the position. Hoar shrugged off rumors that Clinton had decided against him because appointing a Marine would be controversial. "In the end, I think he was just more comfortable with Shali," Hoar said. That was true; Clinton liked Shalikashvili, who'd done well in northern Iraq and came with the recommendation of John Galvin, an influential figure in the military who'd preceded him as the Supreme Allied Commander in Europe. Galvin had watched in awe as Shali, in the walk-up to Desert Storm, had transferred ninety thousand American troops from Europe to the Gulf in just under sixty days, a logistics miracle. Galvin's opinion mattered—he was the closest thing the military had to a diplomat. Then too, as he told Clinton officials, Shalikashvili knew Europe well. With the Bosnia crisis heating up, Clinton needed someone in the military who had a feel for the conflict and experience working with European militaries.[5]

Shalikashvili was perhaps the most underrated senior officer in his service. He'd come to the United States at the age of sixteen, the son of refugees, and learned English by watching John Wayne movies. His father had fought against and then with the Germans in World War II, hoping to liberate his beloved Georgia, but when the Red Army stormed through Eastern Europe he found his way to Peoria, where his son attended Bradley University and enlisted in the ROTC. After graduation, Shalikashvili received his draft notice. Much like Powell, Shalikashvili found the Army to his liking, was awarded a Bronze Star in Vietnam, and made his way slowly, if deliberately, upward. He was steady, certain, but lacked the kind of flashy resume that got one regularly mentioned as a figure of influence. Which is why Powell, when he queried Galvin about Shalikashvili, did so with a distinct hint of surprise in his voice. "Shali is looking good, isn't he? I mean really looking good," Powell said. Galvin agreed, recommending that Powell see for himself. Powell did, visiting Shalikashvili in Turkey during Operation Provide Comfort. He liked what he saw—his never-say-no confidence, informality, fundamental decency, and, a key for Powell, his care for his soldiers. Powell wasn't surprised that, when Clinton told Shalikashvili that he wanted him to head the JCS, Shali said he'd rather stay in Europe. That sealed it: Shalikashvili was Clinton's pick.[6]

Shalikashvili was sworn in as Powell's replacement on October 25, 1993, in the wake of the Somali disaster. The White House was reeling from the incident, Les Aspin was being pressured to leave his job because of it, interservice feuding over the Pentagon budget was heating up, and Serbian militias were besieging Srebrenica in Bosnia. Shalikashvili had his work cut out for him, which included easing the still uncomfortable relationship between Clinton and the military.

That said, Shalikashvili was also fortunate. While he took over a JCS that was in transition (Merrill McPeak had retired and was replaced by Ronald Fogleman; Admiral Jeremy Michael Boorda had replaced the Tailhook-battered Frank Kelso; and Admiral William Owens was the new vice chief), he knew and felt comfortable working with two of America's most important combatant commanders—Army general George Joulwan, a former West Point football guard, who'd taken over in

Europe, and the squeaky-clean former Eagle Scout J. H. Binford "Binny" Peay III, the new head of the US Central Command. Finally, in December, Les Aspin resigned as defense secretary and was replaced by William Perry, who would earn a reputation for being one of the smartest officials to head up the Pentagon in its history. Perry was "focused, articulate, precise and deep" (as one news report noted)—the exact opposite of Aspin.[7]

As crucially, while Shalikashvili felt out of place in White House meetings, Clinton listened closely to what he had to say, even if Shali wasn't always as forceful as Powell. Shalikashvili offered a different approach, and more in keeping with how the military had traditionally dealt with presidents. Like many of his most effective predecessors, Shalikashvili rarely said "no." Rather, when he didn't like an idea he would couch his disagreement with a courteous conditional, delivered in a low-voiced monotone laced with his Eastern European accent—the customary "yes sir, but" that had characterized White House military disagreements since the time of Omar Bradley, the first JCS chairman.

But for Clinton, Shalikashvili's best quality had nothing to do with his modesty, nuanced views, or his almost palpable feel for Europe. It had to do with who he wasn't: he wasn't Colin Powell.

LIEUTENANT GENERAL WESLEY Clark arrived at the Pentagon as the newly appointed J-5, the director of strategic plans and policy, in April of 1994. Along with the J-3 (operations), the J-5 might well be the most important position on the Joint Staff. Each of the directorates (the principle ones are numbered J-1 through J-8) report to the Joint Staff director and operate behind closed doors and at all hours, with colonels toting weighty briefing books for their bosses. Clark spent his first day determining what the JCS should say about the burgeoning political and humanitarian crisis in Rwanda, the African nation suffering through a brutal civil war, where Belgian troops had just landed. He left, finally, at 7:00 am the next morning, a full twenty-four hours after he'd reported for duty. It was, he thought, an exhilarating experience.[8]

Shalikashvili gave Clark the J-5 job despite the widespread dislike of him among his colleagues. The JCS chairman was familiar with the case against Clark: he was a tireless self-promoter, his fellow officers said, who'd gotten ahead by rubbing shoulders with the right people, endlessly polishing his own credentials—and by his singular focus on himself. He was a West Point valedictorian and Rhodes Scholar, had graduated at the top of his class at the prestigious Command and General Staff College, and had served as a White House fellow. He looked the part: clean-shaven, you could see your reflection in his spit-shined shoes, and every ribbon (and there were lots of them) was pinned perfectly in place. He smiled easily, reassuringly, and said he was there to help. The troops he commanded called him "the perfumed prince." In Army parlance, Clark was a "water walker." Which is to say, Clark was brilliant, well spoken, ambitious, and experienced. He was, in many respects, the perfect general. But that, it seems, was his problem. Few liked him, many hated him, and he hadn't been the first choice for the J-5 job among many of Shalikashvili's colleagues. Retired general Dan Christman, perhaps Clark's closest friend in the military, attributes this hostility to the Army's divided culture. "You've got to be able to spit and chew and dip, and wear your cowboy boots, and clip your 'ing's," Christman said. "And, if you didn't do that, somehow you weren't part of the crowd, and certainly you couldn't be a warrior. And that was not Wes."[9]

With the exception of a handful of senior officers like Shalikashvili and Christman, the reaction to Clark was visceral, if intangible. "Have you ever read *Once an Eagle*?" one retired senior Army officer asked when Clark was mentioned. The novel, a bestseller in 1967, is a touchstone for the Army, where it is viewed with reverence. The book was praised effusively by two Army chiefs of staff, reissued by the Army War College Foundation, and appears regularly as a requirement on Army reading lists. *Once an Eagle* describes the career of Sam Damon, a "soldier's soldier" who rises from the ranks but whose talents are thwarted at every turn by Courtney Massengale, who gains high command by self-promotion, political networking, and by saying what his civilian bosses want to hear. The book is an allegory that takes place in a fictional Vietnam, with the principled Damon arguing for a withdrawal from a losing conflict that is destroying the Army, his beloved service. Massengale, meanwhile, uses the war to cut his way through the Army's upper echelons. The message is almost baldly stated: Damon is the true selfless patriot, Massengale gets ahead by self-promotion and by sacrificing the troops. He doesn't love the Army, he loves himself. "You know who Courtney Massengale is? Well, Clark is Massengale," the retired Army officer explained.[10]

Clark knew Bill Clinton and liked him. The two had remarkably similar backgrounds. Both had grown up in Arkansas, lost their fathers in childhood, took on their stepfather's family name, and attended Georgetown University, where they'd first met, in 1965. Clark was well educated, a good talker, confident in his views, and extremely ambitious. Like Clinton. And like Clinton, he chucked his adopted Arkansas twang (Clark was actually born in Chicago) for a throttled-back Georgetown-by-way-of-Oxford voice. But if he ever needed to show where he was from, he would channel Little Rock. "Hi, Wes Clark, how are ya?" was his patented greeting. Clinton and Clark lost touch after Georgetown and were only reintroduced three decades later by actress Mary Steenburgen, who grew up with Clark in Arkansas, then served with him on a commission tasked with finding White House fellows in 1993. That same year, Steenburgen and her mother (Clark's mother's best friend) dropped Clark's name to Clinton during a White House visit. That's all it took: from then on, Clinton started referring to Clark as "my good friend, Wes Clark." Senior military officers regularly rolled their eyes on the unfairness of Washington, where (as they would say) "who you know is more important that what you know." That was true everywhere, but it didn't change the anti-Clark narrative. For Clark's critics he was a Massengale-like "staff puke," the second coming of former White House official, senior Army officer, and Nixon pal Alexander Haig, whom Clark knew, served with, and admired. Haig had gained promotion, leap-frogging his way over more senior and deserving officers, by palling up to Henry Kissinger back in the Nixon years. Clark was just like Haig, his critics said, elbowing his way into the White House by sidling up to the rich and famous. Shalikashvili overruled them all; Clark was an outstanding officer and sophisticated strategic thinker. He needed him.[11]

What Clark offered was a fresh view of the worsening situation in the Balkans. When the Cold War ended, Yugoslavia had broken apart, with its former constituent republics of Slovenia, Croatia, and Bosnia-Herzegovina forming independent states. In Belgrade, Serb leaders vowed to keep the federation together under their leadership, pushing for a Greater Serbia. The Serb-dominated Yugoslav army fought a short war with Slovenia in 1991, then withdrew from Bosnia in 1992 while leaving its weapons in the hands of Serb separatists. The war for Bosnia turned violent, with the better-armed Serb forces overrunning eastern Bosnia, where they imposed a policy of ethnic cleansing on the largely Muslim population. Women were gang-raped, military-aged men murdered or herded into concentration camps, and tens of thousands of Bosnians were starved, beaten, and executed. It was Europe's largest humanitarian disaster since the end of World War II.

In polite conversation, the Serb policy was called ethnic cleansing, but for many what was happening was genocide. A 1991 UN-imposed embargo on the warring parties was designed to end the fighting, but it had allowed Serbs access to weapons stockpiles of the Yugoslav army provided by Belgrade, where Serb president Slobodan Milosevic implemented a policy of "forced removal" of non-Serb populations from Bosnia. In April 1993, the UN responded by imposing a no-fly zone, Operation Deny Flight, which banned military flights in Bosnian airspace. American F-16s downed six Serb jets over Banja Luka in February 1994, but that did not stop the Serbs who, in an echo of the botched Safwan cease-fire, were allowed to use helicopters.[12]

The Clinton administration pushed for a policy of "lift and strike." The UN would lift the embargo on Bosnia, while the United States would strike at Serb forces. But the policy got little support in Europe, where America's NATO allies were hesitant to get involved in a Balkan war. Secretary of State Warren Christopher attempted to sell lift and strike during a tour of NATO capitals in 1993, but the trip was a disaster. The US, the Europeans said, wanted to resolve the problem by flying above it, leaving the dirty job of taking on the Serb military to them. They sensed what everyone in Washington knew: Clinton himself wasn't sold on the policy. Christopher returned from his foray a beaten man. Author David Halberstam quoted Richard Perle on Christopher's failure: "Warren Christopher went to Europe with an American policy," he said, "and he came back with a European one." And so the crisis deepened. Nearly every day, the administration's Principals Committee, the chief deputies in the major national security departments, attempted to come up with a Bosnia policy, and each day they failed.[13]

"Every weekend in Washington in the Spring of 1994, there were frantic White House Situation Room meetings," Clark would later write.

> My first Sunday on the job I was in the Situation Room for three hours, backing up the vice chairman of the Joint Chiefs, Admiral Bill Owens, as the Principals Committee considered the air mission over Bosnia, Operation Deny Flight. What constitutes a threat? When can our pilots shoot? At what point can a pilot legally preempt an attack? In the room were lawyers, policy analysts, military officers and university

professors . . . all gesturing and wagging their hands like fighter pilots as they wrestled with the intellectual challenge of providing sound, effective and legally acceptable guidance to pilots 4000 miles away over the Adriatic Sea.

A part of the problem was that the administration had yet to settle on a national military strategy, a philosophy of when to go to war, and when not to.[14]

In the absence of a national strategy, Clinton's White House had committed itself to "assertive multilateralism," UN ambassador Madeleine Albright's shorthand for when the United States would act. In an era of shrinking defense budgets, she said, it was in America's interest to build coalitions to respond to international threats. George Bush's 1991 intervention in Kuwait was the model, a clearly defined mission with clearly defined operational limits backed by UN resolutions. National security adviser Anthony Lake believed assertive multilateralism would allow the US to implement "a humanitarian led foreign policy." While Albright's term did not preclude the US from unilateral military action, it brought wry smiles from senior officers wrestling with the Bosnia crisis. Clinton's foreign policy team, they said, couldn't quite bring themselves to say the word "war." Predictably, Pentagon wags weighed in: Madeleine Albright wasn't going to bomb the Serbs, they said, she was going to "assert them."[15]

THE FIRST TEST of assertive multilateralism had come in Somalia and it had been a disaster. The second came in Haiti, where a Somali-like coup had imposed a harsh military junta. Haiti was closer to home than Somalia, and seen as a test of America's ability to act decisively in its own hemisphere, but it proved impossible for Clinton's foreign policy team, or the military, to shake off Mogadishu's grisly spectacle. The result was a more hesitant approach to the use of American force, cast now as an option of last resort in favor of diplomacy, economic muscle, and international pressure. So it was that the administration's first response to the burgeoning Haiti crisis was the imposition of harsh economic sanctions on the regime (with the agreement of the UN and the Organization of American States), followed soon thereafter by the threat of force. Rattled by this slow pressure, the Haitian junta decided to negotiate, eventually agreeing to the peaceful return of deposed president Jean-Bertrand Aristide. The settlement, signed on July 3, 1994, called for Aristide's reinstatement, an amnesty for coup leaders, the modernizing of the Haitian army, and a new Haitian police force. On October 11, one week after the debacle in Mogadishu, the USS *Harlan County*, a US Navy tank-landing ship, arrived in Port-au-Prince with two hundred US military police to enforce the agreement. But with Mogadishu still fresh in the public mind, Clinton directed the soldiers on the *Harlan County* to stay aboard their ship when an angry mob protested their landing, shouting "Somalia, Somalia." The hesitation embarrassed Clinton and cost him politically. George Bush, Republicans said, would never have gone "all wobbly" when facing unruly third-worlders.

Clinton retrenched. He accelerated planning for a US military response, but told Shalikashvili and Pentagon chief William Perry to keep the numbers modest—somewhere, he said, under twenty-five thousand men. He did not want to use force, but Haiti would not be another Task Force Ranger. The operation was in place by the time of the *Harlan County* incident, but former president Jimmy Carter interceded, saying he knew some junta members and could get them to step aside. Clinton hesitantly welcomed Carter's help, but believed the former president was simply calling attention to himself, signaling (nose in air) that he could resolve a problem for the young and naïve president. Carter took Colin Powell and Sam Nunn to Haiti with him, which heightened White House worries, so Clinton set a deadline for the end of their talks. The US invasion force (Operation Uphold Democracy) would come ashore on September 19, spearheaded by the 75th Ranger Regiment, whether Carter, Powell, and Nunn were successful or not.[16]

Operation Uphold Democracy's commander was Lieutenant General Hugh Shelton, a non–West Point North Carolinian who'd made his military spurs in the special forces in Vietnam. There was a time when that would have cut against an officer (the special forces were clubby, it was said, and difficult to control), but that had changed. Like many of that elite, Shelton fought a small-unit war in Southeast Asia, hunkered down with a handful of others on long-range reconnaissance patrols, a "lerp" in Army parlance. This was hand-to-hand combat in close quarters. His commander told the broad-chested, six-foot-five Shelton that the Vietcong would kill him for sure, because he made an inviting target. He was just too tall. That hadn't happened, and Shelton went on to touch all the bases, sporting parachute wings, a chest full of medals, and a 5th Special Forces Group combat patch on his right sleeve. But Shelton's finest quality was his brevity. "Been there, done that," he said of his Vietnam experience, and left it at that.

Predictably, perhaps, Shelton mistrusted Bill Clinton, who hadn't been there or done anything. But Shelton's fellow officers were careful not to criticize Clinton to Shelton's face after the former lerp spent an afternoon with Clinton. That had been seven months before Shelton readied his task force for Uphold Democracy, when Clinton came to Fort Bragg to visit soldiers injured when an F-16 collided with a C-130 transport plane, killing twenty-four paratroopers and burning many others. Shelton accompanied Clinton to the Womack Army Medical Center, where the president visited the injured. There were over one hundred patients in all, and Clinton made a point of meeting each one of them. Shelton watched closely. Clinton might not have connected with Colin Powell or the JCS, but he connected with these soldiers. As Clinton was about to leave, he turned to his assistant. "Is that it?" he asked. In fact, it wasn't. There were three other burn victims in intensive care on the top floor. They weren't conscious, and weren't expected to live. "I want to see those three," Clinton said. Shelton and Clinton donned special gloves, gowns, and face coverings, then saw them one by one. Clinton stood over each bed, then sat beside them in prayer. Shelton was moved. "It's just something I had to do," Clinton told him.[17]

Now, steaming toward Haiti aboard the USS *Whitney*, his command ship, Shelton monitored his forces: the 75th Rangers were raring to go, sixty-two aircraft were filled with paratroopers of the 82nd Airborne, Marines aboard amphibious ships were about to come ashore, the USS *America* aircraft carrier with a contingent of Navy SEALs was in position, and radio-jamming aircraft were approaching Port-au-Prince. There was high tension aboard the *Whitney*, where Shelton was monitoring the Carter talks with Haitian strongman Raoul Cédras, whom Shelton had met. As Carter negotiated, Shelton seethed. The former president was bumping up against Clinton's deadline. At one point, watching CNN, Shelton caught a shot of Carter. "Get the hell out of there," he shouted, then checked with Admiral Paul Miller, his commander. Miller got on the telephone with Clinton, Perry, and Shalikashvili. Carter's team, Miller told Shelton, needed "a few more minutes." Shelton was exasperated. "Do they understand what we are dealing with here?" he asked. "Those minutes are critical." Eventually, Cédras relented, but only after an aide burst into the talks. "The 82nd Airborne is on the way," he shouted. That was enough for Cédras, who capitulated.[18]

Shelton was annoyed. He was now required to transform his military operation into a peacekeeping plan, using US soldiers and sailors to ensure stability, not impose it. The US military would enter Haiti, he was told, "in an atmosphere of cooperation and coordination." What the hell did that mean? Shelton wondered. He felt like he'd just been handed "ten pounds of shit in a five pound bag." Shelton hadn't wanted to put his soldiers into combat, but the agreement was a letdown, as it was for the soldiers of the 82nd Airborne, many of whom refused to be disconnected from their parachute rigging even as their transports headed back to Fort Bragg. "We were so pumped up and ready to go," one of Shelton's paratroopers noted. "Now this!" Later, after Shelton returned stateside, a story circulated about his reputation for understatement. Confronting Cédras, Shelton told him to order his military to turn in their weapons, because they now belonged to the Americans. "And pack your bags," he added. "You're leaving."[19]

In fact, while his meetings with Cédras contained many of Shelton's celebrated one-liners, his discussions with him went into great detail about what the departing Haitian dictator should do, and just how he should do it. While Shelton would later write that he appreciated his Harvard University course on "The Art of Negotiating," his actions in Haiti, and his blunt take-it-or-leave-it instructions to Cédras, weren't about "getting to 'yes.'" They were about imposing America's will. Shelton was in his element and Washington noticed. Haiti put him on a fast track to his fourth star. He was now one of Clinton's favorites, a combat officer who'd made the essential transition from fighter to diplomat. Haiti was a turning point for Shelton, but it was also crucial for Clinton, who now jettisoned assertive multilateralism.

The shift came with the *Harlan County* incident. "I'm never going to wimp out like I did in Haiti again," Clinton vowed. In fact, the abandonment of the policy had been under way since the previous spring, when the White House issued Presidential Decision Directive 25 (PDD-25), redefining US support for peacekeeping missions. "Participation in UN peace operations can never be a substitute for the necessity of fighting and winning our own wars," the memorandum stated, "nor can we allow it to reduce our capability to meet that imperative." State Department spokesman Nicholas Burns put it more simply. The UN "can keep the peace," he said, "but when it comes to applying force, it's not a good instrument." The JCS agreed: the Haiti and Bosnia operations (conducted with broad international approval) showed that while there'd been a lot of multilateralism, there hadn't been much assertion.[20]

The administration viewed the restoration of Aristide as a foreign policy win—evidence, they said, of the administration's new decisiveness. But Haiti did little to reverse the Somalia setback, which hung like a dark cloud over everything. Nor did it set aright mounting reports of a genocide in Rwanda, an interethnic bloodletting set in motion in April, just as PDD-25 was in its final draft. Starting on April 7 and for the next three months, Rwanda's Hutu majority slaughtered over eight hundred thousand minority Tutsis. The weapon of choice was the machete, wielded with horrific effect. Writer Philip Gourevitch dubbed it "the most efficient killing since the atomic bombing of Hiroshima and Nagasaki."[21] The United States did nothing. Reports of the mass murders reached Washington, where officials quibbled, debating the definition of the term "genocide." There was a sense that if the murders could somehow be classified as something other than "genocide," then the US wouldn't be required to intervene. Hence, what was happening in Rwanda wasn't actually a genocide, a State Department official patiently explained; what was happening were "acts of genocide." How many "acts of genocide" did it take to make a genocide? a reporter asked. "That's just not a question that I'm prepared to answer," the State Department's spokesperson said.[22]

In retrospect, Somalia, Haiti, and Rwanda are a tragic triptych, panels of decision and indecision bolted together, hinged but related. The central panel of the triptych is Somalia. On the left is Haiti, a smaller wing of the defining centerpiece, with blood-soaked Rwanda on the right. It is Somalia that defines the piece, as it defined the administration's foreign policy: America waded into Somalia, recoiled from it, then waded into Haiti, fearfully and hesitantly, and so did not wade into Rwanda at all. The sense of lurching was profound, a mix of intervention and hesitation that brought on waves of public criticism. For Republicans, Somalia, Haiti, and Rwanda were not so much a triptych as a three-ring circus. The Clinton administration didn't have a clue what it was doing. The public agreed.

Clinton was responsible for the lurching, but so was the military. They were as uncertain as Clinton about when to use force. Shelton symbolized this ambivalence. Indelibly forged by war, Shelton castigated those who recoiled from battle as "sissies," grumbled about civilian meddlers (like Carter, the ultimate in hand-wringing sissies—as Shelton believed—in Haiti), and felt awkward in policy debates. His instinct was to simplify: just give us our orders, and we'll do the rest. In this sense, Shelton represented the best of the US military tradition: he believed in the essential rightness of American power and was disappointed when his troops were ordered back from Operation Uphold Democracy. Yet, like Powell, Shelton was a reluctant warrior. Conducting military interventions to build nations or save lives made no sense to him. The military's job wasn't to build nations, but destroy them, not to save lives, but to take them. The correct question wasn't how many killings does it take to make a genocide, but how many Americans are willing to die for Rwanda? The military's answer to the question was clear: none.

Then, on July 12, 1995, Bosnian Serbs overran Srebrenica, which they'd besieged for three years. Over the next day, over eight thousand men and boys were massacred, a mass murder so heinous that the United States couldn't ignore it. The killings also sparked a crisis among America's NATO allies, whose leaders had proved as feckless over the past years as Clinton. The Serbs had been killing their enemies for years, but Srebrenica was different: trouble in the Balkans had sparked World War I and had been a crucial political battleground during the Cold War. America's European allies were worried and under increasing domestic political pressure to intervene. Through all of the first half of July, British and French military commanders were on the telephone with their American peers nearly every day, urging the US to do something. Two days after Srebrenica, on July 14, Clinton responded. French president Jacques Chirac had called that morning, then given a press conference in Paris, comparing the situation in Europe to the eve of World War II. This was just like 1938, when Nazi Germany was rearming and pressuring its neighbors, he said. Clinton promised Chirac that he'd do something, and now, standing on the putting green on the White House lawn, the president turned on his advisers. "This can't continue," he shouted. "We need a policy." The next morning he huddled with Shalikashvili and Perry, then sent them to Europe. Warren Christopher followed two days later. Clinton's instructions were clear. The US would not simply confer with its allies, he told Shalikashvili, it would lead them. Clinton was tired of "being played" by the Serbs. "The only time we make any progress there is when we threaten to use force," he said.[23]

The Balkans are a military burial ground. The Austrians fought there in World War I, losing an empire, while the Nazis chased legions of partisans there twenty-five years later, conducting mass reprisals when their soldiers were killed. The partisans matched them. The level of brutality was astonishing, even by World War II standards. Belgrade wasn't liberated by the Soviet Red Army, but by a partisan army under Josip Broz "Tito," who fought on two fronts—in a national war against the Germans and in a civil war against his anticommunist Balkan enemies. Over one million Yugoslavs died fighting each other. But despite this history, John Shalikashvili believed that NATO airpower would prove successful against the Serbs and force them to end the conflict, and he told that to NATO leaders in July. On July 16, in London, Shalikashvili and Perry met with their NATO counterparts, then traveled to Holland to meet with Dutch commanders. That July meeting marked a turning point in the senior military's relationship with the Clinton administration, a senior military officer now says, because it "showed how the civilian-military relationship was supposed to work and, when it did, how effective it could be."[24]

More than anyone in the Clinton administration, John Shalikashvili knew this history and understood it in a way that they didn't. In the months ahead, he would become the focal point of American actions, counseling patience, mediating among his feuding commanders (Army chief Denny Reimer wanted a more modest American commitment, NATO commander George Joulwan didn't), defending his most argumentative air commanders, and supporting Clinton. Always a good listener, he was easy to underestimate and quite often, and despite his accent, people forgot who he was and where he'd been. One of the truly memorable stories about Shalikashvili, repeated often in the years ahead, was about a trip he took with William Perry, Warren Christopher, and senior diplomat and Europe expert Richard Holbrooke to Berlin at the end of 1994. The group was there to honor the retirement of the Berlin Brigade, the Army's famed 6th Infantry Regiment, which stood facing the Red Army from the opening of the Cold War until the unraveling of the Soviet Union. It had been there, in 1961, at Checkpoint Charlie, when the Red Army had maneuvered its tanks to the precipice of World War III. As Holbrooke, Christopher, and Perry awaited the beginning of the ceremony, they compared notes on when each of them had first come to the city. The earliest date for each of them had been in 1961, which seemed ages ago. They chuckled at how old they'd become, and how Europe, and Berlin, had changed. And then they turned to Shalikashvili. Did he remember his first visit? He nodded. "It was 1943. During the war," he said. "My father brought me here." The three stood looking at him, taking in his past. Shalikashvili didn't say anything more, but he didn't need to. His father had gone out to fight, while he and his mother huddled together in one of Berlin's basements, as Allied aircraft roared overhead and their bombs thumped through the burning city around them. The memory was important to Shalikashvili because it symbolized an American victory, which had finally brought peace to the continent. His job now was to ensure that peace. His memory brought the group to silence.[25]

Shalikashvili and Perry were back in London on July 21, where they were joined by Warren Christopher, who'd arrived for a meeting with representatives from those European nations who were a part of the UN deployment (UNPROFOR, the UN Protection Force) in Bosnia. French president Chirac had taken the lead in calling the meeting, but French military officers arrived without a plan. Chirac, his defense minister announced, wanted the French military to occupy Sarajevo and fight the Serbs. The British chief of staff, General Anthony Inge, was incredulous. Fight the Serbs? "With what?" he asked. Thirty-nine nations had troops on the ground, but few had heavy weapons. Perhaps, the French suggested, the Americans could ferry their troops to Sarajevo in their helicopters. This was a non-starter for Shalikashvili: he did not want the United States to drib and drab its way into the Balkans, arguing that a helicopter assault would have to be preceded by an air campaign to knock out the Serb air defense system.[26]

The US plan was less ambiguous and more realistic. What Shalikashvili, Perry, and Christopher proposed was a massive and sustained bombing of the Bosnian Serbs. But for this to be successful, they argued, the UN command structure put in place in February 1992 had to be scrapped. The UN had set up safe areas for Bosnian civilians but relied on NATO aircraft to protect them. The structure was unmanageable.

Under the arrangement, the UN had final approval of NATO air missions. Air taskings would move up the separate national (British, Canadian, Dutch, French, and Spanish) chains of command, be coordinated by a NATO tactical office, then given to the UN command. The arrangement was not only unwieldy, it was ineffective, resulting in "tit for tat" Serb reprisals against UN personnel. At the end of May, for example, the UN struck Serb positions at Pale, near Sarajevo. The Serbs responded by taking four hundred UN peacekeepers hostage, parading them in chains for television cameras. Two French soldiers were then killed in fighting with Bosnian Serbs. French general Bernard Janvier, the head of the UN peacekeeping force, was in a quandary: responding with force would simply yield more hostages.

The UN-commanded air campaign hadn't kept the Serbs out of Srebrenica, from being resupplied, from taking hostages, from defying the international community, or from murdering Bosnian Muslims. The reason, Shalikashvili argued, was that the UN was using "pinpricks." The JCS chairman had studied the "UN/NATO Command Relationships" graphic, with its two columns of distinct boxes crisscrossed by arrows, and concluded that it was a prescription for doing nothing. Maybe that was the point, he told senior British and French military commanders. The UN was the wrong organization for the job. He then launched into a defense of NATO. NATO is the peacekeeper in Europe, he told them, not the UN. There should be unity of command with massive air strikes led by NATO aircraft. He used the phrase "carpet bombing." Shalikashvili was nearly eloquent in his argument, working to convince his British, French, and Dutch military counterparts while Perry worked on convincing NATO's gaggle of defense ministers. Warren Christopher, meanwhile, deftly elbowed aside the UN. NATO had been supporting the UN, he said; now the UN could support NATO.[27]

The key to the final agreement rested largely with Shalikashvili, who convinced the British, French, and Dutch chiefs of staff that, after two years of waffling, the United States would back its words with action. Shalikashvili had the same effect on them that he'd had on Clinton's NSC team: he listened closely, commiserated, then spoke in a tone so low his fellow officers had to lean forward to hear him. Shalikashvili also relied on General George Joulwan, the Supreme Allied Commander in Europe and the head of the US European Command, an imposing West Pointer who also served as a kind of unofficial ambassador to the continent. Deep voiced and imposing, Joulwan could dominate a room, and often did. People who knew him believed he was most comfortable in front of a white board, pointer in hand, explaining how things worked—or, in the case of the UN, didn't. By the end of whatever he was saying, the board would be filled with indecipherable circles, arrows, and exclamation points, but they all made sense to Joulwan. Shalikashvili and Joulwan were a formidable team, but to this Shali added Wes Clark, who served as his primary liaison with the European militaries. Clark had spent the weeks prior to the London meeting on the telephone with his counterparts, talking them through the crisis and passing their views on to Shalikashvili.[28]

Four days after the London meeting, UN secretary-general Boutros Boutros-Ghali announced that he was putting the authority for ordering air strikes in the hands of the military commander of UN troops on the ground. That didn't sound like much of a change, but it was crucial—from now on, air strikes in the Balkans would be under the control of Admiral Leighton Smith, the commander of NATO forces in southern Europe. In practical terms, an entire column of the unwieldy command structure was eliminated. For the UN, busily calculating fairness, air strikes were always a last resort. Now, they were on the table from the beginning. The other result of the London Conference was a new ultimatum to the Serbs. If they violated the safe zone in the city of Gorazde, NATO would respond with an air attack. Shalikashvili was disappointed that the ultimatum was so specific, but it is what he could get everyone to agree to—and, in the end, as he calculated, it wouldn't matter. In practical terms, NATO could now package an air attack plan that would punish the Serbs wherever they struck. By early August, the planning for the air campaign (called Operation Deliberate Force) was under way, with America in the lead. "There is a very important lesson that you cannot be in an alliance with nations and somehow step back from a leadership position," Shalikashvili would later reflect.[29]

On August 3, Air Force lieutenant general Michael Ryan (Leighton Smith's air commander) briefed George Joulwan on Operation Deliberate Force, which was agreed to seven days later by the UN force commander in Bosnia. An Air Force Academy graduate and son of a former Air Force chief of staff, Ryan was a classic "airpower air head"—supremely confident and aggressive, he told UN officials that his goal was to drive the Serbs to the negotiating table. His plan was a creative mix of military strikes tied to political goals: he kept NATO aircraft away from targets where civilians might be killed (television shots of civilian corpses would be political fodder for the Serbs, he knew), while flooding the air over Serb positions in Bosnia with fighter-bombers. The Serbs' greatest asset in Bosnia was their military, so he would destroy it. Ryan also understood the vulnerability of NATO members to casualties: the already shaky co-alition would become more shaky if British, French, Dutch, or Italian fliers were paraded as captives, so Ryan prepared a lead-up addendum to the attack plan called Operation Deadeye, targeting Serb air defense po-sitions. And Ryan made it clear to everyone: he would be the only officer in charge of targeting.[30]

On the morning of August 30, after a Bosnian Serb mortar attack on Sarajevo that killed thirty-eight, Ryan ordered his fliers into the air. This was not a "pinprick" operation. Over the next forty-eight hours, NATO bombers hit fifty-six Serb military targets in Pale and around Sarajevo. The first strike was actually launched by the USS *Theodore Roosevelt*, on station in the Adriatic. The strikes were precise, though Dutch fliers used CBU-87s, a clustered bomb that carried 202 submunitions, which cut through large swaths of Serb formations, with unexploded ordnance lit-tering the ground. After two days, the UN requested a bombing halt when the Serbs said they would remove their heavy artillery east of Sa-rajevo. But on September 7, when the Serbs reneged on their agreement, Ryan once again ordered his bombers into the air. For the next seven days they pounded Serb military positions. Eight NATO nations participated, with a total of over 350 aircraft launching more than 3,500 total sorties against 338 targets: communications nodes, radar sites, artillery and air defense emplacements, troop concentrations, and armored formations. At one point, the United States launched a Tomahawk cruise missile strike on Banja Luka at the request of George Joulwan, who believed the use of the missile would convince the recalcitrant Serbians that NATO was serious. The offensive halted after three weeks, when the Serbs agreed to negotiate.

From the outside, and coupled with surprisingly effective Bosnian and Croatian ground offensives against Serb military positions, Delib-erate Force was a victory. But on the inside, the story was different, with deep disagreements aired by US commanders about the intervention.

Admiral Leighton Smith (his colleagues, predictably, called him "Snuffy") called the Bosnia operation "the biggest damn mess in the world." The UN-NATO relationship, he added, was unwieldy ("absolutely, completely unworkable"), military goals were being driven by uncertain political calculations, and the last thing the United States should do is act as a policeman for warring Slavs. Smith could be uncomfortably blunt, answering press questions with a "beats the hell out of me," or, on occasion, "go ask the civilians," and while he hesitantly supported Operation Deliberate Force, he railed that the air attacks should have come sooner, and been more violent. Not all problems could be solved by military force, he thought, and Bosnia was one of them. The enmities went back too far, the hatreds were too deeply embedded. And like many of his colleagues, Smith worried that the US military was being asked to do too much. "Where the hell are the diplomats?" he asked his staff.[31]

The problem for Smith, and for much of the rest of the military, was that the diplomat the Clinton administration put in charge of negotiating a political settlement on Bosnia was Richard Holbrooke, a lifelong foreign service officer and well-traveled diplomatic guru with a reputation for cultivating political allies. There was no one in the State Department, those who knew him said, who was more brilliant. Or more disliked. When Clinton took office he'd named Holbrooke the US ambassador to Germany—a position Holbrooke thought well beneath his station, but he took the position after being assured that Clinton had plans for him. In August, Anthony Lake put him in charge of getting the Serbs to the negotiating table, warning him that not everyone had agreed with his appointment. Peter Galbraith, the State Department's eyes and ears in Zagreb, Croatia, was more direct: "I'm your only friend," Galbraith told him one day. "Everyone else hates your ass." Holbrooke was the State Department's Wes Clark—ambitious and effusive when it came to talking about himself or holding forth on his exciting and brilliant career, but much less enthusiastic when the topic turned to someone or something else. He got on peoples' nerves. "The ego has landed," his staff would say whenever his plane arrived in Belgrade.[32]

"You know, why doesn't this guy come down here [to Naples] and get briefed in on Bosnia?" Admiral Leighton Smith asked Air Force general Chuck Boyd, the deputy at the European Command. "There's probably nobody in this universe that knows more than our staff knows about Bosnia. And he's getting ready to go over there and wade right in the middle of it. It seems to me he might want to come here." Not surprisingly, when Holbrooke finally showed up, Smith was less than impressed.

"Eventually, we got a call that said that he was coming to town," Smith later recalled. "We got all the briefings ready, and met in my office, and we were treated to a couple of hours of Dick Holbrooke on Dick Holbrooke." Holbrooke left without hearing the briefing.[33]

Smith was even less impressed with Holbrooke's military aide, General Wesley Clark, appointed as the JCS's liaison with Holbrooke by Shalikashvili. In early September, Clark overstepped his bounds, conveying Holbrooke's wishes in the form of an order. During Deliberate Force's bombing pause, Holbrooke told Clark to get on the telephone with Smith and tell him to resume the air offensive. Clark should have known better. "Who the hell are you?" Smith asked, then reminded Clark that there was a chain of command that led from the president to the secretary of defense to Joulwan and then to Smith. Holbrooke wasn't in the chain of command, and neither was Clark. "Are you in the fucking chain of command?" Smith asked Clark. "No sir," Clark answered. "This is a NATO operation," Smith told him. "I take my orders from George Joulwan. If you want me to do something, you go through the proper channels. But I cannot, will not, should not, I simply won't take orders from you individually. You want to talk to me, you know how to do that." Clark realized his mistake and gave the required answer: "Yes, sir," he said, "Absolutely, sir."[34]

Holbrooke and Clark were oddly, if perfectly, matched: the administration mistrusted Holbrooke, the military disliked Clark. While their relationship got off to a rocky start (a shouting match over their views on NATO expansion to include former Soviet-aligned Eastern European countries, which Clark was for), they quickly patched up their differences, and by November 1995, when Holbrooke convened Bosnia's warring parties at Wright-Patterson Air Force Base in Dayton, Ohio, they were nearly inseparable. Their bond had been sealed the previous August, when the two set out in a convoy from their hotel in Split toward Sarajevo along the dangerous Mount Igman Road. When a French armored personnel carrier ahead of them rolled off the incline and careened down a mountain, Clark grabbed a rope. As he rappelled down, firing broke out from somewhere, and everyone dove for cover. Clark kept going, pulled some of the peacekeepers from their vehicle, then went back up the mountain, hand over hand, to check on Holbrooke. After he'd sprinted to Holbrook's side, he wasn't even winded. Two French peacekeepers died, but later, in a telephone call to the president, Holbrooke called Clark a hero.

At Dayton, with Holbrooke tirelessly moving between the Bosnian, Croatian, and Serbian delegations, Clark was always nearby, hovering in the background, briefcase in hand. Shalikashvili noticed the hovering and told Clark to get out front. He wanted the military to have a higher profile, he said. "Get out front, be seen," he directed. "You're not an errand boy." Clark complied, moving front-and-center. Shalikashvili noticed: "Wes, you are the most well-known General in Europe," Shalikashvili told him after several weeks. Clark's official mandate was to help Holbrooke draft the military annex to a final agreement, but his unofficial role was as Holbrooke's lobbyist with George Joulwan in Europe and the JCS in Washington. It was an impossible assignment, bringing Clark into conflict with a military leadership opposed to deploying US troops in the Balkans.[35]

At one point in the negotiations, Holbrooke quizzed Clark on the military's opposition to deploying US forces as peacekeepers. It was an early morning discussion in a stuffy Dayton hotel room where both men, exhausted and irritable, turned on each other in a replay of Colin Powell's face-off with Madeleine Albright. "Wes, what's wrong with the Pentagon?" Holbrooke asked. "Don't they understand they have to participate. The President has said he wants an agreement. What's happened to the military since Vietnam?" An eavesdropper later claimed that Clark responded angrily to this, pointing out that if Holbrooke was asking him to take sides he was talking to the wrong person. "This isn't Vietnam," Clark responded. "I'm not going to go around Shalikashvili's back." The incident was quietly promoted by Clark as proof that he stood with the military against the pro-interventionist White House, but few believed him. That was because in private, and when no one was listening, Clark and Holbrooke agreed. The United States needed to do something in the Balkans, and the JCS was dragging its feet. Holbrooke was an interventionist; so too was Clark. Clark later reflected on Holbrooke's views on the military. "There was a lot of truth in what Holbrooke was saying," he said.[36]

Clark's task had been made even more difficult with the appointment of General Dennis Reimer as the Army chief of staff the previous June. Reimer made his views on Clark known to his most powerful patron, John Shalikashvili. Clark, he said, wasn't like Shali or Powell. He might have slogged through a war in Vietnam, but he wasn't a reluctant warrior; in fact, there wasn't anything reluctant about him. Reimer also cited stories about Clark that circulated among his fellow officers—that he was "abusive, condescending and mean" to enlisted personnel, cutting in line in front of them in mess halls, or having aides clear the way for him when he arrived. But it was Clark's friendship with Holbrooke that most grated on his colleagues. Holbrooke praised Clark because he believed in him and Clark welcomed the praise, sidling up to Holbrooke, because he thought it would help his career. It didn't: Holbrooke was a walking advertisement for what senior military officers most mistrusted, a civilian who looked on them as a tool that could be used whenever they needed to score negotiating points—agree with us, or I'll loose these crazies on you. "Clark, more than any other military officer of his rank, was ready to project power in this murky area that we call peacekeeping, or nation-building, or humanitarian intervention" and had a "liberal interventionist attitude toward the use of force," Holbrooke said admiringly. For Reimer, Holbrooke got it exactly right: peacekeeping, nation building, and humanitarian intervention were "murky"—which, he thought, was a damned good reason for not doing them. Madeleine Albright called this kind of murkiness "assertive multilateralism," while Clark dubbed it "compellent diplomacy." It was the same thing, Reimer concluded. Wes Clark was Madeleine Albright with stars on his shoulders.[37]

Holbrooke was right about the JCS, but what he said about the military was also true of the White House, which was as reluctant to send twenty thousand soldiers to the Balkans as Dennis Reimer. Which meant that at the same time that Holbrooke was strong-arming Serb leader Slobodan Milosevic, cajoling the Bosnians, and lecturing the Croats, he was reassuring the White House that a final Dayton agreement, signed in December 1995, did not mean a long-term commitment to Bosnia. The White House pushed back, limiting American involvement to a single year. Clark was a key to the agreement, for during the most difficult negotiations, and particularly with the Serbs, Holbrooke would smile and reach over, lightly touching Clark's elbow—a not-so-subtle signal that, if things didn't go America's way, the United States would use its military to impose its will. Milosevic did not need to be reminded. Holbrooke had been with him in Belgrade when a cruise missile obliterated his command and communications post in Bosnia—a single missile destroying the Serb strongman's ties to his right-wing militias. Holbrooke could see that Milosevic was frightened. "It was your NATO, your bombs and missiles, your high technology that defeated us," Milosevic told Clark when the Dayton negotiations were finally concluded. "We Serbs never had a chance against you."[38]

SHALIKASHVILI KNEW THAT Clark was disliked, but he remained his strongest ally. He defended him to Dennis Reimer, then recommended him for a command slot that would give him his fourth star, making him a full general and bringing him into the military's stratosphere. Shalikashvili fought with Reimer over Clark's future through all of February 1996, then peremptorily overruled his objections by recommending that Clinton appoint Clark as head of the US Southern Command, overseeing US forces in Central and South America. Clark was also helped by General Barry McCaffrey, the celebrated division commander in Desert Storm and Clinton's fellow jogger, whom he would be succeeding at US Southern Command (SOUTHCOM). "Don't worry," McCaffrey told Clark, "I have more pull than Denny. You'll get this." Shalikashvili brought Clark and Reimer together shortly after Clark took up his new command, when Clark wanted to relocate SOUTHCOM's headquarters to Puerto Rico and Reimer disagreed. When the two met and Shali couldn't peacefully resolve the disagreement, he decided for Clark. This was textbook Shalikashvili, who preferred diplomacy over confrontation, until he had no choice. "This whole thing about Shalikashvili being a kindly man with a European accent is a little exaggerated," George Joulwan would later say. "You know, Shali would hear you out and you'd think you'd convinced him and then he'd give you this steely-eyed stare and you'd have to fight. I've seen it a dozen times."[39]

But the dust-up over Clark was nothing compared to what Shalikashvili faced on May 16, when Chief of Naval Operations (CNO) Jeremy Michael Boorda left the Pentagon, returned home, then shot himself in the chest with a pistol. Distraught over claims that he was wearing service awards he didn't deserve, Boorda left two suicide notes. Shalikashvili was stunned. Boorda had come up the hard way, lying about his age to get in the Navy after he dropped out of high school at the age of seventeen, then climbing the greasy pole from seaman to the Navy's highest office. Boorda was the first enlisted man to serve as CNO, which endeared him to the Navy's enlisted ranks. Boorda's sin might have seemed minor (he wore a combat "V," for "valor," over his Vietnam campaign ribbon, a war in which he'd proudly served), but senior officers were always careful to never claim service they didn't have, especially if it had anything to do with showing valor in combat. *Newsweek* reporter David Hackworth got hold of the story, calling Boorda's actions "the worst thing you can do." Boorda's allies defended the CNO, saying the "V" was "a simple mix-up."[40]

Boorda had actually faced far worse pressures in the months preceding his death, including a claim in the pages of the *New York Times* that he'd sidelined the career of Admiral Stanley Arthur, implicated in the Tailhook scandal, to curry favor with Clinton. The allegation was made by James Webb, a former secretary of the Navy under President Ronald Reagan and a Vietnam veteran, who then repeated the criticism during a Naval Academy address. Webb's anti-Boorda campaign was ugly and personal, but it had little to do with Boorda. Webb hated Clinton with something close to a personal obsession. That wasn't a surprise, as he publicly referred to everyone who opposed the Vietnam War (a demographic that included the president) as "cowards."[41]

Webb's attacks and the *Newsweek* investigation weighed on Boorda, as did allegations that senior Navy officers had mismanaged the Norfolk Naval Exchange (a massive retail outlet for Navy service members and their families) and that he failed to adequately defend the service against a probe of overspending on its F-18 fighter program. He had also had to face down supporters of an anonymous senior officer who claimed in the pages of the *Navy Times* that Boorda had lost the confidence of the service. Finally, Boorda had to answer challenges to his leadership because of a series of scandals at the Naval Academy, where five midshipmen were accused of "criminal activity." Within days of the Boorda suicide, Shalikashvili convened the JCS in an executive session, with just the chiefs in attendance. A close colleague of Shalikashvili says that the JCS chairman remained "absolutely tight-lipped" about what he told his colleagues, but speculated that "Shali said that 'we have to look at ourselves, and ask whether we did enough to help Mike.' For him, the answer was obvious."[42]

THE FIGHT OVER Clark and the Boorda suicide added to Shalikashvili's headaches, coming as they did in the midst of the deployment of US troops to serve as peacekeepers in Bosnia—and the opening of the US election season. Clinton had effectively defanged Bosnia as an election issue by promising to bring the twenty-thousand-plus troops he was deploying there home by December 1996, a pledge he'd reasserted during a visit to Europe in the wake of the Dayton agreement. The visit included an appearance, with General George Joulwan at his side, before US soldiers and their families at the Baumholder Army Base in Germany. In the wake of his sure-handed handling of the Bosnia crisis, Clinton showed his newfound confidence during his address to US troops. "You are strong, you are well-prepared, and the stakes demand the American leadership that you will provide," he said, and the troops responded with their patented "Hooo-ah" cheer. Clinton then added a standard personal touch, telling his audience about Zlata Filipovic, a young Sarajevo girl he'd met at the Dublin airport. She had asked him to deliver a message: "Mr. President," he related, "when you are in Germany, please thank the American soldiers for me. I want to go home." Joulwan applauded on cue, the perfect commanding officer escorting the commander in chief. But privately he was impressed. Clinton had "the touch," as Joulwan called it: he knew how to reach people.[43]

At the end of his address, the troops gave Clinton a sustained ovation, while the generals standing behind him joined in. For many senior military officers, the visit symbolized how Clinton had changed. This was the ultimate irony: George Bush, who'd led America into Desert Storm and served as a naval fighter pilot in World War II, seemed much less comfortable talking to privates and corporals than Clinton, who hadn't served a day. Gone too was the lousy salute, discarded in favor of a patented Clinton move, perfected through years of campaigning. As soldiers came to attention Clinton would nod and smile, sometimes throwing back his head in a huge grin, while reaching out with his left hand, touching the shoulder and subtlety pivoting the subject toward the camera: a picture with Bill. He wasn't the president of the United States, he was one of them. He was "Bubba." It was masterful.

But it wasn't only Clinton who'd changed: so too had the military. While senior military officers retained a deep mistrust of Clinton's liberal views, they now kept their doubts private, as if in deference to the popularity Clinton had with the troops. Enlisted personnel, in particular, treated him like he was a celebrity. Seated surrounded by soldiers at a long table during a lunch, he traded jokes with them, knew all about their music, and told them stories about who he'd met in Hollywood, and what they were like. He dropped names, swapped stories, asked about their families. He laughed easily, listened closely, and smiled. He was back in Arkansas, working potential voters, talking football. Even George Joulwan was sucked in, telling Clinton about how, when he was a cadet on the Army football team, they'd played Syracuse and about that "terrific running back they had." He shook his head, searching for the name. Clinton leaned in. "Ernie Davis," he said. Years later, Joulwan would wonder at this, still surprised by his own judgment. "Yeah," he said. "Yeah. I liked Bill Clinton."[44]

The military's senior leadership had it wrong: Clinton wasn't out of step with those in uniform, they were. Clinton was in high form at Baumholder, trading jokes and anecdotes as the soldiers around him leaned forward, hanging on his every word, thrilled to be talking to Bill Clinton. For them, Vietnam was a fading legacy, the military's fight over gays a wasted effort, and Bosnia a proud moment when they'd saved the lives of women and children. Bill Clinton had made that possible and they were proud of him: he was the comeback kid.

CHAPTER FOUR

Hugh Shelton: Clinton's General

"The lights are going out, the
bridges are coming down."

THE NOVEMBER 1996 reelection of Bill Clinton sparked a reshuffling
of the president's national security team. Warren Christopher was
out as secretary of state, and Madeleine Albright in, William Perry was
replaced at the Pentagon by Maine Republican senator William Cohen,
and Sandy Berger was named Clinton's national security adviser, replacing Tony Lake.[1]

The appointments of Albright and Cohen were a surprise. Senators
George Mitchell and Sam Nunn had been mentioned as Christopher's
likely successor, with Nunn sliding over to the Pentagon if Mitchell took
on the job of secretary of state. In truth, neither of them was in the running for either position, as Republicans signaled they would fight Mitchell's appointment, while Clinton thought Nunn was too conservative.
Then too, Nunn had sided with Colin Powell in the fight over gays in the
military, a fact that Clinton would not forget. For a time it appeared that
Richard Holbrooke would become Clinton's new man at Foggy Bottom,

but as reporter David Halberstam later noted, "the temptation to name the first woman secretary of state was irresistible."[2]

Cohen's appointment was puzzling. While his nomination was viewed as an attempt by the president to reach out to the Republicans, Cohen had been an outspoken critic of Clinton's Bosnia policy. Cohen criticized Clinton for failing to provide an exit strategy for US soldiers, for overspending in a time of Pentagon austerity, for sending US soldiers on a nation-building mission, and for failing to induce America's NATO partners to increase their share of the costs of the military alliance.[3] Then too, Cohen had no experience running a bureaucracy as complex as the Pentagon, nor was he seen as a strategic thinker, something the administration desperately needed.

The appointment of Cohen was a gamble, but it was one that Clinton was willing to make. The president calculated that the Maine senator would turn into a team player, taking the hard edge off his criticism of Clinton's decision to deploy peacekeepers to Bosnia once he was ensconced in his Pentagon office. The Bosnia deployment, dating from the signing of the Dayton Accords, had begun in December 1995, with US troops making up one-third of the sixty-thousand-soldier contingent. The Republicans were shrill in their condemnation of the move, saying US soldiers would be caught in the Serb-Bosnian cross fire. It hadn't turned out that way ("our troops have a different problem: They're bored," defense analyst Robert Kagan noted), but the criticisms continued, and Clinton's date for their departure kept changing. Initially, Clinton pledged the US deployment would end in December 1996 (conveniently, one month after the election), but that deadline had slipped. The changing situation on the ground, he announced, would mean the United States would have to keep its soldiers there until mid-1998. To make this digestible, he ratcheted down the number of US troops involved (to some 8,500) and renamed their deployment—they were no longer the International Force (or IFOR), they were now the Stabilization Force, or SFOR.[4]

The 1995 deployment was controversial on Capitol Hill, unpopular among the general public (a poll found that 70 percent of the American people opposed it), and viewed with disdain by the senior military. The Bosnia mission smacked of Mogadishu, placing US soldiers at risk in a part of the world where vital US interests weren't at stake. Evidence of the military's deep antipathy for the assignment had been most pronounced among senior American commanders in Europe. Several months after the Dayton Accords were signed, Bosnian Serb president Radovan Karadzic, who had been indicted for war crimes, drove through several NATO checkpoints without being detained. In Washington, an enraged Holbrooke said the military was purposely impeding Dayton's implementation. But in Europe, Admiral Leighton "Snuffy" Smith, the commander of allied forces in southern Europe, had a different view: the United States had mounted operations against public officials before, he said, and they had ended up costing American lives. That had happened in Somalia, and he didn't want it to happen in Bosnia.

Smith denied that Karadzic had ever gone through any NATO checkpoints and told General George Joulwan (the supreme allied commander in Europe, or SACEUR), as well as JCS chairman John Shalikashvili, that the Dayton Accords didn't require his troops to arrest war criminals. It wasn't his job and, moreover (as he'd once said to Wes Clark), he didn't take orders from Holbrooke. If Holbrooke wanted him to arrest someone, he could talk to the president, who could then call him and order him to do it. "Holbrooke wanted very much for us to have the kind of autonomous powers that we had in Germany, post World War II. [But] we didn't . . . and I think Holbrooke knows that," he later argued. "He also knows, precisely, that General John Shalikashvili, the chairman of our Joint Chiefs of Staff [and] General George Joulwan . . . were clear and unequivocal: soldiers do not make good policemen, this is not a good idea."[5]

American troops weren't good policemen and they weren't good firemen either. When Serb militias burned down Bosnian Muslim houses in Sarajevo, Holbrooke complained that Smith could have stopped them. NATO didn't have fire trucks, Smith responded testily, and while there was one at the Sarajevo airport, it was the only one in the city. If Holbrooke wanted to use the fire truck, Smith said, he had to agree to close the airport. "It's too bad that Holbrooke wasn't on the ground more," Smith told a reporter, "and had a better understanding for what was really going on." The nasty back-and-forth symbolized what was most controversial about the US deployment. The administration looked at the military as a means of enforcing international agreements, promoting human rights, and building respect for the rule of law. It called on America's soldiers to be nation builders, a prescription for failure, the military thought. As one of Smith's senior officers explained, the Clinton White House "wants American soldiers to wage a moral crusade" in Bosnia. The military, he said, "just isn't interested."[6]

Smith was a problem for Holbrooke, and he was a problem for John Shalikashvili. In public, Shalikashvili defended Smith, saying he would "draw the line" on rounding up war criminals, but he believed Smith's fight with Holbrooke undermined the military's mission. "I know there has been ambivalence among some of your people about Bosnia," the president had told Shalikashvili after the signing of the Dayton Accords, "but that is all in the past. I want everyone here to get behind the agreement." Shalikashvili looked at this as an order, not a suggestion, and so in April 1996, as the election season was heating up, Shalikashvili told Joulwan to quietly put out the word among his NATO colleagues that Smith would be removed. Who would they suggest as a replacement? In a short time, Joulwan had his answer: a number of NATO defense ministers, he said, had suggested that Smith's slot should be taken by a French officer. Shalikashvili groaned: that would never be acceptable in Washington, he said. But in June, Smith was nudged aside, bowing to entreaties from Joulwan that he retire. Shalikashvili moved quickly to put Smith in the past, recommending that low-key US vice admiral Thomas J. Lopez take his place.[7]

George Joulwan was the next to go. One month after Clinton's reelection, the SACEUR announced he would retire, which meant that Shalikashvili could shape the US command structure in Europe to his liking. Joulwan's announcement gave Shalikashvili six months to mull over his replacement. Then too, Shalikashvili had to think about his own successor, as a new JCS chairman would be named by Clinton in the fall of 1997. The situation in Bosnia gave the search for a new JCS head an added intensity. On January 29, just four days after Cohen's swearing-in, Clinton held an audition of sorts, traveling to the Pentagon with Al Gore for a meeting with the nation's top commanders, then had dinner with them at the White House. In the dinner's wake, the press dubbed Air Force general Joe Ralston and Marine Corps general John J. "Jack" Sheehan the frontrunners for Shalikashvili's job.[8]

As it turned out, Shalikashvili was less concerned about who would take over as JCS chairman than he was with who would take over as SACEUR. Troubles were again brewing in southeastern Europe, where separatists in the former Yugoslav republic of Kosovo (with a population divided between ethnic Albanians, commonly referred to as Kosovars, and minority Serbs) were battling the Serb army (it was still called the Yugoslav army, but it was nearly all Serb) over control of the territory. Shalikashvili wanted an activist in place of Joulwan, who had been only minimally cooperative in monitoring Dayton. In fact, Shalikashvili wanted Wesley Clark as Joulwan's replacement, but when the JCS chairman asked Army chief of staff Dennis Reimer to suggest three names for the SACEUR job, Clark's name was not on the list. During a private conversation with Reimer in February, Shalikashvili confronted the Army chief. Clark had done a good job at SOUTHCOM, he said. He was ready. "I want Clark on that list," he said, insistently. "Well, you won't get him," Reimer responded. Shali did not need to ask why, but he didn't need Reimer's permission either, and sent Clark's name to the White House. Clinton was aware of the Clark controversy and gently probed his JCS chairman over the choice. "Is he the right guy for the job?" he asked. Shalikashvili said that he was.[9]

CLARK'S APPOINTMENT AS Joulwan's successor led to speculation that he might eventually take over for Shalikashvili. Senior commanders dismissed the reports, though without saying what everyone in the Army knew: that naming Clark as Shalikashvili's successor would lead to an open revolt in the Army, which might include Reimer's resignation. Then too, appointing Clark would mean the military's top job would have been held by three Army officers in a row. While not institutionalized in law, senior military officers watch carefully to make sure the services take turns as JCS chair, and it was the Air Force's turn. More crucially, the man Clinton wanted for the job was Vice Chairman Joe Ralston, a much-admired and politically savvy Air Force general. Ralston was supported by Cohen, got on well with Clinton, and had proven a loyal deputy for Shalikashvili. But Ralston's candidacy was derailed in May by press reports that he had "a Kelly Flinn problem."

Flinn was celebrated in the media as a female graduate of the Air Force Academy and the Air Force's first female B-52 pilot. In 1995, she was featured in an Air Force promotional video, but in May 1997, after two years as a bomber pilot at Minot Air Force Base in North Dakota, she was forced into retirement when her commander discovered she'd had an adulterous affair with a local soccer coach who happened to be the husband of one of Flinn's subordinates. She was ordered to end the affair, then lied when she said that she had. Charged with multiple violations of the military code, Flinn faced a court-martial for the affair and, more damning, for lying to a superior officer. The press fed off the story, with lurid details of Flinn's steamy sex life. Flinn fought the charges. "I'm not a husband chaser," she told reporter Elaine Sciolino. "I'm not an insubordinate officer. I'm not a sob-story kind of person. I don't have an 'I hate the Air Force' vendetta. I just made a mistake."[10]

Facing a nascent replay of the Tailhook scandal, the Air Force negotiated its way out of the Flinn scandal, agreeing to grant her an honorable discharge in exchange for her resignation. The incident fatally undermined Ralston's nomination. Why was the military pushing him for promotion at the same time that it was purging its ranks of airmen (or women) for doing what he'd done? Air Force prosecutions for adultery had quadrupled over the previous decade, with officers forcibly separated from the service. Why wasn't Ralston among them? "People are throwing stones at my glass house," Flinn said, "and I say take a look at your glass house, too." Ralston, it appeared, was living in a glass house, with the Air Force old boy network prosecuting Flinn at the same time it was supporting him. The vice chairman argued that his case was different: he'd been separated from his wife during his affair and he'd never lied about it to a superior officer. But with women's groups rallying against him, Ralston bowed to the inevitable. He withdrew his name from consideration as Shalikashvili's successor in June. "My regret is that the public discussion surrounding my potential nomination blurred the facts in a number of recent cases and gave the appearance of a double standard regarding military justice," Ralston said in explaining his decision. "I don't believe there is a double standard."[11]

The withdrawal of Ralston left Marine general Jack Sheehan and, an emerging dark horse contender, the soon-to-retire George Joulwan, as Shalikashvili's likely successors, though only by default. The Navy did not have a candidate, because its senior ranks had been decimated by Tailhook, while the Ralston skirmish made the appointment of an Air Force officer uncomfortable for Clinton. Sheehan was a popular choice among senior military officers, because he supported Clinton's more expansive role for the military. Clinton was also attracted by Sheehan's bluntness. Once, during a foreign policy discussion at the prestigious Aspen Institute, a prominent academic had promoted American leadership, so long as it didn't cost too much either in dollars or lives. "I'm sorry, that can't be done," Sheehan said. "If you want the US military to go abroad, it will spend your money and it will put your sons and daughters in harm's way."[12]

Sheehan's opinions made him popular in the Marine Corps ("sacred cows make the best hamburger," he told his aides), but they didn't make for a palatable JCS chairman. More crucially, while Sheehan didn't have "the Ralston problem," as William Cohen delicately phrased it, he had a Carl Mundy problem. After the fall of Srebrenica to the Bosnian Serbs in July 1995, Sheehan had privately excoriated the Dutch military, saying a nearby Dutch unit had failed to respond because it was filled with homosexuals. General Shali knew of Sheehan's views, so when he provided the White House with his recommendations, Sheehan was not on the list. Nor was Joulwan. When asked by a reporter whether he would take the position, Joulwan turned on him, raising his eyebrows and finger. "No," he said, flatly. In desperation, Cohen asked Shalikashvili whether he'd serve another two-year term. By tradition, the JCS chairman served two consecutive terms, but by law the president could name a JCS chair to three consecutive terms so long as he hadn't served as vice chairman. Cohen made the suggestion tentatively, knowing Shali would likely give the same answer as Joulwan. He was right. "No," Shalikashvili said.[13]

During the last week of June 1997 Cohen told an assembled commanders conference that he hadn't yet decided on who to recommend to replace Shalikashvili, though the Ralston incident made finding someone with a clear personnel file imperative. Air Force generals Eugene Habiger and Walter Kross were rumored to be under consideration, as well as Clark and Reimer. In fact, however, Cohen was leaning toward recommending that Clinton appoint Hugh Shelton, then serving as the head of the US Special Operations Command. There were a number of things to recommend Shelton, but the most important was that, so far as anyone could tell, his personal life was unblemished. Clinton and Shelton got on well, which Cohen viewed as a requirement for the job. Cohen also knew that Shelton recoiled from political questions, kept to himself, and was a loyalist. Given the Clinton's administration's courting of military controversy, that in itself was enough to recommend him. And Cohen was an enthusiastic proponent of Shelton's Special Operations Command, which Cohen, as a senator, had helped to establish back in 1987. Shelton would be a good JCS chairman, Cohen told Clinton.[14]

Shelton was unaware he would succeed Shalikashvili until reached by telephone from Cohen's office during a training mission in Namibia. One of Cohen's assistants had been tasked with vetting Shelton's personal life. Later, Shelton said he was first asked whether he'd ever run up a substantial debt, but that inevitably the aide got around to the Ralston problem. Was there anything in his past that would embarrass the secretary, the president, or the country? Shelton cracked a joke, saying that while serving in Vietnam he'd been offered the hand of a Montagnard girl by a village chief, but that otherwise he'd been happily married for over three decades. Shelton found himself on the short list the next week and then, on July 17, he had lunch with Cohen. That afternoon, Shelton and Cohen drove to the White House, where Shelton was ushered into the Oval Office. One hour later, he emerged and was greeted by Sandy Berger. How'd it go? Berger asked. Just then, Berger's telephone rang and when he hung up, he turned to the general. "You've got the job," he said.[15]

John Shalikashvili officially retired on September 30 during a ceremony at Fort Myer; jets streaked overhead, an honor guard marched in review, and Bill Clinton stood, ramrod straight, as the retiring JCS chairman was honored. "From an immigrant learning English, he has become the shining symbol of what America is all about," Clinton said in tribute. "I am convinced that when future students look back upon this time, they will rank John Shalikashvili as among the greatest Chairmen of the Joint Chiefs of Staff America ever had." At the time, Clinton's words seemed like so much puffery. Among the greatest JCS chairmen? After all, Colin Powell was more well known to the public and more celebrated by the press. He seemed a giant, while Shalikashvili was merely his successor. He'd authored no doctrines, stood up to no presidents, garnered no press attention, stayed clear of controversy, and had no political ambitions.[16]

But over the years, Shalikashvili's reputation grew, particularly among his peers. For Powell and for almost every other senior officer of his generation, Vietnam served as a fiery test, a crucible of their service. That was never true for Shalikashvili. While his fellow officers reflected endlessly on their Vietnam experience, Shali only rarely did. His most formative experience was not in Vietnam's jungles, but in a Berlin basement clinging to his mother as American bombers roared overhead. For him, Europe was everything. If there were steadfast principles he followed during his time as JCS chair, if there was such a thing as a Shalikashvili Doctrine, it was simply this: that NATO must be strong and the United States must lead it. And that no matter what, Europe must never again be the cradle of a global war.

"HUGH SHELTON WAS the most secretive, private JCS chairman I ever met," a Marine Corps senior officer says. "He surrounded himself with three or four guys, officers he trusted, and he'd sweep in and out with this retinue and that was that." This secretiveness kept the newly minted JCS chairman out of the public eye and away from controversy, but Shelton was so private that few knew what he really believed. "He never told anyone what he was thinking or, for that matter, whether he was," this same Marine Corps officer says. Shelton's behavior was not a surprise. It's who he was. The new JCS chairman's formative military experience as a part of a small team of elite operators in Vietnam had embedded itself in his personality: Shelton had learned to keep his mouth shut because his life depended on it. For Shelton, silence was survival.[17]

Early in his tenure, Pentagon reporter Elaine Sciolino cited Shelton's past as providing clues to his character: he would "watch his back," build loyalty, and maintain his silence "until he is ready to move." Shelton knew this about himself, but where others saw negatives, he saw positives. He believed the job of the JCS chairman was to advise the president, implement his orders, and then support him. It is what his sergeants in Vietnam had done for him, and it is what he would do now. Shelton admired officers who were team players and "stayed in their lane." It was when good soldiers got out of their lane that they ran into trouble. Powell had not stayed in his lane and Shalikashvili had been too outspoken. He was going to be different. It was enough, he said, to be a "good soldier," like Robert E. Lee and Stonewall Jackson, the two commanders whose portraits he'd hung in his office. "I did my best to isolate myself from the political arena and walk squarely down the middle—not an easy task in a city where one's party affiliation seemed more significant than his blood type," he later reflected.[18]

But the real reason that Shelton isolated himself and walked "squarely down the middle," his colleagues said, is that he was out of his depth in Washington. Shelton had spent a lifetime jumping out of airplanes and wading through swamps. His first vetting for the JCS job had come when he was in a remote Namibian desert, training six hundred foreign soldiers. In Namibia, he knew what to do and how to do it. That wasn't true for Washington. In his first weeks, Shelton relied on JCS vice chairman Joe Ralston for guidance; Ralston showed him the ropes, advised him on how to handle the White House, and prebriefed him on his first meetings in the tank. The difficulty for Shelton, Colonel Martin Dempsey, who later served on Shelton's staff, observed, was "the dash"—the punctuation mark that brings together the political and the military, the dash in "pol-mil." Shelton knew all about the word after the dash, but almost nothing about the word before it.[19]

Shelton first waded into the dash in early 1998 when the Kosovo Liberation Army (KLA) escalated its attacks on Serb forces in Kosovo, which included units of Yugoslav president Slobodan Milosevic's Yugoslav army. The Serbs responded harshly, setting off an increasingly bloody conflict. The Kosovo fight struck many in the military as yet another Balkan morass that the United States should stay out of. The KLA had popped into existence in April 1996 with attacks on Serb militia outposts, then escalated its attacks over the next year. For many in the military, the KLA was no more than a gang, led by thugs; it was listed by the State Department as a terrorist organization. But US views on the KLA began to change when Milosevic deepened the conflict, sending Yugoslav army units into Kosovo to destroy the militia.[20]

Shelton and the chiefs were opposed to yet another intervention in southwestern Europe, a position the JCS chairman made clear in several discussions of the growing crisis with the White House. This wasn't Bosnia, Shelton told Clinton: it was a local fight between two armed gangs. But Shelton was on shaky ground, knew it, and slowly began to shift his views. During his meeting with Clinton prior to being named chairman, Shelton had been asked by the president about his opposition to the intervention in Haiti, which he'd commanded. Shelton hesitated, but only for a moment. In retrospect, Shelton told the president, it was clear he'd been wrong. The intervention had turned out better than he'd anticipated, and he'd rethought the whole concept of humanitarian intervention.[21] It was that admission, a number of his colleagues believed, that had given Shelton the military's top job. But fears that Shelton would soften his opposition to a further Balkans intervention to please Clinton were misplaced. This had nothing to do with Clinton: Shelton was willing to swallow his doubts because of the shift he'd made on Haiti, and because he despised Milosevic. He wasn't alone. Sitting at his headquarters in Mons, Belgium ("it was as big as a football field," one State Department official said), Wesley Clark calculated that Milosevic would do everything he could to remain in Kosovo, even if that meant defying the United States. The United States would have to intervene to stop him.[22]

In February 1998, Berger convinced Madeleine Albright to send Richard Holbrooke to Europe as a special envoy to find a way to end the Kosovo crisis. The Belgrade government responded by flooding Kosovo with Yugoslav army units. Milosevic argued that he was simply protecting the Serb minority from a murderous terrorist organization. At the end of the month, the KLA and the Serbs fought a three-day battle in which the KLA suffered sixteen dead. On March 2, Serbian police, protected by armored troop carriers, cracked down on anti-Serb protestors in Kosovo's capital of Pristina, injuring over 250. Then on March 4, Serbian security forces entered three Kosovo villages and massacred eighty ethnic Albanians, including twenty-five women and children. The international community was caught flat-footed, but on March 9 a European Contact Group consisting of the United States, the United Kingdom, France, Germany, Italy, and Russia met to shape a policy to respond to the crisis. They couldn't. The US and the UK wanted to threaten the Serbs with a bombing campaign, but no one else agreed.

Daniel Serwer, a now retired State Department diplomat who was a part of the US team handling the crisis, remembers that it was in March that the Clinton administration realized that Kosovo was even more important for Milosevic than Bosnia. "Milosevic came to the table in Dayton looking for an agreement on Bosnia, when we thought he would dig in his heels," he recalls. "And we thought that a little pressure on him over Kosovo would push him to negotiate. We got it exactly backwards—we focused on Bosnia, he focused on Kosovo. For him, Kosovo was the deal breaker. Kosovo was far more important than Bosnia. He wasn't going to give it up, and he wouldn't negotiate."[23]

Clashes between the Serbs and the KLA escalated in April, but Holbrooke (engaged in a series of nine exhausting trips to the region) persuaded Milosevic to agree to negotiate Kosovo's status with Kosovar president Ibrahim Rugova and comply with a UN resolution granting Kosovo autonomy. Milosevic and Rugova met in Belgrade in mid-May, shook hands and smiled for the cameras, but once Rugova departed the Serb leader escalated his military campaign. In June, Milosevic reinforced his Yugoslav army units in Kosovo with another ten-thousand-plus troops, along with hundreds of tanks, armored personnel carriers, and artillery pieces. That same month, in a meeting with Milosevic, Holbrooke threatened NATO action, promising air strikes on Milosevic's military positions in Kosovo unless Belgrade withdrew its forces. But the more

Holbrooke talked, the more Milosevic escalated his attacks. In June, Clark met with Shelton at the Pentagon, pushing him and the chiefs to approve air strikes to force Milosevic into negotiations. "Milosevic will pretend to negotiate, but he won't until he's under pressure," Clark told Shelton. "The air threat will provide the crucial leverage for the diplomats to be able to achieve a meaningful agreement."[24]

In the late summer of 1998, Clark signed off on a targeting plan to be used if Holbrooke's negotiations failed. It was an incredibly complex process, involving the Joint Staff's targeting team, a group of planners from Clark's headquarters, Air Force general John Jumper's staff at the European Command, and NATO's air planners in Italy. At first, the target sets were modest, with Clark's staff focusing on Serb air defense and military positions near Pristina. The reason for the modest targeting, Clark told his aides, was that NATO would never approve plans that included direct air attacks on Belgrade. But when Milosevic wouldn't budge on NATO's demands, Clark carefully expanded the plan, calculating that NATO's impatience with the Serb leader would result in a greater willingness to punish him. Inevitably, Clark came up with more detailed and broader target lists. In fact, the more Milosevic dug in his heels, the more expansive Clark's target plan became—and the more willingly NATO defense ministers, and the White House, accepted it. It was a delicate dance, with Clark reassuring Washington that simply threatening Milosevic would be enough to drive him to the negotiating table, while planning an air campaign that would punish him if he didn't. He knew Milosevic, he said. He was scared to death of American airpower. His air plan, he argued, would never have to be used. "We need to put the diplomats out front," Clark said.[25]

So it was that the late summer targeting plan was updated in October, when Milosevic's command and control headquarters in Belgrade was included in the target mix. When this new plan was passed up the chain of command, it sent shock waves through the JCS, whose members concluded that Clark wanted to put the military, not the diplomats, out front. The goal was to force Milosevic to the negotiating table, not to wage a full-scale war. That was especially true for Hugh Shelton, who'd told Clinton that he now favored military interventions to protect innocent populations. But Clark's plan wouldn't protect innocent civilians, the JCS concluded, it would embroil US forces in a Balkan civil war. The chiefs adamantly opposed Clark's target plan and said so. As did Defense

Secretary William Cohen, who cold-shouldered Clark in several of his visits to Washington. Military officers remember that meetings between Cohen, Shelton, and Clark were uncomfortable. The room was always filled with tension. Neither Cohen nor Shelton liked Clark, and they were convinced the US commander in Europe was plotting to take America to war. Clark's judgment was clouded, they said: his hatred of Milosevic and his love of the limelight were driving the US military in a direction they didn't want to go.

The JCS and Cohen breathed easier in October, after Holbrooke pressured Milosevic into an agreement on a cease-fire that included a withdrawal of Serb forces from Kosovo. But Holbrooke didn't believe the cease-fire would hold, and neither did Clark. On December 24, the Serbs deployed nearly one hundred tanks outside the village of Podujeva, fighting a daylong battle with the KLA. Fourteen Kosovo Albanians were killed. Two days later, Clark told the press that "we are seeing the emergence of a new round of possibly significant escalation in the scope and intensity of the violence by the Serb side. The Yugoslav army has broken its promises to NATO."[26] Two days after that, Clark warned Dennis Reimer in a telephone briefing that the United States was "facing a war decision" in Europe, and that he would need additional resources to wage it. "We're going to have to fight in Kosovo," Clark told Reimer, then waited for nearly a minute for Reimer's reply. "But we don't want to fight there," Reimer said.[27]

OPERATION ALLIED FORCE, the US-NATO intervention against the Serbs over Kosovo, might well be America's least remembered conflict. Eclipsed in the national memory by 9/11, the air campaign that began on the night of March 24, 1999, was dubbed by senior US policymakers as "an exercise in coercive diplomacy." Ordered by Bill Clinton after weeks of White House meetings, its intent was to force Serbian president Slobodan Milosevic to yield to the demands of a settlement of the Kosovo crisis laid out by NATO in the Rambouillet Agreement, named for the chateau in southwestern France where it was signed six days before NATO began its campaign. On the first night of that attack, fighter-bombers from thirteen nations flew four hundred missions against Serb air defense systems inside of Kosovo. On the second day, US fighters engaged in combat with two Serb air force jets and destroyed them both.

Wesley Clark predicted a short and painless war. Milosevic, he said, would cave. "This will be over in three nights," he told Air Force general Michael Short, his air commander. Short didn't agree. The air campaign that Clark advocated didn't hit the Serb leader where it would do the most good, which was in Belgrade. Instead, Serb armored and infantry units would play a delicate game of hide-and-seek with NATO fighters, ducking in and out of the forested valleys of the Balkans while Milosevic portrayed himself as a man who stood up for Serb rights. Then too, NATO's air forces were hobbled by the alliance's political bureaucracy. Short struggled to identify targets that would degrade Serb capabilities without sparking political controversy. Thirteen NATO nations deployed aircraft for the March 1999 air offensive, but nineteen nations had a say on what would be bombed and when.

The NATO chain of command for the Kosovo campaign was the most complicated and unmanageable in the history of warfare: the targets were identified first by an American team working at a British air base at Molesworth (who collated satellite imagery and other intelligence reports to identify Serb positions), then passed on to NATO headquarters on the continent. The edited target list was then given to a committee of lawyers who reviewed each target to ensure that bombing it wouldn't violate international law. When this was done, a shorter target list was passed back up the chain of command to a Joint Target Coordination Board—political officials and military officers from NATO nations. The proposed targets would then arrive on the desk of Admiral James Ellis, the commander in chief of allied forces in southern Europe. Ellis reviewed the target list, then passed it to Clark in Belgium. Air Force general John Jumper, the head of the US Air Force in Europe, also reviewed the target list. Finally, Admiral Ellis would transmit the final target folders to the US Air Force's 32nd Air Operations Group at Ramstein Air Base in Germany or to the Sixth Fleet's command ship in the Mediterranean.[28] At any point in the process, a senior political official could veto a target. In one case, a week into the campaign, a target was shifted as an aircraft was in the air over Kosovo. It was an air commander's nightmare. Short complained that he wasn't a warfighter, he was an implementer. The process enraged him.

An "airpower airhead," Short had flown nearly every fighter in the Air Force inventory. But Short coupled his faith in airpower with a Warden-like philosophy that called for targeting an enemy's most important assets in the war's first hours. Operation Allied Force did just the opposite.

The one thing that would persuade Milosevic to end his aggression in Kosovo would be to hit him in Belgrade, Short believed. Instead, Short found himself fighting an air war that targeted a highly mobile ground force that would "shoot and scoot," hiding its most lethal weapons in tunnels, caves, and culverts, where NATO's bombs couldn't reach them. This wasn't cutting off the head of the snake, as Short advocated, it was chopping away at his tail. "The political constraints existed throughout the conflict," Short later said. "Every nation had a vote. An individual nation could say: you can't hit that target. A nation hosting US airplanes could say that US airplanes taking off from their soil cannot strike this target. An individual nation would say, 'Our Parliament won't let us hit that target, but of course they're not going to say you can't hit it.'"[29]

Even more frustrating for Short was that Clark's tortured approval meant that the NATO commander, and not the air commander, was in charge of the air war. This was a distinct change from Operation Desert Storm, where Norman Schwarzkopf had told Chuck Horner what he wanted, then left him alone to do it. That wasn't true for Clark, who not only signed off on a target, but just as often decided which aircraft would hit it and with what weapon. When Short received the final target list, it was unrecognizable from what he'd seen earlier in the day. Short also worried about his son, who was flying an A-10 "Warthog," a tank killer, against Serb positions. Most effective at lower altitudes, the A-10's lethality meant it was regularly "painted" (identified by a laser beam) by air defense crews, who gave it special attention. Then there was the A-10 itself. A-10s didn't fly, Air Force officers said, they crashed. The continued changes in his targeting sets, the terrible weather over Kosovo, and the difficulty of finding camouflaged Serb armor dug into forested hillsides was exacerbated by Short's sense that his mission had little support among his colleagues. In fact, it had almost none.

In America, a bevy of high-profile retired generals and admirals weighed in on the campaign. Retired US Army lieutenant general Robert Gard was among the most outspoken of the dozens of officers who condemned the campaign as "one of the most immoral wars this country has ever fought." Gard and his peers were joined in their judgment by veteran US diplomats who condemned the Rambouillet Agreement as purposely written in order to ensure Milosevic would reject it. One of its key requirements was that the Serb leader accept NATO troop access to his country, a demand its drafters knew he would never accept. Even former secretary of state Henry Kissinger was shocked, saying Rambouillet was "an excuse to start bombing." The joint chiefs agreed: Operation Allied Force was not a war of necessity, it was a war of choice. The intervention's critics point out that Allied Force was being waged without the backing of a UN resolution, because Russia and China opposed it, with the United States acting as "the KLA's Air Force." Clark's predecessor, George Joulwan, watched all of this from afar and summarized the Pentagon's views. "Allied Force was cooked up by Madeleine Albright and Sandy Berger," he said. "Most senior military leaders were dead set against it."[30]

Pentagon reporters called Operation Allied Force "Madeleine's War," and circulated details of an off-the-record conversation the secretary had had with a reporter. The Rambouillet Agreement, she'd told the journalist, "intentionally set the bar too high for the Serbs to comply. They need some bombing, and that's what they're going to get." But while reporters called Allied Force "Madeleine's War," the military concluded it was "Wes Clark's War." Richard Holbrooke agreed. He'd done everything he could to stop the NATO bombing campaign, running headlong into Milosevic's stubbornness and Wes Clark's view of the world. "Kosovo was simply an extension of Bosnia in the mind of Wesley Clark," he later observed. "For Clark, Kosovo was the logical next step in his liberal interventionist attitude toward the use of force. That's why they put him there."[31]

The Kosovo bombing reinforced the JCS's animus toward Clark, deepened by a conflict between Clark and air commander Michael Short. During daily videoconferences on targeting, Clark and Short fought a series of ugly personal battles. In each daily targeting conference (there were seventy-eight in all), Short recited what had been hit during the previous day, but then argued that the air campaign needed to focus on Milosevic. Short was channeling John Warden, who'd made the same argument in the lead-up to Desert Storm. So too, Short argued, the key to victory wasn't in Kosovo, but in Belgrade. The United States needs to end the "tank plinking," he'd say, "and go downtown." In response, Clark would sarcastically read from a menu of targets that Short's bombers had failed to hit. "Are we bombing those ground forces yet, Mike?" he'd ask. Clark would then review the new target list, questioning each entry. "I think that's an apartment building," he'd say, and would cross it off the list. Clark was throwing his weight around, Short and his team concluded: he didn't have a clue whether a target was an apartment building or not. As the stories circulated, so too did tales of how Short's boss, General John Jumper, regularly intervened to calm the arguments. "SACEUR [Clark]," he'd say, during the testy exchanges, "I'll call you on the hotline," and Clark would end his attacks. Short welcomed the intervention. "The boss will take care of this," he'd think.[32]

ONE MONTH AFTER the air campaign began, in late April 1999, NATO ministers met in Washington to mark the fiftieth anniversary of the alliance and to coordinate their next steps on Kosovo. The air war was stalled, with Short running out of targets. Upward of 50 percent of the target list had now been hit twice, with NATO aircraft fighting the weather and the increasingly sophisticated Serbian "shoot and scoot" tactics. The three-day war had turned into a monthlong slog. Clinton's critics savaged the president. Milosevic, they said, was embarrassing America. Worse yet, the limited air campaign had spawned a number of painful tragedies, including the bombing of a refugee convoy that was mistaken for an armored column. The war, begun to end a humanitarian crisis, had actually deepened it. Hundreds of thousands of Kosovo's Albanians had taken to the roads, looking for shelter. The public was getting impatient, criticism of the military was increasing. The outcry reminded senior officers of what had happened during Vietnam: the nation's political leaders were restricting the air war, then wondered why it was so ineffective. Nor was Clinton's national security team willing to pay the price for the war they wanted, or even admit it was a war. Three weeks into Operation Allied Force, William Cohen told the Senate Armed Services Committee that "we're certainly engaged in hostilities" but "whether that measures up to, quote, a classic definition of war, I'm not prepared to say."[33]

The turning point came during NATO's fiftieth anniversary commemoration, when US officials pressed their NATO counterparts to punish Milosevic by targeting the Serb media, his support among Serb security forces, and his economic base. Wes Clark showed up for the celebration, but Cohen and Shelton shunned him. Just one week earlier, Clark had told the *Los Angeles Times* that the bombing had been ineffective and that the United States might have to commit ground troops to win the campaign. He repeated his point in a high-profile television interview. Cohen was enraged, but he didn't want to be the person to upbraid Clark. He'd done it before, and it had proven useless. "You do it," he told Shelton. So Shelton called Clark in Belgium. It was a short conversation. "The Secretary has asked me to deliver the following message, and I quote: 'Get your fucking face off the TV. No more briefings, period.' That's it."[34]

By the end of the NATO conference, Michael Short's target list had been expanded. The person responsible was Sandy Berger. The Kosovo conflict kept him awake at night. It seemed to go on and on. Clinton looked silly. They all looked silly. Finally, exhausted, he decided that, no matter what, the United States (and NATO) had to win. At the beginning of the war, NATO had decided that 169 targets, almost all of them in Kosovo, be destroyed. Serbia itself had been off limits. But because of Berger's April intervention, by early June NATO's master target list had grown to over 950 targets, most of them in Serbia. More crucially, NATO ministers had come to accept what the US military had long known: that a short and bloody conflict, using overwhelming force, was less controversial than a long and antiseptic one. At the NATO conference, Berger circulated among the ministers, strong-arming them into an agreement. The future of the alliance was at stake, he argued. "This isn't about Milosevic, this is about NATO," he told Shelton. "This is about whether NATO is a real alliance or not." No matter what, he told him, "we will not lose. We will not lose. No matter what, we will not lose." The NATO ministers agreed. "After Washington . . . there was no way that NATO was going to let itself fail," John Jumper later reflected. America's Air Force was "going downtown."[35]

On the night of May 3, 1999—one week after the end of the Washington meeting—Short's bombers turned off the lights in Belgrade, dropping CBU-104s, highly lethal cluster munitions, on five electrical transformer yards. It was the beginning of the end. But expanding the target list also brought increasing dangers. On May 7, a US warplane sent five JDAM (joint directed attack munition) bombs into the Chinese embassy in Belgrade, killing four Chinese reporters. The US apologized for the incident while denying rumors it had destroyed the embassy in retaliation for China's lack of support for the operation at the UN. "This wasn't a mistake," an Air Force officer later said, proudly. "We hit what we targeted. It was beautiful. We just didn't know that the building was the Chinese embassy." At the end of the first week of May, the alliance targeted Belgrade's sprawling automobile factory, putting upward of fifteen thousand Serbs out of work. Then, at the end of May, the alliance destroyed the communications net that linked Belgrade with its army forces in Kosovo.[36]

By June 1, the NATO campaign had dropped 14,200 bombs on Serb air defenses, airfields, roads, bridges, ground forces, and other military targets. "We brought down the bridges in Belgrade," an Air Force officer told reporters. "We just dumped them into the Danube. Those people couldn't go anywhere." By early June, Serbia's telephone and computer networks had been destroyed. On June 3, Milosevic gave in, announcing he would comply with NATO demands, withdraw his forty-thousand-man army from Kosovo, and grant the province autonomy. Another week of bombing remained, because NATO ministers doubted that Milosevic would keep his word, but by June 10 the air campaign had ground to a halt. The UN approved the deployment of an international Kosovo Force (KFOR) to monitor the agreement, with British general Sir Michael Jackson as its commander. On June 11, the force, with seven thousand American troops, entered Kosovo.

The war had ended, but the peace was nerve-wracking—pitting NATO in an unpredictable face-off with the Russians, who'd agreed to be a part of the peacekeeping force. On the morning of June 11, 250 Russian soldiers accompanied by armored vehicles left their base in Bosnia and raced to Kosovo's Pristina airport. Their plan was to seize the airport before NATO troops, en route from Macedonia, got there. The Russian move was viewed as a provocation in Washington, which had insisted that Russian troops be a part of a joint peacekeeping force but not have control of their own sector. The Russians agreed with this, but only reluctantly: the Serbs were their traditional allies and they'd grown increasingly wary of NATO's expansion into southeastern Europe. Now they were flexing their muscle. In Belgium, Wesley Clark received word of the Russian deployment and, on June 12, called Admiral Ellis in Naples, ordering him to land US helicopters with a contingent of paratroopers at the airport to block the Russian move. Ellis hesitated, telling Clark that Jackson wouldn't like it. Clark was enraged, called Jackson, and then flew to Skopje, in Macedonia, to confront him. Early the next morning, the two met at Jackson's headquarters, which was in an abandoned shoe factory.

Jackson didn't think much of Clark, but Clark outranked him: Jackson only had three stars on his shoulder, while Clark had four. "Wes Clark was something of a loner," Jackson later wrote, "a driven, intensely ambitious man with a piercing stare. Often described as 'tightly wound,' he seemed to bring a disturbing zeal to his work. He had a reputation as a very political sort of general, antagonizing his military superiors by going over their heads when they did not give him what they wanted." Now, with Jackson the object of his piercing stare, Clark lit into him, demanding he order helicopters to the Pristina airport to block the Russians. Jackson was shocked: Clark was upbraiding him out in front of his own soldiers. It just wasn't done. Jackson shook his head, then led Clark into his office. "We cannot go on like this," Jackson said. "We need to move on. Let me sort it out with the Russians." Clark flashed, demanding that Jackson follow his orders. "I want those helicopters in Pristina, now," he said. Jackson refused.

"I won't do it! Sir, I just won't do it," Jackson said. Clark stared at him in disbelief.

"Mike, these aren't Washington's orders, they're coming from me," he said.

"By whose authority?"

"By my authority, as SACEUR"—the supreme allied commander in Europe.

"You don't have that authority," Jackson said.

"I do have that authority. I have the authority of the secretary-general behind me on this."

It was at this point that Jackson uttered the phrase that would make him a legend inside the US military. He faced down Clark: "Sir," he said, "I'm not going to start World War III for you."[37]

But that wasn't the end of the argument. After a moment, Jackson leaned into Clark, his face just inches away from him, returning his stare: "Sir, I'm a three-star general, you can't give me orders like this," he said. "I have my own judgment of the situation and I believe that this order is outside our mandate." Clark leaned back: "Mike, I'm a four-star general," he said, "and I can tell you these things." The two separated, Clark turning on his heel.

Clark climbed the chain of command, demanding US support. He didn't get it. Hugh Shelton told Clark that the British government controlled their commander, not Clark. That wasn't technically true, but Shelton was on solid ground. US commanders didn't take orders from officers of other nations, whether they were outranked by them or not—it didn't work like that. This was a political question, Shelton explained.

Reminded of the incident nearly two decades later, Clark passed it off as "just another war story." Jackson was tired. "Oh yeah, well, Jackson was overwrought," he said. "He hadn't had much sleep. It wasn't that big a deal." In fact, eight hundred British paratroopers who'd taken up position at the Pristina airport remember it differently, with Clark storming out of his confrontation with Jackson and grabbing the radio of a British soldier. He ordered the British paratroop commander to move against the Russians, to "overpower them." As the British commander later remembered, his unit had "200 Russians lined up pointing their weapons at us aggressively." The twenty-five-year-old British captain, James Blunt, decided to ignore Clark's order and got in touch with Jackson. What should I do? he asked. "Why don't you just surround the airport?" Jackson said. That's what Blunt did, pulling back his soldiers and redeploying them out of the way of the Russians. Several days later, citing the incident, Jackson threatened to resign rather than serve with Clark. His threat was ignored. But in Pristina, his confrontation with Clark had headed off a confrontation with the Russians.[38]

Years later, George Joulwan cited the Clark-Jackson confrontation as the reason behind Cohen, Shelton, and Reimer's anti-Clark views. They believed that Clark wanted to take America to war against the Russians, and the Pristina airport incident proved it. "When I was leaving as supreme allied commander in Europe, I think it was the last two weeks I was there, I got a call from Cohen, who told me that he was going to recommend Clark as my successor because he was Shali's choice," Joulwan remembered. Joulwan was stunned: given Cohen's views on Clark it just didn't make sense. Cohen acknowledged that, but told Joulwan that Shali insisted on Clark's appointment. "I told Cohen, 'Mr. Secretary, please don't do this. It's a mistake.' But it was already done." Joulwan remembered that one day during his retirement, after the Clark-Jackson standoff, he received a telephone call from Cohen. Joulwan remembers being puzzled that a secretary of defense would be calling a retired four-star officer who was about to embark on a day of golf. "I remember the call very clearly," he said. "I got on the phone and Cohen was on the other end. It was a little odd: and Cohen said, 'You know George, you were right about Clark, and I just wanted to let you know that.'"[39]

One month after the Pristina incident, Clark was having dinner with the president of Lithuania when he was interrupted by a telephone call from Hugh Shelton. Clark was surprised—Shelton rarely initiated any contact with him. "You're being replaced," Shelton told him. Clark was confused. "What do you mean? I'm up for reappointment." Shelton was cold-blooded. "No," he said. "You're being replaced." As it turned out, Cohen had convinced the president that Joe Ralston should be rewarded for having withdrawn his name from consideration as JCS chairman. The administration owed him. Why not put him in charge in Europe? Cohen asked. Clinton mulled this over for a minute, and agreed. "Great idea," he said. "You handle that."

In fact, Cohen's Ralston idea had nothing to do with Ralston, and everything to do with Clark. What Cohen had failed to tell Clinton was that Clark was due for reappointment and that naming Ralston as his successor meant that Clark would have to retire. In the up-or-out military, he had nowhere else to go. Then Cohen instructed an aide to leak the information on Ralston to the *Washington Post*, along with an announcement of Clark's retirement. The leak would set the Ralston appointment in stone, as it seemed unlikely that Clinton would want to admit he'd been bamboozled by his secretary of defense. So Ralston was in, Clark was out, and Cohen, Shelton, and Reimer had their revenge. When news of Cohen's maneuver reached Madeleine Albright, she was enraged, as was Clinton. "I'd like to kill somebody," Clinton sputtered. "It was Cohen who did it," George Joulwan later commented. "It was Bill Cohen. It was a hell of a move. Creative. But no one deserved it more than Wes Clark." When Clark retired, few of his colleagues attended the ceremony. Hugh Shelton, the chairman of the Joint Chiefs of Staff, one of Clark's aides told him, just couldn't make it. "He's on vacation," he said.

THAT OPERATION ALLIED Force is now little more than a footnote in the history of the Clinton years should not be a surprise. The campaign was not only overshadowed by other events, not a single American pilot was lost in the seventy-eight-day operation. The United States had scourged Milosevic, freed Kosovo, and strengthened NATO. But for the US military, the Kosovo operation showed how force should not be used. The campaign was desultory and confused, its political goals poorly stated and unconvincing. Allied Force was that most unique of all military campaigns: it was a victory, but it was a failure.

Michael Short provided the most succinct account of what happened. At the beginning of the conflict, Short said, the United States should have made clear to its NATO allies who was in charge. "We, the United States, will provide the leadership, the enabling force, the majority of the striking power, and the technology required. We will take the alliance to war, and we will win this thing for you. . . . In exchange for that, we are going to call the tune. And what that means, ladies and gentlemen from the other 18 nations, is that we are going to conduct a classic air campaign from the very first night. The lights are going out, the bridges are coming down, and the military headquarters are going to be blown up." The US had not done that, Short said, which is why the war had lasted for seventy-eight days, instead of seventy-eight hours.[40]

Other senior officers went further. The problem with the war was not that it was fought poorly, but that it was fought at all. Claiming victory was putting lipstick on a pig. There was no such thing as a "humanitarian war." Allied Force had empowered thugs, thieves, and drug dealers. The KLA was not a liberation movement, but a gang. This was "Madeleine's War," proof that liberals and draft dodgers could be as tough as Republicans. Albright reversed hundreds of years of foreign policy thinking: it used to be that you bombed when diplomacy failed, now you bombed in order to make diplomacy succeed. "Up until the start of the conflict," she'd said, "the military served to back up our diplomacy. Now, our diplomacy serves to back up our military." It was a dangerous precedent.[41]

The war also bared the inherent tensions in the national command authority. The Goldwater-Nichols Department of Defense Reorganization Act gave new powers to the military's theater commanders, taking the JCS chairman out of the chain of command. But strong chairmen, like William Crowe, Colin Powell, and John Shalikashvili, maintained their influence by inserting themselves into White House policymaking debates. Hugh Shelton had ceded the ground. "He was weak," a former four-star Army officer who served with him says. "Weak, weak, weak." Wes Clark took advantage of this weakness; at key points during the Kosovo campaign he simply bypassed Shelton, and at several points he'd even bypassed Bill Cohen. In fact, Wes Clark's primary contact inside the Clinton administration was Madeleine Albright, who was also his biggest fan. Clark would talk to Albright, sharing with her the troubles he was having with Cohen, Shelton, and Reimer, while cautioning her that his views should be kept confidential. He was outside the chain of command, he admitted, but his calls with her were essential. He was simply trying to do what was best for the country. But these conversations were never as confidential as Clark said, or Albright was led to believe. During conversations with Cohen, Clark would use his conversations with Albright to get his way. Cohen would give Clark his views, and Clark would respond by citing Albright: "That's not what Secretary Albright thinks," he'd say. For Cohen and Shelton, this was not simply disloyalty, it was insubordination. Later, in 2004, when Clark ran for president, Shelton not only refused to endorse him, he took the unusual step of criticizing him in public. "I've known Wes a long time," he said. "I will tell you the reason he came out of Europe early had to do with character and integrity issues, things that are very near and dear to my heart."[42]

Clinton, meanwhile, rarely cited Operation Allied Force as a part of his legacy. Other events were more defining. Back in 1993, Clinton brought Israeli and Palestinian leaders to Washington to sign the Oslo Accords, which he hoped would end the Israeli-Palestinian conflict.[43] In 1995, he appointed former senator George Mitchell as the administration's special envoy for Northern Ireland. Mitchell's whirlwind negotiations led to the Good Friday Agreement, which ended the festering conflict. And Clinton had proven that he could be as tough as Bush. In 1993, the United States sent twenty-three cruise missiles into Baghdad in response to reports that Saddam had planned to assassinate Clinton's predecessor, then ordered a sustained attack when Saddam refused to allow UN weapons inspectors into his country. Finally, and in retrospect presciently, Bill Clinton ordered US strikes against al-Qaeda, the terrorist group that, just weeks after his inauguration, had planted a bomb under the World Trade Center. Clinton had downplayed the bombing, calling it "regrettable," but in late 1998, he was forced to take the threat more seriously.

ON THE MORNING of August 7, 1998, bomb-laden trucks attacked the US embassies in Dar es Salaam, Tanzania, and Nairobi, Kenya, killing 224 people, including twelve Americans. Hugh Shelton was in his residence at Fort Myer when told of the incident in a call from the Pentagon. Ninety minutes later he received a briefing on the attack from General Anthony Zinni, the head of the US Central Command, who said that the al-Qaeda terrorist organization had planned and carried out the attack. Later that afternoon, President Clinton convened his national security team to decide on a response. Shelton recommended the president approve a JCS proposal that al-Qaeda training camps in Afghanistan be hit by Toma-hawk missiles. Doing so when the camps were occupied would "kill the maximum number of terrorists being trained there," he said.

The problem with attacking the al-Qaeda camps was that the missiles would have to fly over Pakistan, which might mistake them for nuclear-tipped missiles fired from India. So JCS vice chairman Joe Ralston (who had not yet been officially named as Clark's successor in Europe) ar-ranged a dinner with General Jehangir Karamat, Pakistan's defense min-ister, calculating that he could calm him if the missiles were spotted. So it was that on the night of August 20, 1998, while Ralston was dining with Karamat in Islamabad, sixty-six Tomahawk missiles were passing overhead. When the two parted, the missiles had already reached their targets. Along with the training camps, the United States hit the al-Shifa pharmacy in Sudan, which the CIA had identified as an al-Qaeda weap-ons manufacturing facility. The intelligence was wrong.

The hunt for Osama bin Laden, the founder and head of the al-Qaeda international terrorist group, intensified after the Africa bombings, with Clinton officials pressing the JCS to provide a plan to kill him. Shelton was skeptical that such an operation would work, and so was Tony Zinni. It was one thing for Washington to order bin Laden killed, but if the mis-sion didn't succeed it would cause untold problems for the United States in the region, Zinni said. The problem was getting the intelligence right. During one Sunday afternoon, Shelton sped to the Pentagon after being told that the CIA had located bin Laden at a compound in Kandahar, in Afghanistan. But Shelton wasn't impressed by the CIA report. "This just doesn't look right," he said. William Cohen was also skeptical. By the time we order the missile strikes, bin Laden will be gone, Cohen pointed out. The missile strike was canceled, but Shelton later discovered that if the strike had occurred, it would have missed bin Laden by an hour.

By the last year of Bill Clinton's tenure in office, America's hunt for bin Laden had become the CIA's hunt for bin Laden. The terrorist was nearly an obsession for the agency. Curiously, that was never the case for the military, which viewed bin Laden as just another loudmouthed thug. Al-Qaeda was worrisome, but not a major threat. In late 1999, the year before Clinton left office, Shelton had the Joint Staff prepare a memo list-ing thirteen options for killing the terrorist, presented it to Clinton, then regularly dissented when the president argued it be adopted. "You know, it would scare the shit out of al-Qaeda if suddenly a bunch of black ninjas rappelled out of helicopters into the middle of their camp," Clinton told Shelton. Shelton nodded, but made it clear the military wanted nothing to do with the idea. He thought Clinton and his team had seen too many Hollywood movies.[44]

When Shelton told his JCS colleagues about Clinton's "black ninja" idea, they shook their heads. One of them suggested Shelton remind the president of what happened with "Desert One"—Jimmy Carter's attempt to rescue the US hostages in Tehran back in 1979. In that case, the "black ninjas" had crashed a helicopter into a troop transport, killing eight Americans. So it was that when Clinton again pressed his point, Shelton was adamant. "Whoa," he told Clinton. "I don't think we can do that." Anytime Clinton mentioned the topic, Shelton became a master of delay, telling the president he'd check with his colleagues and get back to him. He never did. "The problem," a colleague of Shelton's would later say, "was that the JCS never really believed the CIA's intelligence, while the CIA said the military was risk averse. That was their term. Risk averse. And we'd say, 'Well, if Jimmy Carter had been risk averse, he'd have had a second term.'"[45]

At the same time that Clinton was focusing on bin Laden, he was also focusing on Saddam Hussein. Despite the attention he gave to Somalia, Haiti, Bosnia, Kosovo, and the hunt for bin Laden, Iraq was another one of those problems that never seemed to go away. Clinton was convinced the Iraqi dictator was shirking UN resolutions and developing weapons of mass destruction. The United States imposed a no-fly zone over much of Iraq and strengthened the economic sanctions imposed on the country after Saddam's invasion of Kuwait. The goal was to ensure that Iraq abandon its chemical and nuclear weapons program. But the sanctions were so punishing that while Saddam was building ever more extravagant palaces, his people were starving. A UN study showed that, by 1995, over a half-million Iraqi children had died from hunger and disease.[46]

In May 1996, UN ambassador Madeleine Albright had appeared on *60 Minutes* to defend the administration's Iraq policy. "We have heard that half a million children have died. I mean, that's more children than died in Hiroshima," reporter Leslie Stahl said. "And, you know, is the price worth it?" Albright's answer spurred a public outcry. "I think it is a very hard choice, but the price—we think the price is worth it." Albright later apologized for the remark, but in a highly contentious 1998 Ohio town hall meeting, held to explain the administration's increasingly interventionist foreign policy, she claimed Saddam was building weapons of mass destruction. She was certain of it. "No one has done what Saddam Hussein has done, or is thinking of doing," she said. "He is producing weapons of mass destruction, and he is qualitatively and quantitatively different from other dictators."[47]

In fact, because of the Clinton administration's increased worries over Saddam's weapons program, key senior US military leaders worried that the United States would launch an invasion to remove the Iraqi government. So, in April 1999, the US Central Command conducted a war game to assess the likely outcome of such a war. The resulting "Desert Crossing" simulation "amounted to a feasibility study for part of the main war plan for Iraq—OPLAN 1003-98—tested 'worst case' and 'most likely' scenarios of a post-war, post-Saddam, Iraq," a press report noted. Desert Crossing was the brainchild of Marine general Tony Zinni, one in a series of high-profile CENTCOM commanders who, with the end of the Cold War, found their AOR (area of responsibility) the center of Washington policy discussions. Zinni was a popular officer with a habit unique to senior officers: he was a terrific listener. He'd hear all points of view, then wave his hand, turn in his chair, and go silent before making a decision. "Okay," he'd say, "here's what we're going to do." These personal characteristics, it was said, were derived from his Italian American heritage, so naturally Zinni was dubbed "the Godfather" by his senior aides. He was never far from small-town Pennsylvania, where his mother (Lilla) had been a seamstress, his father (Antonio) a chauffeur. "Zinni is a wonderful guy and always testing," a staff officer who worked for him says. "His favorite question was 'and then what?' So you want to invade Iraq? Great, we can do that. And then what?"[48]

The results of Desert Crossing were sobering. The study showed that while Saddam's military could be easily defeated, it would require four hundred thousand troops to "keep order, seal borders and take care of other security needs" after the war was concluded. The collapse of Saddam's regime would fracture Iraq along sectarian lines, antagonize "aggressive neighbors," destabilize other Arab regimes, erode US standing with its allies, set Iraq's tribes against each other, and enflame Iran's anti-Americanism. Zinni studied Desert Crossing's conclusions and issued his patented low-key judgment, which amounted to a recitation of why the study was conducted. "I thought we ought to look at political reconstruction, economic reconstruction, security reconstruction, humanitarian needs, services, and infrastructure development," he said. In other word, as Zinni concluded, after the United States went into Iraq, it would shatter around them.[49]

While Desert Crossing gained the attention of the Joint Staff when it was completed in July 1999, its conclusions were all but forgotten until, in the next administration, the dangers Clinton saw in Saddam were revived. But on the eve of the 2000 presidential election, Iraq was viewed as contained, a niggling problem, to be sure, but not a crisis-in-the-making. During the campaign, Vice President Al Gore and his challenger, Texas governor George Bush, focused on domestic issues. Iraq was a foreign policy footnote while al-Qaeda was barely mentioned at all.

NO ACCOUNT OF the Clinton years is complete without mentioning Monica Lewinsky. Lewinsky arrived at the White House in 1995 as a twenty-one-year-old intern. That November, she began a sexual relationship with the president. In 1996, she was transferred to the Pentagon, where she told Linda Tripp, a fellow worker, about her and Clinton's intimate relations. In December 1997, she was subpoenaed as a witness in a lawsuit charging the president with sexual harassment. The relationship was made public in January 1998. Clinton adamantly denied ever having a relationship "with that woman." It was a lie. By September 1998, when the House Judiciary Committee announced it would begin an impeachment inquiry against Clinton, the continuing crises in Bosnia and Kosovo seemed like a diversion. America was consumed by the Clinton-Lewinsky scandal.

For a large number of senior military officers, the Lewinsky scandal reinforced everything they'd believed about the president. How could Clinton demand that their colleagues be dismissed from the service while he remained in the White House? If Joe Ralston couldn't get the top job at the Pentagon, how could Clinton maintain his in the Oval Office? And yet, like many officers before him, Hugh Shelton found himself unaccountably attracted to the president. Like George Joulwan, Shelton believed Clinton had "the touch," the ineffable quality of connecting with people. He'd seen that first at Fort Bragg, but now at the end of the Clinton years, he saw that quality again.

As Shelton later told the story, just before George W. Bush was inaugurated in January 2001, Clinton took Shelton aside during a national security meeting at the White House. They searched for a private place to talk and ended up in the office of the deputy national security adviser. "I just wanted to take a moment to personally thank you," Clinton began. He then referred, elliptically, to the Lewinsky scandal. "Hugh, I know the last few years have put a tremendous strain on you based on my . . . activity. I know the principles for which you stand, and I know the values, and character, that our men and women in uniform expect—and possess—and in truthfulness, I have not lived up to those values; and yet, you have stuck by me. You have never wavered, and you have never judged; you have been the consummate professional about the whole thing. I just wanted to thank you for your service, your great leadership, and . . . " And then, as Shelton told it, Clinton began to cry. "I was completely awed," Shelton said. He told Clinton that he had been honored to have worked for him. Clinton nodded, then turned to leave. It was the last time Shelton saw him as president.[50]

CHAPTER FIVE

Tommy Franks: Rumsfeld's General

"Don't pay attention to those
assholes. You're my general."

T HE MILITARY VOTED overwhelmingly for George W. Bush in the
2000 election, because he was a candidate who reflected their pre-
dominantly southern, rural, and conservative values. Oddly, Bush's failure to serve in Vietnam (a fact that had once plagued Bill Clinton) had
no impact, reflecting a generational shift and voter fatigue with that conflict. Al Gore had served in Vietnam, but that war was now twenty-five
years in the past. So instead of talking about his military service and his
experience on foreign policy, Gore attempted to ride to the White House
on Clinton's economic successes. But Gore was not the campaigner that
Clinton was, or the master of glad-handing that Bush was known for.
Additionally, Gore's expertise on foreign policy issues was checked by
Bush's selection of former secretary of defense Dick Cheney as his vice
presidential nominee. In defiance of stereotype, Gore was the hawk while
Bush sounded like a dove. During his first televised debate against Gore,
Bush critiqued the Somalia intervention, saying that Clinton had been

wrong to shift America's humanitarian effort into a nation-building mission. Then, in the lead-up to the vote, Bush emphasized his opposition to nation building by hinting that Gore would put humanitarian intervention at the top of his foreign policy agenda. It became Bush's brand, his way of saying that his opponent was soft: Gore didn't want to win wars, he wanted to help people. "I don't think our troops ought to be used for what's called nation building," Bush told the public. "I think our troops ought to be used to fight and win wars."[1]

The only foreign policy controversy the campaign generated focused on Bush's pledge to withdraw US forces from Bosnia; keeping the peace there, he said, was the responsibility of America's European partners. The United States had a vital stake in Europe, Bush said, but the Europeans needed to take the lead. Gore attempted to paint Bush as soft on tyrants; Bush countered by saying the US military was "overextended and unprepared for the future." In fact, and not surprisingly, Bush's complaint about nation building had strong support among senior military officers, who hoped the younger Bush would replicate his father's close relationship with the military's officer corps and follow the policies adopted during the Reagan years: that America had a large military not in order to use it, but so that it wouldn't have to. The overwhelming majority of the nation's senior military leaders found the Albright view of American power distasteful, even naïve. For them, George Bush's critique of nation building was a coded rejection of Albright's "assertive multilateralism."

The Gore team celebrated their candidate's toughness by attacking Bush as hesitant to use military force. But it wasn't Bush who was hesitant, it was the military. Gore never quite got it: the military supported Bush because they thought he'd put an end to Clinton's military adventures, not engage in more of them. During the campaign, Gordon Adams, a senior adviser to Gore on military issues, said that Bush was thinking too narrowly about nation building, implying that the Republicans were sadly out of step with current military thinking. "The Bush team has a curiously old-fashioned view," he said. "We will have a well-funded military that is designed to go nowhere and prepared to do nothing, because they are only there to fight the nation's wars, and we are not having any." In fact, a military designed to go nowhere and do nothing was exactly what, with some few exceptions (like Wes Clark), senior military officers wanted. "The linchpin of our policy is forward engagement," Adams said. But after Somalia, Haiti, Bosnia, and Kosovo, the military had had enough of "forward engagement." The linchpin of US foreign policy, they believed, should be diplomacy. "This comes down to function," Bush adviser Condoleezza Rice told the *New York Times*. "Carrying out civil administration and policy functions is simply going to degrade American capability to do things America has to do. We don't need to have the 82nd Airborne escorting kids to kindergarten." Admiral "Snuffy" Smith couldn't have said it better.[2]

The 2000 presidential election was decided on December 10, when the Supreme Court issued a "stay" on a recount of Florida's ballots. The decision made George W. Bush president of the United States. Nine days later, on December 19, Bush arrived at the White House for a meeting with Bill Clinton. The two were filmed striding comfortably along a White House walkway, then sat together for the press. They met in the Oval Office for just over ninety minutes, and hit it off, the beginning of what would be a growing friendship. Clinton liked Bush and admired his political skills. And while Bush had slammed Clinton during the general election, he, like so many before him, was drawn to the man. The two later said they'd only disagreed on their views of the greatest threat facing the country, with Clinton saying he believed that it was al-Qaeda and Osama bin Laden. "I have to disagree with you there," Bush said. "The biggest threat is Iraq."[3]

In the years that followed, senior military officers would reprise this first Clinton-Bush meeting, circulating stories of how their discussion reflected the personalities of the two. But the one story that gained the most traction, and was passed from ear to ear in the Pentagon, had nothing to do with bin Laden or Saddam Hussein. Instead, the story reflected Clinton's continuing resentment of Colin Powell's actions in his administration's earliest days. As military lore would have it, on that rainy December 19, 2000, as the president-elect got up from his chair in the Oval Office to leave, he turned to Clinton with a parting question. If there is one piece of advice that you could give me, what would it be? he asked. Clinton had anticipated the question, and so was ready with the answer. "Whatever you do," he said, "never appoint a strong chairman of the Joint Chiefs of Staff." As it turns out, it was advice that Clinton didn't need to give.[4]

HIS CLOSEST COLLEAGUES in the Air Force were surprised when George Bush nominated the vice chairman of the JCS, General Richard Myers, to succeed Hugh Shelton, as they were convinced the job would go to Air Force general Ralph Eberhart. Eberhart was a wonk, an Air Force Academy "ring knocker," who understood the emerging importance of cyber networks, had received high marks as his service's deputy chief of staff for plans and operations, and was viewed as an Air Force partisan. He'd checked all the boxes, scored at the top in his evaluation reports, and was well liked by his fellow officers. He was in line for the job. But Myers was the pick, while Eberhart retained his job as head of North American Aerospace Defense Command (NORAD) in Colorado.

The other contenders for Shelton's replacement included Admiral Vern Clark, the chief of naval operations; Marine general Peter Pace, the head of the US Southern Command; and Admiral Dennis Blair, the US commander in the Pacific. But Bush liked Myers when he met him, which occurred several months before Shelton was slated to retire, and he came with the personal recommendation of Donald Rumsfeld, Bush's choice to take over the Pentagon. Myers, Rumsfeld said, agreed with the president's defense transformation agenda, which focused on increased defense expenditures for a new generation of weapons, a small and lighter army, and more money for the continuing development of a national missile defense system. Myers, Rumsfeld added, was known as a loyalist and wasn't one of "Clinton's Generals," a derisive term common among Bush officials to describe those in the military appointed by Clinton and who'd signed on to nation building. As if to emphasize this point, Bush appointed Colin Powell as secretary of state, a not-so-subtle reminder of Powell's leadership in Desert Storm (during his father's term) and a subtle nod to Powell's standing as one of Clinton's earliest critics.[5]

Ironically, the appointment of Myers confirmed for the senior military that Bush wouldn't tolerate the kind of public spats between the JCS and the White House that had marred the Clinton years, which had begun with a Powell-Clinton face-off. But then, as Bush had been told, Myers was no Powell. "When you pick a chairman, you want somebody who is sympathetic with your ideas," said Lawrence Korb, the director of studies at the Council on Foreign Relations. "Myers seems to be one of the few folks in there who is sympathetic with what Rumsfeld and Bush want to accomplish." For many in the military, Korb's comment was the first in a litany of backhanded slaps at Myers that policymakers would

make over the years that followed. They all amounted to one thing: Myers wasn't going to be a "yes, but" JCS chairman. He was an agreeable
guy, and he would agree with Bush and Rumsfeld. That's why Bush had
picked him. He would get his orders, snap off a breezy salute, and say
"yes, sir." Dick Myers, it was said, wasn't big on having a discussion.[6]

Articulate, data driven, humorless, and as much a tinkerer as Colin
Powell (he had a degree in mechanical engineering, and loved to fiddle
with engines), Myers's reputation inside his service was as a get-along,
go-along kind of guy. He'd taken a different career path than many of
his predecessors (like Powell, Wes Clark, or Dennis Reimer), who almost
seemed to welcome a political row. Not Myers. As head of the Fifth Air
Force in Japan he'd driven his staff hard, but always toward consensus.
He'd come to Washington to serve as assistant to John Shalikashvili and
then as vice chief under Shelton. In Pentagon parlance, the noncontroversial, hardworking, and utterly predictable Myers stayed in his lane. In the
up-or-out military, where promotion was survival, you didn't get ahead
by disagreeing with your boss, and Myers never disagreed with his boss.
This was particularly true during his assignment as the military aide to
Madeleine Albright, defending her to his fellow officers, keeping his rare
disagreements with her to himself, and advising her on how to handle the
JCS. Albright reciprocated, bubbling away when she learned Myers was
Bush's JCS choice. "Always a pleasure to work with," she said of him.[7]

That Myers wasn't known for being an outspoken advocate on military issues was important for Rumsfeld, who knew that the military's
senior commanders would fight his transformation plans. The biggest
dissenter would be the Army, which was facing pressure to become more
"agile, lethal, rapidly deployable and require a minimum of logistical support," as Bush himself had described it. But problems could also be expected from the Air Force, whose mafias would defend their turf against
the new "platforms, weapons and doctrines" that Rumsfeld wanted them
to adopt, or who took issue with the president's call that the military
design weapons that would (as he said) "skip a generation of technology." For career officers, these lofty goals were mystifying: how exactly
were weapons developers supposed to "skip a generation of technology"?
Didn't scientists need to develop the next generation in order to plan the
generation after? It sounded good, but it didn't make sense.[8]

In the end, as a number of senior officers believed, all the talk about
military transformation would come down to what it had always come

down to: who would buy what and how much it would cost. And, as they later commented, that was true even for Donald Rumsfeld, who spent his first months as defense secretary laboring over the defense department's quadrennial defense review, the famed Pentagon tome shorthanded as "the QDR." Mandated by Congress in 1997, the once-every-four-years study lays out how the military will fight and what it will need to do so. Ultimately, the QDR is about money, shaping the defense department's view of what should get funded in the congressional appropriations process—it was the most significant way that an administration could shape defense policy. Which is why the QDR process was key for Rumsfeld: the review would put his stamp on the military. The Rumsfeld meetings on the QDR went on day after day in a series of highly detailed question and answer sessions that started in the late morning and lasted into the midafternoon. Rumsfeld questioned everything, from the most miniscule expenditure to Air Force plans to develop a new bomber. Why do we need a new bomber? he would ask. Shouldn't we be spending money on unmanned aircraft? When it was explained to him that such aircraft were being developed, he grew testy. He hated being contradicted. Soon, the word got out: Donald Rumsfeld wasn't the smartest guy in the room, he just thought he was. Increasing numbers of officers thought he was insulting. "How difficult can this be? What is it you don't understand?" he'd ask.[9]

What the United States needed, Rumsfeld told Myers, was a new way of thinking about how to respond to threats. He called it a "capabilities-based model." Instead of identifying enemies and studying their capabilities, the military would build capabilities that could respond to the threats posed by enhanced weapons systems, no matter who fielded them. This was music to the ears of the Pentagon's tech gurus, for it was exactly what they were focusing on. In the wake of Desert Storm, the Air Force and Navy assumed that China and Iran would develop weapons to counter the high-tech precision-guided munitions fielded by the US against Saddam. The two nations, which Air Force and Navy officers identified as the most likely challengers to American power, would attempt to deny American ships and planes access to their waters and airspace by developing anti-access and area-denial weapons, fighting America's precision-guided munitions with their own "smart," stand-off munitions. What was disturbing for those who rubbed shoulders with Rumsfeld was that he was convinced that military planners hadn't thought of this, while he had. "You're just not getting it," he'd say during the QDR discussions, and then present his views: "See what I mean?"

One of the new secretary's closest friends, Marty Hoffman, who'd been secretary of the Army back in the 1970s and had known Rumsfeld since they'd been roommates at Princeton, often served as "a kind of blocking back for Don," as one of his Pentagon colleagues described him. Hoffman had done this before, when Rumsfeld was named Gerald Ford's defense secretary in 1975, the youngest man to ever be named to the job. Then, Hoffman's services had rarely been needed, but over the years Rumsfeld's natural abrasiveness had gotten worse. He was outspoken, opinionated, blustery, and rude. Hoffman watched Rumsfeld's moods and found himself intervening to calm officers whom Rumsfeld had offended. "Let me straighten this out," he'd say, and stride out of Rumsfeld's office. For Hoffman, the challenge wasn't explaining the military to Rumsfeld, but explaining Rumsfeld to the military. Within months of Bush's inauguration, Hoffman had a "come to Marty" meeting with his old friend, telling him his outbursts were ruining his relations with the JCS. Hoffman reminded Rumsfeld that the military had celebrated Bush's election, and he repeated Rumsfeld's promise that the Bush administration was going to give the military "the respect it deserved." Don't squander that, Hoffman warned. "I'm just trying to get things done, Marty," Rumsfeld pleaded. "I'm just trying to turn this thing around." Hoffman nodded, but told Rumsfeld he was turning friends into enemies. "Holy Mackerel, okay, I get it," Rumsfeld said. "I'll do better." But that never happened. For Hugh Shelton, who was happy that he was headed into retirement, Rumsfeld was a constant nightmare.[10]

"With the Clinton administration," Shelton would later write, "I always felt that I was free to express my honest opinions and they would be taken into consideration and either accepted or rejected, but I always seemed to get a fair shake. As I transitioned into the Bush administration, it felt more like some members of his team had a particular agenda—a direction they wanted things to go—and if you were going to be part of their team, you had better be willing to vote in that direction, or you probably would be looking for another job." In the weeks before Myers took over as the JCS chairman, Shelton told him what it would take to rein in Rumsfeld. When he shouts at you, Shelton said, stand your ground. If you are "legally, morally, and ethically correct," Shelton said, then stand up to him. In one instance, as Shelton later told it, Rumsfeld had disagreed with a "threat matrix" on Iraq, a voluminous and complex PowerPoint presentation. Shelton agreed to review it, stuck it on his desk for two weeks, then gave it a new title (the "Rumsfeld Auto-Response Matrix") and a new glossy cover and presented it to the defense secretary. "He loved every word of it," Shelton said.[11]

Not everyone in the military disliked Rumsfeld, of course, but even his supporters would later tell stories that provided insights into what drove him. Early in his term as defense secretary, Rumsfeld began to author a flurry of single-page memos asking questions, making points, or demanding answers. Called "snowflakes," the memos became legendary among the Joint Staff, who spent countless hours responding to them. "I really liked Donald Rumsfeld," a now retired Air Force brigadier general says. "You know, I'd come in early in the morning, and there he'd be, dictating a snowflake. He was absolutely tireless. It was a little weird, because this was really old technology. He had one of those, you know, dictaphone like things, and my job was to get the memos transcribed, distribute them, and then track the answers. It became very elaborate." The brigadier would greet the defense secretary ("he was always pretty nice to me," he said), then grab up that morning's snowflakes and distribute them. "He got the idea from Churchill," the general said. "Rumsfeld read somewhere that Churchill did this and you know, what he really wanted was to be Winston Churchill. He idolized Churchill. He was thinking about his legacy the whole time. I think he envisioned some future historian talking about how Don Rumsfeld was America's Churchill."[12]

One of those who regularly received Rumsfeld's snowflakes was Douglas Feith. Rumsfeld had brought Feith on as undersecretary of defense for policy in the summer of 2001 because, as Rumsfeld told one of his civilian aides, "he appreciates that what we're fighting is what we don't know," a phrase that was a Rumsfeld mantra. There were the known unknowns and the unknown unknowns—a whole litany of Rumsfeld-isms that the defense secretary used to explain his ideas to his staff and the military. The phrases struck military officers as downright odd, with Rumsfeld going on and on, but Feith loved them and faithfully wrote them down, then repeated them to his friends. "Here's what the secretary said today," he'd exclaim. What made Rumsfeld unpopular, Feith argued, was that he demanded that the military question its assumptions. The problem for the military is that they hadn't come up against someone as smart as Donald Rumsfeld, Feith said. He was always rethinking things. "Those of us in his inner circle heard him say, over and over again: Our intelligence, in all senses of the term, is limited," Feith would later write. "We cannot predict the future. We must continually question our preconceptions and theories. If events contradict them, don't suppress the bad news; rather, change your preconceptions and theories." Feith made the same point during testimony he gave before the Senate Armed Services Committee soon after taking his job. Committee members had heard complaints about Rumsfeld, and they were concerned. Feith calmed their fears. The defense secretary's goal, he said, was to save American lives; he then worshipfully quoted one of Rumsfeld's sayings: "It is clear that the Defense Department needs to plan, but we must plan to be surprised." Feith beamed at the committee: he was working for a genius. Back at the Pentagon, an officer on the Joint Staff heard this and shook his head. "How the fuck do you plan to be surprised?" he asked.[13]

HUGH SHELTON WAS in the air over the Atlantic Ocean, headed to a NATO conference in Hungary, when American Airlines Flight 11 crashed into the north tower of the World Trade Center on September 11, 2001. The JCS chairman, who had a little less than a month left in office, was aboard a specially modified C-135, the "Speckled Trout," that was normally used by the Air Force chief of staff. Shelton was informed of the incident by Colonel Douglas Lute, a rising West Point graduate who served as his executive assistant. When told that a second plane had crashed into the south tower (seventeen minutes after the first crash), Shelton concluded the incident was a terrorist attack and ordered his C-135 to return to the United States. Shelton's absence made Vice Chairman Richard Myers the acting JCS chairman. "Until I crossed back into United States airspace, all the decisions would be his to make, in conjunction with Secretary Rumsfeld and the president," Shelton remembers.[14]

Myers was on Capitol Hill, headed into a meeting with Georgia senator Max Cleland, when the first plane hit. He saw a report of the incident on a television outside of Cleland's office. Myers's first thought was that the incident was an accident. "I remember the day being beautiful," he later recounted. "I said, 'How could a pilot be that stupid, to hit a tower? I mean, what'—but then you think, 'Well, whatever.'" Myers was in Cleland's office when the second plane hit, and immediately notified his staff to assemble the JCS's crisis activation team (CAT), a half-dozen senior officers who coordinate military emergency responses. He then headed back to the Pentagon. In Colorado Springs, General Ralph Eberhart was at NORAD headquarters at Peterson Air Force Base when the second jetliner hit. After trying to get in touch with Shelton, Eberhart reached Myers just as he was leaving Cleland's office. The two agreed that the United States was under attack.

Myers's directive to assemble the JCS's CAT was followed by similar orders for each of the services. At the Pentagon, Major General Peter Chiarelli, the Army's director of operations, readiness, and mobilization, heard about the New York attack from Major General Julian Burns, the deputy chief for operations of the US Army Forces Command. "Have you seen what's happened in New York?" Burns asked. Chiarelli looked up at a muted television, which showed smoke pouring from the north tower, and called Lieutenant Colonel Kevin Stramara, his operations chief. "It's time to activate the CAT," he said. "Get it set up."[15] The incident must have struck Chiarelli as a dark irony. Just the month before, he'd told his staff that they would be doing an exercise using the CAT during the week of September 11. It had been ten years since the CAT was used, and Chiarelli wanted to make sure everyone knew what to do. At the center of the exercise, he decided, would be an incident featuring an aircraft crashing into the World Trade Center. Now Chiarelli was faced with the same scenario. Chiarelli was floored by the coincidence, but shook it off. Things happen. Within the next minutes, on his orders, Army officers headed to the Army's command and control center, located in a bunker two floors beneath a Pentagon parking lot. Before heading there himself, Chiarelli turned to Stramara: "If there are other aircraft up there that have been hijacked," he said, "or if there are other aircraft getting ready to do this, this building has got to be a target. Who has responsibility for this building?" Stramara didn't know: "I will check," he said.[16]

Donald Rumsfeld was at the Pentagon in the midst of a breakfast meeting with members of Congress to discuss the QDR when Flight 11 flew into the north tower. Deputy Defense Secretary Paul Wolfowitz was present, as was Rumsfeld's senior military assistant, Navy vice admiral Edmund Giambastiani Jr. The breakfast was breaking up when Rumsfeld was handed a note about what had happened in New York, but, like Myers, he assumed the incident was an accident and so headed to his office. It was while he was there that the Pentagon was hit by American Airlines Flight 77. The aircraft plowed into the first floor of the western side of the Pentagon, killing 189 people, including 125 in the building. A fourth aircraft, United Airlines Flight 93, crashed in Pennsylvania twenty minutes after the Pentagon attack, at 9:57 a.m. Seated in his office, Rumsfeld headed outside to assess the damage and could be seen there, in later photographs, helping to carry a stretcher of a wounded victim.

By the time of the Pennsylvania crash, General Eberhart had told Myers that he was grounding all commercial aviation, and directing all fighter aircraft in the United States to "battle stations, fully armed." At the White House, reports that a fourth aircraft was headed to Washington (this was the United Airlines flight that crashed in Pennsylvania) spurred Vice President Cheney's security detail to evacuate him to the Presidential Emergency Operations Center, which is below the East Wing of the White House. Cheney had already talked with George Bush, who was in a classroom at an elementary school in Florida when he'd heard about the first attack. Bush's chief of staff, Andy Card, then told him about the second plane by whispering in his ear. "A second plane has hit the second tower," he said. "America is under attack." Bush made a split-second decision "not to jump up immediately and leave the classroom. I didn't want to rattle the kids. I wanted to project a sense of calm." Later, Bush said that his first reaction was "anger." Who the hell would do this to America? he wondered.[17]

While reporters would pore over the timeline of 9/11 in the years ahead, hoping to find some clue of panic among the nation's leaders, the evidence suggests the opposite—a sense among senior military officers, at least, that they should be careful not to overreact. In Colorado, Ralph Eberhart ordered a limited version of the Security Control of Air Traffic and Navigation Aids system, which would clear all commercial airspace above the United States, while maintaining ground navigation stations to ensure that flights still in the air could land. At the Pentagon, meanwhile, Richard Myers dragged his feet when Donald Rumsfeld recommended raising the defense readiness condition to level three—with defense condition one signifying imminent war. Myers recommended that the order be confirmed by the White House, which slowed the process. Myers later told an aide that while raising the alert level "was appropriate," it would do little to protect the nation from the kinds of attacks it had suffered that morning.[18]

All three senior military officers—Shelton (whose aircraft was not allowed into US airspace until that afternoon), Myers, and Eberhart—

concluded that while what had happened in New York, at the Pentagon, and at a crash site in Pennsylvania was an act of war, it did not constitute an existential threat to the US homeland. There was no reason to "spin up the missiles" (prepare for war, in Pentagon parlance). For both Hugh Shelton and Richard Myers, there was never much doubt about the attacker's identity. Arriving at the Pentagon late that afternoon (his flight had taken him directly over the smoking remains of the World Trade Center), Hugh Shelton assembled his senior Joint Staff officers to hear what they'd learned, then headed to the White House. But later that night, he returned to the Pentagon to quiz them. A bevy of officers ran through the leading suspects as he shook his head—no, no, and no—until they got to al-Qaeda. Somewhere in Afghanistan, he knew, Osama bin Laden had planned the attack, then recruited and trained the attackers. Shelton was checking all the boxes, but the briefing was essential, he recalled, "in the unlikely event that someone other than al-Qaeda was responsible."[19]

TWELVE DAYS LATER, on the night of September 23, 2001, the CIA's Islamabad station chief, Robert Grenier, received a telephone call from his boss, George Tenet. "Listen, Bob," Tenet said. "We're meeting tomorrow morning at Camp David to discuss our war strategy in Afghanistan. How should we begin? What targets should we hit? How do we sequence our actions?" Grenier was surprised by the call, but he'd been thinking about these same questions since 9/11, so he was ready. Bush's speech to the US Congress just a few days before, he told Tenet, was a good starting point: demand that Afghan ruler Mullah Omar stop protecting bin Laden and turn him over to the United States. If he refused, launch a campaign to oust him. Grenier had thought through the plan, but before going into details, he stopped the conversation. "Mr. Director," he said, "this isn't going to work. I need to write this all down clearly." Over the next three hours Grenier laid out the battle for Afghanistan. Included in the paper was a detailed program of how the CIA could deploy undercover teams to recruit bin Laden's enemies among Afghanistan's northern Tajik and Uzbek tribes, supply them with cash and weapons, and use them in a rolling offensive that would oust the Taliban in Kabul. He gave the draft eight-page paper to his staff to review, then sent it on to Tenet in Washington, who passed it through the deputies committee (the seconds-in-command of each of the major national security agencies), then presented it to Bush.

"I regard that cable," Grenier later wrote, "as the best three hours of work I ever did in my twenty-seven-year career."[20]

Three days later, on September 26, the CIA landed a covert-operations team in Afghanistan to recruit local allies in the hunt for bin Laden. Among the first CIA officers on the ground was fifty-nine-year-old Gary Schroen, who'd been on the verge of retiring from the agency when he was given the chance to go after the terrorist. He jumped at it. While Schroen was told that the president had decided the CIA would take the lead in Afghanistan, he knew the Taliban couldn't be ousted without the help of specially trained military commando teams. So twelve days before going into Afghanistan (with $3 million in neatly sorted American cash), Schroen had one of his assistants call his counterpart at the Pentagon. "Reach out to these guys," Schroen said. "Let's talk to the SEALs. Let's talk to Delta. Let's talk to SOCOM [Special Operations Command]. Let's talk to CENTCOM [Central Command]. Anybody you know, let's invite." His assistant made the call, but came up empty. The military's special operations people couldn't get their bosses to agree on who should go, he was told. "The whole US military was caught flat-footed. I don't think that anyone had ever raised the issue how do we go into Afghanistan," Schroen later observed.[21]

Senior military officers, including CENTCOM commander Tommy Franks, would dispute this view. Franks said the military was ready, as evidenced by a briefing he provided to Rumsfeld and the JCS "within days" of the 9/11 attacks. In fact, while Franks presented his plan on the same day that Robert Grenier wrote his, Rumsfeld inexplicably slowed the military planning process. Then too, Franks's briefing of Rumsfeld did not go well, with the defense secretary complaining that the plan wasn't creative and would take too long to implement. Rumsfeld said the same thing to Bush. "You will find it disappointing," Rumsfeld told Bush the day after Franks's presentation. "I did."[22] But while Franks's briefing of Rumsfeld didn't go well, his presentation to the JCS, which gathered to hear him in the tank, was a disaster. For Franks, a tough-talking Oklahoman known for his profanity-laced speeches, the briefing was a painful formality; he didn't need the JCS's approval on how to fight a war and didn't care if he had it. "The concept of operation has our special forces working with locals, tied into CIA operations and supported by airpower," he began, and then went through his slides, some seventy in all.[23]

The members of the JCS, and their roomful of action officers, were taken aback. The Franks plan seemed a hodgepodge of ideas, some taken from what the CIA was already doing and some from CENTCOM's dusted off binders of Taliban target lists. It was off-the-cuff, shoddy. There was muttering around the table, a participant later recalled, and a perceptible shifting in seats. Myers, now officially the JCS chairman, was silent, but Army chief of staff Eric Shinseki spoke up. "No one's ever fought a war using an indigenous rebel force," he pointed out. "What you're proposing is completely unprecedented—" Franks interrupted him: "I'm fighting this war, you're not." Shinseki was taken aback, took the measure of the room, nodded, looked down at his notes, then calmly looked up at Franks. Shinseki knew that Franks was thin-skinned. It was one of his personal characteristics. He decided to be blunt: "We don't think it will work," he said. Franks exploded: "Bullshit," he said. "It's my plan. And I am responsible for its execution." There was an awkward silence around the table, so Franks got up and walked out. No one could believe it. "Shinseki baited him," a participant recalled, years later, "and Tommy took the bait."[24]

After the briefing, Myers approached the director of the Joint Staff, Army lieutenant general John Abizaid, who'd been in the room. "Tommy Franks is a pompous ass," Myers said. The exclamation point to this comment came the next day when Franks faced off against two JCS members. "Yesterday in the Tank," he said, "you guys came across like a mob of Title X motherfuckers, not like the Joint Chiefs of Staff." The two offending chiefs, a Joint Staff officer later reported, were Shinseki and Air Force chief of staff John Jumper, both of whom had seen this kind of arrogance before, with Wes Clark in Kosovo. Franks's criticism wasn't subtle. Title X, the mandate under which the JCS operated, took them out of the chain of command—the result of the passage of Goldwater-Nichols in 1986. By law, their role was to recruit, train, and equip. They didn't command anybody. So, in Franks's world, they didn't count. Inevitably, the story of the Franks confrontation with Shinseki and Jumper made the rounds. As it turns out, Franks himself was the one repeating the story. For him, the phrase "Title X motherfuckers" was a good punch line. It showed people how he could stand up to the services. But for the JCS, Franks wasn't the problem; the problem was Don Rumsfeld, who'd made it clear to Franks that he could bypass the chiefs. The defense secretary hadn't liked Franks's plan for Afghanistan, but he liked how he handled the JCS. It titillated him. Franks was exactly what he needed. "Don't pay attention to those assholes," Rumsfeld told him in the wake of the JCS briefing. "You're my general."[25]

It took another week for CENTCOM to finalize a plan on Afghanistan, and an astonishing two weeks for Rumsfeld to approve it, but when the president announced the beginning of Operation Enduring Freedom, on October 7, the United States had already positioned fighter-bombers from three aircraft carriers and elements of the 10th Mountain Division in the region and recruited help from a host of nations. That same day, five Air Force B-1B bombers, two B-2 stealth bombers, ten B-52 heavy bombers, twenty-five Navy F-14 and F-18A fighters (from the aircraft carriers *Carl Vinson* and *Enterprise*), and fifty Tomahawk cruise missiles hit al-Qaeda training camps, Taliban training sites, and air defense systems in Jalalabad, Kandahar, and Kabul. This three-day campaign was followed by a second target set of Taliban command, control, and communications centers. But even then, the bombing had little impact. The leadership of Afghanistan's anti-Taliban tribes, called the Northern Alliance, complained that the US wasn't hitting the Taliban where it needed to, while Schroen kept pleading with CENTCOM's target officers to focus on Taliban ground forces. This wasn't Iraq, or Kosovo, and the Afghanis weren't the Republican Guard or the Serbs. Mullah Omar wasn't Saddam Hussein: he didn't have a military infrastructure. The CIA could hardly believe it. The military needed to kill Taliban fighters, but that wasn't happening. The Pentagon wasn't getting the message. It was conducting the campaign by-the-book, without any consideration of whom they were fighting.

"Nobody was calling the shots," Schroen remembered. "It was almost useless bombing because we weren't really impacting the front lines, which is where the Taliban fighters were hunkered down." Even the arrival of a contingent of US Marines in Kandahar had little impact, as the Taliban continued to gamely hold their lines. It took until October 20 for the first US special forces team to link up with anti-Taliban Afghan rebels, but it wasn't until the first week of November, when US special forces teams landed in strength, that the targeting shifted. In the next phase of the air campaign US aircraft spread deadly cluster munitions and daisy cutter bombs, shattering Taliban frontline positions. Schroen's team, with the anti-Taliban Northern Alliance's Tajik and Uzbek fighters, saw the results firsthand. "Our guys were listening to the radios and the panic, the screaming, the shouting as bunkers down the line were going up from 2,000 pound bombs, I mean, they were just simply devastated, and they broke," he later recalled.[26]

By early November, the Taliban was on the run, with al-Qaeda units disappearing from the battlefield. On November 13, the Northern Alliance seized Kabul. In nearly every sense of the word, this was a decisive US victory. But Robert Grenier was worried: the conquest of Kabul by northerners, he concluded, would worry the Pashtun tribes in southern Afghanistan, and might even turn them into Taliban allies. Grenier warned Schroen against this, hoping to hold off the conquest of Kabul until the southern tribes could join in. Schroen knew that Grenier was right, but he wasn't about to slow down the Northern Alliance's march, and couldn't have done so if he'd wanted. The campaign had a momentum of its own. Even so, Schroen knew the United States might face chaos in Afghanistan, with southern Pashtun tribesmen bumping up against northerners. "They don't like each other; they don't get along well; it's a much more complicated tribal structure there," Schroen would later say. "There were all kinds of problems. We didn't understand the south like we did the north . . . so we ended up not really winning the hearts and minds of the Afghan people, but destroying the Taliban and then putting a government in place that hopefully would be able to win the hearts and minds."[27]

But the complexity of the Afghan situation was lost on the Pentagon and especially on Donald Rumsfeld. When the CIA had presented its Afghanistan plan during a White House meeting on September 12, Rumsfeld had insisted that the military, and not the CIA, take the lead. Military units couldn't even go into Afghanistan without CIA approval. That bothered him more than anything. Why should the CIA be in charge? "This needs to be a military operation," Rumsfeld said. "And if it's going to be a military op, then it has to be run by the military, not the CIA. I'm not even so sure Afghanistan is the right place to start. What if Iraq is involved?" Seated across the table, Colin Powell could hardly believe what he was hearing. "What are you talking about?" he asked. "We have al-Qaeda to deal with. If Iraq's involved and we know they're involved, then they'll be a part of this war. All we know for now is that al-Qaeda is responsible—and they're in Afghanistan." Bush agreed, repeating one of Rumsfeld's bon mots to make his point. Al-Qaeda was the known known. "Let's deal with one thing at a time. Let's deal with what we know," he said to Rumsfeld. "We know al-Qaeda is responsible. Let's deal with al-Qaeda."[28]

But Rumsfeld wouldn't give up. He was leery about getting involved in Afghanistan, often citing Afghan intellectual Mahmud Tarzi's phrase that the country was "the graveyard of empires." Then too, Rumsfeld thought the idea that bin Laden could pull off the New York attacks without outside help was ludicrous. So, in the wake of the September 21 meeting, Rumsfeld called Tommy Franks in Tampa. "What about Iran?" he asked him. Franks was taken aback. "What about them?" he asked, then went on to explain that he was digging up intelligence on anyone involved in the attack, whether it was "Afghanistan, Iraq, Iran, or anyone else." Rumsfeld seemed satisfied. Then, on September 29, while discussing the situation in Afghanistan, Rumsfeld told Myers that he and the JCS should "begin preparing military options on Iraq." The comment came out of the blue, but if Myers was surprised he didn't show it. The invasion, Rumsfeld added, should be done with a lot less than the five hundred thousand troops used by Norman Schwarzkopf.[29]

By early October, Rumsfeld's plea that the military take the lead in Afghanistan was a constant refrain. "The CIA has to work for me, or this isn't going to work," Rumsfeld said to Bush. He even mentioned his preference to Tenet himself, with whom he had weekly lunches. According to *New York Times* reporter James Risen, Tenet was so intimidated by Rumsfeld that his lunches with him became story-swapping sessions, where Tenet would tell "Don" about the latest scuttlebutt at the CIA, while Rumsfeld nodded in apparent appreciation. Tenet, Risen wrote, "rarely challenged him on festering problems between the Pentagon and the intelligence community." According to one of Rumsfeld's aides, the defense secretary rarely bored in on Tenet, but when he did he was painfully blunt. "You know, I think this is a military operation," he said in early October, referring to the CIA's Afghanistan war. "We have the assets. You don't have them." Tenet told Rumsfeld that he was simply doing what the president wanted. "I want the CIA in there first," Bush had said. After his lunches with Tenet, Rumsfeld would shake his head: "Do I really need to see this guy?" he'd ask his staff.[30]

But Tenet wasn't the only one intimidated by Rumsfeld; so too was George Bush. In what would later be described as a "fiery" mid-October NSC meeting, Rumsfeld lit into Tenet after the CIA director implied that the reason the Afghanistan operation was taking so much time was because the Pentagon was dragging its feet. Rumsfeld took the criticism personally. "What nonsense," he replied, arguing again that the Pentagon should lead the war. In the wake of that meeting, on October 18, Rumsfeld got his wish: Bush told Rumsfeld he now agreed with him; the Pentagon, he said, would take the lead in Enduring Freedom. The decision had an immediate impact. On October 20, two days after Bush's decision, the first US special forces team in the country linked up with the Northern Alliance. At the CIA, senior officers concluded that now that Rumsfeld had gotten his way, Enduring Freedom would move much more quickly. In Afghanistan, Gary Schroen was disgusted. He was convinced the military could have targeted the Taliban's frontline troops much earlier.[31]

Schroen was right, Rumsfeld had been dragging his feet, even though a senior officer described him in this period as "flying around" the Pentagon "screaming at people that we weren't moving fast enough." Even so, after Franks's first briefing it took him nine more days to provide "credible military options" for responding to al-Qaeda, but when he did, Rumsfeld sent them back for more work. He regularly signaled his dissatisfaction with the same two words—"not fulfilled"—then shook his head in exasperation. The problem for CENTCOM was there just weren't that many places to bomb: "a few al-Qaeda training bases, a few leadership buildings, a few tactical aircraft, and some anti-aircraft guns and surface to air missiles," as one senior Pentagon officer described it. Rumsfeld was irritated. "We need more targets," he told Franks. "We don't have any," Franks responded. "Find them," Rumsfeld said.[32]

As the pressure mounted on the military, it also mounted on Don Rumsfeld, with powerful members of the Senate Armed Services Committee among the critics. What was taking so long? they asked. There was even talk that, with complaints against him now common, he would be eased out of his job. Rumsfeld responded by calling on his most powerful allies, including former House speaker Newt Gingrich, a longtime supporter. Rumsfeld was in regular touch with Gingrich, repeating the litany of problems he was having with the military. He was struggling to change the military's culture, he told Gingrich, which had been polluted during the Clinton years. These guys are risk averse, Rumsfeld said. Gingrich, whose admiration of Rumsfeld was nearly slavish, got the message. The problem wasn't Rumsfeld, he told reporters, it was Bill Clinton—and the military. "I think the underlying fact is that you have Bill Clinton's generals designing a campaign that is not very creative, and it's not very clever, and it's very worrisome," Gingrich told reporters. Yet, when the final targeting plan was finished, Rumsfeld dragged his feet again, spending three days reviewing it before passing it on to the White House. On October 2, the president gave it his approval. By then it was too late. Bin Laden was gone.[33]

LATE ON THE afternoon of November 21, after a National Security Council meeting in the White House Situation Room that featured an update on the successes of Operation Enduring Freedom, George Bush pulled Donald Rumsfeld aside. "What kind of a war plan do you have for Iraq?" he asked. "How do you feel about the war plan for Iraq?" Rumsfeld said that he was reviewing all of the military's plans, Iraq included. It sometimes took years to come up with a war plan, he said, and they were often hundreds of pages long. Bush nodded. "Let's get started on this," he said. "And get Tommy Franks looking at what it would take to protect America by removing Saddam Hussein if we have to." This was a sotto voce conversation, held in private. Bush told Rumsfeld his request should remain secret. Rumsfeld said he understood.[34]

At CENTCOM headquarters in Tampa, General Tommy Franks was told about Bush's decision on Iraq by Air Force major general Victor E. "Gene" Renuart Jr. The news had arrived by way of a Rumsfeld memo, reinforced by a call from the JCS director of operations. "You've got to be shitting me," Renuart responded. Franks had much the same reaction. "Goddamn," he said, "what the fuck are they talking about?" This was standard for Franks, whose staff thought of him as a throwback, an Oklahoma good ol' boy with a richly deserved reputation for being curmudgeonly.

Five days after his discussion with Bush, Rumsfeld was in Tampa, reviewing CENTCOM's plan for overthrowing Saddam Hussein; one month later, Franks was at Bush's ranch in Crawford, Texas, for a meeting with the president. In the intervening weeks, Franks and his staff had honed CENTCOM's Iraq plan, cutting it back from an initial deployment of nearly five hundred thousand American troops. Rumsfeld was underwhelmed by Franks's initial offering, which was an updated version of CENTCOM's original OP Plan 1003. "This is old think," Rumsfeld said when Franks told him the numbers. "We need something much more flexible. Fewer troops. And we need to be able to move on short notice."[35]

When Franks arrived in Crawford on December 28, the Iraq plan had been refined into a series of complex slides. Franks and his staff, under constant pressure from Rumsfeld, had cut the numbers of troops, then cut them again. The standard military saying, recited by senior officers as a warning, is that the United States must guard against "fighting the last war." But Franks threw the warning out the window. Afghanistan, he said, showed that it was possible to move decisively against "a broad spectrum of enemy assets" to gain a short and decisive victory. Franks said he wanted to avoid a long build-up of forces by incrementally moving units into the region as a part of normal military rotations. But this wasn't going to be a replay of George H. W. Bush's 1991 war in Iraq, with Desert Shield followed by Desert Storm—with days of bombings followed by a ground invasion. From the moment US and coalition troops reached their start line, they would vault forward, capturing Saddam, destroying his government, and liberating Baghdad. This would be a short war.[36]

However, what was most astonishing about Franks's briefing was that while it focused on the military plan to remove Saddam Hussein, his first slides centered on building political support for the operation. That was unusual. The military didn't provide political options, but Rumsfeld had waved away Franks's concern when he'd first visited with him, citing a paper provided by Deputy Secretary of Defense Paul Wolfowitz detailing how the war would be sold. What was needed, the paper implied, was a good excuse: "Saddam moves against Kurds in north? US discovers Saddam connection to Sept. 11 attack? . . . Dispute over WMD inspections?" Below that, Wolfowitz had written: "Start now thinking about inspection demands."[37] Wolfowitz was looking for a reason to go to war, and Franks aped him, including his points in his Bush briefing. Looped into Crawford from the Pentagon via videoconference, Rumsfeld assured the president that the briefing wasn't the final product. A lot more, he said, needed to be done. Bush liked what he heard. "This is good work," he said. "Keep grinding on it."

When Franks returned to Tampa, he and his staff devoted nearly their entire time to Iraq and, over the next year, provided at least seven different Iraq war plan updates. Fighting the coming war was Franks's job, but providing it with a political grounding was Bush's. Taking his lead from

Franks's briefing and the Wolfowitz paper, he began to lay the political groundwork for invading Iraq during his State of the Union message of January 29, 2002. Iraq, he said, was part of an "axis of evil." Saddam's regime, he argued, "continues to flaunt its hostility toward America and to support terror. The Iraqi regime has plotted to develop anthrax and nerve gas and nuclear weapons for over a decade."[38]

By March, Franks had honed the CENTCOM war plan, shaping it to reflect varying levels of international support: the less support, he calculated, the more Americans would be needed to fight. Franks provided Bush with this approach in a White House briefing. The president, he said, had three Iraq war options: the US could initiate a "robust" operation (with strong international support), a "reduced" operation (with some international support), or a "unilateral" invasion, with no international support. But no matter what, Franks assured Bush, an invasion could begin sixty days after the president gave the order, with or without international support. Bush nodded his head, satisfied. But there was still a lot of work to be done. Franks should keep going. By August 5, 2002, the plan had been refined even further; it was now a "hybrid plan." In this "hybrid concept," as Franks told the NSC, "the US military would quickly mobilize forces in the region, initiate an air campaign, then launch a ground invasion." Bush approved the plan, as did his top national security aides. Secretary of State Colin Powell added his support, but privately thought that Franks underestimated the troops he'd need. And he wasn't impressed by CENTCOM's presentation of what postwar Iraq would look like. Franks and his staff had labeled this "Phase IV" of his operation, the military's standard term for postwar reconstruction. "Phase IV" was a "stability operation."[39]

Powell had a telephone conversation with Franks following the August 5 briefing. Franks was respectful: he wasn't a Powell fan, but that was when the general had been the JCS chairman. He thought Powell was a part of the past, back when the US military needed a half-million troops to conquer a country. Franks had told that to Rumsfeld, echoing the defense secretary's bedrock belief: that America's program of military transformation had transformed the nature of war. But Franks didn't say this to Powell. Instead, now that Powell was secretary of state, he patiently explained his reasoning. Governing postwar Iraq, he said, would be left in the hands of the Iraqis themselves, monitored by the State Department. Franks reminded Powell that this had been included in his briefing. "DOS [Department of State] will promote creation of a broad-based, credible provisional government—prior to D-Day," one of his slides stated.[40]

Franks wasn't the only one to hear from Powell. On the night of his briefing, Powell had had dinner with the president and Condoleezza Rice. This turned into a two-hour session, the most time he'd had with the president without Rumsfeld present. He was worried that Franks was moving too quickly, he said, and he wasn't impressed with the briefing's "Phase IV" assumptions. There was no doubt the United States could win a war in Iraq, but there didn't seem to be a clear answer to the "now what?" question. "You are going to be the proud owner of 25 million people," Powell told Bush. "You will own all their hopes, aspirations and problems. You'll own it all." Bush didn't answer, so Powell continued. The intervention would define Bush's first term as president. "It will suck the oxygen out of everything," he said. "This will become the first term." Then Powell made his proposal. The president, he said, had to look for allies. The way to do that was to go to the United Nations.[41]

Powell's "you'll own it all" comment was later referred to as "the Pottery Barn Rule," as in: if you go into a shop and break the pottery, you own it. In fact, the rule was first used by *New York Times* columnist Thomas Friedman, but Powell had adopted it as his own. Powell and his savvy deputy secretary, Richard Armitage, discussed it often. While Donald Rumsfeld might have called such talk "risk averse," both men had seen shattered nations, dying soldiers, and an America nearly broken by an unnecessary war. Armitage knew what he was talking about. A Naval Academy graduate, he'd served in Vietnam, then returned there in 1975 as a part of a mission to retrieve as much of the US arsenal as possible. He hated what the United States had done in Vietnam, saying the US withdrawal was "like getting a woman pregnant and then leaving town. It is not a beautiful or good image either but I thought that we acted like irresponsible fathers." This was more than simply talk—Armitage and his wife had eight children, six of them adopted. For him, "Phase IV operations" were personal.[42]

But while Colin Powell and Rich Armitage believed in the Pottery Barn Rule, that wasn't true for Tommy Franks, Donald Rumsfeld, or George Bush. None of them had a problem with breaking pottery, but paying for it (they believed) would not be necessary. Franks was a military traditionalist: his job was to break the pottery. Repairing it was the

State Department's problem. Then too, paying for the pottery was a "military operation other than war" (MOOTWA, in military shorthand)— and "real men don't do MOOTWA." Donald Rumsfeld supported this and believed it. As defense secretary, his job was to ride herd on the military. After that, his job was done. Phase IV operations were not a part of his writ. His policy staff, Douglas Feith's shop, reinforced this belief. The Iraqis were more than capable of putting the pottery back together. And the Pottery Barn Rule? Just as "real men don't do MOOTWA," great nations don't do nation building. And so the Pottery Barn Rule was transformed: the Iraq war would show that real men can break as much pottery as they want and then walk out the door.[43]

JCS chairman Colin Powell with General Norman Schwarzkopf and Undersecretary of Defense Paul Wolfowitz on the eve of Operation Desert Storm. *Credit: Getty Images, Corbis Historical*

Secretary of Defense Dick Cheney flanked by Colin Powell and Norman Schwarzkopf in Riyadh prior to Operation Desert Storm. Lieutenant General Calvin Waller, whom Powell had sent to calm the volcanic Schwarzkopf, is on the left. *Credit: Getty Images, David Hume Kennerly*

Admiral Frank Kelso II (left) and Marine Corps commandant Carl Mundy Jr. Kelso spent his last years caught up in the Tailhook scandal, while Mundy remained an adamant opponent of Clinton's program to allow gays in the military. *Credit: Getty Images, Jennifer K. Law, AFP*

Clinton's chairman, General Hugh Shelton. At the end of his second term, Clinton tearfully apologized to Shelton for the Monica Lewinsky scandal. *Credit: Getty Images, Luke Frazza, AFP*

"Yeah, I liked him": NATO commander George Joulwan with Bill Clinton in Baumholder, Germany. Armored commander Major General William Nash is on the left. *Credit: Getty Images, Luke Frazza, AFP*

"The Invisible Chairman": General Richard Myers with Defense Secretary Donald Rumsfeld during Operation Iraqi Freedom. *Credit: Getty Images, Win McNamee, Getty Images News*

Retired General Anthony Zinni explains the Generals' Revolt. *Credit: Getty Images, Alex Wong, Getty Images News*

General Jack Keane, who turned down Rumsfeld's offer of the Army's top job but authored the Surge—and the Keane Coup. *Credit: Getty Images, Jeff Hutchens, Getty Images News*

General David Petraeus and his patron, Jack Keane. Keane believed Petraeus to be the most talented commander he'd ever met. The Iraqis called him "King David." *Credit: Getty Images, Charles Ommanney, Getty Images News*

David Petraeus and General Ray Odierno. "I can't stand that son of a bitch," Odierno would later scream at his staff. *Credit: Getty Images, Getty Images News*

Barack Obama rolls out his administration's new defense strategic guidance (DSG). He is flanked by (left to right) Defense Secretary Leon Panetta, Army chief of staff Ray Odierno, Marine Corps commandant James Conway, and new JCS chairman Martin Dempsey. *Credit: Getty Images, Saul Loeb, AFP*

Air Force chief of staff Norton Schwartz (right) and chief of naval operations Gary Roughead (next to him) plotted out the new AirSea Battle doctrine. The two are shown here with Army chief George Casey and Marine Corps commandant James Conway. *Credit: Getty Images, Mandel Ngan, AFP*

CHAPTER SIX

Richard Myers: The Invisible Chairman

*"The only thing missing
was a firing squad."*

IN EARLY 1917, during World War I, British general Sir Frederick Stanley Maude led an army of sixty thousand British and Indian soldiers from Basra up the Tigris and Euphrates rivers to Baghdad. His enemy was a Turkish army, some twenty-five-thousand strong, defending a province of what was then a part of the decrepit Ottoman Empire. Maude was hardly a creative campaigner (his troops called him "systematic Joe"), but then his conquest of Mesopotamia wasn't much of a fight. "The Turkish Army that was recently before us," he reported to his superiors, "has ceased to exist as a fighting force owing to its casualties, prisoners, demoralization and the loss of a large proportion of its artillery and stores." Maude led his army into Baghdad on a prancing horse on March 11 and then, in the finest British tradition, issued a proclamation: "We come as liberators, not occupiers," it said. The Iraqis thought otherwise.[1]

In 1917, Iraq's tribes began an insurrection that lasted until October 1920. The British responded with a troop surge, then put the war in the hands of its air force, which debated whether to use poison gas on Iraq's restive villages. Winston Churchill, then his country's colonial secretary, thought this just the thing. "I do not understand this squeamishness about the use of gas," he said. "I am strongly in favor of using gas against uncivilized tribes." The revolt failed (and without the help of poison gas) but the British had learned their lesson, turning administration of the country over to their chosen Arab quisling, Faisal I bin Hussein, and then getting out. Faisal was followed by a succession of relatives, but the country's real power was Nuri al-Said, a murderer in a three-piece suit. In 1958, a group of Iraqi officers shot the Faisals in the courtyard of their Baghdad Palace, then hunted down Nuri (who'd escaped the capital disguised as a woman) and executed him. Maude's statue, in Baghdad, was burned. Thus, Iraq.

IT'S UNLIKELY THAT Maude's Iraq campaign was studied by American war planners at the Army's Fort Leavenworth–based School of Advanced Military Studies, though SAMS partisans celebrate their history-laden curriculum. Tommy Franks's planners, the core of whom were SAMS graduates (and thus, "Jedi Knights"), were certainly aware of what Iraq could do to an army, but they had better models than the one provided by a British officer on horseback. These included Desert Storm (George H. W. Bush's Iraq invasion of 1991) and Enduring Freedom (the 2001 intervention in Afghanistan), which taught more important or, at least, more current lessons. A lot had changed in the last one hundred years, and in the last ten. For one, CENTCOM's planners had no need for a John Warden to advise them on how to neutralize Saddam's air force since, after nearly fifteen years of no fly zones, he didn't have one. Nor was Saddam's Republican Guard what it had been in Desert Storm, its power eroded through years of protecting a besieged regime. The SAMS planners put all of this into their mix, then ignored it: victory didn't come from assuming the best outcome but from assuming the worst, in planning for every contingency.

When the outlines for what became Operation Iraqi Freedom began to be drafted in earnest in late 2001, graduates of the Army's School of Advanced Military Studies became the backbone of Franks's CENTCOM planning staff. The head of the group was Colonel Michael Fitzgerald, the brains behind the 2001 Afghanistan plan. His counterpart was Colonel

Kevin Benson, a knowledgeable observer of the Middle East who was heading up the planning staff of the Combined Forces Land Component Command (the CFLCC, or "C-flic"), a by-product of Goldwater-Nichols legislation ensconced in military joint docterine that integrated all Army, Marine, and coalition ground forces. Planning a war is a massive undertaking, its complexity masked by seemingly endless PowerPoint presentations. In the case of what came to be called Operation Iraqi Freedom, Fitzgerald and Benson were flooded with plans and requirements from designated participating units: V Corps, I Marine Expeditionary Force (the IMEF, pronounced "one mef"), Special Operations Forces, and a host of others. Each developed its own plans, then fed them up the chain of command.[2]

It was Fitzgerald and Benson who'd developed Franks's White House talking points that had so impressed George Bush on August 5, 2002, with an emphasis on a simultaneous air and ground campaign (a pointed abandonment of John Warden's Desert Storm precedent) preceded by a surreptitious deployment of special operations units, some of which would covertly contact Iraq's senior military officers in the hopes of convincing them to surrender. Franks worked closely with his CENTCOM planners in advance of his Washington appearances so that he could recite their most important points nearly from memory. The August 5 briefing was 110 slides long, but Franks was so familiar with its high points that he was able to glide through it. He'd even come up with a snappy way of describing the coming war, telling Donald Rumsfeld that Saddam would be defeated by "shock and awe." Rumsfeld used the phrase with Bush and Bush liked it. "Shock and awe," Bush said with a chuckle. "That's a catchy notion."[3]

In fact, the phrase had come from a study done by Navy partisan and Naval Academy graduate Harlan Ullman and a handful of others for the National Defense University in 1996.[4] Included in this group was now retired general Frederick Franks (no relation to Tommy), who'd run afoul of Schwarzkopf during Desert Storm, and Chuck Horner, the air commander in Desert Storm. Tommy Franks read the paper and embraced the phrase, because it fit in with his notion that short, violent wars were the kinds of wars the United States should fight. One of the things that appealed to the CENTCOM commander was the paper's advocacy for the full integration of land, air, and sea units in a combined arms offensive, a requirement of the Goldwater-Nichols reform act that institutionalized interservice "jointness," what military officers called "going purple."

Franks prided himself on going purple, echoing Bill Crowe's claim as the military's most boisterous advocate of joint operations: "There isn't anyone more purple than me," he told his staff.[5]

The object of shock and awe was to stun the enemy so quickly and so thoroughly that it saw no chance of winning—to force enemy "compliance or capitulation through very selective, utterly brutal and ruthless, and rapid application of force to intimidate," Ullman and his team wrote. "The fundamental values or [enemy] lives are the principal targets and the aim is to convince the majority that resistance is futile by targeting and harming the few." Whether either Fitzgerald or Benson actually gave much credence to "shock and awe" as a snappy phrase is open to question, but they embraced Ullman's theme, drafting a plan that would be so "brutal and ruthless" that the war's outcome would never be in doubt. In fact, both men thought it possible that using the phrase itself might lead to a sudden regime collapse, as it would make clear to the Iraqis what they were facing. Iraq would throw up its arms and surrender, "like a balloon pops when poked," as Rumsfeld had once described it.[6]

By the time of Tommy Franks's August 5, 2002, briefing, the campaign plan had gone through countless iterations, each of them more refined than the last. "CENTCOM's main effort would be a ground attack out of Kuwait to defeat Iraqi forces, isolate the regime in Baghdad and, if necessary, the Ba'ath Party home city of Tikrit, remove the regime from control of the country, and transition to security operations after major combat operations were complete," as a postwar review described it.[7] The Third Army would be at the center of the assault, with 1,800 aircraft in support, which included B-2 bombers flying from their base in Missouri to aircraft based in the Persian Gulf. That seemed simple enough, but Tommy Franks remained under constant pressure from Rumsfeld to cut the invasion force even further.

In truth, Rumsfeld's relentless badgering of Franks had little to do with imposing shock and awe on Iraq, but everything to do with imposing it on his competitors in Washington. This was the view at the CIA, where senior officials passed around stories of what Franks said about his boss. Deep into the planning process for the Iraq war, George Tenet made a point of visiting Franks at his Tampa headquarters, accompanied by his senior staff. "How are you getting along with the secretary?" Tenet had asked him at one point. Franks smiled. "If I start every meeting with him with the words 'I'm not worthy, I'm not worthy, I'm not worthy,' and then repeat that for the next thirty minutes I do fine," he said.[8]

The anecdote brought a chuckle from Tenet, but there was something in what Franks said that disturbed him. During Enduring Freedom, Franks had parroted Rumsfeld's views, apparently at the secretary's insistence, and he continued to do so now. In the aftermath of yet another briefing in October, Franks was morose. The plan needed more work, he told his senior staff officers, adopting Rumsfeld's signature phrase: "POTUS is unfulfilled." The rotating team of CIA liaison officers who watched Franks up close in Tampa finally figured out why Franks was such a lamb when it came to Rumsfeld. Franks had "big plans" for his retirement, they decided: he would return to Oklahoma and run for the Senate and Rumsfeld would be there, praising him. "He thought he had a future," as one of these officers put it. "You know, not like Norm Schwarzkopf, who didn't run for squat. That's wasn't Tommy Franks. He thought he was a great leader. Maybe even another Eisenhower."[9] As it turns out, Franks not only thought he was a great leader, he insisted on being treated like one. At the height of the planning process, and while taking a trip to Doha to check in at CENTCOM's semisecret forward headquarters in Qatar, Franks was given a suite at the Sheraton. Unfortunately for his military assistant, it wasn't the best or largest suite at the hotel, which had been reserved for a visiting dignitary. Franks was enraged, and dressed down his military assistant in the hotel lobby. Franks was out of control: "Don't ever let this happen again," he yelled, "or I'll bust you all the way to private." That was "standard operating procedure for Tommy Franks," a retired Army officer who saw the incident said. "But when it came to meeting with Rumsfeld, he was as quiet as a lamb. So I guess if you bleated in the presence of the secretary of defense, it meant your staff had to bleat around you."[10]

The eager to please mentality seemed to seep through every part of the Pentagon, but it was most prevalent with JCS chairman Richard Myers. Myers backed up Rumsfeld during press conferences, and seconded his ideas at White House meetings on Iraq. At one of the latter, in late October 2002, the room was filled not only with the president's primary advisers (Vice President Cheney, Powell, Rumsfeld, Myers, White House chief of staff Andrew Card, and National Security Adviser Condoleezza Rice) but also their deputies, what one observer described as the "back

benchers" who were available to answer specific questions or pass forward
required documents. Cheney and Rumsfeld dominated the meetings, so
that participants began to suspect that the two had conferred in advance.
"It was all in code," one of these back benchers later said. "Rumsfeld and
Cheney never said exactly what they meant. They talked about the 'Iraqi
resistance' and 'democratic forces,' when they meant Ahmad Chalabi;
but they never mentioned him by name. That kept them out of Tenet's
line of fire, because they knew he didn't like Chalabi. The CIA had done
an investigation of him and were convinced he was a fraud."[11]

Ahmad Chalabi was notorious. A former Iraqi official, he headed the
Iraqi National Congress, a small anti-Saddam group of political exiles.
He bragged about his network of Iraq supporters and built the INC into
a powerful group of anti-Saddam lobbyists.[12] His group attracted neoconservative officials at the heart of the Bush policymaking establishment.
For Rumsfeld, especially, Chalabi was "an Iraqi George Washington,"
a phrase used by William Luti, a former aide to Newt Gingrich and an
assistant to Doug Feith. Luti and Feith thought that Chalabi was a celebrated figure in Iraq, and would replace Saddam once Franks's troops
entered Baghdad. Cheney and Rumsfeld agreed. "It was all in code because whenever Tenet or [Condoleezza] Rice called them on their support for Chalabi, they could say 'who said anything about Chalabi?'" The
same back bencher said that Tenet and Rice were often in league against
Cheney and Rumsfeld, "trying to box them in." When Rumsfeld made a
suggestion, this official said, "Condi would pipe up and say, 'You know,
Mr. Secretary, that's a great idea, why don't you follow up and report
to the president what you've found during our next meeting?' And you
could see Rumsfeld would just be seething. The last thing he wanted was
to be told to do anything by anyone, let alone Condi Rice." The back
bencher felt sorry for Rice because he and Tenet would meet her in her
office following NSC meetings where she was constantly interrupted by
calls from the president. "We'd be sitting there and the phone would ring
and she'd apologize and take it. And it was always 'yes, sir,' and 'no, sir.'
It was kind of embarrassing really, and you could see it on her face. She
wasn't the president's national security adviser, she was his secretary."[13]

The same thing could be said of Richard Myers. Throughout the
planning process for the Iraq war, the members of the JCS put aside their
dislike of Franks and diligently met his requirements. But nearly all of
them (the chief of naval operations, Vern Clark, was the sole exception)

harbored doubts about the president's rush to war, including Myers. The hope among the chiefs was that, at some point, Myers would tell Rumsfeld that the whole idea was just foolish. But he never did. "I don't know what happened to Dick," former Air Force chief Merrill McPeak says. "I knew him fairly well. He was an excellent officer, and very competent. And he could always be counted on to speak up. But I'd see him standing there with Rumsfeld and I wondered what the hell he was doing. He would stand there, motionless, during a Rumsfeld press conference, and I thought, 'Well, he's the military ornament.' Otherwise he wasn't a factor. It was like he was invisible." McPeak never told Myers this, following a long military tradition that former chiefs don't give advice to their successors. Even so, McPeak's anti-Rumsfeld views were circulated in the Air Force, along with news that the Iraq war so upset him that he changed political parties. Once a hard-core Republican, he became a more moderate, and then liberal, Democrat. His former colleagues called him "General Ponytail." They had a more vulgar expression for Dick Myers—they called him "limp Dick."[14]

"The senior military was absolutely terrified of Rumsfeld, just terrified," the official who attended the White House national security meeting as a back bencher says. "Rumsfeld held an ax over their head. He could end their careers." A fellow Air Force officer who'd served with Myers denies that the JCS chairman was frightened of Rumsfeld. "He just defined his role differently than McPeak," he says. "He was typically military. He was 'can do.' That was the military way. It's almost second nature. 'Yes, sir. Can do.'" Which is not to say Myers didn't have doubts about the Bush plan for Iraq. He had them, but he covered them up. During a key White House briefing in the fall of 2002, Myers sat unresponsive as Rumsfeld pushed Franks's war plan on Bush. He nearly spoke up when talk turned to a postwar plan for Iraq, which had been taken away from the State Department at Rumsfeld's insistence, but then decided against it. "You could see him struggling," this official says, "but then his face fell and you could see he'd decided to remain silent." Afterward, Myers approached a circle composed of senior deputies. "You know, I often think during these meetings that we're not really serving the president very well," he said. Everyone in the group looked at him, this official says, and they were all thinking the same thing: what did Myers mean by "we"?[15]

NO ONE CAN now agree on when the military began to more openly express its reservations about Iraq, but mid-October 2002 is a good starting point. "On or about October 16, I think it was," a now retired senior Navy officer says, "the joint staff circulated a memo to the CINCs [the commanders in chief of the military field commands] to prepare for war on Iraq. It went to all of their chiefs of staff, senior aides, and military assistants. I don't think anyone anticipated the response. People were angry, really angry." The memo, a "Strategic Guidance for Combatant Commanders," stated that "we are preparing to order that a war with Iraq be considered a part of the war on terror."[16] In effect, the memo was a "warning order" that a war was coming. Over the next few days, the Joint Staff received a spate of messages protesting the warning, including one from a Navy admiral stationed in the Pacific. "What the hell are we doing?" it read.[17]

The reaction had been the same in the Pentagon, where one officer was quoted by *Washington Post* reporter Tom Ricks as asking the same question that had been asked by the JCS for months. "How the hell did a war on Iraq become part of the war on terrorism?" There is no link between Saddam and 9/11, argued another officer, and conflating the two is "going to play hell with the allies. What the hell is going on?" The outcry was so visceral that General George Casey, the head of strategic plans and policy (J-5) decided to put an end to it. Casey stared down his staff: the warning order was justified by the president's own statements, he said. "This isn't a debate," he told one of his senior assistants. "Do your job."[18] At the end of the year, a five-paragraph guidance went out to the CINCs confirming the earlier directive. Iraq, it said, had long been designated as a state sponsor of terrorism. One officer on the Joint Staff described the memo succinctly as the "so keep your mouth shut" order.[19] But for many senior officers, this second guidance put a stain on the earlier warning order: it had gone out because it wasn't obvious why a war with Iraq was necessary.

How did the war on terrorism get transformed into a war on Saddam Hussein? The same question had been asked by Casey's Joint Staff colleague, Marine Corps lieutenant general Greg Newbold, who had helped draft the warning order as one of his last acts as the Joint Staff's J-3, its operations director. Newbold thought he might gain a fourth star, and maybe even become a combatant commander, but five months before the warning memo was circulated he announced he was retiring. Officially,

Newbold said that he needed to spend more time with his family, but in private he was fed up with Rumsfeld. Newbold thought the chiefs should confront Rumsfeld on Iraq. "This is totally unnecessary and it's going to be a disaster," he'd told a fellow officer, after one of Franks's briefings. "I can't believe we're doing this." Newbold vowed that he would tell that to Rumsfeld, but he never did. Newbold blamed himself: How could he demand that Myers and his colleagues stand up to the secretary if he wouldn't do it himself?[20]

In mid-October, at about the same time as the warning order, Rumsfeld told Bush he should meet with the chiefs to hear what they had to say about Franks's war plan. Bush agreed and, at the end of the month, met with them at the White House. Rumsfeld had been telling Bush that while the chiefs were concerned about going to war in Iraq, they supported such a war. Rumsfeld knew that wasn't true, for he'd heard that Army chief of staff Eric Shinseki and Marine Corps commandant James Jones (in particular) had privately expressed deep reservations about the war, but he doubted they would speak up when facing the president. Bush came into the room, trailed by Dick Cheney, Condoleezza Rice, and Andrew Card, greeted the chiefs and then sat at the head of the table. There was a little banter, but then Bush looked from one to the other, asking them their opinion on the Franks plan. Any concerns?[21]

Air Force chief John Jumper spoke up. He was concerned about whether the Air Force had enough high-tech precision munitions for the job. Franks's proposed air attack plan needed "another look-see," but otherwise, no, he said. He thought the plan would work. Marine Corps commandant James Jones said he was concerned about troop protection in the case of a chemical weapons attack, and he was also concerned about fighting in Baghdad. Chief of Naval Operations Vern Clark echoed Jumper, saying the war would likely strain Navy resources. The Navy had used a lot of aircraft carriers for Afghanistan, he said, and he wondered how many they would need for Iraq. It was left to Eric Shinseki to say what everyone else at the table was thinking. He was concerned that Franks's force was too small, he said. Logistics might be a problem. Soldiers would be strung out along Iraq's southern highways, with a long supply line. And that was it. The president thanked them for coming. The discussion never got too deep.[22]

In the years that followed, each of the chiefs would say he had good reason for not confronting the president, and each would be right. The meeting had one purpose: to assess the Franks plan. The president hadn't asked them for their opinion on America's foreign policy, so they didn't give it. And even if he had, they'd have likely given the standard stay-in-your-lane military answer: the nation's foreign policy wasn't their business. Their job was to recruit, train, and equip the force. And that was it. Nor, they said, had Bush asked if America would win. If he had, they'd have been unanimous in their views: of course America would win. Nor had the president asked their opinion of Rumsfeld, but it wouldn't really have mattered if he had. Rumsfeld was not only their boss, he was second in the chain of command. His job was to transmit to them the orders of the president, then make sure they implemented them. What did it matter whether they liked him? Finally, as they all realized, Donald Rumsfeld was appointed by the only official in America elected by the people. No one had voted for them.

Of course, there were some chiefs who not only agreed with Bush, but actually admired Rumsfeld. Among them was the Navy's Vern Clark, a soft-spoken Evangelical Christian who spent his boyhood with his brother and sister singing in the church choir (South Side Assembly of God, in Springfield, Missouri), appearing as "the Clark Trio" on television spots. Clark retained his faith through the years, never wavering from his understated ways. He did his best to get along with Rumsfeld, while knowing that when Bush was looking for a replacement for Hugh Shelton and his name was mentioned, it was Rumsfeld who'd vetoed him. Not a team player, Rumsfeld had said. Clark took this with grace, saying that the defense secretary was welcome to his opinions. As it turned out, and as Rumsfeld came to realize, Vern Clark was the most loyal team player he had. Except for Myers, of course. "Rumsfeld's a tough guy, no doubt about it; he can be prickly," Clark would later say. "You have to gain his respect, but once you gain that, you can work with him. I was thankful I had a tough guy, because we were in tough times." Clark learned the Franks lesson: if you said "I'm not worthy" enough times, Rumsfeld would listen to you. "The way to get Rumsfeld's attention," Clark told one reporter, "was to show that you'd challenged basic assumptions, to admit that you were wanting, and to demonstrate that you were going to do better."[23] When Clark did that, Rumsfeld paid attention to him. Clark could almost hear Rumsfeld forming his words: "Hey, this guy gets it." Vern Clark was proud of that: he'd come a long way from Springfield, Missouri.

Back when Clark took over as CNO, in 2000, Hugh Shelton had given him a copy of *Dereliction of Duty*, a study of how the JCS had failed during the Vietnam War. Written by H. R. McMaster, the celebrated tank commander during the Battle of 73 Easting in the first Gulf war, the book was required reading for senior officers by Shelton, and viewed as a military masterpiece throughout the retired military community.[24] It was passed from hand to hand, and retired senior Army officers went out of their way to host McMaster at a series of afternoon receptions, introducing him to the Washington media. The book was especially popular in the Army, which alternately extolled and condemned General Harold K. Johnson, the Army chief of staff during Vietnam. Johnson was at the center of McMaster's book. Johnson had considered resigning in protest over the war in 1965, held his four stars in his hand when he went to visit the president, intent on putting them on the president's desk, but then decided not to. It was, as Johnson later said, the worst decision he'd ever made. The cautionary statement of General Bruce Palmer, one of Johnson's fellow officers and a senior Vietnam commander, rang through the years: "If you have to explain to your soldiers why they're there," he'd told a reporter, "they shouldn't be."[25] So why now were American troops going to go into Iraq? Could the JCS explain to their soldiers why they were there? Vern Clark read McMaster's book and put it aside, though his aides could tell the book bothered him. Still, he remained silent: the reason we're going to war, he told his staff, is because the president had ordered it.

The JCS was caught, just as Harold Johnson had been in Vietnam. If they refused an order or openly questioned one, they were being insubordinate. If they didn't and things turned out badly, they would be blamed. During the Clinton years the JCS had complained that the draft-dodging, womanizing Clinton didn't know how to salute. The dissenters had pointed out that it didn't matter whether Clinton knew how to salute, it only mattered whether they knew how to salute. Well, did they or not? Nor could the chiefs claim that they were surprised by Bush's Iraq decision, despite the outcry that greeted the October warning order. They'd been present during Bush's January 29, 2002, State of the Union address, when he said the United States would act against any nation "seeking weapons of mass destruction," and they'd read the administration's first major national security paper, where he'd said the US would "exercise our right of self-defense by acting pre-emptively against threats before they are fully formed." They'd said nothing then. A few of them later argued that it didn't really matter whether Saddam Hussein had weapons of mass destruction: Bush had warned that the US would act against anyone "seeking them." Bush was going to take the country to war no matter what they thought. "If we resign, they'll just find someone else," JCS chairman Earle Wheeler told his colleagues during Vietnam. "We have to see this through." That was what the JCS thought now. Their job was to make the best of it.[26]

THE ONLY TRUE dissenter, and the most outspoken JCS critic of Rumsfeld, was the US Army chief of staff, Eric Shinseki. Understated, described often by his colleagues as a "straight arrow," Shinseki's grandparents came to America from Hiroshima in 1901. He remembered that, as a boy, he listened intently as his uncles told stories about their service with the 442nd Infantry Regiment, comprising Japanese American soldiers who fought in Europe during World War II. Shinseki attended West Point but suffered a debilitating sports injury during his plebe year and had to repeat it. Then, when he finally graduated from the military academy, he was shipped to Vietnam, where a land mine ripped off half his foot. He refused to retire, telling the Army he would work until he met the physical requirements allowing him to stay in. Prior to being named chief of staff, he served as Hugh Shelton's vice chief.

From the moment that Shinseki became chief of staff, he'd battled his service's traditionalists, arguing that the Army needed to be lighter, faster, and, as he phrased it, "more deployable." His first efforts were slow, deliberate, and gauged at getting his fellow officers used to his ideas. But after his first year in office, he'd become more insistent. "If you don't like change," he'd told the dissenters, "you're going to like irrelevance a lot less." Shinseki's ideas were initially supported by Lieutenant Colonel Douglas Macgregor, H. R. McMaster's commander at 73 Easting. Macgregor was more extreme than Shinseki, but he thought Shinseki had made a good start. When Shinseki was vice chief of staff, Dennis Reimer had passed around copies of Macgregor's 1997 book, *Breaking the Phalanx*, which argued that simply adopting new technologies wasn't enough; the Army would have to be reconfigured into lighter and more mobile units. Macgregor's book was enormously influential in Army circles where, like McMaster's *Dereliction of Duty*, it appeared on all the service's required readings lists.[27]

Shinseki agreed with Macgregor that the Army needed to get faster and lighter, but he thought the lieutenant colonel went too far; his ideas were too extreme. But he met with the 73 Easting commander in his office soon after *Breaking the Phalanx* was released. Macgregor was already notorious in the Army, but not simply as an author or innovative thinker. He was increasingly outspoken about what the Army could do with lighter and faster forces, and he used his influence with members of Congress. He briefed Newt Gingrich, the influential Republican and former speaker of the House of Representatives, on his own plan for Iraq on New Year's Eve of 2001, telling him that Saddam could be toppled with an army of fifteen thousand soldiers. Gingrich reported this to Rumsfeld, who lined up a meeting for Macgregor at CENTCOM. Twelve days later, Macgregor briefed his war plan to CENTCOM planners in Tampa. During the question and answer session, Colonel Mike Fitzgerald asked Macgregor why there wasn't anything in his plan about Phase IV operations. "Because we're not going to need Phase IV operations," he'd answered. "We're going to turn the governing of Iraq over to the Iraqis, then we're going to get out."[28] Fitzgerald looked at Macgregor, then got up from his chair and left the room. "I think it was at that point that Doug's career ended," a fellow West Point graduate says. After the meeting, Franks met with Macgregor, issuing his standard staccato sentences: "Attack from a cold start. I agree. Straight at Baghdad. Small and fast. I agree. Simultaneous air and ground. Probably. Not sure yet." Franks then smiled and ended the meeting: "thanks for coming," he said.[29]

Shinseki heard about Macgregor's Tampa briefing, of course, but he thought it was important to talk to him. So when Macgregor presented his views on transformation, Shinseki listened intently. When Macgregor was finished, Shinseki told him that he underestimated the number of soldiers the Army would need in case of a major war, arguing that their service's "doctrine, tactics and organization" had been validated by Operation Desert Storm. "I was completely shocked," Macgregor later noted, "because I didn't see much evidence that Desert Storm validated anything other than that any European army can quickly dispatch any Arab army in the world."[30] Macgregor was proud of the 73 Easting fight, but over the years he'd anguished over the country's missed opportunities. Later, when Shinseki aired his transformation proposals, Macgregor said they didn't go far enough. Thus, the Army's straightest arrow faced off against its most notorious iconoclast. It ended badly for Macgregor, who spent his time during the Iraq war teaching at the National Defense University, while his classmates commanded in Iraq.

Shinseki put his transformation plans in place in his first year as chief of staff, in October 1999, ordering that two brigades be transformed into new and lighter units, of the kind the Army had been experimenting with since Gordon Sullivan was chief of staff during the earliest days of the Clinton administration. In effect, Shinseki created a new medium-weight unit called an Interim Brigade Combat Team or, more simply, a Stryker Brigade (named for two unrelated soldiers with the last name of Stryker who were killed in Vietnam), a kind of way station between his service's heavy divisions and more mobile and lighter units. Simply outgunning the enemy wasn't good enough, Shinseki argued; you had to get there first, and the new Stryker Brigades were designed to fix that problem. These IBCTs came complete with a new Stryker light-armored vehicle, which could be easily shipped to any point in the world. It was a brave call; Shinseki knew there would be howls of protest among senior officers who'd grown up in and commanded heavy divisions, but he went ahead anyway, and found that the more he pushed his program, the less the Army protested.

It made sense then that Shinseki would have supported Rumsfeld's transformation efforts, but the relationship had always been tense. "Shinseki and Rumsfeld really didn't like each other, that's a big part of it," a fellow officer says, "and that was true from the minute that Rumsfeld walked in the door." Shinseki thought that Rumsfeld was arrogant, underhanded, and a bully. His verbal tics ("see what I mean?") were grating. Then too, Shinseki noticed, Rumsfeld was all in favor of new ideas, so long as they were his. Shinseki's ideas, honed through years of experience, weren't good enough. Rumsfeld didn't kill Shinseki's Stryker decision, but he regularly derided his ideas. Shinseki partisans believed Rumsfeld didn't kill the Stryker decision because he actually agreed with it, but because it wasn't his idea, he could never bring himself to say so. After a while, Shinseki couldn't even bear to be in Rumsfeld's presence, and simply stopped coming to his transformation meetings.[31]

The first week after 9/11, Rumsfeld invited Stephen Herbits, a close friend and successful businessman, to visit him at the Pentagon. Rumsfeld wanted Herbits to construct a presentation on which senior officers commanded what, when they were due to retire, and who was in line to replace them. The 9/11 attacks had changed everything, Rumsfeld said, and the military needed new leadership. Herbits reported back after several months, showing Rumsfeld an elaborate chart of who was who in the military. Herbits recommended several possible changes. Eric Shinseki was due to retire in eighteen months, he pointed out, which would give the secretary a chance to name his replacement. Herbits recommended General Jack Keane, the Army's vice chief, for the job. Rumsfeld found the idea appealing, but he didn't want to wait eighteen months. Rumsfeld thought about firing Shinseki, but when JCS chairman Richard Myers heard this he was shocked. It will buy you a lot of trouble, Myers told Rumsfeld. The vice chairman, Marine general Peter Pace, agreed. Firing someone simply for disagreeing with you wouldn't wash, he said. The JCS was there to disagree; that's what providing advice meant.[32]

Rumsfeld mulled this over and conceded the point, but he was desperate to get rid of Shinseki. So in early April 2002, fourteen months before Shinseki was due to retire, Rumsfeld directed one of his staff to tell the *Washington Post* that he'd appoint Keane as his replacement. The story, Rumsfeld calculated, would make Shinseki a lame duck, undercutting him in his own service. It might even force him into retirement. No one cared about a chief who didn't have sway with the defense secretary. "It was all very indelicately done, really ham-handed," a top civilian aide to Rumsfeld at the time says, "but that's what the secretary wanted." Shinseki was one of "Clinton's Generals."[33]

Shinseki fought back, facing down Rumsfeld over his decision to cancel the Army's new Crusader artillery system. The Crusader was the Army's next-generation weapon, a light, lethal, and self-propelled howitzer whose prodigious rate of fire could lay down more than ten artillery rounds a minute. A standard battery of six Crusaders could deliver fifteen tons of munitions in five minutes. The Army had spent years developing the weapon. But during the first week of May 2002, Rumsfeld cancelled the Crusader, arguing that it was too big and too slow. In fact, Rumsfeld was parroting the views of Deputy Secretary Paul Wolfowitz and Stephen Cambone, the head of Rumsfeld's policy department and Doug Feith's boss. Both told Rumsfeld that cancelling the artillery system would reinforce his transformation agenda. Their reasoning seemed sound: mobile formations were light and fast, they argued, while the Crusader wasn't. Rumsfeld agreed, but his cancellation decision took Shinseki and the Army by surprise. When they heard Rumsfeld's explanation, they concluded that he didn't understand artillery.[34]

Crusader wasn't a behemoth: two of them could fit into a C-5 or C-17 transport plane. Then too, artillery wasn't meant to be mobile, or even precise. That's what jets were for. And precision, as Shinseki later told Congress, was fine if you knew where the enemy was. "If you have imprecise locations or if you just know that there's an enemy force out there, but you don't have them accurately located, precision doesn't help you very much," he said.[35] Other Army officers put this differently: if the United States had had artillery on the ground in Afghanistan during Operation Anaconda (the military offensive aimed at destroying al-Qaeda in eastern Afghanistan), bin Laden might not have gotten away. As it turned out, the Army didn't have artillery in Afghanistan because, reading Rumsfeld's mind, Tommy Franks said it wasn't needed. So it was that when forward units believed they had bin Laden located, it took twenty-five minutes for fighter jets to arrive. Then too, as one study noted, you could blanket a target with ten artillery rounds fired from a Crusader for the same cost as a single precision-guided munition, which took longer to arrive.[36]

Shinseki made these points to members of Congress, covertly meeting with a handful of them after Rumsfeld's announcement. Rumsfeld found out and one week after the cancellation announcement, he directed the Army's inspector general (1G) to investigate who had circulated a two-page memo defending the Crusader program in Congress. Several days later, the IG determined the offending memo (it called its language "inappropriate, inaccurate and offensive") was Kenneth Steadman, the principle deputy in the Army's office of legislative liaison. On May 11, Rumsfeld demanded Steadman's resignation, then held a press conference with Army secretary Thomas E. White, announcing it. It was like a scene from *The Caine Mutiny Court-Martial*, except instead of talking about strawberries, Rumsfeld was talking about artillery. Waving at White ("he has addressed the subject"), Rumsfeld promised further action. "This would complete whatever might be done from a disciplinary standpoint," he said, "although I would not say it's [all that] will be done." White quickly grabbed the lectern, saying he supported his boss: "I have made clear within the Army that this action was repugnant and contrary to the interests of our troops and country," he said.[37] Rumsfeld's message was chilling: dissent would be punished, careers ended, offenders disgraced. "The only thing missing," a Joint Staff officer said at the time, "was a firing squad."[38]

Shinseki faced off against Rumsfeld in private, but he never talked about the confrontations with the press, and rarely with his staff. But one of Rumsfeld's civilian special assistants later described them as "pretty ugly," with the defense secretary "absolutely furious, dressing down the chief; Shinseki just stood there and took it." There was a lot of admiration inside the retired community for Shinseki, particularly as the Bush administration edged closer to a showdown with Iraq. And there were growing fears that, with Shinseki's departure, Rumsfeld would have successfully surrounded himself with a group of officers who not only agreed with his transformation program, but who would support his march to war. That view was already prominent inside the Joint Staff: "When you're the Secretary of Defense and you personally interview everybody for three and four stars, you politicize your general-officer corps," a top Army official told *New Yorker* reporter Peter Boyer. "That's what they accused Clinton of doing, and now *they're* doing it. If you're asking general officers if they agree with political decisions, then you're not asking for the best professional military advice."[39]

THE MARINES WERE also concerned about Rumsfeld, and about the Iraq war. For the Marines, the concerns started at the top, with the commandant of the Corps, General James Jones. Jones was infuriated by Rumsfeld, but he kept his views private, going so far as to tell reporters that the Rumsfeld-JCS tussle was more of a family spat than a real break. In private, and in discussions with retired Marine commanders, he told a different story. He was disgusted. He wanted out. What angered him the most was Rumsfeld's habit of asking the JCS their advice and then criticizing them for giving it. He would openly laugh at them: "You've got to be kidding," he'd say. For Jones, this was a classic bait and switch; it was what led Myers and his colleagues to tell Rumsfeld what he wanted to hear. In the summer of 2002, some of this leaked into the press, with the *Washington Post* reporting that senior military officers believed a war in Iraq would fracture that country, that the intelligence on Saddam's weapons programs was exaggerated, and that invading Iraq would be a diversion in the war on terror. There was even a report of an unofficial alliance between the State Department and the senior military in opposing the war—a back channel of story swapping that focused on Rumsfeld.[40]

Rumsfeld and his top assistants (Wolfowitz, Feith, and Cambone) thought that Jones was the one talking to the press, but they couldn't prove it. So Rumsfeld dispatched conservative intellectual Richard Perle, the chairman of the Pentagon's Defense Policy Board, to counter the articles. Perle weighed in against the military, as if reminding them of their place. The decision on Iraq, he said, is "a political judgment that these guys aren't competent to make." Rumsfeld then had his assistants, Feith and Cambone, brief leading scholars at Washington think tanks about his relations with the JCS. Within weeks Rumsfeld's strategy started to yield benefits, with a prominent policy guru intoning that "if there are more than one or two" members of the JCS opposed to confronting Saddam "I'd be surprised." The number was not insignificant: one or two members would comprise one-third of the JCS members. Jones would make three. Jones told a Marine colonel on his staff that he thought all this was laughable. "If the military isn't competent to judge when we should go to war, then who the hell is?" he asked. Later, Jones would tell reporter Bob Woodward that Rumsfeld had "emasculated" the joint chiefs. And that's what he told his retired colleagues, among them Tony Zinni and retired lieutenant general Paul Van Riper, a highly respected forty-one-year veteran of the Marine Corps.[41]

During the long walk-up to the war in Iraq, Tony Zinni, the Marine "godfather" and author of the Desert Crossing postconflict war game, and his good friend Paul Van Riper compared notes on Rumsfeld (Van Riper regularly called him "Rumsfield," even when corrected by reporters) and worried that he and Bush were leading the country into a disaster in Iraq. The two lived in the same neighborhood in Williamsburg, Virginia, and could often be seen together on weekends, when they went bass fishing. Van Riper didn't look the part: his official Marine portrait shows a bespectacled man under a traditional green cap. But underneath, Van Riper sports a shaved head and open manner, fearless in battle and in his opinions. He was wounded in 1966 in Vietnam, charging a North Vietnamese machine-gun nest. Like Zinni, Van Riper enjoyed his role as a tough-talking Marine. In private, his friends and colleagues say, he was and is much more cerebral, thoughtful, and almost erudite.

A closely knit service with two hundred years of tradition, the Marines hold a special place in American military history. Traditionally an arm of the Navy, they'd gained semi-independence during the Cold War. While they still rode to battle on Navy ships, they were the only truly integrated, combined-arms service, with their own air wing. They prided themselves on being expeditionary and able to deploy quickly to any crisis. In the wake of Desert Storm they focused on urban combat, a specialty that set them apart from the other services. And they were known for producing independent-minded and outspoken officers. Van Riper was one of these.

As the Iraq war was being planned, Van Riper took on the role of the "red team" enemy commander during a war game called Millennium Challenge 2002. To that point, Millennium Challenge was the most expensive and complex war game ever staged, involving nearly fourteen thousand soldiers, airmen, and sailors and costing $250 million. The goal of the war game was to simulate the military's new high-end technologies in wartime conditions. As the red team commander, Van Riper's role was to deny the US military (the "blue team") access to the waters and airspace of his fictional Middle East country. Van Riper had played his role before and knew he was supposed to lose. But that's not what happened. During the exercise, Van Riper used motorcycle scouts to transmit messages to his commanders (thereby evading blue team electronic eavesdropping), ordered his flotilla of small boats to flit in and out amongst the blue team's lumbering behemoths (confusing Navy targeters and making use of their lack of maneuver), hid his armor under highway overpasses (to dampen their heat signatures), and attacked first, just as the blue team carrier task force deployed. The strategy worked. In what one participant called "the worst naval disaster since Pearl Harbor," Van Riper's red team sank nineteen blue team ships. "The whole thing was over in five, maybe ten minutes," Van Riper later said. At that point, the game's referee called off the simulation and started over. This time, according to Van Riper, the blue team had a decided advantage, because they were given new technologies, which were only then being developed, that showed what the red team was going to do. And Van Riper was replaced as the red team commander.[42]

Oddly, and despite the controversy the war game sparked, Van Riper thought that, in a strange kind of way, it was a success. "Yeah, sure it was fixed," he says. "The guys who ran it wanted blue to win. That's right. But don't look at the outcome, look at what happened. You know, we always say that a plan doesn't survive the first shot. Well, this proved it. So you need to plan knowing that what you think is going to happen never does. Ever." In his weekend talks with Zinni, Van Riper made this point again and again, then emphasized it when talking with reporters. "You all focus on numbers, whether we have the right number for Iraq. And the answer is 'no,' not by a long shot. But that's not the whole story, because once you start thinking you need 400,000 troops you impose some new thinking. And the new thinking is 'well, if it's going to take that many, maybe we shouldn't do it.' So, you see, this isn't about numbers."[43]

NUMBERS MIGHT NOT have been an issue for Paul Van Riper, but they were key for General David McKiernan, the commander of Tommy Franks's ground force. After reading, editing, and rethinking CENTCOM's war plan, McKiernan believed the United States simply didn't have enough troops to take on Saddam. He'd come to that conclusion in late November 2002, after a Kuwait-based command exercise (aptly dubbed "Lucky Warrior") showed that the current "hybrid" deployment plan would stretch ground deployments. He needed to flow reinforcements into southern Iraq more quickly after the invasion, or start the war with more troops. This wasn't a matter of opinion, it was what Lucky Warrior showed. The Kuwait exercise was attended by a number of senior, now retired, officers who'd served in Desert Storm. After a November 22 briefing conducted by McKiernan himself, he was approached by Frederick Franks, who'd led Schwarzkopf's left hook in 1991. Franks, who'd followed McKiernan's career for many years, wasn't impressed by his briefing, or the Iraq war plan. "Is this your plan?" he asked. McKiernan shook his head. Of course it wasn't—it was Tommy Franks's plan, and after his briefing in Kuwait, McKiernan wanted it changed. On December 5, McKiernan met with V Corps commander William Scott Wallace and Marine commander James Conway to air his worries. He didn't have enough soldiers, he told them. When they agreed, McKiernan went to Franks.

Franks was inclined to follow the advice of his ground commander, but warned him that if, soon after the invasion, Saddam's regime collapsed, Washington would "look for an off ramp," Rumsfeld-speak for stopping the flow of troops into the war zone. McKiernan understood that, he said, which is why he wanted more troops at the outset. Rumsfeld had wanted a "just in time" approach to deployments, but McKiernan disagreed. "I don't want 'em just in time," he said. "I want 'em a little bit early." On December 12, McKiernan made his pitch to Rumsfeld in

Kuwait. Rumsfeld was uncomfortable with the request, but with reports of JCS dissent reaching the newspapers, he was coming under increased scrutiny. The dissent was becoming more public.

Two months previously, he'd received word that senior officers had spent two days at the Army War College in Carlisle, Pennsylvania, criticizing his "piecemeal deployment plans," the primary reason, they said, for the poor handling of the Afghan operation. "The possibility of the United States winning the war and losing the peace is real and serious," they warned. So at the end of December, McKiernan got his wish. An entire division, a helicopter regiment, and a battalion were added to the mix. Franks's hybrid plan now became Cobra II, named for the massive 1944 operation that had breached German defenses at Normandy.[44]

While McKiernan lobbied Franks and Rumsfeld, the V Corps prepared for its deployment in a training exercise in Germany. "Victory Scrimmage" was "a walk up to the conflict," one of its participants remembers, with the entire corps practicing the same maneuvers they would employ in Iraq. The new technical capabilities in command and control, and the advent of the Internet and high-speed communication were all tested, but the template for the fight would be an accelerated version of Desert Storm. This time, the "shock and awe" scenario meant a shorter air campaign, followed by a vault forward, with overwhelming airpower and tank formations cutting through the Republican Guard. These ground exercises were followed by simulation-driven tests ("Gotham Victory") of how to command troops in urban combat, what Wallace assumed might happen when his troops penetrated Baghdad. The plan had V Corps bypassing major urban centers in southern Iraq, but they couldn't do that with the capital. Unless the Iraqi military collapsed, Baghdad would be a necessary fight, and Wallace wanted to make sure it was quick. The war games were rehearsals, conducted by every major assault unit equipped with the latest technical advances—Blue Force Tracking (a battlefield system monitoring friendly units); the Army Battle Command System (ABCS) with digital command, control, and coordination of battlefield functions; and testing and fielding of the D9 armored bulldozer, a massive piece of armored engineering that could take down entire houses.[45]

In December, as McKiernan was briefing Franks, US units began to arrive in Kuwait. The 3rd Infantry Division arrived from Fort Stewart, in Georgia, followed on February 6 by the 101st Airborne, with its twenty thousand soldiers coming from Fort Campbell, Kentucky. It was followed by the 82nd Airborne. The 4th Infantry Division, in Germany, was ordered to deploy to Turkey, as a part of McKiernan's plan to strike at Iraq from multiple directions, but its deployment was delayed as Turkey debated whether to join the coalition—a hodgepodge of forces that included units from the United Kingdom, Australia, Spain, Poland, Portugal, and Denmark.

Even at this late stage, Rumsfeld continued to argue about troop numbers. In January, Rumsfeld hesitated in calling up Army Reserve units who'd be responsible for overseeing the striking force's long supply arm. McKiernan worried that after the initial punch into Iraq, his forces would be slowed and unable to mount a final assault on Baghdad. Now, with Rumsfeld's hesitation, a number of reserve units were rushed through their training.[46]

McKiernan's doubts about troop numbers were reflected at the State Department, though Donald Rumsfeld attempted to freeze Colin Powell out of the planning process, scooping up paper copies of Franks's presentations as soon as his briefings were concluded. "This is highly secret and classified," he'd say, grabbing at Franks's presentation. At one meeting, as Powell leafed through the briefing, Rumsfeld held out his hand. "I'll take that," he said. "Highly secret."[47] Rumsfeld knew that Powell was likely to criticize the Franks plan, particularly given the former JCS chairman's oft-stated view that the best way to achieve a quick victory with a minimum of casualties was to use overwhelming force. Franks's plan relied instead on speed and violence, an American blitzkrieg that would puncture the Iraq balloon. For Rumsfeld, "shock and awe" would redeem his vision for military transformation. The invasion would be light, but its violence would make up for what it lacked in numbers. That's not the way Powell saw it. In December, as McKiernan was pressing Franks to give him more soldiers, White House aide Frank Miller asked Marine Corps colonel Thomas Greenwood to surreptitiously obtain copies of the Franks plan from a Pentagon colleague and join him for a drive to an unknown location. Miller, a savvy political insider known for his keen intelligence and complex network of Washington contacts, told Greenwood that he wanted the entire Franks plan, all of the annexes and maps. Bring it all, he said. Every bit of it. The two ended up at the State Department, where Greenwood nervously provided copies of the Franks plan to Colin Powell and his deputy, Richard Armitage.[48]

Greenwood was one of the Marine Corps' most respected rising officers. He'd been to Harvard, served on the National Security Council, and had a fistful of medals. His fellow Marines believed that he was one of their service's best prepared soldiers, no matter what their mission. It seemed that no matter what country they ended up in, Greenwood knew all about it. Greenwood now presented Powell with the Franks plan. After he was finished, Powell turned to Armitage. "Can you believe what you're hearing here?" he asked. Powell knew a little about Iraq, so looked at the maps Greenwood had presented and calculated the distances. The way he saw it, Tommy Franks was going to take an American army three hundred miles up two highways and hope for the best. He was almost openly contemptuous. Miller was overjoyed by the briefing, but Greenwood was shaken.

As Greenwood was briefing Powell, doubts about the Franks plan continued to ripple through CENTCOM. A part of the problem with the planning was the constant interference from the defense secretary. Most disturbing of all was that Rumsfeld's micromanagement affected nearly every aspect of not simply what they were doing, but the system they used to do it. Rumsfeld even wanted to bypass the military's Timed Phased Force and Deployment List, called a "tip-fiddle." The tip-fiddle is a complex menu of which units would go where, and how and with what they're to be supplied. While the tip-fiddle was now computerized, during the 1950s it was among the most voluminous and closely held of the Pentagon's secrets. It not only dictated how America's troops would be transported, it actually listed in detail what was needed first and how it would get there. The tip-fiddle was the military's bible; if you studied it in detail you could figure out how America would wage its wars. The information was crucial in other respects: no one wanted to unload a ship filled with toilet paper when troops needed ammunition, or unload artillery shells from a ship that was listed as carrying tank shells. "The deployment system is large, complex, and sensitive to mistakes and serendipity," the Army's postwar study of the Iraq fight, entitled *On Point*, noted. "A unit showing up at the airfield out of sequence or late causes a ripple effect that can take days to overcome." During one briefing, a logistics officer explained to Rumsfeld the complex sequencing of a unit and its gear, explaining the difficulty of transporting thousands of soldiers tens of thousands of miles and marrying them up with their gear, which would be aboard a ship in a totally different place. Rumsfeld shook his head: "Yeah, but how do you know that?" he asked. The officer wanted to scream, "Because I've been doing this my whole fucking life," but instead patiently explained his reasoning. Rumsfeld was (as he might have said) "not fulfilled," telling one of his civilian aides that he thought the tip-fiddle was a remnant of the Cold War. Planning could be done without it, he said.[49]

For McKiernan, the flow of who and what would go where and how was a constant and consuming worry. Despite the often dismissive talk that "bean counters" weren't "real soldiers," McKiernan knew better. While "real men" might not do "MOOTWA," he knew that history's best commanders worried about logistics and mastered its intricacies. Back in 1980, Marine Corps commandant Robert H. Barrow uttered a phrase now common among senior officers: "Amateurs talk about tactics," he said, "but professionals study logistics." Frederick Franks, who'd raised his eyebrows after McKiernan briefed him on the CENTCOM war plan, said it even better: "Forget logistics, you lose," he said. That's what McKiernan worried about now. By mid-January 2003, his normally taciturn demeanor was turning ugly, as the arguments over force numbers continued. He pleaded with Tommy Franks: he needed additional combat support. Tempo is everything, he said. He didn't want his soldiers slowing down waiting for supplies, he didn't want to have to worry about reinforcements, he didn't want to have to shift gears in the middle of a fight. Franks agreed, but shifted McKiernan's priorities, saying he could call on the 101st Airborne if necessary. "It'll be there," he assured him, confidently. "You won't need it, but it'll be there."[50]

Eric Shinseki was as worried about the flow of troops into Iraq as McKiernan. He'd mentioned his concerns to Bush (twice) and to Rumsfeld, and then in formal sessions of the joint chiefs.

He repeated his warnings to Franks. Shinseki's concern wasn't about whether the United States was capable of toppling Saddam, but whether the forces who'd toppled him could secure and run the country. It was a massive job and, so far as he could tell, people weren't planning for it. Instead a set of best-case assumptions was being put in place: that US troops would be welcomed as liberators, that Iraqis would cooperate with the American occupation forces, that Saddam's Iraq was much like the Soviet Union—a little nudge and all the air would go out of it, "like a balloon that pops when poked."

Shinseki was the highest-ranking military officer to question these assumptions, but his doubts rippled through the Joint Staff and were particularly prominent among those who knew their services would be the ones called on to fight. On February 25, 2003, the JCS testified on the looming war in Iraq before the Senate Armed Services Committee. During the hearings, Michigan senator Carl Levin asked Shinseki how many troops he thought would be needed to stabilize Iraq after the fighting was over. Shinseki's response sparked national headlines, and a slap from civilian Pentagon officials. The Army chief was matter of fact, saying it would take about three hundred thousand troops. "Assistance from friends and allies," he said, "would be helpful."[51] The first salvo fired at the Army chief came from Deputy Defense Secretary Paul Wolfowitz. "Some of the higher end predictions that we have been hearing recently," he said, "such as the notion that it will take several hundred thousand US troops to provide stability in Iraq, are wildly off the mark."[52] To rebut Shinseki, Wolfowitz then played the "Clinton's Generals" card, reminding people the Army chief had served in Bosnia. "There has been none of the record in Iraq of ethnic militias fighting one another that produced so much bloodshed and permanent scars in Bosnia," Wolfowitz said, "along with the continuing requirement for large peacekeeping forces to separate those militias."[53]

Wolfowitz's words seeded a piling-on from Rumsfeld allies, including Douglas Feith and Stephen Cambone, who issued off-the-record comments on Shinseki's testimony to journalists. Shinseki doesn't know what he's talking about, they said. "This is more bullshit from a Clintonite enamored of using the army for peacekeeping and not winning wars," an unnamed Pentagon official was quoted as saying. In the offices of the chief of staff, senior military officials believed the quote had come from Stephen Cambone. Cambone was despised by the military, but his comment sealed their views. "If I had one round left in my revolver, I'd take out Stephen Cambone," a senior officer told one reporter.[54]

IN THE LATE summer of 2002, as Tommy Franks's staff was in the midst of drafting its plan for the invasion of Iraq, Major General Raad al-Hamdani was summoned from his headquarters by Saddam Hussein. Hamdani, an urbane Iraqi Sunni, was the commander of one of Saddam's elite Republican Guard divisions and among the few military officers the dictator believed he could trust. Hamdani had earned that trust, serving for over twenty-five years in the Iraqi military, fighting in six of his country's wars, and becoming acknowledged as one of the regime's most loyal soldiers. He was the Iraqi military's leading strategist and intellectual. Which is why Saddam enjoyed talking to him. Hamdani was a student of military history, and he would often tell the dictator what he was reading and what it meant.[55]

In the summer of 2002, Hamdani was focused on the World War II battle for the Ludendorff Bridge, which spanned the Rhine River at the town of Remagen. In March 1945, the bridge was the last standing structure across the Rhine, and the Allies were intent on capturing it intact. If the Germans blew the bridge, the Allies knew, it might take weeks to breach Germany's borders. The Germans knew this too, and so guarded the approaches to the bridge, fighting tenaciously to deny US units positions on the opposite bank. As the Americans approached the bridge, they got a taste of German artillery, ranged in on their positions that now crowded the Rhine's western bank. At worst, the Germans calculated, they would destroy the bridge at the last minute. The Americans would then be caught on the river's opposite shore, and would get a taste of more German artillery. In early March, German army engineers had planted explosives on the bridge pillars, stringing the wires leading from the charges into the water and along the bridge's structure.

Hamdani told this story now to Saddam. And so, he said, the Americans came and the Germans set off their explosives. But the charges failed to detonate and the Americans stormed the bridge. At that moment, Hamdani concluded, Germany was doomed. Saddam heard all of this, then shrugged. So Hamdani explained what he meant. The Americans are coming up those highways from the Kuwait border to Nasiriyah, he said, and they're going to be aiming for the bridges over the Euphrates River. Or they will come from the southwest. But however they come, he said, they will have to take the bridges over the Euphrates and we will fight for the bridges and push the Americans west, into the desert, where it was harder to maneuver. "When they come," he said, "we've got to blow those bridges." Saddam waved him off. The Americans aren't coming, he said. "They don't like to shed blood, they've had their fill of it," he said. Saddam was confident, certain. Don't worry, he said, there's not going to be a war.

Operation Iraqi Freedom started March 19, 2003, with a bombing campaign that targeted Iraq's political leadership. The bombing was followed at dawn, on March 20, with the ground invasion.

On the right, the I Marine Expeditionary Force aimed for the southern oil fields, with the British 1st Armored Division securing the Faw Peninsula, on the far southeastern part of Iraq, in the IMEF's rear. On the left, the 3rd Infantry Division (a part of General William Wallace's powerful V Corps) swung slightly west, then pivoted north. But its key aim point were the bridges across the Euphrates River, just as Hamdani had predicted.

On April 2, Hamdani received word that Saddam wanted to see him in Baghdad. Hamdani was annoyed; his soldiers were fighting and needed him. But he was a good officer and loyal, and Saddam was his commander in chief. When he saw him, Hamdani noticed that Saddam had changed little from the previous summer. But now he had his son, Qusay, at his side, and next to him the head of the army, who was Hamdani's boss. Saddam asked him to report, so Hamdani summarized the fighting so far. Then he went through his battle plans. The Americans were coming fast from the south, he said, with larger units to the west. Tough fighters. He was going to contest their thrust, then blow the bridges across the river and pummel them with artillery from the other side. The key to his defenses was the al-Qaed Bridge over the Euphrates River, just to the northwest of Nasiriyah. Hamdani was emphatic. We have to blow that bridge, he said.

Saddam heard him out, then shook his head, turning to his son and to the head of the army. The Americans are going to make their major thrust from Jordan and from Turkey in the north, he said, and that's how they plan to capture Baghdad. You need to redeploy your troops, Saddam said. Pull them out of the line and defend Baghdad from the north. Hamdani looked at the head of the army, but he said nothing. The Americans are right next to me, Hamdani protested, we are fighting them now. Saddam shook his head. Don't blow those bridges, he said, we're going to need them. Qusay then spoke. We have plans for the Americans, he said. Three hours later, Hamdani returned to oversee his command, which stretched from Nasiriyah 130 miles to the south.[56]

Later, during his first years in exile in Amman, Jordan, Hamdani would remember this conversation in Baghdad, telling it over and over to the Americans who visited him. He had never liked Qusay, he would contend, because he was bloodthirsty and influenced his father. Not blowing those bridges was his idea, he would say, and it led to the fall of Baghdad. But over the years, and as Hamdani thought about it, he added his own reflections to the story. He thought about the war a lot. There was a reason why Qusay ("God bless his soul," Hamdani would always add) was at that meeting, and there was a reason why, even in the face of defeat, Saddam still appeared confident. "I think now that Saddam certainly understood the Americans would have their victory," he said, speaking in Arabic. "He wasn't a fool. And while he predicted we would win and said this often and convinced many people of it, he knew the truth. The Americans would ride into Baghdad and celebrate their victory. But succeed? They would never succeed. In the end they would do as so many others have done. They would win, and then they would fail. And he was right. You got your victory, and then you failed."[57]

CHAPTER SEVEN

"Mad Dog" Mattis and the Fight for Iraq

*"We're not only losing, we're on
the wrong side."*

RAAD HAMDANI WAS right when he told Saddam that the Americans
would come up the highways from the south and head toward the
bridges over the Euphrates River. That's exactly what they did. But he
was also wrong, for he faced not only the Marines coming up the highway, but also the US Army's 3rd Infantry Division, the 3rd ID. That's the
force that Hamdani wanted to push into the desert, where it was hard
to maneuver. In fact, the desert is precisely where it wanted to be. As
commander of the 3rd ID, Major General Buford "Buff" Blount oversaw
twenty thousand soldiers and eight thousand vehicles, a mobile striking
force that had been training in the desert for months. Blount's goal was
to reach Baghdad as fast he could. From the moment the 3rd ID started
into Iraq, Blount kept it moving, knowing that stopping would allow the
enemy a chance to regroup. The 3rd ID was going to feint north, brush-
ing up against the outskirts of Iraq's southern cities, then swing west, into
the desert, sprinting toward Baghdad.[1]

"I would leapfrog the brigades, so for a couple of days one brigade would be in the lead until they got to their objective, then they would secure that, then I would pass another brigade around until they could secure the next objective, then I'd pass another brigade around so there was constant movement," he remembers. "We wanted to stay out in the desert, to stay west of the Euphrates, to try to keep away from the canals and the urban areas that existed between the Euphrates and the Tigris, and so I figured the fastest route would be through the desert." His plan was to head north, swing west of the Euphrates River, then veer north again and attack the Republican Guard from the rear. In his wake, the cities he punched into, then bypassed, were left in the hands of the 1st Marine Division, the powerful striking arm of the I Marine Expeditionary Force, or IMEF.[2]

On April 2, with the desert just off their left shoulder, units of the 3rd ID pushed into Musayyib, a crossroads town in the Karbala Gap. The gap defined the area between Razazza Lake on the west and Highway 1 on the east. Punching through the gap would give the 3rd ID a clear shot at Baghdad. Just back from meeting Saddam, Hamdani rushed units to counter the Americans, but US tanks arrived first and tore into the Iraqis. Hundreds of Iraqi soldiers were killed. The US V Corps commander, Lieutenant General William Wallace (Blount's superior) then ordered Blount's forces to seize "Objective Peach," the last of southern Iraq's major bridges over the Euphrates.

Objective Peach was Hamdani's Remagen, the al-Qaed Bridge that he was intent on destroying. But as he issued his orders, the forward elements of the 3rd ID launched themselves across the Euphrates in a made-for-Hollywood cross-river assault and seized the span. The next morning, Hamdani organized a desperate counteroffensive aimed at pushing the Americans out of Musayyib. But by the time Hamdani's attack was launched, Blount's 3rd ID was already headed north. Hamdani, his forces destroyed, spent the next two weeks walking home. As the Americans celebrated in Baghdad, he was sheltered by a sympathetic family in a palm grove. He refused to surrender, saying his honor wouldn't permit it. Finally, he made his way to the capital. Baghdad, he remembers, "was in total chaos."[3]

Buff Blount has a different narrative. "Going into Baghdad was very, well . . . it was one of the highlights of my life, of my career," he later recalled. "We crossed the Euphrates, we had about seven different crossings of the Euphrates where we seized bridges, where we did limited crossings, but the crossing at Objective Peach, that's really the last place the Iraqis could have stopped us, the last good defensive area they had . . . so we seized that and that opened the door for us to attack to the city."[4]

This was a tough fight. As the 3rd ID moved north, it left Iraq's urban areas to the IMEF. Its commander was Lieutenant General James Conway, a career Marine and looming hulk of a man admired by his peers, the most important of whom was Major General James Mattis. A legend inside the Marine Corps, Mattis was commander of Conway's 1st Marine Division and Task Force Tarawa—a powerful air-ground component matching speed with power. Called "Mad Dog" by his troopers, the Marine was a fearless fighter and plain talker. His personality was shown during morning combat conferences. He'd stride to the head of the room, pointer in hand, and pivot to face his audience: "The reason we're fighting today," he once said, "is that so those fucking Army colonels down in Kuwait can have cream for their morning coffee." It was just the right touch, easing the tension in the room and bringing laughs from his Marines. Mattis barely cracked a smile, leaving his listeners wondering if he thought it was true. In Iraq, Mattis proved he was arguably the best combat commander in an American uniform since George Patton. "Tempo," he would yell. "This is about tempo." If his Marines weren't moving he wanted to know why. Once, striding through a forward Marine position, he noticed his men were hugging the ground as Iraqi mortars landed nearby. He went to the unit's commander. "What the hell?" he said. "This is indirect fire. They're not actually aiming for you. Don't take it personally." The commander stared at him. "Yeah, right," he said, "but indirect fire can still kill you." Indirect fire? "We took indirect fire all the time and Mattis would just pass it off, talking about 'tempo,' 'tempo,' 'tempo.' And we'd think: 'Yeah, tempo, but if you could just call in the Air Force to bomb those fuckers that would be great.'" One of Mattis's Marines had a different take: "I was always under the impression when I talked with Mattis that he was about to leap on me and beat my brains out."[5]

Years later, Mattis's reputation for bluntness would get him mentioned as a potential presidential candidate. But Mattis also had his detractors, including members of the press who thought he was more pose than substance. Some of his subordinates agreed. Mattis had once come into a bar near Quantico (the Virginia Marine base), one of them remembers, and traded stories with them about women they knew, "laughed heartily, slapped us on the back and then breezed on out." Mattis was just trying to be "one of the boys," this officer says, but it seemed a bit odd that he felt he needed to parade his masculinity. One reporter came across Mattis in Kuwait, on the eve of the war, and told him that he'd just visited Marines sheltered in a nearby warehouse, sleeping on the cold concrete. Perhaps Mattis might arrange to get them some cots. "Good Christ," Mattis grumbled, "they're Marines. They don't need soft beds." The reporter noted that that particular unit later suffered increased incidents of bronchitis, an illness that "didn't seem to know these guys were Marines."[6]

Mattis maneuvered his 1st Marine Division toward Basra, but then shifted his units west, following the major highways north in the shallow valley between the Tigris and Euphrates Rivers. Battle tempo is everything, he told his commanders. "Get going, move," he'd yell over and over. The division worked its way through the swampy ground of southern Iraq, then bumped up against Nasiriyah, where the fighting intensified. Just as the Marines arrived, an Army maintenance unit was ambushed. Eleven soldiers were killed and Army private Jessica Lynch was taken prisoner. Lynch was later rescued, but her capture suggested that what Mattis's troops faced in the city would be different than what they'd come across further south.

The 1st Regiment of the 1st Marines was supposed to take the lead in Nasiriyah, but the fighting was so intense on its southern outskirts that its commander, Colonel Joe Dowdy, ordered a halt. This is not what he'd expected. US commanders had been told by CIA briefers that they'd have little trouble with Iraq's southern cities, which had been the scene of Saddam-ordered reprisals after the end of the first Gulf war, and they could expect that entire Iraqi units might voluntarily surrender. That was clearly not true, and Dowdy now debated whether to skirt the city and continue north. The hesitation irritated Mattis, who sent an aide to check on him. When he arrived, Dowdy was still stuck. Turning to one of Dowdy's subordinates, Mattis's aide told him that if Dowdy "doesn't get this column moving, I'm gonna pull him." Dowdy eventually moved, heading through Nasiriyah, where the bodies of US soldiers from Buff Blount's command were just being collected. Over the next two days, Dowdy and his men faced off against thousands of Iraqi fighters, spurring (as the official Marine account described it) "a running gunfight through the Mesopotamian mud." In the middle of the fight, an exhausted Dowdy nodded off at the wheel of his vehicle. It was an accidental nap, but Mattis's aide reported it to him. During the first week of April, Mattis called Dowdy to his headquarters. "We're going to give you a rest," he said, and then instructed him to remove his sidearm. Dowdy could hardly believe it. "I've been fighting my way up this motherfucking road for the past two weeks," he said. But Mattis didn't change his mind.[7]

Removing an officer from command is not unusual, but doing it in the midst of a combat operation, and demanding an officer's sidearm, was unprecedented. News of Dowdy's firing swept through his unit. The way it was handled suggested that Mattis thought Dowdy was not a real man. Dowdy, they thought, had been sacrificed because the Iraq fight was becoming nasty and embarrassing. This wasn't the way it was supposed to be; no one was being greeted as liberators. The firing of Dowdy took place because, as one Marine later said, "someone has to pay the price for this fuck-up and it isn't going to be Jim Mattis." Mattis's actions were defended by his aides: Dowdy was slow and victory depended on speed. In Washington, Tony Zinni heard of the incident and expressed his doubts. "I trust Jim Mattis," he told a colleague, "but he made a show of this. I don't like shows." The incident, Zinni said, is "not going to add to Jim Mattis's luster."[8]

In time, three unrelated events came to symbolize what the military thought was wrong with Operation Iraqi Freedom. The first was the capture and rescue of Army private Jessica Lynch, the second was the relief of Joe Dowdy, and the third was a seemingly matter-of-fact statement by V Corps commander William Scott Wallace in the middle of a military campaign.

For the first days after her capture, Lynch was described as a hero who'd gamely defended her fellow soldiers in a tough fight. In fact, as she noted, she hadn't been a hero at all; she'd been knocked unconscious before the real fighting started. Her unit, she said, had simply taken a wrong turn. Dowdy, on the other hand, had commanded his unit in a fight he hadn't expected. What he and his men had trained for was a fight with the Republican Guard, a classic face-off of tanks and artillery; instead he'd faced waves of "Saddam Fedayeen"—lightly armed guerrilla fighters.

The fedayeen (in Arabic, those who sacrifice themselves) flitted in and out of American units, rode to battle on Toyota flatbeds, unleashed massed fire from chain guns (a kind of machine gun), and prowled the streets of Iraq's cities forcing young men into battle. The American high command described them as "fanatics." The word was a telltale: what the Marines were facing were tenacious fighters, willing to sacrifice themselves to kill Americans.[9]

Raad Hamdani didn't think the fedayeen were fanatics, he thought they were patriots; in the months prior to the American invasion, he'd had his soldiers bury caches of weapons in southern Iraq that could be dug up during the battle for their use. The fedayeen turned Nasiriyah into a tough fight. Marines of Task Force Tarawa came into the city from the south but were immediately met by sustained fire, forcing them to call in air support. The road into Nasiriyah took on the name Ambush Alley, with the Marines and fedayeen engaged in close combat. This was not the US Marines' proudest moment: units became mixed, intelligence was poor, cooperation with Army units in the western part of the city was nonexistent, there were several friendly fire incidents, unit cohesion was minimal, and the command directives detached from reality. A number of Marines compared the fight to what had happened in Mogadishu in 1993.[10]

On March 26, V Corps commander Wallace told David McKiernan that they should delay the attack on Baghdad. He noted that the 4th Infantry Division, currently aboard ships in the Mediterranean, could be used as reinforcements. McKiernan said no: it would take months for the 4th ID to get to Kuwait, he said. But McKiernan rejiggered his campaign plan, an admission that CENTCOM's original strategic concept had met an unexpected tactical reality. "The plan was shit, and I mean absolute shit," an Army officer said at the time. "It made some assumptions that turned out not to be true. McKiernan threw it in the trash." Over the course of March 26, McKiernan and his chief of staff sketched out an operation that would bring a brigade of the 82nd Airborne into Samawah, replacing one of Blount's units that would rejoin the 3rd ID for the push to Baghdad. This additional unit would take on the fedayeen, while a brigade of the 101st Airborne, under Major General David Petraeus, would take on the Republican Guard's Medina Division. But until those units deployed, there would be a pause.[11]

McKiernan got Tommy Franks's approval for the pause, but not without reassuring him that the fight against the Republican Guard was still his focus. The reassurance was essential, as McKiernan knew he couldn't get Franks's agreement without it. Franks was refighting Desert Storm, and the appearance of the fedayeen wasn't going to change that. McKiernan informed Wallace and Conway of the changes, and the pause. After talking with McKiernan, Wallace spoke with reporters from the *New York Times* and *Washington Post*, telling them that the pause was temporary and would be used to bring forward food, fuel, water, and ammunition. No one had anticipated that "the paramilitary forces would fight with the fanaticism they showed"—and no one had anticipated that, in the midst of combat operations, "the mother of all sandstorms" would blow into Iraq from the western desert, Wallace said.[12]

Wallace was unusually candid about the problems he faced. "The enemy we're fighting," he told reporter Jim Dwyer, "is a bit different than the one we war-gamed against, because of these paramilitary forces. We knew they were here, but we didn't know how they'd fight." The admission shook the Pentagon. Predictably, Rumsfeld was furious and, just as predictably, he landed on Franks, who then landed on McKiernan, who called Wallace. No more talking to the press, McKiernan told him. But that didn't solve the problem. "Shit flows downhill in this man's Army," a Joint Staff officer said, "and it's going to land on Wallace." After receiving another Rumsfeld complaint, Franks told McKiernan he might relieve the V Corps commander. "Who the hell gave him permission to talk to the press?" he asked. McKiernan argued with him. Wallace's only sin was telling the truth, he said.[13]

In Washington, Rumsfeld shoved responsibility elsewhere. "It was not my plan," he told reporters. "It was General Franks' plan, and it was a plan that evolved over a sustained period of time, which I am convinced is an excellent plan." Franks stuck to his guns: the pause was simply a pause, he told reporters, with victory near. But Franks was irate when he met with McKiernan. It's time to get moving, he told him. At one point in their conversation, Franks said he didn't want to hear anything about casualties. McKiernan's staff thought that was a set-up: Franks wanted to tell Rumsfeld the problem was that his commanders were worried about casualties. But no one had mentioned casualties, and the comment was resented.[14]

On April 1, the 3rd ID and the Marines resumed their offensive, while Dave McKiernan sketched out the final assault on Baghdad. His plan reflected battlefield realities: the eastern side of Baghdad would be in the hands of the Marines, with the Army coming in from the west.

By April 4, Jim Mattis's Marines had fought their way into the south-eastern part of the city, where they were met by well-armed and particularly tenacious paramilitary militia. The Saddam fedayeen now took on a new name: they were called "jihadists."

BY APRIL 3, Buff Blount believed that the 3rd ID's appearance in western Baghdad had unhinged the Republican Guard and calculated that the capital would collapse with a little push. In this case, the push would come from the 3rd ID's 2nd Infantry Brigade Combat Team. On April 4, Blount called in the 2nd BCT's commander, Colonel Dave Perkins, and told him to conduct a "thunder run" from his position at the intersections of Highway 1 and Highway 8 (called "Objective Saints") to the airport, where the brigade had taken up position. The idea of a thunder run, a sprint into the enemy's defenses, had worked beautifully further south, in Najaf, and Blount thought he could replicate that now. In fact, the plan for the toppling of Baghdad had come from Brigadier General Lloyd Austin, Blount's expert on maneuver warfare. "Austin was the brains behind the assault on Baghdad," a senior Army officer later explained. "He was always pushing Blount, pushing, pushing, pushing. We could have stopped outside of Baghdad and had a siege for the next twelve months. Lloyd wasn't going to let that happen." Austin was always underestimated. A huge figure with hands the size of boxing gloves, Austin was in his element in combat, as he was now outside of Baghdad. When Blount turned to him for advice on whether to conduct the thunder run, Austin leaned in. "Do it," he said. "Absolutely, do it." The run would test Iraqi defenses, signal to Baghdad residents that the Americans were on their doorstep, and silence Iraqi propaganda that Saddam was winning the war. Perkins and Austin understood what Blount wanted. If the thunder run worked, the next one would take them into the very heart of the city and Iraq's governing center. No one made the comparison at the time, but this was John Warden's concentric circles theory translated into Army-speak. The way to defeat Saddam was to move from the center out.[15]

   Perkins made his run on the morning of April 5, taking his men into a maelstrom. The fighting was more intense than anyone in the brigade had ever experienced, with Iraqi soldiers pummeling Perkins's column with light arms fire and rocket-propelled grenades (RPGs). The Saddam fedayeen were everywhere, running their flatbeds toward the column and then, when it passed, shoving concrete barriers across the highway to block its retreat. In several instances, the column came across civilians caught in the cross fire: a family destroyed in their car, a child blinded, a father whose skin was burning, melting off him, a mother rocking in tears at the side of the road. But the column made it to the airport while suffering one dead and two wounded. Perkins lost a tank, while upward of two thousand Iraqis died in the fight.

Two days later, on the morning of April 7, Perkins made another thunder run, this one into Baghdad. Wallace had told Blount that this time Perkins was to head toward the city center and then turn around. Wallace emphasized this point: Perkins wasn't going to go all the way. It was too dangerous. But Perkins never got the word. In mid-operation and with Saddam's "Crossed Sabers" victory arch just ahead, Perkins contacted Austin: "I'm going in," he announced. At that point Austin calculated it was too late to order him back. The same conclusion was reached by Blount and Wallace. As Perkins's soldiers fanned out, occupying the city center, Perkins told Blount he wanted to stay. Blount relayed the request to Wallace. Wallace agreed, knowing that ordering Perkins out now might actually be more dangerous than keeping him where he was.[16]

Over the next hours, an Iraqi counteroffensive was organized and launched, with fedayeen and Iraqi soldiers of the Special Republican Guard, the elite of the Iraqi army, coming out of the eastern side of the city with mortars, RPGs, and AK-47s. They were no match for Perkins, but the fedayeen were as ferocious as the ones encountered by the Marines in Nasiriyah. Then too, as Perkins's soldiers discovered, many of the paramilitary fighters were not even Iraqis, but Syrians and Jordanians who'd come to Iraq to fight the Americans. The Americans weren't liberators, but "shit magnets," as James Mattis termed it.[17]

On April 9, McKiernan, Wallace, and Conway decided to exploit the opportunity presented by Perkins. The plan was for the Marines, on the eastern edge of the city, to fight their way into Baghdad while Blount's units on the west were doing the same. By now the resistance faced by the Americans was tenacious, even as Iraqi civilians emerged from their homes to begin the systematic looting of the regime's treasures. By dawn on April 10, the Marines were fanning out through the government ministries along the Tigris River. The last major fight took place that morning, as the Marines captured Saddam's palace, then fought a gun battle with Iraqis holed up in the Abu Hanifa Mosque. One Marine was killed and twelve wounded. That night, though resistance continued, it was clear that Saddam's government was finished.

As with so many of America's wars, Operation Iraqi Freedom was defined by its images. World War I is remembered in films showing British Tommies going over the top, World War II by landing boats bobbing in the swells off Omaha Beach, Vietnam by rain-drenched grunts standing in soaking jungles, and Desert Storm by Norman Schwarzkopf, pointer in hand, giving the "mother of all briefings." Iraqi Freedom would be remembered for the toppling of Saddam's statue—and by George W. Bush's "Mission Accomplished" speech aboard the USS *Abraham Lincoln* at the end of the war. But for senior US military officers, the most persistent memory of Operation Iraqi Freedom is not an image, but William Wallace's declaration: "This isn't the enemy we war-gamed against." There are three unforgiveable sins that can be committed by a military commander. The first is refusing to obey a direct order, the second is cowardice in the face of the enemy, and the third is being surprised. "Planning for every contingency" is the military's holy writ. Of course, being surprised in the midst of a battle is one thing, but underestimating your enemy, or not even knowing who he is, is quite another. That kind of surprise can cost the life of the nation.

After the Japanese attack on Pearl Harbor in 1941, the commanders in charge of the American naval base were relieved of duty and demoted. Their punishment remains controversial, but they were in charge and they failed. In 2002, during the Millennium Challenge war game (which prefigured the kind of resistance US troops would meet in southern Iraq), Paul Van Riper's fedayeen had adopted unusual tactics, and won. Van Riper's tactics had been a surprise. It wasn't what the game was supposed to show. So the Millennium Challenge referee stopped the game and changed the rules. But it was too late to do that now in Iraq, where mobs of Iraqis were looting Saddam's palaces while American soldiers stood watching. No one had told them what came next, no one had answered the question then on everyone's mind: and then what?

IN JANUARY, RETIRED lieutenant general Jay Garner had been appointed by George Bush to head the team tasked with the postwar reconstruction of Iraq. His new organization was called the Office of Reconstruction and Humanitarian Affairs, with offices at the Pentagon. Garner was a solid choice: brainy, authoritative, and charismatic, he'd helped the Kurds in northern Iraq after Desert Storm and knew the country well. Garner also had a vast network of experts to draw on in the US government, with a mandate to cherry-pick whoever he wanted. He chose experts in health care, administration, infrastructure, the economy, agriculture, industry, and natural resources. In all, there were nineteen experts heading up different reconstruction areas, while below them were teams of implementers. His was a small group, but they were dedicated. For many of them, Garner seemed almost too modest for the job; rumpled but authoritative, his leadership was intoxicating. More crucially, Garner had the support of the president.[18]

On March 10, nine days before the beginning of the military campaign, Garner briefed his reconstruction plan for postwar Iraq at the White House. It was essential, Garner said, that the United States retain the loyalty of Iraqi civilians. They needed to stay on their jobs. Civil servants and local police would be paid out of American funds to provide political stability. His team would vet Iraqis to ensure that none of Saddam's thugs returned to power. The Iraqi army, he said, would be taken out of uniform, but kept intact and put to work rebuilding Iraq's infrastructure. The plan was to organize Iraqi soldiers into two-hundred-man construction squads, like the young men recruited as a part of America's Civilian Conservation Corps during the Great Depression. They would repair Iraq's pipes, sewers, and electrical grid. They'd be paid. Bush said he thought that was a good idea.

Garner was pleased by Bush's support. But his closest aides were skeptical. Garner's point person at the Pentagon, Rumsfeld policy deputy Douglas Feith, never seemed to produce what he promised. "We'd sit there in a meeting and say 'we need this or that' and Feith would say, 'absolutely, great idea, I'll get right on it,' but nothing would happen," a CIA officer who was a liaison from the agency to Garner's team later said. There were other problems. Rumsfeld disagreed with Garner's staff choices. Two days after briefing Bush, Rumsfeld told Garner he wanted him to remove two members of his team: Thomas Warrick, the head of the Future of Iraq Project at the State Department, and Meghan O'Sullivan, who worked in the State Department's Office of Policy Planning. They were both senior State Department officials answering to Colin Powell. Garner was puzzled: he'd been working with both of them for weeks. Powell talked with Rumsfeld: "Don, we're only trying to help," he said. But Rumsfeld got his way. Then on March 15, the day before Garner was due to leave the United States for Kuwait, Rumsfeld called him into his office. "I'm going to give you a new set of ministry officials," he said. The offices were listed on a memo Rumsfeld held in his hand. "I want to run all these," he said. Garner decided to ignore his demand. The officials he'd worked with would head to Iraq with him. If Rumsfeld's replacements showed up, he'd deal with it then.[19]

The next morning, Garner's team gathered in the Pentagon parking lot, where Rumsfeld saw them off. "Rumsfeld was all smiles," one of Garner's team later noted. The team then took a charter flight from Washington's Andrews Air Force Base to Kuwait, but when Garner arrived he was told that Rumsfeld was reviewing all of his staff appointments. Garner again ignored what Rumsfeld had to say; he was tired of fighting him. A US intelligence officer arrived to brief Garner and was shocked by what he saw. "These people didn't even have radios," he remembers, "and no one had made arrangements for where they would stay." During the next three weeks, as American troops fought their way north, Garner and his team met around the clock. They focused on three issues: to get the Iraq government in place, to provide humanitarian relief to internally displaced refugees, and to provide fresh water, sanitation, and electricity to the population.[20]

During the first week of April, Garner met with Jaber Awad, a key Iraqi American who knew his country's most important Sunni leaders (the dominant branch of Islam throughout the Middle East, but a minority in Iraq, where they were outnumbered by the Shias). Garner persuaded Awad to be a part of his outreach effort to the Sunni tribes and to identify officials who'd served in key ministries but didn't support Saddam. Awad agreed to help, saying he would provide introductions to Sunni leaders in Iraq's far western province of Anbar. For Garner, Awad was a key find. Then, on April 15, Garner traveled to Nasiriyah to meet a group of Iraqi political leaders put together by Zalmay Khalilzad, Bush's special envoy to Afghanistan. Khalilzad was a career diplomat and former scholar whose neoconservative views and outspoken opinions had endeared him to both Rumsfeld and Vice President Dick Cheney. In Afghanistan, he'd worked wonders, putting together groups of political officials to hammer out a postconflict government. Now he was going to do that in Iraq. "This was a kind of an oil spot theory," a US intelligence officer who worked with Khalilzad says. "Zalmay was going to go from city to city talking to leaders, bringing them together, and putting local governments in place. Eventually, he'd create a network of Iraqis who'd have political legitimacy." Khalilzad said the local leaders would form an Iraqi Interim Authority, slowly taking control of the country from the Americans.[21]

While Khalilzad had organized the Nasiriyah meeting, held in a large tent, Deputy Assistant Secretary of State Ryan Crocker chaired it, calling on Garner to open the conference with some remarks. "A free and democratic Iraq will begin today," Garner said. Khalilzad followed, telling the attendees that the United States had "no interest, absolutely no interest, in ruling Iraq." At the end of the meeting, he announced there would be another gathering in ten days in Baghdad.[22]

But in Washington, unbeknownst to either Garner or Khalilzad, Dick Cheney had already shifted America's postwar Iraq strategy. During the first week of April, Bush had convened the members of his national security team, including the JCS chairman, in the White House Situation Room. Bush said he wanted to discuss the plans for postwar Iraq. At this point, Cheney took over the meeting, issuing a terse opening. It was the first time anyone could remember him being so blunt. He was no longer talking in code. "It seems to me that we have two choices in Iraq," he said. "Legitimacy or control. I'm for control. Anyone disagree?" No one said a word. Later, one of the participants said this was the first time he realized that Garner and Khalilzad were going to be replaced.[23]

Garner and his team arrived in Baghdad on April 20, with the city in chaos, but the next day he traveled north to meet separately with rival Kurdish leaders Massoud Barzani and Jalal Talabani, whom he knew from his 1991 humanitarian mission. Garner wanted to convince them to help in his mission, and to cooperate with each other. It was a tall order, but both leaders were used to being strong-armed by the Americans. Before the war they'd been cajoled by Paul Wolfowitz, who'd assured Rumsfeld that he could persuade Turkey to join the fight in Iraq, which meant he had to convince the Kurds to allow the Turkish military to pass through their territory. It didn't work: no matter how much Wolfowitz insisted, the Kurds remained adamant. "We won't do that," Barzani told him. As it turned out, the Kurds had little to fear. Wolfowitz's talks with the Turks did not go well: they refused to join the US-led coalition and said they wouldn't allow the American military to enter northern Iraq from their country. Now here was Garner, strong-arming them again. He told them about his plans: he was going to keep Saddam's ministries in place and he wanted their cooperation. They hesitated, but agreed. They trusted Garner. Then too, it was too late to object, as the Americans were already in Baghdad.

Garner returned to the capital on April 22, where members of his reconstruction team were waiting. He gave them their assignments. "We have to do this fast and do this well," he said. "The Iraqi people are watching us." But two days later, Garner received a telephone call from Donald Rumsfeld. "Hey, I'm calling just to tell you what a great job you're doing," he said. "It looks like things are really moving. Watched everything going on, and just keep up the good work and all that. And by the way, I wanted to let you know that today the president chose Jerry Bremer to be his presidential envoy, and he'll be coming over there." It was all very matter-of-fact. Rumsfeld said this was the president's decision; in fact, it wasn't—he and Colin Powell had argued about the change for three days. Rumsfeld had not picked Garner, so now he insisted he be allowed to choose his own man in Baghdad. He won the argument, with Cheney backing Bremer. Jerry Bremer was L. Paul Bremer III, a career foreign service officer, diplomat, and outspoken terrorism expert. In fact, his appointment was the result of a classic turf battle—a part of the battle being waged by Rumsfeld against the State Department for control of Iraq.

But for Donald Rumsfeld, it wasn't Iraq that was at stake, it was his standing in the administration. He wanted to make sure he was in charge. Others in the administration came to a similar conclusion. When CIA director George Tenet heard about Bremer's appointment he turned to an assistant: "Who the fuck is Jerry Bremer?" he asked. Tenet was in his armored SUV, surrounded by his aides and security team, headed to the CIA's Virginia headquarters. Tenet called the president. It was a short conversation: Bush said that Bremer would answer to Rumsfeld. Tenet hung up the phone. "Well, that explains that," he said.[24]

Garner was stunned by Rumsfeld's call, but shouldn't have been. "Rumsfeld never liked Jay," a senior Pentagon official later said. "You know, Garner had agreed with Shinseki about troop numbers, and had told that to Rumsfeld. He was pretty blunt about it. Right there in his office. He told him he needed twenty-two thousand soldiers just to deal with Kurdistan back in 1991 and that was a small part of Iraq. The US would need twenty times that number for the entire country. Well, it really nagged at Rumsfeld. It showed that Garner wasn't one of his guys, he was one of 'them.' From that moment, Garner was doomed."[25]

Garner stayed on in Iraq because he'd promised he would cooperate with Bremer during a transition, but his hands were tied. As soon as the Iraqis learned about Bremer, they ignored what Garner said. The one thing that bothered Garner was that some members of his team "were trying to locate the [Iraqi] army and bring it back"—that is, arrange for their formal surrender, their pledge not to fight the Americans and ensure that they remained on the Iraqi government payroll.

A key team member was Army colonel Paul Hughes, a dedicated officer with a strange specialization: he focused on humanitarian issues. Tall and politically savvy, Hughes had met with Iraqi commanders to talk about the Iraqi army's demobilization. "The idea was to keep them on our side," Hughes says. "So we would meet with the commanders and talk about what they needed." By the end of April, Hughes and senior Iraqi military officers were close to an agreement. "We had decided on most of the details," Hughes says. "We thought the soldiers would come in, we could organize them, put them to work, that kind of thing. They would continue to get paid. Well, that was the plan."[26]

As Hughes was conducting his negotiations, Bremer met with Bush in the Oval Office. What he needed, Bremer told Bush, was full control. Keeping Garner and Khalilzad in Baghdad to oversee an Iraqi interim administration violated the cardinal principle of unity of command. One guy needs to be in charge, he said. Bush agreed. "You've got it," he said. And with that, Bremer became America's proconsul in Baghdad, with virtual dictatorial power. Colin Powell was not consulted on the decision, nor was Condoleezza Rice, nor even Donald Rumsfeld—who'd pushed Bremer, but never intended that he be given the power to rule Iraq by decree. Four days later, on the afternoon of May 10, Doug Feith, Paul Wolfowitz, and Walter Slocombe met in Feith's office where Slocombe, Feith's predecessor, well-known Washington insider, and a defense department consultant, presented a paper outlining the disbanding of the Iraqi army. All three agreed that Iraq must be "cleansed of Baathist influence," as Slocombe said. Two days later, Feith gave the paper to Bremer, who took it with him to Baghdad, arriving there on May 13. As the head of the new Coalition Provisional Authority (CPA), he issued CPA Order No. 1, which barred officials from Saddam Hussein's Baath Party, which many Washington policymakers compared to the Nazis; they were arch-criminals that needed to be cleaned out of Iraqi society. With Slo-combe's paper as his guide, Bremer then issued CPA Order No. 2, dis-banding the Iraqi military.[27]

"Bremer changed everything," Jaber Awad, picked by Garner as an emissary to Iraq's Sunni leaders, remembers. "One day Garner was there and the next day he was gone. I had my first meeting with Bremer and he made it clear to me that the Sunnis were not going to be listened to. There would be no pay to civil servants, no pay to the Army, no pay to the police and all the government departments would be cleaned out. He reversed all of Garner's plans." Awad told Bremer that "his plan for the Sunnis was a mistake. 'This won't work. It's going to be a disaster.'" Standing behind his desk, his window looking out on what would soon be called the "Green Zone," Bremer dismissed Awad's worries. "Every Sunni is a Baathist, every Baathist is a Saddamist, and every Saddamist is a Nazi," Bremer told him.[28]

By then, Garner's team had begun to break up; most members sim-ply went home. They had a new name for what Bremer had done: de-Garnerfication. Zalmay Khalilzad had his meeting with Iraqi leaders in Baghdad, but then Bremer arrived and he was told there would be no more meetings, so he returned to Washington. Paul Hughes was already in Germany. "I heard about the [Bremer] decision [on the Iraqi army] on television," he remembers, "and I was just enraged. I couldn't believe it." He knew that things would now change in Iraq, and that it was likely the Iraqi officers he'd negotiated with would take up arms. He'd heard reports that an emerging insurgency had promised to pay former Iraqi army offi-cers $100 a day. The United States would pay them nothing. For Hughes, the Bremer decision was a signal that what the US had done in Iraq was more than a simple mistake. He'd been skeptical that Saddam had had weapons of mass destruction, or that the White House was interested in bringing democracy to the Middle East. It was all a lie. "Iraq was a war of imperial aggression," Hughes told a reporter. "It was a criminal act."[29]

In Baghdad, a senior defense official who'd been helping Hughes had to explain to Iraqi officers that Garner's work was finished. "What else could I do?" he asks. "I didn't really have a choice. So I told the Iraqi officers I knew that they should go home." This official then goes on to recount: "I can remember one of the senior officers just looked at me for a few seconds and then he said, 'Do you know what this means? Do you know what you've just done? There are 340,000 soldiers out there who need to feed their families. What do you think they're going to do?"[30]

What they were going to do was already obvious to Lieutenant General John Abizaid, Tommy Franks's deputy commander. Those Iraqis who hadn't been killed, surrendered, or walked home had fought the Americans through southern Iraq, and there was no sign they were going to stop. Bremer's order made that worse. Abizaid had arrived at CENTCOM's forward headquarters in Doha, Qatar, in January from his position as director of the Joint Staff. The CENTCOM assignment was a relief: the Middle East was where he wanted to be. The descendant of a Lebanese American family, Abizaid had grown up in California and earned money by tending sheep and roping cattle. His flight to West Point was the first time he'd been on a commercial airliner. Abizaid's life took off at the academy. One of those he'd gotten to know as a cadet was George Joulwan, and Abizaid admired him, citing his example regularly in the years after his 1973 graduation.

Rumsfeld was a fan of Abizaid, finding him easier to work with than the blunt-speaking Shinseki. Abizaid never courted controversy, and no one knew the Arab world better than he did. He'd traveled in the region as a young officer, mastered Arabic, and stuck his nose in everywhere, including western Iraq. Abizaid understood and respected Arab culture. When more conservative officers made outlandish claims about Islam, he corrected them, asking them how many years they'd served in the region. At one point as a young officer he'd jogged across Jordan, just to get a feel for the country. The Bedouins he met and shared meals with were astonished that an American knew them so well. They called him "Abu Zaid." If Abizaid hadn't chosen the Army, he could have easily been a scholar of Arab studies at a leading university.[31]

Abizaid knew the answer to the "and then what" question, and he'd tried to give it during a White House video briefing in late March, in the midst of Operation Iraqi Freedom. During the conference, Abizaid mentioned that he was concerned about what would happen when the war ended. The United States needed to focus on what to do with all those Baath Party members. They needed to be put to work, he said. That didn't sit well with Doug Feith, who lectured him. "The policy of the

United States government is de-Baathification," he announced. Abizaid struck back. "This is not Nazi Germany," he said, "and what's needed is not de-Nazification. You have to hold this place together and if you don't keep the government together in some form, it won't hold." Feith dug in: "Let me repeat to you what the policy of the US government is: de-Baathification." Abizaid let it go. This was not the first time the two had clashed. On the day after 9/11, Abizaid was flying back from Europe with Feith, who'd been in Russia. The two were talking about the response to 9/11 when Feith mentioned that going after Saddam was an option. Abizaid turned on him: "Not Iraq," he said. "There is not a connection to al-Qaeda." Feith hadn't changed his mind, but neither had Abizaid. Abizaid never made his doubts about the later Iraq invasion public, but his closest friends, including classmates from West Point, never doubted his views. "He was a good soldier," one of them says, "but he just thought the whole thing was nuts."[32]

In May, when Tommy Franks announced he was going to retire, Abizaid told Rumsfeld he wanted to be his successor. Abizaid said that if he didn't get the job he would quit. Rumsfeld agreed, but he tried to get Franks to change his mind about retiring, saying he wanted him to take over as Army chief of staff. In fact, Franks was actually Rumsfeld's second choice for the slot after General Jack Keane, the Army vice chief (whom Rumsfeld had once hoped would take over for Eric Shinseki as head of the Army), who turned the job down for personal reasons. But Franks could not be persuaded. He was headed home to Oklahoma, where he was being mentioned as a possible candidate for the Senate. Spurned by Keane and then by Franks, Rumsfeld searched for an officer who supported his transformation agenda and came up with Peter Schoomaker, a retired general and former head of the Special Operations Command. Such a move, while not unprecedented (Maxwell Taylor had come out of retirement in the early 1960s to become JCS chairman), was rare. Schoomaker symbolized what Rumsfeld wanted the Army to become—a light and lethal force, like the ones that Schoomaker once commanded. During a talk with Rumsfeld, Schoomaker reminded him of how well special operations units had done in Afghanistan. We need more of that, he said. Rumsfeld was convinced and announced Schoomaker's appointment in June, passing over the entire senior Army leadership. Schoomaker, many officers thought, was Rumsfeld's way of giving them a vote of no confidence.[33]

Abizaid became CENTCOM commander during a ceremony in Tampa on July 7, where Franks's valedictory was laced with his patented tough talk. "Twenty-two months ago the United States of America, in fact the free world, looked into the face of evil," he said. "We came on that day to recognize our vulnerability. And the world came to recognize an America with attitude. As President Bush said recently, 'Bring it on.'" Seated behind Franks, Abizaid remained impassive, but he knew that what the United States now faced was a second war for Iraq, with former Baath Party members taking up arms against the Americans. This second war would be as important as Operation Iraqi Freedom itself. In Washington, senior military officers, including Jack Keane, had come to the same conclusion. Keane had visited Baghdad a little over one week after the war's end and was shocked by what he saw. The looting was out of control, a nascent resistance was starting to form outside of the capital city, and no one was doing anything about it. Buff Blount, whose troops had toppled the Baghdad government, was frustrated by the lawlessness, but he told Keane he didn't think that shooting the people they'd come to liberate was a good idea. Keane reluctantly agreed.[34]

So too did Rumsfeld, who said that the spreading chaos was the natural result of Saddam's removal. The people of Iraq were now free, he said, and "free people are free to make mistakes and commit crimes and do bad things." That was too much, even for the conservative Keane. After the attacks on the US military began, and then persisted, Keane was the first to describe them as an "insurgency." His claim came during a meeting in the tank, with his fellow chiefs. "I said, 'This is a low-level insurgency,' and I told them what the definition of that was, and what it looked like," reporter Peter Boyer quotes Keane as saying. "They were targeting Americans, and it was organized. It was being done at multiple locations, which meant that there had to be some general guidance. . . . They were killing us."[35] A participant in the meeting later said that JCS chairman Myers "got really, visibly angry. I mean, really angry. He told Keane 'don't say that, we don't know that.'" Keane told Myers that he knew an insurgency when he saw one. Keane and Myers stared each other down, but Myers finally dropped the topic. "It was an uncomfortable moment," this participant remembered, "because it showed just how in-the-bag for Rumsfeld Myers had become. He thought there would be hell to pay if anyone said this out loud."

Abizaid came to the same conclusion as Keane, telling reporters in his first days after taking command that the Iraqis were conducting "a classical guerrilla-type campaign." He called it "a low-intensity conflict, in our doctrinal terms, but it's war, however you describe it. But it is getting more organized, and it is learning." The reporters found Abizaid a refreshing change from Franks, who'd never wanted to contradict the defense secretary. Abizaid said he would be different. He was now the CENTCOM commander, he told one of his aides, and if Rumsfeld didn't like what he said he could fire him. In fact, Abizaid knew that was unlikely, but he faced Rumsfeld's ire, which included a blizzard of memos lecturing him about his claim that stretched on for weeks. Some of the memos were downright weird, going on and on about the definition of an insurgency, and how what was happening in Iraq didn't fit the definition.[36]

After becoming the head of CENTCOM, Abizaid regularly visited Baghdad to check on Lieutenant General Ricardo Sanchez, who'd taken over as coalition ground commander (the CFLCC or "C-flic" was now called MNF-I: Multinational Forces, Iraq) soon after the end of the war. A Texan with deep religious convictions, Sanchez's whole life was the Army. Now, just a few months after taking over in Baghdad, his command was embroiled in a series of escalating and bloody battles against an increasingly well-armed enemy—and he found himself wondering why Washington seemed so unconcerned. But his worst problem wasn't in Washington, it was in Baghdad, where Bremer treated him with disdain. "Don't I outrank this guy?" Sanchez asked one of his aides. "I'm the guy who's in charge here, not him." The aide nodded: absolutely, he said, you're in charge. But in fact, Sanchez wasn't, and eventually the aide decided to tell him the truth. If you want to talk with the president, he told Sanchez several weeks later, "you have to make the request to the commander at CENTCOM, who will pass on the request to the Joint Staff, who will ask the Army chief of staff, who will ask the JCS chairman, who will then tell the president you want to talk to him. But if Bremer wants to talk to Bush, he just picks up the phone." Sanchez glowered, but his aide continued. "So no, sir," he said, "you're not in charge here."[37]

Sanchez argued for an increase in the new Iraqi army (which the United States had begun organizing), which was pegged at forty thousand soldiers, lobbied for more money for his troops to use on reconstruction, and told Bremer that the government-owned factories should be reopened. Bremer dismissed every appeal. If the military would just do its job, Bremer said, the fighting would end. After a time, Sanchez simply refused to talk to Bremer, and they would pass in the hall of the CPA headquarters without saying a word. Eventually, Sanchez's discomfort turned into disbelief, then bitterness. He blamed Bush for the war, Rumsfeld for his ill-prepared troops, and Bremer for the insurgency.

Abizaid might have agreed, but he also had his doubts about Sanchez, which were reinforced by Jack Keane. On one of his visits to the region, Keane (who was in his final months in the Army) told Abizaid that Sanchez was in over his head. "He's flailing. We need someone else," Keane said. He reminded Abizaid that he could bring in his own man. "You're the CINC, you don't need my permission." Abizaid considered this, but instead of relieving Sanchez he tried to help him, defending Sanchez in videoconferences with the president. Abizaid was not above sugarcoating the news. "We'll get there," his staff remembers him saying to Bush during one call. Bush was skeptical. "Do these people even want us here?" Bush asked. "Can you find anybody to thank us for giving them democracy and freedom?" Abizaid didn't respond and tried to hide his surprise. Giving them freedom and democracy? At the end of one conference, Abizaid turned to his aide, his usual coolness gone. "There are corpses in the streets," he said, "doesn't this guy know that?"[38]

While historians and reporters put specific dates on the beginning of the Iraqi insurgency, there was actually little pause between the official end of the war and the fighting that followed. At first, Sanchez and his soldiers faced a niggling opposition centered on Saddam's home city of Tikrit, where regime supporters chipped away at the American presence. In June, US forces responded with a sweep of the area. In October, the violence spread, with the suicide bombings of the International Red Cross headquarters and four police stations in Baghdad. The troubles now moved into Baghdad's overcrowded Shia neighborhoods, where young Iraqis were arming against what they described as an American occupation. Eighty-two Americans died in November, with 337 wounded. Saddam Hussein was found hiding in a so-called spider hole in December, but he seemed an afterthought now, as attacks on the US military increased. The fighting escalated into the next year. At the end of March 2004, four American contractors were killed in Fallujah, their bodies strung up by their killers. On March 28, in apparent retaliation, Bremer announced he was closing *al-Hawza* newspaper, the voice of cleric Muqtada al-Sadr's Shia movement. Bremer said that *al-Hawza* was inciting violence against the coalition.[39]

One week later, on April 4, fighting broke out in Najaf, Kufa, Kut, and Sadr City (in Baghdad), when al-Sadr's Mahdi Army stormed public buildings and police stations. By April 5, the United States was fighting to control the country it had overrun in 2003. The coalition struck back, but the bloodletting went on. Worse yet, in late April, CBS News published photographs of American soldiers abusing Iraqi prisoners at the Abu Ghraib prison outside of Baghdad. One of the photographs showed a collar around a prisoner's neck, with a female soldier posing nearby holding a dog chain. The photograph was published and republished worldwide. The public response was overwhelming, with the Bush administration unable to explain away the incident. The president and secretary of defense apologized for the incident and the Army conducted a thorough internal investigation. In fact, the abuses at Abu Ghraib, which included torture, rape, sodomy, and even murder, were not only systemic, they were known at the highest levels of the US government, and almost certainly by Donald Rumsfeld, prior to their being made public. Yet even with this, senior military officers seemed in denial, shunning Major General Antonio Taguba, who was in charge of the investigation—a classic case of killing the messenger. Taguba stood his ground, telling reporter Seymour Hersh that the defense secretary and his aides had abused their office and had "no idea of the values and high standards expected of them." In this case, gravity was reversed, with "the shit" rolling uphill to Sanchez—but no further. After Abu Ghraib, the White House decided the US needed a new commander in Iraq and began to search for a replacement. Bush broke the news to Sanchez on May 20 in the White House Situation Room, after meeting with him, Abizaid, and Rumsfeld in the Oval Office.[40]

The meeting with Bush had gone well, with Sanchez and Abizaid telling the president that the situation in Iraq, while difficult, was well in hand. The only negative was a report from Rumsfeld that he'd received a memo from Bremer requesting that an additional two divisions of troops be sent to Iraq—some thirty thousand to forty thousand soldiers in all—a revelation made public years later by reporter Peter Baker. The Bremer memo was unexpected. Abizaid and Sanchez knew nothing about it. Bush was surprised and irritated: Bremer had not followed the chain of command, he said—conveniently forgetting that he'd promised

Bremer that he could report outside of it. "What are you going to do about it?" Bush asked Rumsfeld. The defense secretary shook his head in disgust. "Well, this is amazing," he said. "Mr. President, you don't have to do anything. He addressed [the request] to me. I'll take care of responding to him." Bush nodded his approval, dropped the subject, then talked to Sanchez privately in the White House Situation Room. Sanchez wasn't going to get his fourth star, Bush said, and would instead be leaving Baghdad. Bush softened the news, saying that the new command arrangement had been planned for some time. Bremer would also be leaving, he said. Sanchez got the message: he was being held responsible for Abu Ghraib. Rumsfeld, meanwhile, passed on the Bremer memo asking for more troops to Richard Myers. Myers said he would take care of it. When Rumsfeld brought it up, two months later, Myers said that he'd asked Abizaid if he needed another two divisions. Abizaid had said no, informing Bremer his request was denied.[41]

As the situation on the ground in Iraq worsened, members of the Joint Staff scrambled to find a solution. The Joint Staff's head of intelligence, its J-2, was Major General Ronald L. Burgess. A career intelligence officer, Burgess concluded that the postwar strategy adopted by the United States in Iraq wasn't going to work. After weeks spent reading battle reports, Burgess wrote a memo on the insurgency and sent it up the chain of command and into Rumsfeld's office. Entitled "Sunni Outreach to the Governing Council, and Coalition Provisional Authority," Burgess catalogued the contacts the US had been receiving from Sunni leaders in Anbar Province, suggesting that reaching out to them might dampen the violence faced by US troops. Rumsfeld flipped through the report, passed it on to a special intelligence cell reporting to Sanchez in Baghdad, then forwarded it to Paul Wolfowitz. A few days later, Wolfowitz returned the memo to Rumsfeld. In the margins he'd scribbled three words: "They are Nazis!"[42]

PAUL WOLFOWITZ MIGHT have thought the leaders of Anbar's Sunni tribes were Nazis, but a handful of senior officials close to Rumsfeld didn't. One of these was Jerry Jones, a gangly and urbane Texan, lifelong Republican, and Rumsfeld's friend.

Jones had known Donald Rumsfeld for more than thirty years, meeting him back during the Nixon presidency when Rumsfeld was head of the Office of Economic Opportunity. A die-hard Republican, Jones had "always been a friend of Don." When Rumsfeld became defense secretary, he asked Jones to serve as his special assistant, which included being his liaison with Vice President Dick Cheney. In fact, Jones had the run of the Pentagon, taking on special tasks for Rumsfeld and serving as his eyes and ears in the building. Jones served Rumsfeld loyally, but by early 2004 he'd begun to take on projects without Rumsfeld's knowledge. He worried about the mounting death toll among American troops in Iraq.[43]

One day in April 2004, Jones received a call from Marty Hoffman, Rumsfeld's former Princeton roommate and best buddy, who told him he wanted him to come down to his office to meet a Texas businessman. When Jones arrived, Hoffman introduced him to Kenneth Wischkaemper, who owned an international agricultural seed company. Wischkaemper told Jones that he'd recently met an Iraqi by the name of Talal al-Gaood in Amman, Jordan. Al-Gaood told him that Anbar's tribes were interested in economic cooperation with the Americans. We should do something, Wischkaemper said. Jones was intrigued, contacted al-Gaood by e-mail, accepted his invitation to attend a business conference he was holding in Amman in July, and put together a small group of officials to accompany him, which included several Marine officers serving in the region.

Coincidentally, IMEF commander James Conway directed Colonel Mike Walker, the commander of the Marines 3rd Civil Affairs Group, to attend a conference of Iraqi businessmen in Bahrain. There Walker made contact with al-Gaood's Amman group, met with al-Gaood in May, and was invited to attend the same business conference as Jones. So it was that, in what would turn into a strange confluence of events, Jones, Wischkaemper, Washington lawyer Larry Meyers, Evan Galbraith (Rumsfeld's defense adviser in Europe), and James Clad (an official of the Overseas Private Investment Corporation), ended up in the lobby of Amman's Sheraton Hotel on the morning of July 19, 2004, along with a handful of Japanese development officials—and the team of Marines put together by Walker.

Jones had cleared his team's meeting with the State Department as well as the deputy chief of the US mission in Baghdad. This was going to be a conversation about business, Jones told them, that would focus on business opportunities for US companies. That's what he told Rumsfeld, who eyed him suspiciously. "Okay Jerry," he said. "But don't embarrass me. You're not going to embarrass me are you, Jerry?" Jones shook his head. "Of course not, Mr. Secretary," he said. In fact, the July meeting with al-Gaood was far from innocent. For when the meet-and-greet coffee in the lobby concluded, Jones and the Marines entered a large conference room with a table, behind which sat a group of Anbar tribal leaders. Al-Gaood, Jaber Awad, and Raad Hamdani stood in the crowd nearby. This, clearly, was not a business conference. "I was really shocked," Marine colonel Mike Walker later reflected. "I remember thinking, 'Well, this is not exactly what I had in mind.'" Walker looked around and knew that he was in a meeting with the leaders of the Anbar insurgency. These people were killing Americans. Later, in a memo to General Conway, Walker put the number of Iraqis in the room at seventy-eight, twenty-three of whom were a "core opposition group." They were "very well organized and prepared," he wrote. Walker eyed the room, looked at those behind the front table, and had to make a decision. If he walked out the door, no one would be the wiser. He decided to stay.[44]

Al-Gaood began the meeting with a short speech, then turned it over to his colleagues who, one by one, trooped to the front of the room to speak. "I have never heard such denunciations," attendee James Clad said. "We sat there and took it, allowing them to have their say. We were like department store mannequins. We just kind of looked at our shoes." Later in the meeting the Americans responded, sometimes harshly. "You can't say that Saddam was good for Iraq," Mike Walker said. "For all the things that we got wrong, the one thing we didn't get wrong was getting rid of him." At the end of the morning, Tadashi Maeda, a senior Japanese banking official, turned to the Iraqis. "I have heard and we have all heard what you have said, and so now I think that I should like to say something," he said. "My mother was in Hiroshima. And I can remember when it happened and I lost her. And I thought that when the bomb was dropped that Japan was absolutely finished. . . . The Americans are not perfect people. But they wanted to help us. So now your country is also in ruins. But you must put the past behind you. You must rise from the ashes. You have to build your new country, as my people built mine." He then sat down. "You could have heard a pin drop," Clad recalled.[45]

Later that afternoon, a small group of Americans gathered in Jones's room to meet with a man described as "a messenger from the insurgents." The meeting started poorly, with the Iraqi eyeing the Americans warily. Walker later learned that the man, "Dr. Ismail," thought he would be

killed. Finally, Dr. Ismail opened up, starting with the standard denunciations of the United States. But then his tone softened. After a two-hour
dialogue, he made an offer: "We are not your enemy," he said. "Al-Qaeda
is your enemy. If you let us, we will get rid of them. But you can't fight
us at the same time. We're different. We will stop shooting and take care
of the real terrorists. We're not terrorists, we're the insurgents. There's a
difference."[46]

The cease-fires that Ismail promised seemed like a good idea, but
they were poorly coordinated. Some of them worked, some didn't, and
convincing the leaders of Anbar's tribes to turn their guns on al-Qaeda
turned out to be a much longer, slower, and more painful process than
Jones or Walker or anyone anticipated. But after the Amman meeting,
Walker got a buy-in from Conway's chief of staff, Colonel John Coleman, and from Conway himself. Conway's fighter, James Mattis (whose
Marines were under fire every day), agreed. One month after the Amman meeting, Mattis had a meeting with Anbar's religious leaders. "How
could you send your worshipers, some of them young boys, against us
when their real enemy is al-Qaeda?" he asked. The religious leaders said
nothing and continued sipping their tea. Mattis shook his head in disgust. "They're kids," he shouted. "Untrained, undisciplined teenagers.
They don't stand a chance." When Jerry Jones heard of the meeting,
he emitted an off-handed chuckle. Mattis was right, he concluded, but
he was also wrong. "I suppose you might ask the same question of us," he
said. "How could we have sent our young men and women into battle in
Iraq when our real enemy was in Afghanistan?" Later, reflecting on his
conversation with Anbar's religious leaders, Mattis told former Marine
Bing West that the tribes "only saw us as the enemy." What the Marines
needed, Mattis said, was for "the real enemy to make a mistake and ex-
pose themselves for what they were."

The mistake came in July 2005, when a group of tribal fighters were
pushed out of al-Qaim, near the Syrian border, by an al-Qaeda militia.
The tribal fighters pleaded for help from Talal al-Gaood, whom they
reached in Amman, who then called Wischkaemper in Texas. The tribes
needed help, he said. The tribal militia was in danger of being slaughtered. Wischkaemper called Jones, who was in his car with his son,
driving to the airport. His son, a Marine, was on his way to Iraq. Jones
listened to Wischkaemper's news, then called Camp Pendleton, where a
senior officer notified the Marine senior command in Iraq. Within an

hour of al-Gaood's telephone plea, Marine Cobra helicopters from Camp Fallujah were in the air, headed toward al-Qaim. One hour later, they were strafing the al-Qaeda position. Coleman called al-Qaim "a turning point." After al-Qaim the tribes in Anbar started to turn against al-Qaeda. This was the beginning of what would come to be called the Anbar Awakening.[47]

The Anbar Awakening will be remembered in American military history as a creative shift in strategy that quieted the Anbar insurgency, with Jerry Jones and John Walker among its many heroes. In fact, however, credit for the awakening is shared by a large group of military officers. In Tal Afar, in far northwestern Iraq, Colonel H. R. McMaster (the hero of the Battle of 73 Easting and the author of the celebrated *Dereliction of Duty*) applied a new strategy for dealing with the insurgents. The way to defeat them, he believed, was to coopt them. He insisted his soldiers work among the people, instead of remaining in well-protected bases. The Americans needed to be seen as peacekeepers, not just trigger-pullers. He schooled his officers in Iraqi history and insisted they treat Iraqi leaders with respect, then assigned one of his squadron commanders, Lieutenant Colonel Chris Hickey, to open talks with the city's Sunni leaders. Hickey's job was to convince them to provide recruits for a new Tal Afar police force that would fight the jihadis. After hours spent with them over Arabic coffee, they agreed.[48]

Further south, in the Anbar city of Ramadi, Army colonel Sean Mac-Farland, who commanded the 1st Brigade of the 1st Armored Division, began to recruit Ramadi's Sunni leaders to cooperate with the Americans. A 1981 West Point graduate and one of the School of Advanced Military Studies' "Jedi Knights," MacFarland's instructions from Casey were straightforward: fix Ramadi, he was told, don't destroy it. MacFarland sealed off the city, built a complex social and political network of tribal leaders to cooperate with the Americans, established Iraqi-led neighborhood watch groups, and recruited young Iraqis into a police force. "You name it, I tried it," he later said. By July, his police force was beginning to fight back against al-Qaeda. Then, in August, one of his senior commanders visited Sheik Abdul Sattar al-Rishawi, a key Anbari tribal leader. The senior commander arrived just as a meeting of about thirty tribesman was under way, and asked what was going on. "We are forming an alliance against al-Qaeda," Sheik Sattar said. "Are you with us?" In September, Sheik Sattar announced the formation of the Anbar Salvation Council, a Sunni-led anti-al-Qaeda coalition.[49]

The impact of the awakening was profound, but not simply in Anbar. In the midst of a war, senior US military officers in Iraq—Walker, Conway, Mattis, McMaster, MacFarland, and others—had quietly adopted a strategy that purposefully reversed Dick Cheney's call for "control" over "legitimacy." Bremer's decision to disband the Iraqi army, purge Baathists from Iraqi government positions, and suspend Zalmay Khalilzad's political program—opting for "control" over "legitimacy"—not only hadn't worked, it had fueled the insurgency against the Americans.

The Anbar Awakening took root and got stronger, but it didn't bring peace, or victory. For as Anbar quieted, the rest of Iraq exploded. In November 2004, the same month that George Bush was elected for a second term, 137 American soldiers died in Iraq, the highest number of combat casualties since the beginning of Operation Iraqi Freedom. The bloodletting continued into 2005, even as the Marines sent their helicopters to al-Qaim. In August 2005, when Anbar's tribes announced that they'd banded together to fight al-Qaeda, 85 Americans were killed. The next month, another 49 Americans died, even as Richard Myers, the invisible JCS chairman, was replaced by General Peter Pace, the first Marine to hold that position. In all of 2005, 823 Americans died in Iraq, more than had died during the invasion almost three years earlier.

The spiraling death count stunned the nation's military leaders, who were deeply divided about what to do. A large number of them concluded that the United States should simply cut its losses and get out; or, as they phrased it, turn Iraq over to the Iraqis. The new JCS chairman, Peter Pace, agreed with this, as did most of his JCS colleagues. More crucially, so did George Casey, in Baghdad. During one videoconference with Bush, in early March 2006, the US ground commander observed that every time a US soldier crossed paths with an Iraqi there was friction. In truth, Casey's observation came by way of John Abizaid—whose influence and experience as a Middle East hand was enormous. The way to end the violence, Abizaid told Casey, was to keep Iraqis and Americans apart. Casey now repeated that to the president. Bush thought about this for a moment, until what Casey was implying dawned on him. "By that logic," Bush said, "the insurgency would disappear if we brought all our troops home." Casey did not respond.[50]

CHAPTER EIGHT

Jack Keane's Coup

"Winning. This is about winning.
We need to win."

WHAT CAME TO be known as the Generals' Revolt began on March 19, 2006, when retired Army major general Paul Eaton called for the resignation of Donald Rumsfeld in the pages of the *New York Times*. Rumsfeld "has shown himself incompetent strategically, operationally and tactically," Eaton wrote, "and is far more than anyone else responsible for what has happened to our important mission in Iraq. Mr. Rumsfeld must step down."[1] Eaton blamed Rumsfeld, but he also blamed the military. Senior military officers always tried to answer the "what's next" question, Eaton pointed out, but "the supreme commander, General Tommy Franks, either didn't heed that rule or succumbed to Secretary Rumsfeld's bullying." For Eaton, who admired Hugh Shelton, Rumsfeld and Franks were an insult to Shelton's legacy: they had thoughtlessly sent America's best men and women into harm's way. Shelton—secretive, private, poker-faced Hugh Shelton—would have never done that.

Eaton's call was reinforced two weeks later, when retired Marine general Anthony Zinni appeared on *Meet the Press*, the Sunday morning news program, where he described the war in Iraq as "a series of disastrous mistakes." Zinni pointedly contradicted Secretary of State Condoleezza Rice, named as Colin Powell's successor after Bush's reelection, who'd appeared in the show's previous segment. The administration had gotten things wrong in Iraq, she said, but these were "tactical mistakes," thus implying that the worsening situation in Iraq was the military's fault.

"These were not tactical mistakes," Zinni said, angrily. "These were strategic mistakes, mistakes of policies made back here. Don't blame the troops. They've been magnificent. If anything saves us, it will be them." The show's host asked Zinni if someone should resign. "Absolutely," Zinni said. Who? he was asked. "Secretary of Defense to begin with," Zinni answered.[2]

Zinni's charge sheet touched on all of the military's complaints: the years of planning "thrown away," troop levels "dismissed out of hand," Eric Shinseki "insulted for speaking the truth," the "lack of a cohesive approach" to postwar planning, belief in a group of exiles that "were not credible on the ground," and the decision to "disband the [Iraqi] army." Four days later, retired Marine lieutenant general Greg Newbold, who'd served under Rumsfeld as the Joint Staff's J-3, and then left the service in disgust, penned an article in *Time* magazine that broadened the Eaton-Zinni indictment. The military high command, Newbold said, had blundered.

"Flaws in our civilians are one thing, the failure of the Pentagon's military leaders is quite another," Newbold wrote. "A few of the most senior officers actually supported the logic of the war. Others were intimidated, while still others must have believed that the principle of obedience does not allow for respectful dissent. The consequence of the military's quiescence was that a fundamentally flawed plan was executed for an invented war, while pursuing the real enemy, al-Qaeda, became a secondary effort." Newbold never named the officers who were intimidated, but his colleagues identified them as Iraq war commander Tommy Franks and JCS chairman Richard Myers.[3]

By mid-April the rebellion included an additional four retired officers: Major General Charles Swannack Jr., the former commander of the 82nd Airborne; Major General John Batiste, the former commander of the 1st Infantry Division; Lieutenant General John Riggs, who'd spent his last years in uniform focusing on Army transformation (and had run afoul of Rumsfeld on the issue); and Marine general Paul Van Riper. In fact, however, the circle of dissenters was much larger, including senior

officers on the Joint Staff, high-profile field commanders, and former civilian officials. The list was impressive: generals Joe Hoar, Wesley Clark,
Robert Gard, John Johns, Merrill McPeak; Army lieutenant general
William Odom, the former head of the National Security Agency; and
former Army secretary Thomas White, who told reporters that Rumsfeld had been "contemptuous of the views of senior military officers"
since the day he took the job. "It's about time" the generals "got sick and
tired," he said.[4]

The network of dissenters was most prominent inside the Marine
Corps, where Zinni, Newbold, Van Riper, and Hoar were hearing from
Marine officers inside the Pentagon. Hoar spoke regularly with senior
Marines who were close to Marine Corps commandant Michael Hagee,
who made a point of traveling regularly to Iraq to make his own assessment. Baghdad was in chaos, Iraq's leadership was corrupt, and the
country was on the verge of a civil war. Astonishingly, Hagee chose to
say nothing. Part of the reason, his staff said, was that he was out of
his depth. He'd been a dark horse pick as commandant, the first one to
come into the office without serving in a powerful three-star command.
Rumsfeld had reached down and plucked him out of his combat position,
knowing he would be uncomfortable in Washington. "We kept waiting
for Hagee to say something," a senior Marine who served with him at the
Pentagon said, "but he never did."[5]

The other elusive Marine was JCS chairman Peter Pace, a self-effacing
officer who maintained his loyalty to the defense secretary. The "stay-
in-your-lane" phrase was a favorite of Pace's, who regularly used it to
warn his fellow officers. When James Conway's chief of staff, John Coleman, was in the midst of his dealings with Anbar's tribal leaders—at the
suggestion of Conway, who commanded the Marines in Anbar—Pace
warned him about what he was doing. "Stay in your lane, John," he'd said
when he met him in a Pentagon hallway. One week after Zinni's television appearance, Pace told reporters that if the dissenting generals didn't
like the way things were going in Iraq, it was their own fault: "We had
then, and have now, every opportunity to speak our minds, and, if we do
not, shame on us, because the opportunity is there."[6]

Rumsfeld went on the offensive, casting his opponents in his standby
language as "Clinton's Generals," and telling reporters that while he'd ruf-
fled feathers in the military, he'd only done it to reassert civilian control
of the services in the wake of the Clinton years. The real problem was that

the military was uncomfortable with being told what to do by civilians, Rumsfeld said. They'd walked all over Clinton, and now wanted to do that with Bush. Unwitting reporters aped this theme, casting the Generals' Revolt as an angry reaction by officers who objected to Rumsfeld's desire to "establish more clear-cut civilian control over the Pentagon," as one press report described it.[7]

To counter Zinni and the generals, Rumsfeld's office assembled seventeen senior retired officers to appear on major news programs to defend the secretary. Among the group were retired generals Wayne Downing, Bob Scales, William Nash, Montgomery Meigs, Barry McCaffrey, and Don Sheppard. The group met with Rumsfeld in his office in mid-April, praising him ("you're our guy," one of them said), then fanned out across Washington, repeating the bullet points they'd been given. But after meeting with Rumsfeld, Major General William Nash began to understand why Eaton and Zinni were worried. Rumsfeld came across as imperious and insecure. He was more concerned about what was being said about him than about what was happening in Iraq. The generals were told to emphasize that Rumsfeld was consulting "frequently and sufficiently" with senior military leaders. The secretary then added that if anyone asked about the meeting, they should say that it was about "more important topics" than his leadership. This isn't about me, he said, and that is what you should say if you're asked. But, of course, it was about him. Nash was disgusted. "I walked away from that session having total disrespect for my fellow commentators, with perhaps one or two exceptions," he later told reporters.[8]

When retired Marine Joe Hoar heard about the meeting, his judgment was venomous. "This is the ultimate irony," he said, "and I think it's pretty much the key to that man [Rumsfeld]. Everyone says he hates the criticism. That's a crock. When everyone should be debating what we can do in Iraq, we're debating what to do about him. He loves it. He loves playing the role of the embattled leader." Other officers came to a similar conclusion, including retired Army lieutenant general William Odom. Odom took on Rumsfeld with the press, but then gamely refocused his comments on Iraq. In May, he penned an article calling the Iraq war a failure. The solution, he said, was to leave. In his article, entitled "Cut and Run? Why Not," Odom said in public what many senior military leaders were saying in private. "This isn't about Rumsfeld, it's about the decisions the administration made on Iraq," he said. "Rumsfeld failed, but so too did the Congress, the Democrats, the media, the military. The result is that we're losing in Iraq. The solution is to get out."[9]

At about the same time that Paul Eaton was writing his op-ed for the *New York Times*, Virginia congressman Frank Wolf was finalizing plans for the creation of an independent group to study the Iraq crisis. Funded by Congress, the group would be bipartisan, independent, and cochaired by former secretary of state James Baker and retired congressman Lee Hamilton. After a bit of wrangling about what the gathering would be called, Wolf's idea became the Iraq Study Group, the ISG, an eclectic collection of ten high-profile Washington insiders that included former CIA director Robert Gates, retired Supreme Court justice Sandra Day O'Conner, former attorney general Edwin Meese, former secretary of defense William Perry, and former Virginia senator Chuck Robb. The ISG's chief of staff was Paul Hughes, now retired from the military. The group began conducting intensive interviews of experts in April, taking testimony through the next months, then traveled to Iraq in August to interview US military commanders and Iraqi officials.[10]

The first person interviewed by Baker and his team in Baghdad was General George Casey, the US ground commander. Casey, whose father had also been a general and was killed in Vietnam, was highly respected in his service, where he was viewed as a tireless worker. "He worked his staff to death," a colleague said. Casey had had a stellar career, leading a division in Germany, heading up US Army forces in Kosovo, serving in a prestige position on the Joint Staff and then as the Army's vice chief. His subordinates groaned when they saw him coming, as it almost always meant more work. Casey admired CENTCOM commander John Abizaid and served with him in Kosovo but, unlike him, he knew next to nothing about the Middle East. That didn't seem a requirement: Rumsfeld's parting message to him repeated the defense secretary's anti-nation-building mantra. Iraq, Rumsfeld said, should be turned over to the Iraqis.[11]

As Casey soon learned, Rumsfeld's laconic advice was belied by Iraq's reality. When he arrived in Baghdad (in June 2004), Iraq was spiraling into chaos and outgoing commander Ricardo Sanchez had left no strategy to deal with it. Casey was starting from scratch. The day after his arrival, Casey told the president during a videoconference that his first priority was to develop "recommendations for the way ahead," because there were none. "That sounds good," Bush said. The moment, largely uncommented on by historians, is as disturbing as the one in 1969, when newly appointed defense secretary Clark Clifford asked JCS chairman Earle Wheeler the plan for winning in Vietnam. "There is no plan," Wheeler had said. Clifford could hardly believe what he was hearing. The United States was five years into the war, and there was no plan to win it. The same was true for Iraq in 2004. One year into the insurgency, there was still no plan to deal with it.[12]

It got worse from there. During his time in command, Casey had had to scramble US troops to respond to the Sadrist uprising—begun when Iraqi politician Muqtada al-Sadr's Shia movement took up arms against the Americans. Al-Sadr's militia, the Mahdi Army, fought the Americans from its base in the slums of Baghdad, but the uprising then spread into Iraq's Shia-dominated southern regions. The Americans were forced to quell disturbances during the 2004 battles of Sadr City, Najaf, Fallujah, and Samarra, as well as the 2005 fights against Sunni militias in al-Qaim, Haditha, and Tal Afar. But the turning point came in February 2006, with the bombing of the al-Askari Shrine, a Shia holy site in Samarra. After that bombing the violence in Iraq reached staggering levels. Each morning the streets of Baghdad looked like a morgue, with bodies left by Shia death squads. Casey helicoptered his way into Iraq's cities, where he sat down with privates, corporals, and sergeants, trying to get a feel for the war. He supported the Marines in Anbar and H. R. McMaster in Tal Afar, but even as he supported political reconciliation in some parts of Iraq, he deployed his units to fight insurgents. But when he learned that Marine general James Conway was seeking an opening to Anbar's tribes, he told him he'd heard the effort was a "goat rope."[13]

Conway replied angrily, telling Casey by e-mail that if he had a better idea on how to fight the insurgency, he would love to hear it. Conway was speaking from experience: he'd been in a goat rope, which is how you trained kids for the rodeo. Anbar wasn't a goat rope, it was a dirty and bloody fight. Conway had seen it up close, while Casey was off in Baghdad giving advice. The exchange was blunt, and ugly. Conway's Marines had fought two bloody battles in Fallujah (in April 2004 and then again in December) and (as both Conway and Mattis knew) their performance was often less than stellar—and below Marine Corps expectation. But then, so Conway thought, the battles had been unnecessary—

ordered from the top. Now George Casey was lecturing him on goat ropes. Mattis agreed. He wasn't having any of it. It was one thing to get advice from John Abizaid, but both Conway and Mattis didn't have nearly the same respect for Casey. Abizaid knew what he was doing, but Casey? Well, as Mattis told one of his officers, "Casey is as dumb as a box of rocks." Mattis wasn't the only one who thought so.[14]

Watching from afar, Army colonel Doug Macgregor called Casey's solution for Iraq "a big base strategy," with American soldiers coming into Iraq's cities from their bases, then heading back to their barracks at night. It was like Vietnam: when the Americans left, the insurgents returned. The result was that Casey's soldiers were killing insurgents, but not killing the insurgency. How many did we get today? Bush would ask. Casey recited the numbers, as Bush nodded his approval. "Good, good," he'd say. Casey would end the videoconferences frustrated. None of this was working, but he couldn't bring himself to say it: the more insurgents the US killed, the stronger the insurgency got.

Despite this, when Iraq Study Group members asked Casey whether he needed more troops to control the violence, he said "no," and then, when asked again, said "no" emphatically. He reasserted his view that the best response to the violence was to accelerate the training of Iraqi security forces. This was a replay of what he'd told Bush: that every time an American soldier interacted with an Iraqi, the result was friction. The solution, Casey reiterated, was for the Americans to get out of the way and put Iraq's future back into the hands of Iraqis. Officially, the strategy was called "clear, hold and build," but in reality, it was "hold and get out." Defeating an insurgency usually took ten to twelve years, Casey told the Baker-Hamilton group, but the training of the Iraqi security forces was going well. The United States, he said, could turn Iraq over to its newly trained security services in eighteen months.

No one in the ISG quite believed that, but no one had a better solution. It wasn't simply that Casey was persuasive (he wasn't, actually), but that no one had come up with a credible alternative; and Casey's ground commanders supported him. That group included Lieutenant General Peter Chiarelli, an optimistic go-getter whose focus on the Iraq economy provided a refreshing tonic from the same-same views of Casey. "We've got to put these people to work," Chiarelli told the group.[15] But he agreed with his commander: the way forward was to put Iraq back in the hands of the Iraqis. The positive assessment of Major General Marty Dempsey, in charge of training the new Iraqi army, also carried weight. The training process was slow and exacting, but that wasn't surprising, Dempsey said. And, like Casey, he was not convinced that additional US troops would actually do much good. The problems in Iraq, he said, were political. Until those were sorted out, the violence was likely to continue. As the Iraqi security forces stood up, the United States would stand down. Baker and Hamilton went along with this, if only reluctantly, concluding that sending additional US troops to Iraq would not solve the country's fundamental problems. But there was one dissenter.

In the long history of American politics, Virginia senator Chuck Robb is unlikely to garner much more than a footnote. Robb's political career was propelled, in part, by his marriage to Lynda Bird Johnson, the daughter of President Lyndon B. Johnson, a Democrat. But Robb was a talented, educated, and ambitious man; he'd served capably as lieutenant governor and governor of Virginia before winning election to the Senate in 1988. But his term was stained by allegations that he'd had an affair with a former Miss Virginia USA, and that he'd been seen at a party where cocaine was used. Robb denied the affair and claimed that he'd never seen the cocaine. No one provided evidence to suggest otherwise. Three years later, he was implicated in a scandal that involved wiretapping his opponent in his bid for reelection, but he skirted a grand jury investigation. Despite this, Robb built a reputation for being a serious foreign policy thinker, a status reinforced by his two years of service as a Marine platoon leader in Vietnam. He'd won three Bronze Stars.

Robb was the only member of the Baker-Hamilton group who insisted on seeing Iraq for himself, and several days after the group's arrival he helicoptered out of Baghdad to visit Marines at Camp Fallujah. While there, he met with Bing West, a fellow Marine in Vietnam and an accomplished military analyst. The two compared notes, commenting on the unlikely similarities between Iraq and Vietnam. Robb had wanted to go on to Ramadi, but US officials stopped him. It was too dangerous, they said. Robb returned to Baghdad, where he burst in on a group meeting, sputtering his disgust at the decision. He'd be damned if someone else would control his schedule, he said. He was being managed, just like General Westmoreland had orchestrated visits to Vietnam. The next day, conceding the point, Casey had a military patrol accompany Robb in a walking tour of a Baghdad neighborhood. The two forays convinced Robb that the United States was losing the war. The training of Iraq's soldiers wasn't going well, US troops weren't getting out among the people, and the security situation was getting worse. After Casey said that his strategy of disengagement was working, Robb shook his head. "I don't believe him," he said. "I don't buy it."[16]

The one thing that had worked in Vietnam, Robb remembered, was the American military's combat action patrols. The CAPs were small units of US troopers who mingled with the local population, untethered to their bases. Security didn't consist solely of killing insurgents when they appeared, but also of securing an area before it could be penetrated. To build the confidence of the people, Robb learned in Vietnam, you actually have to get to know them. You have to be there, where they live, twenty-four hours a day. But to do that effectively you need a lot of troops, and certainly more than Casey had. The United States, Robb argued, should deploy an additional twenty thousand troops right away. Their focus should be Baghdad.[17]

While Robb's recommendation was added to the ISG's final report, he later said that his views, presented in the groups' private sessions, were more outspoken. It's not that he wanted to "add a few troops here or there," it's that he believed the United States needed a new battle plan. Few had seen the former senator like this. Normally, claiming a failing memory, he would scratch out his thoughts in a small notebook, holding his hand up for the speaker to slow down. "Need to get this," he'd say. Now, after his visit to Camp Fallujah, Robb's Marine instincts were on full display. "Jesus Christ, Bill," he said to William Perry, "we're not winning." His right fist pounded his left palm for emphasis. "Winning. This is about winning. We need to win." His final recommendation, a paragraph in length, was right out of the Marine playbook: "Without being overly dramatic," he wrote, "I believe the Battle for Baghdad is the make or break element of whatever impact we're going to have on Iraq and the entire region for at least a decade. . . . My sense is that we need, right away, a significant short-term surge in US forces on the ground."[18]

Jack Keane agreed. The former vice chief of staff of the Army had always punched above his weight. Conservative, opinionated, and likely to go his own way on controversial issues, Keane had turned down Rumsfeld's plea that he succeed Eric Shinseki as Army chief of staff, citing the illness of his wife. But when he left the Pentagon, Keane was worried that the war was being mishandled. As the former vice chief, he felt partly responsible. Over time he concluded that in order for the United States to win, its commanders needed more troops. That's what Keane told the Baker-Hamilton group before they visited Baghdad in August. "Clear, hold, and build is good," he'd said, "but there are not enough forces." On September 19, Keane told Rumsfeld and Pace about his concerns during a meeting he had with them in Rumsfeld's Pentagon office.[19]

Rumsfeld shifted uncomfortably as Keane read off a list of what was wrong in Iraq and how it could be solved. "We have to win the Battle of Baghdad," one of his points argued. "We have to absolutely stabilize Baghdad by control of the population." This was counterinsurgency's central tenet: that in an insurgency, the center of gravity is the people. The United States was failing because it had lost the faith of the Iraqi people. Rumsfeld listened to Keane, the worry sketched out on his face, but he was on his best behavior. The reason had to do with Keane himself, who wasn't easily intimidated. His fellow officers regularly commented on this: Keane, they said, had "gravitas." Keane reminded older officers of General Creighton Abrams, one of a constellation of Army generals considered among the best fighters in American history. Abrams was mentioned in the same breath as Grant, Sherman, and Patton. Abrams had come to Washington in March 1968 to tell Lyndon Johnson that the US was losing the war in Vietnam. Coming from Abrams, everyone knew it was the truth. Keane had that same stature.[20]

Two days later, Keane sat down with Pace. "If you could grade how I'm doing," Pace asked him, "what grade would you give me?" Keane never hesitated: "An 'F,'" he said. Pace sagged. You're focused on your job as JCS chairman, Keane explained, when there's a war going on in Iraq. The job of the joint chiefs is to train and equip the military, Keane said, but in wartime your focus has to be the war. You have to be involved, and you're not. We need new leadership in Iraq, Keane said; Abizaid and Casey were exhausted and their strategy was failing. He recommended that Pace replace Abizaid at CENTCOM with Admiral Fox Fallon, the head of the US Pacific Command, and Casey with the 101st Airborne commander, David Petraeus.[21]

Keane's meeting with Pace left the JCS chairman distraught. He knew he'd raised worries among Marines about his leadership, was seen as too close to Rumsfeld, and was losing the trust of his JCS colleagues, who'd concluded that Pace wasn't being tough on the White House or

Rumsfeld. The chiefs saw this during sessions in the tank, where their questions to Pace about the administration's polices were met with shrugs, silence, or puzzled looks. He couldn't tell them what was going on in the White House, because he didn't know. In the years ahead, Pace's tenure would be adjudged a failure by his peers, but in fact he was trapped in what many senior military officers believed was a rigid system that punished dissent. The fact that a group of prominent generals had felt the need to make their dissent public reflected that view—and Pace's failure.

The Generals' Revolt sent shockwaves through the Pentagon because it was seen as a repudiation of Rumsfeld—and the military—and was evidence that military leaders had abdicated their responsibility to provide their best advice to the nation's civilian leaders. The abdication started with Peter Pace. "I find it absolutely astonishing that a JCS chairman can stand toe-to-toe with a president over the issue of gays in the military," retired general Joe Hoar said, "and yet, when it comes to a war, with American lives at stake, no one will tell our political leaders that they've made a mistake." Yet, here too, JCS and Joint Staff officers believed their inability to act flowed from a system where disagreement, or even reasoned dissent, was viewed as inappropriate, or worse. They were faced with an impossible choice. If they spoke out while in uniform, they were derided as insubordinate, but if they didn't they were derelict in their duty. Who would they rather be—an insubordinate officer who stood up for his principles, or an officer who was derelict in their duty and never stood up to anyone—like Dick Myers?[22]

The crisis in Iraq, coupled with the Goldwater-Nichols reforms, had shifted the JCS's role to the point where their mandate clashed with the priorities of the warfighters. At key points in the conflict, America's Iraq commanders found themselves asking for more, more, and more, and not getting it. In many cases, the JCS didn't have it to give, but in other cases they didn't want to, because more for Iraq meant less for the force. Why provide more if we were going to get out? The inherent tensions in the system had played havoc throughout the first two years of the war and had a subtle effect on George Casey. By 2006, Casey's strategy fed into JCS worries that the war was cutting into military readiness. Building and maintaining the military was in the JCS's interest; fighting a war undermined that.[23]

Urged on by Keane, Pace convened a group of young officers in early September 2006 to review the US strategy for the war on terror and come

up with recommendations on how to fight it. Keane thought that the
JCS's mandate made them unlikely allies in an effort to shift America's
Iraq strategy, so he told Pace that the group should come from outside
the Pentagon. Among those chosen were Army colonel Peter Mansoor,
who'd headed up the US Army and Marine Corps Counterinsurgency
Center, and Colonel H. R. McMaster, recently returned from Tal Afar.
The key Marine was Colonel Thomas Greenwood, White House policy
adviser Frank Miller's unwilling back channel to Colin Powell. The three
of them were the only officers on what came to be called the "council of
colonels" to have combat experience in Iraq. The sixteen-member council
(the Air Force provided five members, the Navy four) first met in the
basement of the Pentagon, just below the JCS's offices, on September 27.
"Our mandate was to focus on the global war on terror," Mansoor later
reflected. "But all of our discussions always looped back to one thing—
what to do about Iraq."[24]

The council's sessions went from morning to night in extended discussions on American military policy, on the nature of the enemy, the
strategy to defeat him, and the obstacles faced by policymakers in doing
so. The council, Mansoor later wrote, "discussed and debated a wide va-
riety of issues: the wars in Iraq and Afghanistan; the Israeli-Palestinian
conflict; various terrorist organizations, including al-Qaeda; the role of
Islam in fomenting extremism." But inevitably, the group reached an im-
passe on what to do about Iraq. The choice came down to finding a way
to win, or finding a way to leave. The difference generally split along service lines: the Air Force and Navy wanted the military to begin a phased
withdrawal, while Mansoor and McMaster advocated varying levels of
reinforcement to stabilize the country. Near the end of one of the discussions, Mansoor walked to a white board and wrote down the differing
views. There were three, and he labeled them "Go Big" (heavy reinforcement), "Go Long" (engaging in the conflict for a protracted period), and
"Go Home," which called for a withdrawal. Surveying the room, Mansoor realized the council was split.[25]

The split among the colonels was obvious to JCS members, who met
regularly with the council to get briefings on their deliberations, which
were followed by question and answer sessions. The meetings were uncomfortable, with the chiefs hosting the colonels in the tank, which
many in the JCS considered sacrosanct. Air Force chief of staff T. Michael Moseley reflected the military's view that the Bush administration

too often looked to the military to solve the nation's foreign policy problems. "Whatever happened to diplomacy?" he asked during one session. "Why is it always up to us?" Moseley was reflecting the thinking of senior Air Force officers, who were heavily influenced by the thinking of previous commanders, including Merrill McPeak and Chuck Horner. McPeak thought that Iraq was a mistake, while Horner worried that whatever happened in Iraq, the military would get the blame. Moseley agreed.[26]

Many of the chiefs, Mansoor thought, were oddly detached from the crisis, except for Admiral Mike Mullen, the chief of naval operations. "I found him intellectually engaged," Mansoor remembers. "He was very interested in our debates, asked penetrating questions. In his own league, I thought, and worried about the strain the war was putting on our forces. He was impressive."[27] On several occasions, the colonels found themselves in the position of having to remind the service heads of why they were there. During one briefing, with the JCS's aides in full array, the option of providing more troops for the war was broached. "That's not going to happen, no way," Army chief Peter Schoomaker said. "More troops? Forget it. It would break the Army." The briefer was visibly taken aback. "Well," the briefer said, "maybe if you'd have made that point before we got into this mess, we wouldn't be talking about it now." The room fell silent, but the colonel didn't back down. Along the back wall, an aide to the Marine Corps commandant turned to a younger colleague. "What you have just witnessed," he whispered, "is the end of a very fine career."[28]

The colonels provided their recommendations to the chiefs on November 3, 2006, outlining the three options: "Go Big," "Go Long," or "Go Home." The options reflected the views of McMaster, Mansoor, and Greenwood. The council also provided a slide of the six overarching trends in the war: (1) Our current strategy is not working; (2) the government of Iraq is unable to provide tangible and credible results in the eyes of the Iraqi people; (3) Iraqi security forces remain weak and ineffective; (4) ethnic and sectarian conflict is increasing; (5) the rule of law is lacking; and (6) economic progress is lacking. The most important part of the briefing, however, was summarized on the last slide, and was the one point the entire council agreed on: "After three years of sacrifice, we think we are running out of time. As the invading foreign power the burden is on us to win or at least show credible progress in Iraq. Because this is not happening at a rate that is convincing the Iraqi people, the American people, and the international community, our group of colonels think we are losing in Iraq today." The JCS listened, stony-faced, but without objection. They agreed: the United States was losing the war in Iraq.[29]

GEORGE BUSH HAD come to the same conclusion. What was needed, he decided, was a change at the top. New thinking. He wanted to start at the defense department. The president had shown enormous confidence in Donald Rumsfeld, supporting him at every turn and even working to calm his outbursts. "That's fine, Don," he'd say. "It'll be okay."

But by the end of September, Bush decided he needed a new defense secretary, and by mid-October he'd decided to replace Rumsfeld with Robert Gates, the former director of the CIA during his father's administration. The two met at Bush's ranch in Crawford, Texas, on November 5, where Bush offered him the job. Gates, then serving as president of Texas A&M University, accepted. The next day, the Democrats won control of the House and Senate in the midterm elections, a stark repudiation of Bush's strategy in Iraq. Twenty-four hours later, with Rumsfeld standing next to him, Bush made the announcement: Bob Gates would take over as defense secretary. One month later, after being confirmed by the Senate, Gates appeared at the Pentagon. Standing in front of a group of senior civilian officials, Gates gave a short introductory talk and asked for questions. How long, he was asked, did he think it would take to get his own team confirmed? "We don't have time for that," he said. "We have a war on in Iraq, and that's my top priority. I'm going there tonight."[30]

A palpable sense of relief washed through the military. Gates could be tough, but he never silenced dissenters and worked hard to shed his need for public recognition. He was also devoid of Rumsfeld's habit of facing off against pretend enemies. For six years, Rumsfeld had found himself at war: with George Tenet, Colin Powell, Eric Shinseki, or Condoleezza Rice. Gates would have none of it. "I like Condi," he told his Pentagon staff, then turned on an aide who suggested that Rumsfeld believed "she was in over her head." Gates dismissed this. "That's not true," he said. "It's my job to work with her, and that's what I'm going to do."[31]

BY EARLY DECEMBER, the idea that a surge of fresh troops was needed in Iraq was gaining momentum. After his meetings with Rumsfeld and

Pace, Keane met with Frederick Kagan, a policy intellectual and former West Point professor who was ensconced at AEI, the conservative American Enterprise Institute, a Washington think tank. The meeting was fortuitous: Kagan was studying alternative strategies for Iraq and was upset about the conclusions of the Iraq Study Group, which had presented its report to Bush one week after Gates's appointment. The group's recommendations were a strange mix of "stay the course" and "do better." The ISG endorsed Casey's strategy, but cautioned against an early withdrawal. The only substantive dissenting view came from Chuck Robb, who'd recruited former attorney general Ed Meese as an ally. Meese had leaned on William Perry to include Robb's argument for a surge in the final report, then hammered out language to make the idea palatable to other group members.

Kagan disagreed with the report and thought Keane (and Robb) had it right—the US military should surge troops into Iraq. He'd convened his own group of experts, who began crunching deployment numbers. According to Kagan's estimates, the Army had five brigades that it could use for the surge. Keane looked at Kagan's numbers and was surprised that he was able to determine troop availability from public sources. Armed with Kagan's report, Keane showed up at the White House on December 11 as a part of a five-member group of military experts for a meeting with Bush. The group included author, State Department official, and historian Eliot Cohen; retired Army generals Barry McCaffrey and Wayne Downing; and Stephen Biddle, a foreign policy analyst at the Council on Foreign Relations. Alone among the five, Keane pressed Bush for a surge. "We need a fundamental shift in strategy," he said, "and we need to start in Baghdad." A surge would allow US troops to patrol Baghdad neighborhoods around the clock and stand between the warring groups. No matter what, Keane told Bush, the United States had to stabilize Baghdad. If that wasn't done, nothing else would matter. Keane left Bush with a warning: the JCS will tell you they don't have the troops for a surge, he said. Don't believe them.[32]

Unbeknownst to Keane, Bush's national security team had been thinking about a surge for several months. Beginning in late May, key White House staffers had been turning over ideas on how to shift US policy in Iraq. The group regularly reported to Bush's national security adviser, Stephen Hadley. In fact, according to National Security Council assistant Peter Feaver, separate strategy reviews were launched not only by AEI and the council of colonels, but also by General Ray Odierno in Iraq, by Condoleezza Rice at the State Department—and by the White House. In late October, Hadley and some of his key staff made a trip to Iraq to talk with George Casey and his senior commanders. They arrived at the same conclusion as the council of colonels: the United States was not winning in Iraq, so it was losing. In early November, Bush gave Hadley's assistant J. D. Crouch the job of collating the different views as a part of an interagency team, a roving deputies committee. For the next six weeks, Crouch's team met six to eight hours a day, and often six days a week, studying the war. The interagency team was to report its findings to Bush in early December 2006, Feaver writes, "but the timeline was extended to the third week of December," and then into January 2007. There was never any doubt where the president stood: he'd been talking about "winning" in Iraq for months. "I want to know how to win," he had told Keane during their White House meeting, then repeated the phrase at a meeting at the State Department on the same day.[33]

Meanwhile, at the Pentagon, the chiefs were increasingly angered by the debate over the surge, and were enraged that Keane had met with Bush. Why hadn't the president asked their opinion? "What are you going to do about this?" Army chief of staff Peter Schoomaker asked Pace. "Since when does AEI get to have its say and we don't?" Keane had helped Schoomaker navigate his transition from retirement to Army chief, and Schoomaker owed him. Because of this Schoomaker was uncomfortable criticizing Keane, but he put that aside: the retired vice chief had his chance to talk about Iraq when he was in uniform and hadn't said a word. It was easy to take shots when you were out of uniform, a lot harder when you were in charge. Schoomaker made the same point during the Generals' Revolt. "I was retired, and you didn't see me doing it," he told reporters. Keane was out of line. Many on the Army staff agreed. The Keane-Bush channel, one of them noted, reminded him of the notorious "Taylor Coup." Jack Keane might have appeared as a latter day Creighton Abrams to civilians, but he was more like former Army general Maxwell Taylor, who'd undermined the JCS during the Kennedy administration. In 1961, Taylor was directed by President Kennedy to investigate the US failure at the Bay of Pigs, the disastrous invasion of Cuba by a US-supported Cuban exile army. In his report, Taylor blamed the chiefs for the failure. Kennedy got the hint: he pushed aside JCS chairman Lyman Lemnitzer and named Taylor as his replacement. Taylor came out of retirement, put on his uniform, and then proceeded to drag the United States into Vietnam. It was a coup. Now it was happening again: a retired general was undercutting his colleagues for the purpose of dragging the military ever deeper into Iraq. That had been the Taylor Coup, this was the Keane Coup.[34]

Angered by Keane's interference, Schoomaker was emerging as the most outspoken opponent of the surge. Schoomaker had standing, in large part because he'd been a surprise success as the Army's chief. He'd been less of a special forces ideologue than many suspected. He'd shuffled troops, deployments, rotation schedules, and recruiting policies to meet the demands of Iraq, fine-tuned unit cohesion, and held the hands of Army reservists, who were posting "One Weekend A Month, My Ass" signs on their Humvees in Iraq. "This is spinning out of control," he told a colleague. "Our soldiers are exhausted, our equipment is wearing thin, no one has any solutions."[35] By late November 2006, the outline of what the president wanted was apparent. In a meeting with the chiefs in the tank, Pace confirmed the rumors: Bush was leaning toward sending an additional five brigades to Iraq. Schoomaker shook his head. "This will break the Army," he told Pace. Admiral Mullen also objected: What about our other threats? he asked. The Air Force chief was embittered: you watch, he said, the civilians are going to put this in our lap, just like they did in Vietnam. Faced earlier in the year with a Generals' Revolt, Pace was now faced with a revolt of the JCS. He'd lost the confidence of the officers around the table. "Do they listen to you over there [at the White House]?" Schoomaker asked him. "I'm having a hard time getting a hearing," Pace admitted. He was chagrined.[36]

To salvage his position, Pace asked Bush to visit the JCS on their turf. It would show he valued their advice. Bush agreed and the meeting was set for December 13. Bush was accompanied by outgoing secretary Rumsfeld, Stephen Hadley, Bob Gates, and Dick Cheney. The two sides arrayed themselves on either side of the tank's long meeting table. Cheney had convinced Bush he should take the lead in the discussion, and Bush had agreed, so he began the exchange by pointing out that the violence in Iraq showed that the Iraqi government needed more help. The chiefs disagreed—adding troops now would just reward the Iraqi government's nonperformance. The chiefs singled out Iraqi prime minister Nouri al-Maliki. Maliki, they said, didn't seem interested in accommodation with his political enemies. That was a big problem. Bush was abrupt. He was there to hear his military views, not take political advice. "Maliki is my job," he said," not yours." Schoomaker broached the subject of the surge.

"Mr. President," he said, "you know that five brigades is really 15." He explained: as five brigades were surged to Iraq, another five had to be brought to readiness, with five behind them as a reserve. And surging five brigades into Iraq would mean that those already there would have to remain until the new brigades arrived. That meant extending combat tours and planning for multiple deployments. Schoomaker was precise in his explanation, locking his eyes on Bush. This is what Keane had warned Bush about. "This stresses the army, and makes it impossible for us to respond to other crises," Schoomaker said. "We don't have the time it will take to do this," he added. There was a moment's hesitation. "I've got the time," Bush said, then leaned back with a half-smile on his face. "Pete, I'm the president." Schoomaker nodded. "Fine," he said. "You're the president." Tension radiated through the room. The discussion shifted. North Korea could be a problem, Mullen said. If we have a crisis with North Korea, we won't have the forces to meet it. Bush shook his head. There isn't going to be a crisis with North Korea, he said, and if there was, he would deal with it then. The crisis now was Iraq. Inevitably, the discussion turned to Vietnam. The force had been broken in Vietnam, the chiefs reminded Bush, and it had taken twenty years to rebuild the military. Bush nodded: so what would really break the force, he asked—"sustaining the surge over the next several years, or another humiliating defeat similar to Vietnam?" The chiefs conceded the point. The discussion turned elsewhere, but Schoomaker and Bush were still locked in battle. "You don't agree with me, do you?" Bush asked. "No, I don't," Schoomaker responded. "I don't know how we're going to get those 15 brigades. I just don't. This could break the force, Mr. President." Bush nodded. "This is my decision," he said.[37]

Later, the president told reporter Bob Woodward that he hadn't gone to the Pentagon with his mind made up. "They may have thought I was leaning, and I probably was," he said. "But the door wasn't shut." That wasn't precisely true; Bush had his mind made up, but if the chiefs had locked arms and threatened to resign over his new strategy, Bush might well have rethought his position. Bush had depended on Pace to prepare them. "The president's goal was to bring the chiefs on board," Feaver says, "not order them on board. Peter Pace doesn't get much credit for it, but he'd done that."[38] The JCS had been thinking about a surge since late November, but while they opposed it, not one of them was willing to walk out the door over it. Additionally, their objections had already been considered by the president and J. D. Crouch's interagency team, including the stress the surge would place on the military. The process, "a virtual twenty-four hours a day deputies committee," had heard every voice. It had been an intensive effort. Schoomaker had presented his fifteen-brigade worries believing it would be the first time the president had heard them. It wasn't. Then too, Bush had been given a draft copy of the council of colonels report by Pace, identifying the surge as an option they'd considered. But when the council's final report was presented, the surge option wasn't included. The JCS had simply taken it out. That was their prerogative, but it was dishonest. Additionally, the president had an offer "in his back pocket" that would make the surge more palatable: he had arrived at the Pentagon saying he would increase the size of the military and that there would also be a surge of civilians, to handle the reconciliation issues and beef up humanitarian efforts. The military wouldn't be the only ones asked to make a sacrifice. The State Department was on board. But the increase in the size of the military was crucial. "The offer was more than a trade-off, or even something the president did to make the surge more palatable," Feaver reflects. "He was telling the military he wasn't willing to break the ground forces in order to save Iraq."[39]

That said, Bush made it clear during the meeting that he wasn't interested in having a discussion. His body language in the tank showed it. When Bush wasn't interested in something, he took on the air of a disinterested student. The ISG had noticed this in its final session with him. He did that now, in the tank. Peter Feaver notes that there are varying accounts of what happened in the tank between Bush and Schoomaker, but those who say that the Army chief was insubordinate, he says, exaggerate what happened.[40]

By 2006, the influence of the chiefs had been eclipsed by the power of the combatant commanders, the Joint Staff, and the JCS chairman. The joint chiefs were fourth in the pecking order, their previous power pared away by law, and war. Nor was Donald Rumsfeld a factor: "he was the Lion in Winter," Feaver says, comparing him to the Peter O'Toole movie character depicting an aging and powerless Henry II. "He'd begun to lose influence by mid-2006, and when Gates was named as his replacement he was a lame duck." As crucially, Bush had concluded that

Rumsfeld's mistake had more to do with his policies than with his character. After 9/11, Rumsfeld should have scrapped his transformation program, but instead he announced the Afghanistan and Iraq interventions would serve as transformation's laboratory by showing that smart weapons could replace soldiers. It was a fatal decision: it propelled the invasion of Iraq with fewer forces than were required, was a budgetary debacle, and placed enormous stress on military forces.[41]

After Bush's December 13 meeting with the JCS, the surge was on. Or not quite. This was a tradition of the JCS, a predictable part of its operational method: its members would reluctantly agree on a policy and then carefully slice away at it until they got their way. They'd done it for years, perfecting their methods through multiple budget fights. The Joint Staff had a word for the tactic: they called it "salami slicing."[42] The JCS did that now, with the surge. After their meeting with Bush, the chiefs fought back. In late December, urged on by Schoomaker, Pace diddled with the five-brigade concept, winnowing it to what was called two-plus-two: an additional two Army brigades, supplemented by two Marine battalions. It seemed like a good idea—it gave Bush the surge, but it eased the pressure on the Army. On December 28, Pace promoted the two-plus-two proposal to the president at Bush's ranch in Crawford. It went nowhere. Bush knew what the JCS was doing, and he was irritated. The idea was to surge five brigades into Iraq and see what happened, Bush said. If they went with two-plus-two and it wasn't enough, then they would have to add more brigades anyway. Then Bush announced that there would be a change in the commander in Iraq, saying Casey would be replaced by General David Petraeus. Everyone would move up a notch. When Petraeus took over in Iraq, Casey would become Army chief of staff. The Petraeus choice was nearly unanimous: Petraeus was supported by Jack Keane, Bob Gates, Ray Odierno (the Iraq ground commander), and Casey himself.

Petraeus had commanded the 101st Airborne in Iraq, had successfully dampened the insurgency in Mosul, knew how to implement postconflict operations, and was in the forefront of developing the Army's new counterinsurgency doctrine. He was a courageous combat commander, was respected by his service's most influential leaders, and was admired by his soldiers. His staff nearly worshipped him, and there was a regular scramble among Army colonels to serve under him. He had new ideas and new approaches. Casey was out, Petraeus was in, and the surge was on. "We're going to do this," Bush said to Pace during his meeting with him in Crawford. "Yes, sir," Pace said.

WHEN DAVID PETRAEUS was growing up, his friends called him "Peaches," but senior Army officers took to calling him "King David." In fact, the nickname originated with the people of Mosul, in northern Iraq, where Petraeus and the 101st Airborne found themselves after the fall of Baghdad. For Mosul's citizens, Petraeus was a problem solver and purse holder, liberally doling out funds to get the city up and running. When he didn't have the money, he spent it anyway, approving expenses in the belief the Pentagon would find a way to refill his division's coffers. It always did. Broken windows, smashed sewers, burned houses, destroyed electrical generators, burst pipes, unpaid salaries—no matter what the problem, there would be Petraeus, paying for it out of his congressionally mandated cash clip, the Commanders Emergency Response Program. Petraeus urged his subordinates to spend, spend, spend. Money is what the United States had, and spending was better than shooting. "Money is ammunition," he said. He was "Malik Daoud": King David.[43]

Petraeus was destined for high command: he had graduated near the top of his West Point class, married the daughter of the academy's powerful and intimidating superintendent (General William Knowlton), distinguished himself at the Army's Command and General Staff College, earned a PhD in international relations from Princeton, served as an assistant to the celebrated General John Galvin in Europe, breezed through Ranger school, commanded troops in Bosnia, attended the School of Advanced Military Studies, received a fellowship to Georgetown University, was part of the US military contingent in Haiti, served as an assistant to JCS chairman Hugh Shelton, commanded the 101st Airborne Division during Operation Iraqi Freedom, and then headed up the mission to train Iraq's new security forces. He was a SAMS graduate (a "Jedi Knight"), Army Ranger, paratrooper, and PhD. He wore his life on his uniform, as a cascade of ribbons—six rows in all. But that told only a part of the story: he'd been accidentally shot during a training exercise, but survived the chest wound that nearly killed him (Jack Keane, who'd witnessed the incident, had delivered him to the hospital) and, as a paratrooper, fell sixty feet through the open air, cracked his pelvis, and limped away. He ran six miles every morning, challenging men twenty years his junior to beat him: they rarely did. David Petraeus was everything an officer should be: he was smart, tough, respected, and experienced. And he was nearly universally disliked by his peers, particularly those West Pointers who competed with him for influence and rank.[44]

This wasn't professional jealousy, but the reaction of officers to a personality trait common among generals and admirals. David Petraeus was a tireless self-promoter. There are perhaps five commanders in US military history whose ego became a personal characteristic: Revolutionary War commander Horatio Gates (who plotted to replace Washington), Union commander George McClellan (who talked of dictatorship), World War II general Mark Clark (photograph me from my right side, he told reporters), Douglas MacArthur (who spoke as if he were an oracle)—and David Petraeus. Petraeus's yen for self-promotion made Wes Clark look like an amateur. But unlike Clark, Petraeus was admired by his superiors, who recognized and rewarded his competence. Petraeus wasn't Courtney Massengale, he was Sam Damon. Oddly, however, Petraeus climbed the command ladder not simply because he was viewed as competent, but because he cast himself as a go-it-alone rebel who developed dangerous ideas—like mixing light infantry forces among US heavy units in a war with the Soviet Union. European commander John Galvin loved the idea and had adopted it. Or breaking down large units into local patrols to mix with the people to undermine an insurgency, an idea that appealed to both Peter Schoomaker and Jack Keane. The two might have disagreed on the surge, but they agreed on Petraeus. Petraeus would shake things up, they thought.

For some officers, it was a bit too much. King David was a Jedi Knight? His fellow officers rolled their eyes. "The real heroes in Iraq were the privates, corporals, and sergeants who fought a war while the self-appointed Jedi got the damn thing wrong," one of them said. "Let me see if I have this right," an Army colonel who served with Petraeus said. "David Petraeus is the unrecognized rebel outsider who bucked the system and triumphed against the odds. Give me a break." He then went on to explain: "This guy was promoted by Galvin, anointed by Schoomaker, ushered around by Jack Keane, and married the superintendent's daughter: you can't get more inside than that." An Army officer on the Joint Staff authored this appraisal: "Yeah, David Petraeus gets up before the rest of us and runs six miles," he says. "That's great. So how many miles did Napoleon run?"[45] Petraeus's self-promotion was of a different type, his detractors claimed. When he figured out that bucking the system was the way to get ahead, that's what he did. And his attachment to counterinsurgency as a new doctrine was a pose. Counterinsurgency wasn't a doctrine, and it wasn't new. Mix with the locals? US soldiers not only mixed with the locals in Germany and Japan in World War II, they married them. And Petraeus's vaunted interpretation of Vietnam got Vietnam wrong: it wasn't the Vietcong that overran Vietnam's cities in 1975, but the North Vietnamese Army—led by tanks given to them by the Russians. A senior Pentagon official had much the same reaction to Petraeus as any reporter first meeting him. Petraeus struck him as unassuming and, at five foot nine, underwhelming: "This is King David? This guy? He's a little-un."[46]

None of this mattered to Petraeus, who reaped the benefits of Mosul. A 2004 issue of *Newsweek* featured him on the cover with the question: "Can This Man Save Iraq?" The headline rubbed Petraeus's peers raw. Ricardo Sanchez called him "the messiah," George Casey thought him vain, Ray Odierno believed he'd taken credit for quieting a city that was already quiet, and Peter Chiarelli couldn't bear hearing his name. For outsiders, the criticism was puzzling: each of his detractors, and even some of his biggest critics, cited him as the only officer who could replace Casey. Petraeus was an asshole, they said, but then, when asked who could turn the Iraq war around, they were unanimous: that vain self-promoter, David Petraeus.[47]

After returning from Iraq in September 2005, Peter Schoomaker had assigned Petraeus to the Combined Arms Center at Fort Leavenworth. Petraeus was disappointed. It sounded like he was being shunted aside. In fact, he was. His *Newsweek* appearance had put him in the line of fire, turning his peers against him. Schoomaker needed to give him a lower profile, if only temporarily, before his career was derailed. Go out to Leavenworth, Schoomaker told him, and figure out how to win this war, because your next assignment will be commanding it. Petraeus set to work with Marine lieutenant general James F. Amos revising the Army/ Marine counterinsurgency (or COIN) manual—what would become FM 3-24. It was to be the bible for how to win in Iraq, incorporating what the Marines had learned in Anbar and what Petraeus had learned in Mosul. Petraeus conferred with an eclectic team of experts: retired lieutenant colonel Conrad Crane, who sported a doctorate in history from Stanford; West Point wunderkind John Nagl (author of the celebrated

book on counterinsurgency, *Learning to Eat Soup with a Knife*); Sarah
Sewall, the director of Harvard University's human rights center; Australian soldier-scholar David Kilcullen; Harvard PhD and special forces
officer Kalev Sepp; prominent Army War College instructor and counterinsurgency theorist Steven Metz; Janine Davidson, who worked in the
Pentagon's Office of Stability Operations; Eliot Cohen, the storied expert
on civil-military relations; and Colonel H. R. McMaster, who was still
on assignment in Iraq but whom Petraeus conferred with via e-mail. It
took Petraeus and his team five months of thinking, researching, writing,
rewriting, and editing to complete their tome.[48]

In mid-February 2006, Petraeus gathered a group of scholars, journalists, academics, and heads of nongovernmental organizations for an
intensive two-day session to review the draft of FM 3-24 and recommend
changes. The resulting manual, published in December 2006, was an
instant hit, in large part because Petraeus's group of self-styled outsiders
had suddenly become insiders; they now called themselves "coindinistas."
Counterinsurgency was now all the rage. In Pentagon cafeterias, soldiers
and sailors had their pictures taken eating soup with a knife, while the
media celebrated the book, the only military field manual to be reviewed
by the *New York Times*. But all of this was prologue, yet to be tested fully
in Iraq. On February 10, 2007, David Petraeus got his chance when he
assumed command of US and coalition forces in Iraq.

"THREE FACTORS MADE the surge a success," Peter Feaver says. "The first
was Petraeus's strategic innovation, the second was the changed behavior
of the Iraqi leadership, and the third was the awakening." When he arrived in Baghdad, Petraeus huddled with Ryan Crocker, newly assigned
as the US ambassador, and hammered out a joint campaign plan that
focused on security, politics, diplomacy, and economics. Ray Odierno (the
commander of Multi-National Corps, Iraq) would handle the military
campaign, and Crocker would handle the Iraqi government, with Petraeus serving as coordinator, strategist, and spokesperson. Petraeus then
gathered an entourage of twenty advisers, a Joint Strategic Assessment
Team, to help him with the day-to-day fine-tuning of the fight. Included
in the group were Peter Mansoor, H. R. McMaster, and David Kilcullen.[49]

The additional five brigades (some twenty-four thousand troops) did
not bring the surge to full force until June, but Petraeus hit the ground

running, instructing Odierno to establish a string of joint security bases ringing Baghdad (there were more than seventy in all), ordering that concrete barriers be erected to separate Baghdad's warring sects, and doling out money to Anbar's tribal leaders, who were forming the anti-al-Qaeda Sons of Iraq. The plan was based on Petraeus's Fort Leavenworth template, which was included in a two-page, twenty-eight-point guidance for US troops—a kind of short course on counterinsurgency. At its center were four key advisories: "live among the people," "foster Iraqi legitimacy," "employ money as a weapon system," and "learn and adapt." Every decision was debated, monitored, and constantly assessed, with Petraeus getting a detailed daily early morning briefing. He ignored criticisms that he was doling out money to former regime thugs in Anbar, was deaf to grumblings from the Iraqi political establishment, and ignored complaints that he was straining US units to a breaking point. In fact, he was. The strain on the Army and Marines was enormous. The operational tempo was grueling, chewing up units, weapons, and ammunition at nearly unsustainable rates. Some soldiers were on their third tour in Iraq, and four thousand Marines in Anbar had their tours extended by seven months. But Petraeus desperately needed the troops, whose job it was to break the back of the insurgency.[50]

On June 16, Odierno ordered US units to begin Operation Phantom Thunder, a series of combat-intensive clearing operations in central Iraq. The key was taming the city of Baqubah and areas northeast of Baghdad, as well as the area near southern Baghdad where al-Qaeda held sway. The operation lasted until August 13, with a precisely tabulated enemy casualty list of 1,196 killed and 6,702 suspects detained. Phantom Thunder disrupted the insurgency by clearing its sanctuaries, interrupting its troop flows, and removing its top commanders. It "ripped the heart of al-Qaeda," Peter Mansoor later wrote. But US casualties remained at their pre-surge levels. "We knew this would take time," Mansoor says, "with the results coming slowly." While it wasn't obvious at the time, Mansoor adds, Phantom Thunder was a turning point. "In the annals of military history," he later wrote, "Phantom Thunder may not rise to the level of the Normandy invasion, but it was an enormously important and successful operation that in the summer of 2007 turned the tide of the war in Iraq."[51]

For David Petraeus, the surge strategy was a race against time, which, he concluded, was measured differently in Baghdad and Washington.

In Baghdad, the clock needed to be accelerated. Political reform, sec-tarian reconciliation, institutionalizing his new thinking, recasting the US military's relationship with the Iraqi people, reaching political ac-commodations with a host of local leaders, and fighting the insurgency couldn't wait—everything needed to be done now, right away. "We need to do this yesterday," he'd tell his staff. But in Washington, the clock needed to be slowed, to ease the political pressure Petraeus was feeling to show immediate results. "We have to be patient," he said. "This will take time." He needed time to allow what he'd put in place to work. The US commander made this clear in September when he and Crocker appeared before the House and Senate to provide an update on the war. It was the most unusual of hearings: millions of Americans tuned in to hear Petraeus, with the hearing rooms crowded for two separate all-day appearances. Petraeus's first appearance, on the afternoon of September 10, was overshadowed by the publication of a full-page MoveOn.org ad-vertisement (the organization is known for its progressive public policy positions) in the pages of the *New York Times* that morning. The ad ac-cused Petraeus of cooking the books on Iraq, then labeled him "General Betray Us." Every independent report on the ground situation in Iraq, the ad said, "shows that the surge strategy has failed."

The "General Betray Us" line detracted from the advertisement's cen-tral message—which was that the surge wasn't working—and turned out to be counterproductive: if anything, it subtly tipped congressional sympathy in favor of the Iraq commander. Petraeus had been in Iraq for just six months, which was hardly enough time to judge whether the surge was working. And Petraeus was quick to deny the ad's main points: the books weren't "cooked," and his remarks to Congress had not been seen by the White House. "Although I have briefed my assessments and recommendations to my chain of command, I wrote this testimony myself," he said. "It has not been cleared by, nor shared with anyone in the Pentagon, the White House, or Congress." Petraeus's nine-page pre-sentation was unambiguous. The US was making progress, he said, with the levels of violence in Iraq coming down. The surge was working. But at the heart of his presentation was a plea. "It will take time," he said. "Our assessments underscore, in fact, the importance of recognizing that a premature drawdown of our forces would likely have devastating consequences."[52]

Petraeus's use of the term "our" was purposeful, though not simply because Ryan Crocker testified with him. Petraeus's view of the State Department echoed the cooperative position taken by Robert Gates. When he arrived in Baghdad he teamed with Crocker, telling his senior aides that this would be a partnership. Once, when he arrived at a meeting with Crocker already present, the room was called to attention. Petraeus was mortified and afterward pulled aside a major from his staff. No one is to stand at attention for me when the ambassador is in the room, he told him. "Do you understand why?" The major shook his head. "Because he outranks me," Petraeus said. When it happened again, Petraeus patiently repeated his requirement, but decided the best way to stop the practice was to ensure that he arrived at meetings with the ambassador, or before him, so that when people stood they were standing for both of them. Petraeus wasn't Franks or Sanchez or Wes Clark; he didn't care about the size of his hotel suite, or who outranked whom. While he may have had a large ego, and it often got out of control, he commanded it when it counted.[53]

While Petraeus partisan and Army colonel Peter Mansoor later called Petraeus's two-day appearance before Congress a "tour de force," its members were not wholly convinced by his testimony. This was not a matter of partisan disagreement: both Republicans and Democrats reflected the views of the electorate, which was skeptical of the American effort and disenchanted with the war.

If there was one false note, it was Petraeus's answer to the question of whether the Iraq war had made America safer. Petraeus's answer was long, rambling, and uncertain. "I don't know, actually," he replied, "I have not sat down and sorted it out in my own mind." He then fidgeted a bit, before adding that he was doing what all commanders do, which is to give the best recommendations "to achieve the objectives of the policy from which the mission is derived." Later, Petraeus sounded more upbeat. The United States, he said, had "very, very clear and very serious national interests in Iraq. Trying to achieve those interests—achieving those interests has very serious implications for our safety and for our security." The answer wasn't believable, but it didn't need to be. Petraeus's job was to buy time, and he'd done that. He was confident, self-assured, and in control. Exiting the hearings after the second day, Mansoor turned to him. "Sir," he said to Petraeus, "you just bought us six more months."[54]

THE CLOCK WAS running for David Petraeus, but it was also running for Bob Gates, whose first months on the job left him deeply troubled. The sense of urgency he thought he would find in the Pentagon simply wasn't there: it was as if nearly everyone had concluded that, since the United States would be leaving Iraq eventually, there was no requirement to meet the war's needs. The services, he concluded, were preoccupied with planning, training, and equipping while, as he said, "assigning lesser priority to current conflicts." That was an understatement: Iraq was in crisis, but for many senior Pentagon civilians and senior military officers it seemed like business as usual.

Addressing this issue—signaling a sense of urgency to the military command, as Gates later wrote—was at the heart of nearly everything he did. Gates imposed this sense of urgency in his language and schedule, but over time his frustrations would get the better of him, and he would simply bypass, relieve, or fire officials who didn't understand his requirements. He never did this cavalierly, but always openly and only after checking with other military leaders and after conferring with the president. He kept his rage in check, in part, by making certain he was holding a cup of coffee in his right hand while meeting with top officials.

Gates's first crisis resulted from a *Washington Post* investigation of "squalid living conditions" at Walter Reed Army Medical Center in Washington. After a personal investigation, which included a walk-through of the facility, Gates forced the relief of the hospital commander, reversed the appointment of his successor by the secretary of the Army, and then insisted on the Army secretary's resignation. It was a salutary signal: failure would be punished, not rewarded.

Nearly a year into his tenure, Gates learned that the Air Force had mishandled nuclear weapons on a B-52 flight from North Dakota to Louisiana. Air Force personnel in North Dakota, it turned out, loaded actual nuclear missiles instead of mock training rounds on the B-52. Gates was told that three colonels and four noncommissioned officers had been relieved of command. Several months later, Gates learned that "forward assemblies" of ICBM nose cones had been inadvertently shipped to Taiwan. When a subsequent investigation showed "an overall decline in Air Force nuclear weapons stewardship," Gates relieved Air Force secretary Michael Wynne and fired Air Force chief of staff T. Michael Moseley, a controversial commander. Gates was at his pithy best, reaching Moseley while Gates was on an overseas flight. Moseley's assistant took the call, saying the chief of staff was then engaged in a ceremony, and would call him back. Gates was nonplussed, issuing what a civilian official who was accompanying him described as "the four most important words" in recent Air Force history—"this won't take long," he said.[55]

And when the Army dragged its feet on providing upgraded MRAP (mine-resistant, ambush-protected) vehicles to soldiers in Iraq because of fears that this purchase would cut into their readiness budget, Gates pulled rank. "This isn't a suggestion," he said. The MRAPs were purchased and shipped. It cost the Army $15 million, a small price to pay, it seems, to save the lives of the soldiers the Army said it cared for.

But Gates's most important command decision was far less controversial, though he found it as uncomfortable as any he'd made. In June 2007, even before the final tranche of US surge forces had arrived in Iraq, Gates was told by members of the Senate Armed Services Committee that Peter Pace's reappointment as JCS chairman for a second two-year term would be met with congressional opposition. Pace had become a lightning rod of dissent for the way the war was handled, Gates was told, and as a symbol of Bush's controversial surge policy. Pace wanted to fight for reappointment, but Gates told him that his chances of winning were no better than 50–50. Reluctantly, he stepped aside, and the president announced he would not be reappointed. His successor, Bush said, would be Chief of Naval Operations Michael Mullen.[56]

The appointment of Mike Mullen was popular with the Navy and welcomed by nearly everyone: Mullen, it was said, was intelligent and articulate. Mullen was pure Navy, an officer and a gentleman. He was tested, savvy, willing to take on the tough assignments, and selfless. He understood the Navy, had led a life of impeccable good judgment. But most important of all, his admirers claimed, he was a modest man who didn't care for the trappings of office.

CHAPTER NINE

Mike Mullen: The Navy's George Marshall

"We weren't searching for the right
strategy, we were searching for
the right number."

A DMIRAL MIKE MULLEN had an agenda. He wanted to "fix the Army," develop a defense strategy for the Middle East, and "rebalance" US forces. "It's all linked," he told a reporter, "and at the heart of that is the need to be successful in Iraq and Afghanistan." The two wars, he noted, had strained the Army, whose soldiers were facing multiple deployments. Mullen's views were the primary reason he was recommended by Bob Gates as the new JCS chairman. What is your top priority? Gates had asked him when they met to discuss the JCS job. The Army, Mullen said. Mullen was not only a good strategic thinker, Gates concluded, he wasn't a service partisan: hearing a Navy officer talk about the Army was refreshing.[1]

But Mullen also had another item on his agenda. During his first days as chairman, Mullen told his senior staff that he wanted them to remodel his office, with a new desk built to his specifications and televisions arrayed so that he could look up at them. And some of the walls needed to come down, replaced by oddly jutting bookcases. Like the bridge of a ship. He was expansive, gesturing, explaining what he meant. The JCS chairman's old desk, in place since Omar Bradley headed up the chiefs in the late 1940s, was packed up and a new one, built to Mullen's specifications, put in its place.[2]

The aides scrambled to get the job done, and soon walls came down, new wiring was added, and large paintings of great moments in the US Navy's triumphant history were mounted. But Mullen's aides worried that the tens of thousands of dollars spent on the remodeling would be leaked to the press followed by a spate of stories asking why Mullen was spending money on an office when he should be focusing on Afghanistan and Iraq. That never happened. Nor, it seems, did Bob Gates say anything about the changes, though he undoubtedly knew of them. Gates was a Mullen partisan and the two were close. When named as JCS chairman, Mullen was to have moved into Quarters Six, at Fort Myer, but he decided to stay in the house reserved for the chief of naval operations near the State Department. Mullen's decision created havoc among senior commanders, who now shuffled command billets to accommodate him. But the arrangement had its positives: Gates had leased the house next door, and would wander over and sit with Mullen on his porch, smoking cigars.[3]

A 1968 Naval Academy graduate, Mullen had served in nearly every Navy position at sea and in Washington, and was the first JCS chairman to attend the Harvard Business School's executive program. The Harvard Business School program had a special place in his biography. But Mullen's career had not started well: in his first command, he'd run his ship into a buoy, received a negative evaluation, and spent the next twenty years getting it expunged from his record. Mullen was well spoken and savvy when it came to dealing with the press. But that wasn't a surprise: it was in his blood, as his parents had been Hollywood press agents, with his father Jack counting Bob Hope, Jimmy Stewart, Phyllis Diller, and Carol Burnett among his clients.[4]

This background helps to explain why Mullen was at ease with journalists, deflecting tough questions with a quick answer, followed by a subtle pivot. Was the US military overstretched by Afghanistan and Iraq? Mullen would bring his hands to a peak, shifting the question from Iraq and Afghanistan to military families. Being in a combat zone, he said, was like raising children. "There's no group that's quicker to tell me what's really going on than a group of spouses," he told one reporter. Mullen put great confidence in naval commander John Kirby, as savvy a press handler as anyone in Washington. At Mullen's direction, Kirby fanned out across Washington, talking with reporters and historians. What Mullen wanted was to reassert the influence of the chairman's office and be "an independent voice," Kirby said. "Like George Marshall."[5]

Marshall became one of the most influential officers in US military history not only by shaping the US military in World War II, but also by speaking directly to the American people in occasional radio addresses. He was a masterful Washington insider, artfully navigating Congress. During hearings, Marshall would repeat the administration's talking points, but then add that if the questioner wanted his personal views, he would be happy to provide them in private. He never did, of course, but he left the impression that what he said in private was new and unique, and his listeners went away convinced they had the inside story—directly from George Marshall himself. In the years ahead, as Mullen served under both President Bush and his successor, Barack Obama, Mullen would follow the same script, though, as it turned out, with far less discipline than Marshall. Like Marshall, Mullen was anxious, Kirby said, to present a more public profile. And that's what Mullen did, speaking at policy forums in Washington, flying to military bases to speak with military families, and appearing before local associations, clubs, and foreign policy groups. Mullen was public, effusive, high-profile; he was the anti-Shelton.

In his first public address as JCS chairman, Mullen appeared at Washington's Center for a New American Security. His speech repeated the standard recognition of America's soldiers and their impressive morale. But Mullen was blunt about what Afghanistan and Iraq were doing to the military. "Are the ground forces broken? They are not," he said. "And I will do everything I can to keep them from breaking." While Mullen didn't say so directly, he was convinced that one of the ways to keep the "ground forces" from breaking was to make sure that Afghanistan and Iraq were the last wars of their kind. He was even more outspoken in private. "No more adventures," he told George Casey, the new Army chief of staff.[6]

"NO MORE ADVENTURES"—OR, at least, that was the hope. The problem, of course, is that (as military professionals regularly note), in any conflict "the enemy gets a vote." That was increasingly obvious in Iraq during George Bush's last year in office, where the Americans had a vote, the Iraqis had a vote, the insurgents had a vote, and so too did Iran.

On July 2, 2007, US forces captured Ali Mussa Daqduq, a senior Hezbollah commander, along with several other Iranian-backed operatives. Daqduq's capture was proof of Iranian meddling in Iraq, for the Lebanese-based, Shia "Party of God" had close ties with the Islamic Republic that dated from the early 1980s. Then two weeks later, in a Baghdad briefing, Brigadier General Kevin Bergner announced that the al-Quds Force, a wing of the Iranian Revolutionary Guard, was providing anti-armor weapons to Shia extremist groups in Iraq. In fact, both Hezbollah and the al-Quds Force had been operating in Iraq almost from the moment of the US invasion. Iranian special forces officers were training Iraqi militiamen to fight the Americans at camps near Tehran and shipping sophisticated explosive devices to their Iraqi proxies. Army and Marine units increasingly found themselves in firefights with militias supplied by the Islamic Republic. Senior members of the al-Quds Force had been seen in southern Iraq as advisers, with Iranian logistics officers running supplies to Iraq's Special Groups—Shia militias operating in alliance with al-Sadr's Mahdi Army—which US military officers identified as Iranian-directed killing squads.[7]

In fact, the United States and Iran had been heading for a military confrontation since 2003, when Bush named Iran as part of an "Axis of Evil." But Iran had been a problem since the 1979 Islamic Revolution, with US Marines facing off against Iranian-supported Shias in Lebanon in the early 1980s, and CENTCOM fighting Iranian naval assets in the Persian Gulf later in the decade. Now US soldiers were being killed in Iraq by Iranian proxies. The situation was likely to get worse, with the US pressing Iran on its nuclear program. When, in Bush's first term, Iran balked at European demands that it suspend its program, the president had supported four separate UN Security Council resolutions to slap economic sanctions on the Islamic Republic. The administration then pressured foreign banks to stop doing business with Tehran. Through all of 2007, Bush had insisted the military regularly update him on Iranian military capabilities, supplementing these briefings with regular CIA background talks on Iranian politics. This was a "deep dive," according to reporter Peter Baker, with Bush learning as much as he could on the topic. The more he learned, the more convinced he became that Iran was developing a nuclear capability.[8]

Bush's conviction was reinforced in September 2007, when Israel bombed a nuclear site in Syria. Outside of Hezbollah, Syria was Iran's most important ally. If Syria's nuclear program was a threat, then so too was Iran's. During a press conference after the Israeli strike, Bush told reporters that if people wanted to avoid "World War III," they should prevent Iran from "having the knowledge necessary to make a nuclear weapon."[9] The anti-Iran offensive was supported by Israel's friends in Washington, who pushed hard for a tough line on Tehran, saying the Islamic Republic was developing a bomb. Israel, they argued, would be the target. But while these groups received a warm hearing on Capitol Hill, few in the military believed them. "The Israelis and their friends have been saying that Iran is a few years away from a nuclear bomb every year for the last ten years," a CENTCOM war planner said at the time, "and it's never been true." But this skepticism wasn't based solely on what military officers actually knew. Rather, their views reflected a growing mistrust of Israel inside the American high command. The belief that the Bush White House had launched the Iraq war to make the Middle East safe for Israel had taken root among a growing number of influential military officers. Increasingly, Israeli Defense Forces officers visiting Washington found themselves unwelcome in military circles.[10]

At the beginning of the Iraq war, senior Israeli military officers were regularly invited by American officials to brief CENTCOM officers on what they'd learned about Arabs in dealing with the Palestinians. "The IDF were everywhere," a CENTCOM officer remembers, "handing out advice, giving briefings"—including several on how to handle Iraqis in American custody. A senior colonel remembers one such briefing. "They said they had three rules for 'dealing with Arabs,'" he remembers. "The first was that when you took them prisoner make sure to blow up their houses, then strip them naked before you question them, and always use dogs—because Muslims hate dogs." Inevitably, the presence of the IDF was resented. The US military was the best in the world, its officers felt, and didn't need advice from anyone. The growing resentment toward Israel was now translated into doubts about Israel's influence on American policy on Iran. In one incident, in early 2008, a senior Israeli military officer gave an Iran briefing at the National Defense University. The room

was filled with three dozen senior military officers and a handful of civilian officials. When the Israeli finished his briefing, the first comment
came from a Pentagon civilian. "If you think we're going to do this for
you again you're wrong," he said. The Israeli officer was startled. "Do
what again?" he asked. The civilian explained: "You think we're going
to fight your wars to the last drop of American blood. Well, you've got
it wrong. You have a lot of friends in the Pentagon," he said, "but not as
many as you once had."[11]

But while Israel's claims about Iran's nuclear program were greeted
skeptically by the military, they were believed by the White House, even
after the administration received a national intelligence estimate (NIE)
reporting that Iran had suspended its nuclear program in 2003. "Iran:
Their Intentions and Capabilities," was put on the president's desk in late
2007. Bush had trouble believing the report, so he ordered the CIA to
take a more critical look at its sources. When the NIE returned with the
same conclusion, the White House was disappointed. "This is a disaster,"
national security adviser Stephen Hadley told Bush. Fearing the report
would be leaked, Bush's team decided to release a sanitized version of it
to the press. Bush then pushed CENTCOM to focus on three catego-
ries of Iranian meddling in Iraq: attacks from Iranian units disguised as
Iraqis, attacks from Shia militias with ties to Iran, and attacks from Shia
militias "inspired" by them. The word "inspired" was now a part of the
lexicon, with attacks by Iraqi Sunnis "inspired" by al-Qaeda and attacks
by Iraqi Shias "inspired" by Iran. Bush made the link: "isn't it interesting," he said, that al-Qaeda and Iran were both killing Americans.[12]

By December 2007, the prospect of a US-Iran military confrontation
in the Persian Gulf was the talk of Washington. Joseph Cirincione, the
director of nonproliferation at the Carnegie Endowment for International
Peace, was telling reporters he was convinced that the administration's
strategy was to repeat what it had done in Iraq; the administration would
make claims about Iranian capabilities as an excuse to launch a war, just
as it had done with Saddam. All of this gave Bob Gates fits. With the US
military tied down in Afghanistan and Iraq, the last thing the United
States needed was a war with Iran. He'd worked to dismiss speculation
that the administration was planning an Iran war through all of 2007,
then visited Israel and Saudi Arabia to dampen their anti-Iran animus.
Gates wasn't as worried about a US attack on Iran as he was about an
attack from an ally that would require an American intervention. After

his visit to Israel, Gates concluded that the US, Iran, and Israel were operating "on different clocks." The US goal, Gates believed, was to "slow down both the Iranian nuclear and Israeli military clocks, while speeding up the [US] sanctions/pressure clock."[13]

But Admiral Fox Fallon, who'd taken over as head of CENTCOM when John Abizaid retired, had a different clock. Fallon's goal was not simply to slow the clocks, but to stop them altogether. Fallon said as much during a series of interviews even before he took on his new command at CENTCOM. The idea that the United States would engage in an attack on Iran, he said, "strikes me as not where we want to go, and not what we want to be engaged in."[14] Over the next months, as the Bush administration escalated its anti-Iran rhetoric, Fallon escalated his. Nine months into his tenure at CENTCOM, Fallon told a *Financial Times* reporter that hitting Iran would be a mistake. An Iran war, he said, would not be "the first choice in my book," implying that that wasn't necessarily true for the president.[15] For Gates, serving out the Bush administration's last months in office, Fallon's statements on Iran were exasperating. Every time Fallon said that he opposed a war with Iran, Gates had to say that the administration wasn't planning one. Gates had the same problem with Mullen, who was as irritating on Afghanistan as Fallon was on Iran. Mullen focused on Afghanistan nearly from the moment he took over as JCS chairman. The US was being whipsawed in the Middle East, Mullen said: at the same moment that US casualties were falling in Iraq, they were increasing in Afghanistan. In public, Mullen said that the administration was right to focus on Iraq, but he then pivoted to Afghanistan where, he pointedly noted, there were shortfalls in "capability and capacity."[16]

During a meeting in the Oval Office in January 2008, Gates noticed that "something was bugging Bush," so he asked him about it. Bush gave a pointed response: were Fallon and Mullen "on the same page" as the White House? "What is it with these admirals?" he asked.[17] The next day, Bush asked Gates if Petraeus should replace Fallon at CENTCOM. Gates defended Fallon, adding that Petraeus wanted the job as supreme allied commander in Europe. Bush dropped the suggestion, but he wasn't the only one concerned with Fallon: so too was David Petraeus. Fallon and Petraeus had a testy relationship, primarily because while Fallon was Petraeus's boss, the Iraq commander had the president's ear. A JCS officer characterized the relationship as "absolutely dysfunctional." Fallon, he said, "would push Petraeus on something, and Petraeus would play his president's card. 'Well, I just talked with the president,' he'd say, 'and that's not what he says.' Sometimes [Petraeus] would mention his discussions with the White House just to make Fallon squirm." Fallon knew what Petraeus was doing, but he couldn't help himself. Their conversations were abrupt, disrespectful. "That little pissant really gets under my skin," Fallon told his staff.[18]

In mid-February, Gates received a call from Fallon warning him that *Esquire* magazine was publishing an article about him that might cause problems. The piece, by military reporter Thomas Barnett, appeared at the end of the month. The article's lead repeated Fallon's worries that the White House was planning an Iran attack. "If, in the dying light of the Bush administration, we go to war with Iran, it'll all come down to one man," Barnett wrote. "If we do not go to war with Iran, it'll come down to the same man." Fallon, Barnett implied, stood between the US and the apocalypse, the one sane voice in an administration whose president "regularly trash-talks his way to World War III." The article also focused on the Fallon-Petraeus relationship, quoting the admiral as calling his Iraq commander an "ass-kissing little chickenshit." Fallon denied the quote, but not the sentiment.[19]

Gates read the article and knew it would anger the White House. On March 6, with Mullen present, Bush talked to Gates about it. "Do we have a MacArthur problem?" Bush asked. Gates gamely tried to defend Fallon. No, the administration didn't have a MacArthur problem, he said, adding that Fallon wanted to apologize. Bush waved that off. He didn't want to humiliate Fallon, he said, "but he kind of boxed me in." Mullen said he thought Fallon should offer to resign, but Bush put off making a decision: "Let's see what happens." The next day, Gates received a letter from Fallon apologizing for his remarks and then, three days later, and after an extended discussion with Mullen, Gates announced that Fallon was retiring. The next month Bush named Petraeus as Fallon's successor at CENTCOM, with Ray Odierno taking over as the commander in Iraq. Gates later said that Fallon was well within his rights to provide his candid advice to Bush, but was wrong to do it in the press. Few senior military officers would have disagreed, even if Fallon became a kind of folk hero in the Navy. But he was never a MacArthur, and the Fallon incident was never a MacArthur moment. Bush had his history wrong:

MacArthur had been dismissed for trying to expand a war; Fallon was forced to retire for trying to prevent one.[20]

IN ANY OTHER era, Arizona senator John McCain might have been a shoo-in for president. Certainly, he would have been the military's choice. A naval aviator, decorated combat veteran, and former prisoner of war of the North Vietnamese, McCain knew more about the military than any other elected official—and certainly more than the junior senator from Illinois, Barack Obama. It seemed inarguable that, in the 2008 campaign for the presidency, no one was as prepared to be commander in chief than he was. Yet, while postelection polls showed that the majority of military families voted for McCain in large numbers (just as they'd voted for George Bush in 2004), those most affected by Afghanistan and Iraq voted for Obama. According to one report, there was a significant shift in six of fifteen military communities whose personnel contributed the most to the conflicts. "Combat-experienced military communities sent a message in 2008," one analyst noted: "Keep the year-long deployments going, keep the bellicose rhetoric up, and you will lose elections to Democrats." No more adventures, Mike Mullen had said, and the public agreed.[21]

In fact, opposition to the Bush administration's military policies among senior officers was significant. Retired officers flocked to Obama during the campaign, a follow-on from the Generals' Revolt of 2006. As crucially, Obama's election was greeted with relief at the Pentagon, many of whose officers had clashed with the outspoken McCain over the years. Mike Mullen flew to Chicago for a forty-five-minute meeting with Obama prior to the inauguration, and came away satisfied that the president-elect was "a pragmatist," a sure signal that he believed Bush hadn't been. Officers were also pleased by Obama's appointment of retired Marine general James Jones as his national security adviser, and his decision to retain Bob Gates as defense secretary. The appointments would mean they would be listened to in the new White House.

Obama's campaign had focused on the nation's economic crisis, which had begun with a financial meltdown in the housing industry in 2007. The contagion spread through all of 2008, with the car industry on the edge of a financial abyss, banks collapsing or near collapse, and businesses unable to get loans. In any other time, the spiraling economy would have resulted in the repudiation of the previous administration, but to this was added America's deep disenchantment with the Bush administration's wars. Obama laid out his military and foreign policy vision just as he secured his nomination: "ending the war in Iraq," refocusing the nation on "the fight against al-Qaeda and the Taliban," making sure terrorists and rogue states didn't obtain nuclear weapons, achieving "true energy security," and "rebuilding our alliances."[22]

By Obama's inauguration, in January 2009, Afghanistan had become the incoming administration's top priority, particularly since Bush had signed a status of forces agreement with Iraq in December that pledged the United States would withdraw its troops from the country by the end of 2011. But even before that, the US commander in Afghanistan, General David McKiernan, had issued a request for a four-brigade reinforcement. This sounded like a plea: McKiernan had been reporting to new CENTCOM commander David Petraeus since the summer of 2008 that the Afghanistan fight was escalating, with foreign fighters pouring into the country from Pakistan. "This thing is headed in the wrong direction," he'd told Petraeus. "If you want me to turn it around, I'll need more troops."

Gates agreed that Afghanistan was reaching "a tipping point"—where the presence of US soldiers sent to stabilize the country (he thought) could actually destabilize it. It was only a matter of time before American troops were viewed as occupiers. "Given Afghanistan's history," Gates later reflected, "if the people came to see us as invaders or occupiers, or even as disrespectful, I believed the war would be lost." Gates counseled McKiernan to pay more attention to the impact of US operations on local populations, directing that compensation be paid to families of those caught up in the cross fire even before they filed a grievance.

The Afghanistan problem was agenda item number one when Obama and Vice President Joe Biden arrived at the Pentagon for their first post-inauguration meeting on January 28. A line of service members greeted Obama in the hallway outside the JCS offices, as Obama smiled and joked with them. "He knows how to turn on the charm," Chief of Naval Operations Gary Roughead told an aide. Norton Schwartz, now ensconced as head of the Air Force after Gates's relief of Michael Moseley, agreed. "Now we know why he won the election," he muttered to no one in particular. In fact, the meeting failed to make headlines, with Obama reassuring the service heads that he welcomed their views and that he would be focusing on "getting it right" in Iraq and Afghanistan, a promise he'd made during the campaign.

If anything, the new administration's earliest days were eerily reminiscent of Bill Clinton's. The day following the inauguration featured news reports speculating on whether Obama would repeal Clinton's "Don't Ask, Don't Tell" policy on gays in the military. Mullen, meanwhile, told his staff the story of his first Clinton-like meeting with the president-elect, which had taken place at Obama's transition office in Chicago. It was always good for a laugh. He'd arrived early for the meeting and was greeted by a young staffer. "Mike Mullen," he said, "here to see Mr. Obama." The woman checked her scheduling book: "And you are?" The story hearkened back to Barry McCaffrey's Clinton anecdote, sixteen years before. But Obama was not Clinton: his staff was more well-organized and he was more self-confident. Obama wasn't a womanizing, draft-dodging good old boy, and he wasn't intimidated by anyone, in or out of uniform.[23]

IN HIS ADMINISTRATION'S first days, Obama assigned CIA veteran Bruce Riedel to conduct a review of the Afghanistan war and come up with recommendations on how to fight it. Bald, wonkish, and intense, Riedel was an expert interrogator, "all give and no take," as one JCS officer said. "You'd sit there with him for two hours, and before you knew it you'd spilled everything and he wouldn't have said a word. When he got what he wanted, he was out the door. He was smart and competent, but an intellectual bully." The Riedel study wasn't due for another two months, but in the meantime Obama approved a request from McKiernan for another seventeen thousand troops for the Afghanistan fight. Obama made the announcement three weeks into his term, saying the United States needed to stabilize the "deteriorating situation," while adding that Afghanistan had "not received the strategic attention, direction, and resources it urgently requires," a nearly word-for-word echo of Mullen's advice to Bush. But Obama worried that Afghanistan might pull him into a morass, consuming his presidency. He would own it.

Riedel provided his assessment to Obama on Air Force One during a trip the president took to California in March. Riedel didn't round off the corners: the situation in Afghanistan was bad and was likely to get worse. Al-Qaeda remained a threat and Pakistan was a problem: the latter was harboring Taliban fighters and allowing al-Qaeda to regroup. The Taliban, Riedel said, was making gains. Obama had asked for a recommendation, so Riedel gave him one: a military and civilian surge that would reverse the military trends and push back on the Taliban. Even then, Riedel said, Afghanistan could be a problem for a very long time. The real challenge for the administration, Riedel insisted, was Pakistan. For a brief moment, the discussion turned to JCS chairman Mike Mullen, who had developed a close working relationship with General Ashfaq Parvez Kayani, Pakistan's powerful Army chief of staff. Mullen aired his Kayani discussions at nearly every meeting, saying he and the general were developing a close relationship. Riedel was skeptical. Don't rely on what Mullen tells you about Kayani, he warned Obama.[24]

On March 20, Obama announced his decision, telling his national security team that he would be sending another four thousand military trainers to Afghanistan. The lone dissenter was Joe Biden, who thought the war politically untenable and expressed his fear that the United States would "overcommit." It was a constant refrain with Biden, repeated so often that the president would snap back. "Got it Joe," he'd say. "Noted." For Biden, the problem was not in Pakistan, but in Kabul. Biden could be emotional, hectoring, blunt. "Why are we sending more troops when we don't even have a strategy?" he'd asked during one Afghanistan meeting, then dipped into his hallmark speaking style, asking a rhetorical question and answering it in his patented somber voice. "Does that make sense? I submit that it doesn't." But now, after the Riedel study, there was a strategy. It was revealed by Obama on March 27. His words reflected Riedel's findings: the announcement was about Afghanistan, but the focus was Pakistan. "The future of Afghanistan is inextricably linked to the future of its neighbor, Pakistan," Obama said in a nationally televised address. "In the nearly eight years since 9/11, al-Qaeda and its extremist allies have moved across the border to the remote areas of the Pakistani frontier." Obama pushed Congress to approve $1.5 billion in aid to Pakistan (an inducement, it was thought, to support Pakistan's cooperation in the anti-Taliban fight), then said he was directing his special envoy for the region, Richard Holbrooke, to work with CENTCOM commander David Petraeus "to integrate our civilian and military efforts."[25]

Bob Gates approved the policy, but thought it didn't go far enough. The defense secretary was worried that the United States had the wrong commander in Afghanistan. Dave McKiernan was admired for his blunt style and willingness to speak his mind. He'd done so during Operation Iraqi Freedom, when he'd taken on Tommy Franks over troop numbers. Franks, who'd rarely deferred to anyone, deferred to McKiernan. But troop numbers had become a constant refrain for the Afghanistan commander, who never thought he had enough. Then too, McKiernan had a testy relationship with David Petraeus, his nominal commander, in a replay of the Fallon-Petraeus competition. "The two couldn't be in the same room together," a McKiernan aide said at the time. "We knew there'd be a fistfight if we left them alone." The disagreement was personal: McKiernan resented answering to an officer whom he'd once outranked.[26]

But the two also disagreed about how to fight in Afghanistan. Both McKiernan and Petraeus agreed that the Taliban posed a security challenge, but McKiernan gave weight to competent governance. Nor was McKiernan a fan of the surge, doubting claims that it had made the difference in Iraq. "This isn't Iraq," he would snap.[27] What Afghanistan needed, he said, was "a sustained commitment." When Petraeus pushed McKiernan to engage Afghanistan's tribes, McKiernan rejected the advice. "I don't want that," he'd said, explaining that it "wouldn't take much to go back to a civil war." And McKiernan didn't give a fig for those US allies, including a number of NATO nations (like Canada, the United Kingdom, and Germany), who provided military support as a part of the anti-Taliban coalition. "Some come to conduct war; some come to summer camp, quite frankly," he told reporters. It was true, but it wasn't the kind of thing you say in public.

In mid-April, Gates told Obama that he, Mullen, and Petraeus had agreed that McKiernan should be replaced by Lieutenant General Stanley McChrystal, a celebrated special operations officer. Mullen admired McChrystal; he was responsible for getting McChrystal the job as director of the Joint Staff, and was his chief Pentagon defender. McChrystal was also admired in the Army. He was known for shaking things up: he'd taken over the Joint Special Operations Command and, according to one of his senior assistants, "had really turned it into something." He was universally admired. "If you were to ask me who was the finest officer of his generation, I'd say Stan McChrystal," a retired senior officer says now. "David Petraeus would be number two." Mullen talked him up with Gates, suggesting he replace McKiernan. Gates agreed. The only drawback for McChrystal was his recommendation that Pat Tillman, a former NFL safety and Army Ranger, be given a Silver Star for battlefield heroism. McChrystal had signed off on the commendation, but later regretted it when it was determined that Tillman was killed by friendly fire. It was an embarrassing moment, but Mullen believed McChrystal had gotten past it. "He's solid, absolutely solid," Mullen told one of his staff, "and he's the right guy for Afghanistan."[28]

Gates and Mullen had received a briefing from McKiernan in the closing days of the Bush administration, and neither of them was impressed. When Mullen flew to Kabul to meet with McKiernan in mid-April, senior Joint Staff officers put two and two together: since replacing McKiernan was Mullen's idea, Gates said he should be the one to break the news to him. Mullen was confident he could convince him to step aside. But McKiernan dug in his heels: his tour would end in 2010 and he'd stay until then. "You're going to have to fire me," he told Mullen. McKiernan was disgusted: here was the JCS chairman deciding on who should fight America's wars. What did Mike Mullen know about war? "This is a guy who steers boats," he told his staff.[29]

Gates followed up in May, and McKiernan finally agreed. Hearing that he should retire from Mullen was one thing, hearing it from Gates was another. While he submitted his retirement papers, all of Washington knew he'd been fired, and the press searched for adjectives to describe it: "defenestrated," "axed," "executed," "ousted," "shown the door." For senior Army officers, the man responsible was Mike Mullen, who said that McKiernan wasn't up to the job. "There are those who would have waited six more months," Mullen told reporters, "but I couldn't. I'm losing kids and I couldn't sleep at night. I have an unbounded sense of urgency to get this right." It was a breathtakingly insulting thing to say. If he thought American deaths were keeping him awake in Washington, he might have imagined what it was doing to Dave McKiernan in Kabul. "You could feel the chill right away," a Joint Staff officer observed. "The army guys could hardly look at Mullen. It was grim." Mullen's aides told reporters that one of McKiernan's problems was that he wasn't willing to adopt the strategies that David Petraeus had used in Iraq. So McChrystal was a step up. Like Petraeus he was admired in Congress and knew how to handle the press. He was, as Mullen said, a part of the military's "'A' team." But that's not what McKiernan's soldiers thought. When McKiernan addressed them just before his departure, he was blunt. He didn't want to leave, he said, but when the people in charge in Washington made a decision, good soldiers obeyed. At the end of his speech, he noticed a line had formed. "What's this?" he asked. "They want to shake your hand," his aide said. McKiernan complied, going soldier-by-soldier for the next ninety minutes.[30]

STANLEY MCCHRYSTAL ARRIVED in Kabul in early June 2009 with instructions from Gates to conduct a sixty-day study of the war. His staff fanned out in the country, along with a fourteen-person team of outside thinkers assembled from Washington think tanks. "They absolutely flooded the zone," a US development officer said. "They were in every province, every village, talking to everyone."

But Stan McChrystal not only flooded the zone in Afghanistan, he'd also flooded the zone in Washington. In his second month as director of the Joint Staff, McChrystal had established the Pakistan-Afghanistan Coordinating Cell (PACC), a thirty-person military-civilian operations group housed in the Pentagon's National Command Center. "This isn't a place you just wander in and out of," a senior Pentagon official said. The PACC reported directly to McChrystal. For senior Joint Staff officers, McChrystal's PACC seemed like the perfect setup. "Anytime anyone had a question about Afghanistan," a Joint Staff officer noted, "there would be Stan McChrystal with the answer. He was always angling for McKiernan's job."[31]

But McChrystal had as many admirers as critics, especially among those who'd served with him. McChrystal was a tough fighter, smart, and cared about his soldiers, they said. If there was one negative, it was his lack of political experience. Contrary to what reporters had been told by Mullen, McChrystal seemed out of place in Washington. His first meeting with Obama had not gone well; the president had cracked a joke and McChrystal had stood confused, not knowing whether to laugh. "McChrystal has a solid reputation for knowing the fight," a special operations officer wrote at the time of his appointment. "Unfortunately, though our special operators are the best in the world . . . they only stumble and fumble with the press. With media, our special operations forces are clueless and self-defeating. This is crucial. McChrystal can win every fight on the ground and still lose the war." The comment, as it turned out, was prescient.[32]

By the end of the summer, McChrystal's team had concluded that the United States was in a crisis in Afghanistan that could only be reversed with more troops. Senior State Department officials rolled their eyes. "What a shock. When has a military commander ever said he doesn't need more troops?" one of them asked. For McKiernan partisans the rumored request brought knowing nods: McKiernan had asked for more troops and been stiffed, but now that McChrystal was asking for them, everyone was invested in his success. He'd been anointed. "From the minute that McChrystal showed up in Kabul, he drove the debate," a White House official confirms. "It was no longer a question of whether we should follow a military strategy or deploy additional troops. It was always, 'should we do 20,000 or 30,000 or 40,000, or even 80,000'? We weren't searching for the right strategy; we were searching for the right number."[33]

A senior State Department official, watching from her perch in Washington, remembers the frustration among the department's top policymakers, who believed the Afghanistan war called for a political solution: "We kept saying 'this is about politics,' and the Pentagon would say, 'that's right, but to do politics you have to have security.' We were going around in circles." The frustration permeated the US embassy in Kabul, where US ambassador Karl Eikenberry concluded that McChrystal was too full of himself to listen to anyone. The appointment of Eikenberry in March 2009 had been greeted with skepticism in the State Department because of his background as a West Pointer and a retired lieutenant general. If anyone would be sympathetic to McChrystal, it would be Eikenberry. But that's not what happened: Eikenberry won friends among diplomats for his quick understanding of their problems and his open irritation at McChrystal's imperious manner.[34]

"McChrystal came in and he just thought he was some kind of Roman proconsul," an Eikenberry colleague notes. "He didn't need to consult with the State Department, let alone the ambassador. This was not just the military's show, it was his show." Often, Eikenberry and McChrystal would cross paths as McChrystal was coming out of a meeting with Afghanistan president Hamid Karzai. "Don't you think I should be a part of these meetings?" Eikenberry would ask. "I'll keep you informed," McChrystal would say, and he would breeze on by.[35]

By the summer of 2009, with its focus almost solely on Afghanistan, Barack Obama's national security team began to splinter. It was the Clinton years, but in reverse. Then, the military had mistrusted the White House; now the White House mistrusted the military.

The problem started with Mullen, who was too public and too unpredictable; he seemed to always be going off script, leaving the impression that he wasn't quite in sync with the White House. Worse yet, Obama's staff had learned via the State Department grapevine that McChrystal's sixty-day Afghanistan study would call for more troops. Mullen had replaced McKiernan because he was always asking for more; now here was McChrystal doing the same thing. Obama, White House aides thought, was being boxed in. Gates, Mullen, and the military, on the other hand, were bewildered by the White House's focus on "messaging," on how a policy would play with the public. Messaging was an obsession for Obama and his team and, senior military officers feared, the single most important factor in policymaking.

But the divisions were also personal: Thomas Donilon, the deputy national security adviser, didn't get along with James Jones, his boss, while Jones felt Donilon was going around him to the president. Jones seemed tentative, overly formal. Donilon, on the other hand, knew Obama well. The Donilon-Jones competition was mirrored throughout the decision-making process. Biden, Biden's staff, Obama chief of staff Rahm Emanuel, foreign policy adviser Mark Lippert, strategic communications assistant Ben Rhodes, and Donilon were on a different page than Gates and the military. Inevitably, Mullen's high public profile and rumors that McChrystal would ask for more troops spurred Obama's staff to mutter about the emergence of a military "bloc" that was maneuvering the president into a corner on Afghanistan.

In mid-July, Obama talked with Gates about Mullen. Obama said that he wanted to name the JCS vice chairman, Marine general James "Hoss" Cartwright (the name came from the character "Hoss" in the television western *Bonanza*), as Mullen's successor. What did Gates think? Gates was alarmed. Mullen wasn't due for reappointment to a second two-year term until October, he said. If Obama's views leaked before then, it would make Mullen a lame duck. Rumsfeld had done that with Eric Shinseki during the Bush years, and it had been a disaster. Obama agreed to wait, but Gates realized that the president was more comfortable with Cartwright than with Mullen. More than once in an NSC meeting, Obama had turned to Cartwright, soliciting his views. "What do you think, Hoss?" he'd ask. Cartwright, who grew up on a farm in Iowa, was a plug of a man, standing half a head shorter than Obama and Mullen, and was an outlier in the Marines, having climbed the command ladder as an aviator. Cartwright was easygoing, Mullen was ponderous. Cartwright used a homey twang, Mullen was deep voiced, going on and on. Cartwright was Des Moines, Mullen was LA.[36]

In July, Mullen flew to Afghanistan for a briefing from McChrystal about the situation in the country. McChrystal gave a sobering account: nearly all of southern Afghanistan was in the hands of the Taliban. We need to turn this around, McChrystal said, but to do that I need more troops. How many more do you need? Mullen asked. Forty thousand, McChrystal said. When Mullen told this to Gates, the defense secretary was floored. Two weeks later, Gates and his staff met McChrystal at an air base in Belgium. McChrystal repeated what he'd said to Mullen. McChrystal's briefing lasted five hours, a Bush-like "deep dive" that covered every aspect of the war. It was compelling, convincing, and included political as well as military recommendations.

Gates might have been surprised by McChrystal's request, but he'd already set the stage for it, having a blunt talk with Rahm Emanuel on the need for Obama to take "ownership" of the war. Gates told Emanuel that he was going to ask the president to approve a deployment of five thousand "enablers" (medics, intelligence personnel, explosives experts) for Afghanistan. The request, he emphasized, was necessary to protect American troops. Gates reiterated these points in a meeting with Obama and Biden. The president was focused on options, while Biden was focused on messaging. A second meeting took place in early September and once again Gates said he needed Obama to approve the deployment of five thousand enablers. Obama was irritated. Enablers? Why do we need enablers? he asked. This sounded like "mission creep," he snapped. Gates was upset by the meeting. Deploying five thousand enablers wasn't a military issue, he told Biden, but a moral one.

Even before Obama had a chance to grapple with the McChrystal review, David Petraeus weighed in. Petraeus was set off by a September 2 column in the *Washington Post* by David Ignatius, suggesting that a counterinsurgency campaign wouldn't work in Afghanistan. "Even in Iraq," Ignatius wrote, "the successes attributed to counterinsurgency came as much from bribing tribal leaders and assassinating insurgents as from fostering development projects and building trust." Petraeus "absolutely had a fit," one of his aides remembers. "The Ignatius piece was a personal affront. It made Petraeus sound like a two-bit mobster, doling out money to the locals." These people, Petraeus said, "need to get their history right."[37]

Petraeus called the *Washington Post* columnist Michael Gerson to correct the record. Petraeus was worried that McChrystal would see him as niggling away at him from the sidelines, but he was most concerned that the triumphant surge narrative in Iraq not be questioned, one of his aides remarked at the time. On September 4, 2009, Gerson's column ("US Has Reasons to Hope for Afghanistan") reflecting the Petraeus position was published: "only a fully resourced counterinsurgency strategy" will work in Afghanistan, Gerson quoted Petraeus as saying. Doing anything else would ensure defeat. Obama's aides were irritated: King David wasn't niggling away at McChrystal, he was niggling away at them; he made it sound like Afghanistan was lost unless Obama followed his advice. Worse yet, at least from the White House point of view, Petraeus had used Gerson, a former Bush administration official, to convey the message. But while this was irritating, it should not have come as a surprise: Petraeus was chummy with all kinds of folks in Washington, but most especially with its neoconservatives, the same people who'd gotten the United States into Iraq. "This was the Keane and Kagan crowd," a White House aide later complained, then compared Petraeus and his followers to religious fanatics. "You know, the Congregation for the Propagation of the Faith"—the Inquisition.[38]

One week after the Gerson column appeared, McChrystal's assessment, sixty-six pages in length, was circulated to Obama's team, along with the endorsement of Gates, Mullen, and Petraeus. McChrystal's assessment was just that: it did not include troops numbers. On September 13, Obama convened the first in what would be nine intensive meetings on the Afghanistan war. The gathering included Biden, Secretary of State Hillary Clinton, special envoy Richard Holbrooke, a senior intelligence briefer, Mullen, Gates, Cartwright, and Obama's top advisers, about a dozen officials in all. Obama wanted to hear every opinion. By the end of the meeting, it was clear that the debate would come down to whether to adopt McChrystal's troop-heavy counterinsurgency strategy or Biden's argument that the United States refocus it efforts away from the Taliban to al-Qaeda, Pakistan, and enhanced training of Afghanistan's army. Biden called his strategy "counterterrorism-plus."[39]

Obama laid out the issues, an intelligence officer presented his community's views on Pakistan, and Mullen gave a PowerPoint presentation of McChrystal's assessment. Biden then spoke up. It takes ten years for a counterinsurgency strategy to work, he said, and lots of troops. He tapped a copy of McChrystal's study. "This is all about Afghanistan," he said, "but if you don't get Pakistan right, you can't win." It was a restatement of Riedel's conclusions. Obama ended the meeting by laying out the options and asking questions. The key one, posed by Biden, was on the agenda: "Is pursuing a broader counterinsurgency the best way to advance our goal?"[40]

If there was any doubt among Obama's staff that a "military bloc" had already decided the issue, it was dispelled during Senate hearings on Mullen's confirmation for a second two-year term as JCS chairman. During his testimony, Mullen came down on the side of McChrystal. "The Taliban insurgency grows in both size and complexity," Mullen said. "That is why I support a properly resourced, classically pursued counterinsurgency effort." A "classically pursued counterinsurgency?" That sounded like Petraeus. The president's advisers were enraged. Mullen was defensive: he'd given the White House a copy of his remarks before the hearing. "What's the problem?" he later asked Donilon. Donilon couldn't believe it. "The problem?" he said. The problem is that "you've sandbagged the president of the United States."[41]

Then, on September 21, the *Washington Post* published a declassified version of the McChrystal assessment, under the headline "McChrystal: More Forces or Mission Failure." This was followed by an October 1 statement from McChrystal during an appearance in London before the prestigious International Institute for Strategic Studies. Not surprisingly, McChrystal backed his proposed counterinsurgency strategy, but his off-the-cuff remarks were puzzling. For an officer who was appointed, in part, because he knew how to handle the press, McChrystal seemed ham-handed. He had no problem in making his views public, he said, and appreciated the fact that he was able to speak out. Of course, he added, "they may change their minds, and crush me someday." It was meant to elicit laughs, but no one in the White House thought it was funny. Sensing his misstep, McChrystal told David Petraeus that he would "lay low for a time." Petraeus said he thought that was a good idea.[42]

But the officer feeling the most pressure was Mike Mullen. Following McChrystal's London speech, Mullen had had a long discussion with James Jones, who reminded him that the job of the JCS chairman was to prevent a civilian-military breach, to "act as a kind of translator" for the military, as Jones put it. That's your job, and you're not doing it, he said. While Obama needed McChrystal, he said, that wasn't true for everyone. He was explicit: if it were up to him, someone would be fired, implying it would be Mullen or Petraeus. Mullen knew he was right. Preventing a civilian-military breach was the job of the chairman. So the next time Mullen met with the president, he went out of his way to reassure him that the military welcomed the Afghanistan review. Obama pointed out that he felt he was being pressured by the military to approve their recommendation, that Mullen, McChrystal, and Petraeus were purposely arrayed against him, forcing his hand. "We would never do that," Mullen said. In fact, as Mullen knew, that's exactly what they were doing. But Mullen's pledge put Obama at ease, reassuring him that while he remained uncomfortable with the admiral, that was no reason not to reappoint him for a second two-year term as the JCS chairman. Then too, as Obama knew, Mullen was popular among many senior officers, particularly in his own service.[43]

MULLEN WAS BELOVED by the Navy, whose officers described him as one of the JCS's greatest chairmen. Diplomat Richard Holbrooke said Mullen was the only officer he'd ever met who was as interested in other countries as he was in his own service. "He has the widest-ranging intellectual curiosity of any chairman I've known," he told one reporter. "He'll invite members of my staff to his office and discuss Afghan agriculture for hours." Mullen partisans cite five reasons for their praise: his work to repeal Don't Ask, Don't Tell, his focus on the Army, his support for the operation that killed Osama bin Laden, his handling of Pakistan, and his opposition to the Obama administration's decision to intervene in Libya.[44]

Mullen began pressing for the repeal of Don't Ask, Don't Tell during his first year as JCS chairman, urging President George Bush to revisit the issue. But with the nation consumed with Iraq, Bush wasn't listening. When Obama took office, allowing gays to serve became a Mullen priority. He reversed the long-standing opposition to gay service among JCS chairmen and pushed Obama to take action. In February 2010, Mullen reframed the controversy. "No matter how I look at this issue," he told the Senate Armed Services Committee, "I cannot escape being troubled by the fact that we have in place a policy which forces young men and women to lie about who they are. . . . For me personally, it comes down to integrity—theirs as individuals and ours as an institution."[45]

Mullen's testimony spurred resentment among his colleagues, who felt their views had been ignored. Repeal of the act was opposed publicly by retired general Chuck Horner, and in private by Air Force chief Norton Schwartz and Army chief George Casey. "You're fixing a policy that isn't broke," Schwartz argued. Marine Corps commandant James Conway also opposed Mullen. "I will fight you on it," he told him. Mullen was unfazed. In a meeting in the tank on May 25, 2010, he faced his colleagues. "This is going to happen," he told them. "The president is committed to it and so am I." Told of the meeting afterward, Horner said he couldn't remember a time when the chiefs were so divided. Mullen was "doing Obama's bidding on this one," he told reporters. But when Obama convened the JCS to hear their views, each of them lined up with Mullen, and when the president signed the repeal during a gathering at the White House, Mullen received a standing ovation.[46]

Mullen made the Army his focus, emphasizing increased attention to postcombat psychological care and shorter deployments. "He'll be remembered as one of the best JCS chairmen in history, just because of that issue," fellow Naval Academy graduate Harlan Ullman says. "What other chairman can you cite who made the entire military his business?" But Mullen also egged on the Army's top leadership to increase its focus on building special operations capabilities, one of the reasons he'd supported McChrystal's appointment in Afghanistan.[47]

After the successful operation to kill Osama bin Laden at his Abbottabad compound in Pakistan in May 2011, senior Army officers believed one of the reasons why Mullen was so outspoken in supporting it was because it was being conducted by a twenty-three-person team from the Naval Special Warfare Development Group (the "Devgru"). This was a matter of service pride and parochialism: the Navy would get the credit for the operation, when the war in Afghanistan had been fought by the Army. But in this case, the Army's paranoia about the Navy was misplaced. When the operation was in its infancy, one of the first calls made by CIA director Leon Panetta was to Vice Admiral William McRaven, who was in charge of the military's Joint Special Operations Command. McRaven then requested a plan from a prominent Devgru officer, who made the assignment. Mullen flew to Nevada to watch SEAL Team Six practice the operation. He liked what he saw. A devout Catholic, Mullen had stood fingering his rosary beads in the White House Situation Room during the operation, leaning down to talk to Joe Biden, who'd pocketed his after it was announced bin Laden was dead. "Mr. Vice President, not yet," he'd said: the SEAL team had not yet cleared Pakistani airspace.[48]

Mullen is also celebrated for expanding the JCS chairman's mandate, as a kind of unofficial Obama administration envoy to Pakistan, where he befriended army chief Ashfaq Kayani. Mullen's goal was to wean Pakistan away from supporting terrorist groups the United States was fighting in Afghanistan. He cajoled and feted Kayani, pressuring him to take steps against the Taliban and al-Qaeda in Pakistan's far western provinces, where the groups had taken refuge after the US invasion of Afghanistan after 9/11. Mullen thus established himself as one in a long line of sailor-diplomats, a tradition begun by Captain James Biddle, who negotiated the first trade treaty between the US and China; Commodore Matthew Perry, who opened Japan to the West; and Fox Fallon, who rebuilt US military ties to China.

But Mullen is most consistently praised for opposing the US intervention in Libya. What came to be called Operation Odyssey Dawn began on March 25, 2011, when the United States and its NATO partners enforced a no-fly zone in the country to keep Libyan dictator Muammar Qaddafi's military from slaughtering prodemocracy rebels in Benghazi, the nation's second largest city. The Libya uprising was the third in a series of events marking what came to be called the "Arab Spring." The Libya protests followed by two months a series of popular uprisings that had replaced the dictatorships in Tunisia and Egypt, as well as burgeoning conflicts in Syria and Yemen. The protests, particularly those in Egypt and Syria, had taken the White House by surprise, but none of them had spurred calls for intervention, except Libya. The intervention was supported by White House special assistant Samantha Power (the author of a Pulitzer Prize–winning book on genocide, *A Problem from Hell*) and UN ambassador Susan Rice. Gates and Mullen were opposed. At one point during the Libya debate, Gates pointedly reminded Obama's staff that the US had its hands full. "Can I finish the two wars I'm already in before you guys go looking for a third one?" he asked. Mullen agreed, channeling Colin Powell's face-off against Madeleine Albright: this isn't a game where you move pieces around a board, he said.[49]

Secretary of State Hillary Clinton joined Gates in opposing intervention, but then broke with him after she met with Libyan opposition leader Mahmoud Jibril in Paris on the night of March 14. Clinton grilled him on his vision for Libya, posing a menu of pointed questions. One by one, the American-educated Jibril answered her. She was impressed. On March 15, during an NSC meeting on the crisis, Clinton (who joined the meeting on video from Cairo) weighed in on the side of intervention. For Obama, her shift was the tipping point. Pressured by Great Britain and France, and with Power, Rice, and Clinton in favor of stopping a slaughter, Obama instructed Rice to seek a UN resolution backing the US position. Two days later, UN resolution 1973 gave the United States and NATO a free hand in Libya, and on March 19, 120 US cruise missiles slammed into Qaddafi's air defense systems. At the end of March, the US ceded control of the operation to NATO, and Odyssey Dawn became Operation Unified Protector. The US, the administration said, was not taking the lead in Libya—it was "leading from behind."[50]

But Odyssey Dawn was not a success. After Qaddafi was hunted down and then ignominiously executed the next October, Libya descended into chaos, with Obama admitting the United States "had not adequately planned for the day after." In private, he called Libya a "shit show." Odyssey Dawn also had a pernicious impact on the military, which stood behind Mullen in opposing the intervention. Senior military officers were embittered by Clinton's about-face on intervention, by Susan Rice's micromanagement of the conflict, and by Samantha Power's advocacy for "R2P," the US "responsibility to protect" vulnerable populations. For senior officers, Libya was a replay of Bosnia, a dark repeat of Madeleine Albright's assertive multilateralism. In military shorthand, Clinton, Rice, and Power were "cruise missile liberals," or worse: "the coven." Retired Army colonel Andrew Bacevich, a professor at Boston University (and perhaps the most respected commenter on America's Middle East interventions), called them "the three harpies"; from good intentions, he said, they'd created a "Somalia on the Mediterranean."[51] But, unlike previous controversial interventions (and especially the one in Iraq), at least the military leadership had taken a more careful view and stood its ground in opposition to Clinton, Rice, and Power. And while Mullen had lost the debate, he'd stubbornly reflected the military's views.

The president and his aides might not have been able to answer the question "and then what," but Mullen and the military had—as Libya, they predicted, would end up in chaos.

Mullen partisans cite him as one of the great JCS chairmen, but his critics are as vocal, saying he was responsible for the mistrust of the military that Obama developed in his first term. The charge sheet starts with Mullen's decision to replace David McKiernan in Afghanistan, but includes what many military officers view as his competition with and personal animus toward Vice Chairman James Cartwright, "Obama's favorite general." In mid-October 2010, Cartwright proposed the president adopt a "hybrid option" on Afghanistan: opting for 20,000 fewer troops than the 40,000 requested by McChrystal with a focus on rebuilding the Afghan military. McChrystal, Petraeus, and Gates opposed Cartwright's recommendation and Mullen pressured Cartwright to keep it under wraps. "I don't want that to leaving the building," Mullen told Cartwright when he heard about his plan. Cartwright wasn't intimidated. He told Mullen that it was his duty to provide his advice and that was what he was going to do. "I have an oath," he said. But instead of going directly to Obama, he provided his option to Biden and James Jones.[52]

The president welcomed Cartwright's 20,000-troop plan, primarily because it reset the debate: it was no longer 40,000 or nothing—and it was a way to respond to critics who said his real choice was to do what the military wanted or "cut and run." It was not only a good middle ground, it set more modest and reachable goals. On October 30, Obama called the joint chiefs to the White House. It was an unusual meeting. In effect, the president was going around Mullen, who was now relegated to onlooker. Mullen was noticeably uncomfortable during the meeting: he hadn't kept his colleagues briefed on the Afghanistan debate, on the differing troop numbers, or on the disagreement over what reasonably could be accomplished. They were out of the loop. Army general George Casey told Obama that he didn't think that another 40,000 troops could defeat the Taliban. Obama nodded, noting that the goal now was to "disrupt" them. That was "Stan's advice," Obama added. Casey hadn't heard this, hadn't been informed. He was embarrassed and there was a long silence: "Oh, well," Casey said, looking at Mullen, "that makes a huge difference."[53]

But the most important advice given Obama during the meeting came from Marine Corps commandant James Conway. He was unconcerned with the debate over troop numbers, and instead focused on the military's mission. He'd seen what happened when US troops had been given responsibility for rebuilding a country. "Don't get caught up in nation building," he told the president. "There are things there that we can't solve. They have to do it, it's their country." Obama was pleased—the military was no longer providing a common front. It was Mullen, Petraeus, and McChrystal versus Cartwright, Casey, and Conway. The Cartwright-Casey-Conway list soon grew to include US ambassador Karl Eikenberry. In early November, Eikenberry forwarded a memo on Afghanistan to Hillary Clinton. It was a stunning repudiation of McChrystal's advice. The counterinsurgency strategy proposed by McChrystal wouldn't work, Eikenberry wrote: there was too much reliance on increased US troops, the Afghanistan president was not a reliable partner, and the proposal didn't address the problem of enemy sanctuaries in Pakistan. "I am concerned," Eikenberry wrote, "that we have not fully studied every alternative."[54]

Eikenberry was convinced he was right, but the memo was also his response to McChrystal's "I'll keep you informed" comment: McChrystal had stiffed Eikenberry, now Eikenberry stiffed him. Mullen was incensed. "This is outside the chain of command," he sputtered. Of course, Eikenberry was not only not in the chain of command, he was perfectly within his rights to give the president his advice. David Petraeus told Mullen to calm down. It was worse than that, Mullen said: Eikenberry had just destroyed whatever trust he'd had with McChrystal. The team in Kabul was splintered. But the State Department sided with Eikenberry. "You can only be treated like a bunch of idiots for so long before you get fed up," one State Department diplomat remarked. "It was briefing after briefing, PowerPoint after PowerPoint, all filled with this military lingo and it all sounded pretty empirical and data driven. But it was all nonsense and it all amounted to the same thing—who do we kill. Well, it won't work."[55]

The Eikenberry memo shifted the debate, but it was James Cartwright who organized the opposition. The differing opinions that Obama had sensed in his meetings with the JCS were made official in an NSC meeting on November 23. Prior to the meeting, Cartwright had privately polled his JCS colleagues on McChrystal and Mullen's argument that it was troop numbers that would make the biggest difference. The JCS was unanimous: McChrystal and Mullen were wrong; it wasn't the numbers that mattered, it was the strategy. The JCS supported "flexibility" on the troop deployment, Cartwright told the NSC, downplaying the troop numbers issue. This wasn't about numbers, but whether the deployments could be used effectively to rebuild the Afghan military. Around the table, Obama's advisers suddenly realized that Cartwright was speaking for the joint chiefs, while Mullen was speaking for McChrystal.

At the end of the November 23 meeting, Obama said he would make a decision on Afghanistan in the week ahead. Then, on December 1, he announced the United States would be sending thirty thousand more troops to Afghanistan in a speech at West Point. The troops would be deployed "at the fastest pace possible," he said, "with the goal of starting to withdraw forces from the country in July 2011." This was Cartwright's "hybrid-option," with a plus. But the real message was that Obama was not going to commit the nation to a troop-heavy, long-term, and expensive commitment.[56]

The loser in the debate, senior officers felt, was David Petraeus, whose counterinsurgency crusade had taken a hit. There wasn't going to be an open-ended surge in Afghanistan, with the military in charge. Instead, there was going to be a more modest deployment, focused on political ends. But the other loser was Mike Mullen, who'd stood with McChrystal. This was not a surprise, for once Mullen supported McChrystal he was wedded to his ideas. "You know, when a captain appoints an exec [the second in command, an executive officer] he never gives him a bad evaluation," a Navy colleague of Mullen noted. "Why would he? It reflects poorly on his choice. So Mike stood at the altar with Stan, and that was that. For better or worse."[57]

"YOU KNOW, I like Mike Mullen, I really do," a classmate of his at the Naval Academy says, "but he can be vengeful. It's who he is." The Joint Staff saw this first hand, and not just during the debate over the Afghanistan surge.

On January 16, 2010, a senior military officer and a State Department official from CENTCOM arrived at Mullen's office to brief him on the Israeli-Palestinian conflict. The team was dispatched by David Petraeus to underline his worries at the lack of progress in resolving the issue. The briefers reported that there was a growing perception among Arab leaders that the United States was incapable of standing up to Israel, which was jeopardizing US standing in the region. The briefers told Mullen that their conclusions followed from a December 2009 tour of the region where, on Petraeus's instructions, they spoke to senior Arab leaders. The real problem was that Israel was continuing to build settlements on Palestinian land in the West Bank, and the US was perceived as doing nothing about it. Mullen was surprised and puzzled, and wasn't sure that he agreed. Was it really that bad? he asked.[58]

Petraeus, as it turned out, was as surprised as Mullen. He'd noticed illustrations of the al-Aqsa Mosque in Jerusalem in a large number of Iraqi houses when he was in command there and had asked his staff about them. When told they were a standard symbol of Arab solidarity with the Palestinian cause, he was taken aback. "Is this issue really that important?" he'd asked. His staff told him it was: the mosque was in East Jerusalem, which had been occupied by the Israeli military since 1967. Mullen expressed the same disbelief during the January briefing, turning to a young woman whom he relied on for her expertise on the region. She knew Israel well, and was a dual Israeli-American citizen. This whole thing about settlements, is that true? he asked her. She shook her head. "No, Mr. Chairman," she said. "These concerns are exaggerated."

When a story about the briefing was published two months later, Petraeus e-mailed author Max Boot, expressing fears the story would undermine him with Israel's friends in Washington. "Does it help if folks know that I hosted Elie Wiesel and his wife at our quarters last Sun night?" he asked. "And that I will be a speaker at the 65th anniversary of the liberation of the concentration camps in mid-Apr at the Capitol Dome." Boot reassured him: don't worry, he said, it will pass. But Mullen was livid, telephoning Petraeus at his headquarters. The article, he said, made him look like an idiot and he insisted the general discipline the leakers. Petraeus did. "Go home and stay there," he told the officer who gave the briefing. Later, speaking from his Tampa residence, the Army officer was contrite. "I'm a big boy, I can take it," he said. "But I'm only getting out of here when Mike Mullen says I can." His sin wasn't leaking a story that made Israel look bad, he added, but one that made Mike Mullen look bad.[59]

But there were limits to Mullen's vengefulness. He'd recommended Lieutenant General Stanley McChrystal as Dave McKiernan's replacement in Afghanistan, then supported him in the Pentagon, telling him he could have the pick of anyone on the Joint Staff to take with him on his new command assignment. The support continued even after McChrystal's 2009 London statement that while the White House supported him in Afghanistan, "they may change their minds, and crush me someday." The crisis passed when Obama met McChrystal aboard Air Force One during a presidential trip to Europe. Obama's confidence in his Afghanistan commander was also buoyed by Mullen's reassurance that McChrystal's London gaffe "won't happen again."

But it did. In June 2010, *Rolling Stone* magazine, in a full-length portrait of McChrystal, quoted the Afghanistan commander and his staff uttering beer-fueled judgments of Washington's civilian leaders. Obama was intimidated by the military, McChrystal told reporter Michael Hastings, while his staff referred to Vice President Biden as Vice President "bite me." McChrystal, the article reported, was surrounded by staff sycophants (one of whom called Jim Jones "a clown") who played follow-the-leader in taking pokes at the White House. The article's title, "The Runaway General," said it all. On June 23, Obama met with McChrystal at the White House, thanked him for his service, but said he would be replacing him as the US commander in Afghanistan. Obama then huddled with his national security team before telling an aide that he needed to see David Petraeus. Petraeus arrived just as Obama's team was filing out of the Oval Office. When Petraeus arrived, Obama began: "As your president and commander in chief," he said, "I am asking you to take over command in Afghanistan." Petraeus had always wanted to be JCS chairman, but now that was out of the question. Obama's appointment was not a suggestion. "Yes, sir," Petraeus responded.[60]

DAVID PETRAEUS WAS the hero of the Iraqi surge, the military officer who, in the midst of a crisis, had turned around a losing effort. He was photogenic, brash, outspoken, the darling of the media. If he seemed taken with his own fame (he kept a pile of signed photographs to pass out to admirers), it was at least hard-earned. When he became the commander in Afghanistan, he was the most admired and recognizable American in uniform. But as Petraeus knew, Afghanistan was not Iraq. During the NSC meetings on the Afghanistan surge, a back bencher had observed that Petraeus's normal self-confidence was noticeably absent. He knew he was inheriting a mess.[61]

The first McChrystal offensive had taken place in Helmand Province, where, in February 2010, US, Canadian, British, Danish, and newly trained Afghan troops took control of Marja, a city of fifty thousand; defeated the Taliban after a five-day battle; and installed what McChrystal dubbed a "government in a box." At first all went well. Coalition troops built schools, set up health clinics, dug wells, and repaired roads. But the government in a box was a disaster: the official picked by McChrystal as the district governor was despised by the locals and spent most of his time holed up under US protection. Inevitably he was removed and then, six months later, murdered.[62]

The Taliban responded to the Marja offensive by inserting themselves in northern Helmand while battling the coalition with a torrent of explosive devices. Worse yet, McChrystal's efforts to recruit Pashtun tribal members, a replay of the Anbar Awakening, yielded few results. Nor did passing out money to Afghan businesses, which had worked so well in Mosul. By July 2010, Marja was lost, with some two thousand US Marines and their coalition partners controlling the city by day while the Taliban controlled it at night. McChrystal called the city "a bleeding ulcer."[63]

David Petraeus said he was going to reverse this by doing what he'd done in Iraq: urging American troops to protect the population while he strong-armed the government into political reforms. As crucially, Petraeus said he would focus his efforts on keeping local populations out of the line of fire, imposing strict controls on when US units could use air, artillery, and helicopter strikes that might result in civilian casualties. McChrystal had accepted these strict guidelines during his time as commander, despite the grumbling of his subordinates, because winning the support of the local populations was the Nicene Creed of counterinsurgency doctrine.

But that's not what Petraeus actually did. When he took command, he discarded the strict rules of engagement, increased the number of US air strikes, deployed additional tanks to the battlefield, accelerated the training of the Afghan army, and sent special forces teams into the countryside on kill-or-capture missions. Petraeus didn't replicate the Anbar Awakening, but he made deals with local warlords and turned a blind eye to Afghanistan's massive drug trade. Like McChrystal, he sidelined US ambassador Karl Eikenberry, but unlike McChrystal he faced off against Afghanistan president Hamid Karzai in a series of long arguments about government corruption. During one particularly stormy session, Karzai said he was going to call Obama and have him replaced. "I will get you fired," Karzai yelled. Petraeus just smiled.[64]

Petraeus's goal was to force the Taliban to the negotiating table, which meant he was willing to use his forces not simply to "secure the population," but to kill the enemy. As in Iraq, Petraeus was on the clock. A successful counterinsurgency strategy takes years to show results; but Petraeus didn't have years, he had months: the Obama-imposed drawdown in US troops would kick in in mid-2011, which meant that he had to show significant progress in less than a year. In effect, Petraeus jettisoned FM 3-24, the counterinsurgency doctrine he'd written back at Fort Leavenworth, and put a more heavy-handed counterterrorism strategy, the Biden-Cartwright option (which he'd argued against), in its place. Over a period of nine months, Petraeus's, strategy yielded noticeable results. The uptick in US casualties that marked McChrystal's short tenure as Afghanistan commander leveled off, the nation's southern provinces quieted, and at least some of Afghanistan's new brigades proved battlefield ready. That was good enough for Petraeus, who in March 2011 told the Senate Armed Services Committee that his actions had reversed the tide of war, with the Taliban's momentum now fading in large parts of the country. Gates followed this up with a statement of his own: the good news on Afghanistan meant that the United States could begin withdrawing its troops from the country, as planned, by July. Afghanistan wasn't a victory, and Petraeus never claimed it was—it was "Afghanistan good enough," which is what King David had said about Iraq. In mid-2011, at least, and after ten years and thousands of American lives, it looked like the US was on its way out of the Middle East.[65]

Obama had made little secret of his desire to replace Mullen, first broaching the topic with Bob Gates back in mid-2009. The president had said he was toying with announcing Marine general and JCS vice chairman Cartwright as Mullen's eventual successor. Gates thought that was a bad idea, and Obama reluctantly agreed, but in three different conversations with Cartwright in the two years that followed, the president pushed him to take the job. Cartwright had said no twice, telling the president he was looking forward to retirement. But the third time that Obama asked, Cartwright said yes. Obama was pleased: "you're my guy," he told Cartwright.

But while Cartwright was Obama's guy, he was also under a cloud. In the middle of the Afghanistan debate, the Pentagon's inspector general opened an investigation to determine whether Cartwright had acted improperly with a young female staff member. The accusation included a tawdry report that, while overseas, the young woman had once passed out drunk at the foot of Cartwright's bed. Cartwright ordered other staff members to haul her off, then issued a directive that any of his staff caught drunk while in uniform would be dismissed from the service. The IG's report cleared Cartwright of the charge of acting improperly, but cited him for maintaining "an unduly familiar relationship" with a subordinate. At the same time, rumors circulated in Marine circles that Cartwright's wife, in the midst of divorce proceedings, was going to "drop a bomb on Hoss" in a tell-all article about her wayward husband's conquests. By mid-2011, what was tawdry had become ugly.[66]

No one knows who fueled these stories, but senior Marine officers blamed Mullen. The chairman, they maintained, resented Cartwright for going around him during the Afghanistan debate. The stories reached into the daily press, which talked of a behind-the-scenes lobbying campaign among the military to get rid of Cartwright. The clear implication was that Mullen was the campaign's instigator. Mullen partisans rejected the claim. "Mullen didn't need to do a damn thing," one Navy officer says. "Cartwright did it for him." Gates agreed, becoming angry with reporters who suggested that Cartwright was being punished for being "Obama's favorite general." The reports, he said, were "garbage." That was true, but it was not what the Marines thought. A now retired Marine colonel remembers a day in March 2011, seven months before Mullen's retirement, when he was escorting a Marine major general to the commandant's office for a briefing. Coming toward them down the hall was Mullen. The major general confronted him. "Got him, got good ol' Hoss, didn't you, Mike," the major general said. Mullen was angry and moved toward his accuser, but thought better of it and kept walking.

In fact, Cartwright had two problems. The first was the gossip surrounding the reported incident with his female staffer. This was a sore subject for military officers, and had been since the Tailhook scandal was made public during the Clinton years. It set the chiefs against him. But Cartwright's second problem was actually much worse. Cerebral, bookish, an outsider in his own service, he'd not only done little to gain friends in Washington, he never got to know his fellow chiefs. Gates told this to

Obama when the president asked him about who should succeed Mullen. "You need a team player," Gates said. Cartwright wasn't. On May 21, 2011, in a private meeting at the White House, Obama told Cartwright that he wouldn't get the JCS job. Cartwright had seen it coming, and wasn't surprised. But the decision left Obama in a quandary. He wasn't comfortable with anyone else in the military's senior leadership. He considered naming Admiral James Stavridis, the head of the European Command, to the job, but Obama's meeting with him had not gone well. Norton Schwarz, the Air Force chief, was also a consideration, but he seemed to fit better as Cartwright's successor as vice chairman.

A few days after Obama's meeting with Cartwright, retired lieutenant general Doug Lute, who'd been appointed by Bush as his administration's military adviser on Afghanistan and Iraq (a "war czar," as the press dubbed him) and then stayed on under Obama as a civilian adviser on Afghanistan and Pakistan, got up from his desk in the White House and made his way to the Oval Office. This wasn't unusual for Lute, who got along with Obama and had faced off against Gates and Mullen during the Afghanistan debate. Gates called Lute a huge disappointment, primarily because Lute disagreed with Gates's pro-McChrystal views. But as far as Obama and his staff were concerned, Lute had gotten McChrystal right, while Gates had gotten him wrong.

Lute told the president he wanted to make a suggestion on who should succeed Mullen. Obama didn't respond, so Lute plunged ahead. He knew the perfect guy, a low-key general and team player. He was loyal. "Marty Dempsey," he said, "would be perfect for the job." Obama had heard this before, from Robert Gates, who had also mentioned Dempsey's name. That two officials who'd faced off over Afghanistan, and who clearly didn't like each other, could both recommend Dempsey was interesting, and the president was intrigued. Dempsey had recently taken over as head of the Army for George Casey, and had only been in that job for a month. But Obama had met with Dempsey and liked him. Of course, what Lute didn't tell Obama (though the president must have surely known) was that he was not only a friend of Dempsey (they'd been a year apart at West Point), they'd been brothers-in-law, having married the Sullivan sisters, Deanie and Maggie, of Monroe, New York. "You should think about it," Lute told Obama. The president said he would.[67]

CHAPTER TEN

The Rise of Martin Dempsey

"All of this stuff about building
trust is a bunch of bullshit."

O N June 22, 2011, Barack Obama told the American people that
he would withdraw 10,000 troops from Afghanistan by Christmas and a further 23,000 by the next summer. That would bring US
troop numbers in Afghanistan down from just over 100,000 to 77,000.
The announcement was not a surprise, though a number of senior military officers thought the deadline could be fudged. In fact, they'd taken
steps to ensure it: David Petraeus had provided an optimistic briefing to
Obama on the Afghanistan fight, and Mike Mullen, in his last months
as JCS chairman, had extolled the progress Petraeus had made. There
would be even more progress if the president kept the troops where they
were, they told Obama. And both officers quietly assured Congress the
president could be pressured by his secretary of state, Hillary Clinton,
and his secretary of defense, Bob Gates, to back off the withdrawal.
"Don't worry," Petraeus told Republican senator Lindsay Graham, "we'll
take care of this."[1]

Petraeus was wrong: Obama's June announcement kept his withdrawal pledge, and began to end the wars that started with 9/11. Iraq and Afghanistan had cost the United States $2 trillion and taken the lives of nearly five thousand Americans, one million Iraqis, and nearly fifty thousand Afghanis. The US failed to destroy al-Qaeda, plunged Iraq into a civil war, deepened the conflict in Afghanistan, divided the American people, sowed mistrust between military and civilian leaders, and nearly bankrupted the nation. So while the president claimed the withdrawals were the response to the progress made by David Petraeus, few in the Pentagon believed him. Obama had promised the American people as a candidate that the US would end its wars in the Middle East, and now he was keeping that pledge.

Obama was a poor bluffer: you could read his emotions on his face. Watching him through his first two years in office, senior military officers concluded that he never really believed the Afghanistan surge would work, and he didn't believe his military commanders when they told him they supported his decision to withdraw US troops beginning in July 2011. The pledge had come during one of the final meetings on the surge, when Obama had asked each of his top advisers, one by one, whether they supported him. And one by one they'd said "yes." But the Afghanistan debate left the impression that the military had maneuvered Obama into adopting a surge he didn't think would work. In exchange, the military had agreed to a withdrawal date they didn't support. Both sides saved face: Obama showed he would support the military, while the military showed it could get its way with the new president. For senior officers who'd monitored the process, what happened during the debate reminded them of a tale told often in the Pentagon. Taken from the ubiquitous management books studied by military leaders who hoped to thereby glean the intangible qualities of leadership they described, the tale offers a dark commentary on the dysfunctional relationship between the president and the military in the Mullen era.

In the early 1970s, according to the tale, a major US car manufacturer hired a consultant to advise it on its management techniques. Paid a substantial fee, the consultant had the run of the executive offices. So he decided, quite randomly, to observe a group of a dozen engineers debating what carburetor to use in a new car. It was a highly technical issue and the sometimes contentious debate went on for weeks, but finally the group reached a consensus. After the decision, the consultant spoke individually to each of the group's members. Not one of them, he discovered, agreed with the final decision. He gave his report on the incident to the company's management team. "You're broken," he said.

A now retired CIA officer made the same point about the Obama administration's Afghanistan debate. "It's the one thing I hold against Obama," he said, "because as he went around the room to each of the guys in uniform I could tell he just didn't believe them. And, really, it's not clear they believed themselves. Obama knew that. But he sat there and said, 'Well, okay.'" In the management example, the consultant was confronted by the company's executives. How should we change our system? they asked. "You don't need to change your system," he responded, "you need to change your people."[2]

WHILE A PRESIDENT can shape the military chain of command as he sees fit, that rarely happens. When Barack Obama became president, he inherited officers appointed by George Bush: Mike Mullen, James Cartwright, George Casey, the Air Force's Norton Schwartz, Chief of Naval Operations Gary Roughead, and Marine commandant James Conway. But by the spring of 2011, Obama had the opportunity to appoint their successors: General James Amos succeeded Conway, Admiral James "Sandy" Winnefeld replaced Cartwright, Ray Odierno took over for Casey, and Marty Dempsey succeeded Mullen. It was different for America's combatant commands, where the changes had a domino-like impact. This was especially true for Afghanistan, where David Petraeus's pending retirement shuffled the command deck.[3]

In April 2011, Obama named CIA director Leon Panetta to succeed the retiring Robert Gates as secretary of defense, then named Petraeus as Panetta's replacement at the CIA. Petraeus's appointment left Obama partisans puzzled: the general was a member of the Kagan-Keane set of neoconservatives, among the president's most outspoken critics. Obama was now inviting them into his administration. But the president's political advisers calculated that the move would make it difficult for Petraeus to run for president. General Doug Lute, still serving as a special assistant to Obama, had a different take, telling his military colleagues that the appointment showed that Obama had a "Powell problem." Obama didn't want to face off against Petraeus in the general election, and he didn't want to give him Powell's old position as JCS chairman. Everyone moved up a step: Odierno replaced Casey as Army chief of staff, James Mattis replaced Odierno at CENTCOM, and Petraeus's place in Kabul was given to Marine general John Allen.[4]

There were other changes. After firing Stanley McChrystal, Obama had replaced James Jones as NSC head, putting trusted political adviser Thomas Donilon in his place. Jones had never been a good fit for Obama because he was uncomfortable with the informal world the president and his team inhabited. In time, Jones had clashed with Donilon. Inevitably, Donilon and those around him worked to force Jones out, circulating stories implying he was lazy. Jones was embittered by his treatment, which his Marine colleagues viewed as shabby, a view that Jones did little to dampen. For Jones's closest friends at the top of the Marine Corps, Donilon became a marked man.[5]

The key change for the military was Marty Dempsey, who was sworn in as the new JCS chairman on October 1, 2011. Confident, understated, and modest, Dempsey had graduated from a Catholic high school, where he was a track star, and had never wanted to make the military his career. But he applied to West Point anyway, and when he received a letter notifying him of his acceptance his mother teared up in pride and that was that. He spent the next thirty-plus years out of the limelight commanding armor units, but had once spent two years teaching literature at West Point, and loved it. If Mullen was the anti-Shelton, then Dempsey was the anti-Mullen, a reputation he sealed by ordering that the JCS chairman's office be put back the way it was. His single vanity was his request that Mullen's desk be replaced by the one used by Douglas MacArthur in the Philippines. Dempsey admired MacArthur, and he wanted to show it. But the transition from Mullen to Dempsey was more than cosmetic. Mullen had once introduced a comedian to an assembly of soldiers by announcing that they would find the comic's humor "impactful." That wasn't Dempsey, who was at ease in public. Oddly, he became known as the "singing chairman" because he was an accomplished tenor. He would sing "Danny Boy" to his troops, who loved it, and was once introduced at a Washington Nationals baseball game: "Ladies and Gentlemen, please rise and join with the Chairman of the Joint Chiefs of Staff, General Martin Dempsey, in the singing of our National Anthem."[6]

Dempsey's appointment was welcomed by Obama's national security staff, which was exasperated by Mullen's habit of saying the wrong thing at the wrong time and by his seeming to have an opinion on everything.

Just weeks before Dempsey was sworn in as his replacement, Mullen told the Senate Armed Services Committee that Pakistan's intelligence service was providing support for the notorious Haqqani terrorist network which, he then added, was behind a recent suicide bombing in Kabul. The statement shocked the White House, though not because Mullen had said in public what everyone was saying in private. The problem was that the "credible intelligence" that Mullen cited didn't exist. At CENT-COM headquarters, an infuriated James Mattis described Mullen as "a complete idiot" who'd just "dropped a manhole cover" on Pakistani army chief Ashfaq Kayani. Repairing the damage was now in Mattis's hands.[7]

A part of the problem was that since the unexpected death of envoy Richard Holbrooke the previous December, Mullen had proven difficult to control. Holbrooke had acted as a brake on Mullen, tempering his public statements and advising him on his relations with the Pakistanis. Now, with Holbrooke gone, Mullen showed increased frustration in his meetings with Kayani, who constantly promised to move against the Taliban but never did. So after a while, the White House simply ignored the Mullen-Kayani channel. Bruce Riedel had been right when he'd told Obama that he shouldn't believe half of what Mullen said, especially when it came to the progress he said he made with the Pakistanis. That is what had spurred Mullen's testimony: he didn't like being embarrassed. Despite this controversy, Mullen's defenders pointed out that the retiring JCS chairman had much to his credit: the repeal of Don't Ask, Don't Tell, a focus on the Army, and a reassertion of the JCS chairman's influence. Well-informed, dignified, and articulate, Mullen was the highest-profile JCS leader since Colin Powell. But when he retired, he left behind a chasm of civilian-military mistrust as deep as any in the post–Cold War era.

DEMPSEY INHERITED A military struggling to recover from war. These kinds of transitions had never been easy, but they were most difficult when the wars were politically contentious. Bad wars spark years of re-thinking, igniting sometimes ugly exchanges over what went wrong, who was responsible, and what must be done to correct it. So the internal military debates over the US wars in Afghanistan and Iraq were entirely predictable, though different in one respect: they began even as the fighting raged.

In May 2007, as the first surge troops were headed to Iraq, Army lieutenant colonel Paul Yingling had published an article in *Armed Forces Journal* that laid the responsibility for the Iraq failure at the feet of the nation's military's leaders. Entitled "A Failure of Generalship," Yingling's article was the opening shot in the military's war over the war on terrorism, an ugly internal Army fight waged by the service's most prominent thinkers. In Iraq, Yingling argued, America's generals failed to "envision the conditions of future combat," failed to correctly estimate how to achieve "the aims of policy prior to beginning" the war, and failed to provide "an accurate assessment of the conflict." It was a damning indictment: "The intellectual and moral failures common to America's general officer corps . . . constitute a crisis in American generalship," he wrote.[8]

Yingling's argument gained a crowd of adherents in the Army, but Colonel Gian Gentile, a highly respected West Point professor, disagreed. In the year that followed, Gentile issued a series of responses condemning Yingling for not having the courage to identify the generals who'd failed, and for masking his central thesis, which was to promote the views of David Petraeus and his counterinsurgency apostles. Yingling's "failed" general, Gentile concluded, was George Casey, while David Petraeus was his messiah. Over the next years Gentile and Yingling debated "A Failure of Generalship" in a spate of contentious back-and-forths on military websites, the heart of a larger discussion about what kind of military America needed. Pro-counterinsurgency advocates (or "coindinistas") led by Petraeus apostles Lieutenant Colonel John Nagl, Australian infantryman David Kilcullen ("the Crocodile Dundee of counterinsurgency"), Pentagon policy guru Janine Davidson, and a gaggle of supporters at *Small Wars Journal* ("the town square of counterinsurgency") advocated a turn away from conventional military doctrines to meet the "challenges of the Long War" (as they dubbed the war on terrorism), requiring the military to intervene in nations destabilized by extremist insurgencies. It also meant using the military to engage in nation building—a policy that had been fought by senior military leaders since Colin Powell became JCS chairman.[9]

The debate rippled through Martin Dempsey's first two years as JCS chairman, culminating in 2013 with the publication of Gian Gentile's book, *Wrong Turn: America's Deadly Embrace of Counterinsurgency*, a searing indictment of the "coindinista cult." At the heart of the cult, Gentile argued, was the myth that military interventions "can be done in a precise and clean way." The myth that counterinsurgency works, Gentile wrote, "is catnip for advocates of US intervention overseas because it promises the possibility of successful 'better wars.'" Gentile was blunt: "Don't kid yourself," he said, "war is violence, fear, hatred, death and destruction," and "any doctrine that says otherwise is a lie." For those who'd fought in Afghanistan and Iraq, Gentile's critique had the ring of truth. Among that number was General Ray Odierno, the commander responsible for implementing the Iraq surge. While the coindinistas counted Odierno as one of their apostles, that wasn't exactly true. Odierno was a Petraeus skeptic and a classic, gruff warfighter. In 2008, as US soldiers began to surge into Baghdad, Odierno faced off against Muqtada al-Sadr's Jaysh al-Mahdi (JAM) militia in Sadr City, the sprawling Baghdad district al-Sadr controlled. To secure Baghdad, Odierno's soldiers would have to defeat the Sadrists.[10]

The tension between Odierno and Petraeus is one of the most well-known, if little talked about, backstories of the surge, for while Petraeus was in overall command of the campaign, its day-to-day implementation was in the hands of Odierno. The two had entirely different personalities: Odierno was gruff and a throwback to the Army's Pattonesque traditions. "All this stuff about building trust is a bunch of bullshit," he'd explode. But Odierno had another side. For him, the Abu Ghraib scandal was a personal embarrassment, spurring him to talk about morality and ethics with his officers. His key assistant, Emma Sky, quotes him speaking with a group of American officers at Camp Taji, just north of Baghdad. "Our Army, our Marine Corps," he told his officers, "is based on morals and ethics. We must teach what that means at all times." He was right, of course, but his talks were a sign that what the United States had done in Iraq bothered him. He was known for supporting Petraeus's counterinsurgency principles, but he didn't believe they were either new or radical. The tactics he followed had been used in every one of America's wars. Securing the population meant fighting its enemies, he said, while the surge was really "a surge in cement" that was used in the Baghdad walls his soldiers erected. The walls didn't bring people together, it kept them apart. King David was not his favorite person.[11]

Odierno's reactions to his daily talks with Petraeus were, in fact, legion. One reporter remembers standing outside Odierno's office for the sole purpose of observing his daily Petraeus tirade. On cue, Odierno emerged, crashing through the door. "I hate that God damned

son-of-a-bitch," he screamed. This was a classic rivalry between two opinionated and ambitious officers; one felt slighted, the other paraded his
intellect. Which is to say that Odierno is exactly what Petraeus needed:
a no-nonsense combat officer who would do what it took to win. In fact,
Petraeus knew that Odierno had been a quiet critic of George Casey's
plan for Iraq (in effect, turning the war over to the Iraqis), going behind
his back (and outside the chain of command) to share his doubts during
regular telephone conversations with Jack Keane. He'd pushed Casey and
Abizaid for more troops, and when they turned him down he complained
to Keane. When the surge was announced, Odierno took the credit. "I
did it here and [Petraeus] picked it up," he explained patiently to doubting reporters.[12]

While a large portion of the surge's new troops were deployed in the
belts surrounding Baghdad (where networks of Shia supporters were con-
structing IEDs and sending them into the capital), Odierno focused on
Sadr City, the sprawling Shia slum. For him, it was the heart of the fight.
In March 2008, Odierno sent his soldiers into Sadr City in the first of
two offensives: Operation Striker Denial, followed by Operation Gold
Wall. Their goal was to defeat Muqtada al-Sadr's Shia militias and build
a barrier that would wall off Sadr City. Retired colonel David Johnson,
who wrote an influential account of the fight, describes it as "six weeks
of intensive and punishing combat," during which the Army built a five-
mile barrier separating the militant-infested neighborhoods from the rest
of the city.[13]

Odierno used the bluntest of instruments, deploying M1 Abrams
tanks and M2 Bradley fighting vehicles for the effort. "We're not here to
pass out fucking candy," Odierno instructed his subordinates. The wall
became a magnet for JAM fighters, who assaulted Army positions and
were bloodily repelled. "What you have to do is complete the sentence
'securing the population,'" Johnson said, in summarizing Sadr City's lessons. "In the case of Baghdad, securing the population meant securing
them from the Jaysh al-Mahdi, which meant defeating JAM in battle."
By early May, Odierno had accomplished his goal, killing seven hundred
JAM fighters. In the years that followed, the Battle of Sadr City would
become a mantra of the anti-coindinista lobby inside the Army. It was
Odierno's bloody fight and not Petraeus's new doctrine, they argued, that
made the difference in Iraq. The same was true for Afghanistan, they
said, where Petraeus himself abandoned counterinsurgency's principles

in his fight against the Taliban. The Afghanistan surge proved what Petraeus's detractors had always claimed: King David had used FM 3-24 not to promote a new way of fighting, but to promote himself. When he'd reached his goal he discarded it. For Petraeus partisans, the criticism was patently unfair: what the Afghanistan fight showed, they said, was that when faced with a choice between doctrine and victory, Petraeus chose victory.

The last act in the coindinista drama took place in May 2013, when John Nagl and Gian Gentile faced off on the issue at Grinnell College, in Iowa. This celebrated "Cage Match in a Cornfield" focused on the single question, "Is COIN dead?" Ironically, while most accounted the debate a draw, the question was already decided. COIN was dead, but it wasn't Gian Gentile or his followers who killed it. It was killed by the Air Force and Navy. And by Barack Obama.[14]

IN MID-OCTOBER 2011, Marty Dempsey was told that the president wanted a comprehensive review of US military policy. Dempsey knew it was coming, because the previous April Obama had said that fiscal constraints meant the Pentagon would be required to cut its budget by some half-a-trillion dollars over the next ten years. Dempsey and his colleagues had to find a way to do that. But Obama's tasking went further: the president wanted the military to write a new defense strategic guidance (a DSG) that would reshape its "10-year strategic outlook in response to changes in the global security environment." The directive consigned the war on terror to a second-tier military challenge, with a "shift in overall focus from winning today's wars to preparing for future challenges." In fact, the DSG was the outcome of a series of intensive internal discussions involving Obama, Secretary of State Hillary Clinton, and the Pentagon's Bob Gates within months of Obama's election. The driver of the discussion was Clinton, whose first overseas trip as secretary of state was to Asia, where she focused on trade and economic growth. Clinton argued that the United States should pivot away from the Middle East, and toward Asia. Clinton debuted the "Asia pivot" in the pages of *Foreign Policy* in October 2011, at nearly the same moment that Dempsey launched the Pentagon's strategic review. Clinton was the public face of the pivot, while Gates's job was to institutionalize the pivot as a part of the strategy shift.[15]

An accomplished amateur historian and voracious reader, Gates was convinced the interventions in Afghanistan and Iraq were mistakes; it was China that posed the greatest future challenge to American power. Gates had said as much in September 2009, at an Air Force Association convention, where he noted that China's investments in "cyber and anti-satellite warfare, anti-air and anti-ship weaponry, and ballistic missiles could threaten America's primary way to project power and help allies in the Pacific—in particular our forward air bases and carrier groups." The United States, he said, had to counter China's progress. Obama agreed. While White House officials would later contend that Obama's idea for a new defense strategy was necessitated by the looming budget deficit, the DSG reflected the president's view that "stabilization operations" were too expensive, their outcomes too uncertain. Clinton, Gates, and Obama were on the same page: fighting endless insurgencies was a prescription for going broke. So was nation building.[16]

Following the president's directive, Dempsey convened a group of defense officials to focus on laying out the DSG. The resulting eight-page document, "Sustaining US Global Leadership: Priorities for 21st Century Defense," reflected Obama and Gates's thinking. Gates's successor, Leon Panetta, guided the final result, which received the president's endorsement during a January 2012 Pentagon news conference. It was the first time that any president held a news conference at the Pentagon. While "Sustaining US Global Leadership" confirmed that the United States would "take an active approach" in countering terrorist threats, it emphasized that "US forces will no longer be sized to conduct large-scale, prolonged stability operations." Instead, the military would focus on "projecting power in areas in which US access and freedom to operate are challenged by asymmetric means."[17]

The coindinistas knew this meant that the kinds of "large footprint," long-term deployments required for Army and Marine forces were dead. But it wasn't only the coindinistas who were being eclipsed: the January announcement signaled that future defense budgets would favor the Air Force and Navy—at the expense of the Army. The Army's leaders never saw this coming, but they should have. For what Obama announced in January 2012 had been in the works for two decades, and was the result of a behind-the-scenes collaboration between the Air Force and Navy to change the way America fights wars. Counterinsurgency no longer symbolized the new thinking that would lead the American military in the new century. It had been eclipsed by a new doctrine, called AirSea Battle (ASB).[18] The doctrine wasn't promoted by a group as celebrated as the Jedi Knights, but its adherents proved as influential. The military had come full circle: almost all of ASB's adherents were the intellectual inheritors of the revolution in military affairs that was symbolized by the planning of John Warden's Checkmate staff twenty-five years before.

In the aftermath of Operation Desert Storm, a small group of defense intellectuals had raised a series of uncomfortable questions about the war. What if Iraq had been able to mount a sustained anti-naval and anti-air campaign that denied the United States access to the waters of the Persian Gulf and the unfettered use of air bases in nearby countries? What if Iraq had had a strong air force, or a suite of hardened anti-ship and anti-aircraft missiles? Would the operation have been as successful? The questions reflected the war's premier lesson: the US won because its weapons dominated the battlefield. But there was no guarantee that that would always be true.

The ease of the US victory in Operation Desert Storm was celebrated in America, but it sent shudders through the Chinese defense establishment, whose top officers studied how the United States had won. Beginning in 1992, senior officers of the Chinese Academy of Military Science, the country's prestigious military think tank, initiated a weapons development program to challenge the US Navy's access to the Taiwan Strait and the waters of the South China Sea. Iran did the same by starting a modernization and anti-ship missile program to contest US military access to the Persian Gulf. The new Chinese weapons included increased numbers of anti-ship cruise and ballistic missiles, more submarines and surface ships, technical upgrades in electronic warfare capabilities, the development of advanced sea mines, and the use of more sophisticated command, control, surveillance, and reconnaissance systems. A senior Marine officer and Middle East policy expert explained that Iran followed the same path, adopting the equivalent of sea-based counterinsurgency operations, deploying "mines, swarms of small boats and land-based cruise missiles" that would "overwhelm the much larger and sophisticated American warships."[19]

Predictably, China's and Iran's decisions to develop and deploy anti-access and area-denial weapons (A2/AD, in Pentagon parlance) spurred a countermove by the United States. Over twenty years, until Obama's 2011 DSG, senior officers inside the Air Force and Navy shaped an ASB doctrine to meet the A2/AD challenge. ASB replaced the "AirLand Battle" doctrine that had guided the military's thinking during the Cold War by creating a war plan that would enable the Air Force and Navy to respond to countries developing weapons that would deny the US access to the globe's commonly held air, sea, land, space, and cyberspace resources. Even as the US military implemented the Afghanistan surge, ASB celebrated its coming out as a part of the Pentagon's 2010 Quadrennial Defense Review. ASB, the Pentagon said, would "address how air and naval forces will integrate capabilities across all operational domains . . . to counter growing challenges to US freedom of action." That sounded simple enough, except that the new doctrine removed the Army from its premier role in America's war fighting equation, with pride of place suddenly given to the Air Force and Navy—which meant less money for the Army in future defense budgets.[20]

So it was that, in the wake of the release of the DSG, the Army did everything it could to shoot down ASB. The effort started at the top, with Army chief of staff Ray Odierno. The DSG "sent Odierno into a tizzy," "chilled relations" between him and his JCS colleagues, and sparked "real resentments toward the Air Force and Navy among Odierno's staff," as a Joint Staff officer described it. The resentment was fueled by Odierno's view that his service was now fighting a two-front war: one in Afghanistan against the Taliban, and another in Washington against the Air Force and Navy. For Odierno, the adoption of ASB was the ultimate betrayal: while the Army was fighting the war on terror, the Air Force and Navy were conspiring to grab a greater share of the defense budget. While the Army was surging troops into Iraq, the Air Force and Navy were surging in Washington. While young men and women were dying in the Middle East, the Air Force and Navy were nibbling away at the money to support them. Odierno was irate.[21]

"There's always tension between the service heads," an Odierno colleague said, "but this was on an entirely different level. Odierno looked at senior Navy and Air Force officers as plotting against him." For Odierno and the senior Army leadership, the ASB threat was a simple numbers game: with the wars in the Middle East winding down, with counterinsurgency advocates in retreat, and with proposed budget cuts that would slash Army end strength from 570,000 in 2011 to 450,000 in 2017, the

Army faced a future in which large-scale deployments of US troops were passé. Then too, when Odierno said that he believed the Air Force and Navy were plotting against him, he wasn't being paranoid. They were. When Bob Gates's Air Force Association speech was circulated inside the Pentagon back in 2009, it was as if a starting gun had sounded. Shortly after Gates's remarks, in September 2009, Air Force chief of staff Norton Schwartz and Chief of Naval Operations Gary Roughead signed a classified memorandum directing their services to develop ASB. The memorandum was classified for a reason: they made sure the Army didn't see it, because the Army wasn't included.[22]

Schwartz and Roughead were unlikely revolutionaries. Schwartz was appointed by President Obama on Robert Gates's recommendation after the defense secretary fired his predecessor, T. Michael Moseley, ostensibly over nuclear security issues. But the real reason that Moseley was fired, senior Air Force officers believed, was because he opposed Gates's decision to cancel production of the F-22 fighter. The F-22, Gates said, was too expensive and would not be relevant in future wars, where the United States would need to rely on unmanned aerial reconnaissance and attack vehicles—drones. Moseley had taken on Gates on the issue on Capitol Hill, believing the aerospace jobs the F-22 provided would trump Gates's views. So (as senior Air Force officers claimed) Gates fired him and replaced him with Schwartz, who supported increased drone research and production. As crucially, Schwartz was not a part of his service's fighter mafia, so was open to ideas that did not necessarily fit their agenda. The Air Force reeled from the appointment, not least because its most influential officers had pushed General John Corley as Moseley's replacement, calculating that Gates would need to appease their service's traditional power center. He didn't. "He stiffed us," a retired Air Force brigadier general noted.[23]

Roughead was cut from the same cloth as Schwartz, though with a different pedigree. A Naval Academy graduate, the white-haired intellectual was Pacific-focused and a follower of Alfred Thayer Mahan, the nineteenth-century historian, sea power theorist, and Navy icon. Mahan claimed that what made Great Britain a nineteenth-century superpower was its command of the sea, which gave it access to overseas markets—a model the United States should follow in the Pacific. Roughead agreed, referring to Asia as "the Indo Pacific" region, whose oceans are "great highways" of commerce. America, Roughead argued, was a Pacific power, its future a competition with China for resources, port access, and trading partners. The Navy would be the key to success in the competition, protecting America's Pacific markets. But it couldn't do that without support from the Air Force. The Schwartz-Roughead partnership sealed the Air Force–Navy coalition, providing the security underpinnings to the Obama administration's Asia pivot.

In early 2010, five months after Schwartz and Roughead signed their secret memorandum, the influential Center for Strategic and Budgetary Assessments published a monograph written by Andrew Krepinevich, a West Point graduate, retired senior Army officer, and one of Washington's leading defense thinkers. "Why AirSea Battle?" highlighted China's and Iran's A2/AD capabilities. The spread of "advanced military technologies and their exploitation by other militaries," Krepinevich wrote, posed a challenge to "the US military's ability to preserve military access to two key areas of vital interest, the Western Pacific and the Persian Gulf." The monograph put Washington's leading center for military thinking squarely on the side of ASB. While the Gates speech, the Schwartz-Roughead memorandum, and the Krepinevich monograph put ASB on the Pentagon's agenda, it also sealed a deeper integration of Navy and Air Force capabilities. Beginning in the mid-1990s, the two branches had institutionalized joint air operations; eventually, the two services began swapping air crews, tacticians, and intelligence officers in a joint-service partnership. The new cooperative environment ironed out differences in naval (carrier-based) and Air Force (land-based) air operation, strengthened command and staff relationships, integrated air asset strike operations, and pooled common air resources. The Army, meanwhile, was nowhere to be found.[24]

IN OCTOBER 2011, within weeks of his swearing in as the new Army chief, Ray Odierno drafted a strategy that would either undermine ASB or, if that couldn't be done, make sure the Army had a role in it. Some of Odierno's strategy worked. In January 2012, in the wake of President Obama's appearance at the Pentagon, the Army won an agreement elevating the commander of the US Army in the Pacific to a four-star slot, a rank equal to that of his Navy counterpart. The designation expanded the Army's role in what had been traditionally viewed as the Navy's area of operation. The decision left Navy officers fuming. "The Army has no business having a four-star slot in the Pacific," former Desert Storm war planner and influential senior Air Force officer David Deptula said. "They're just setting themselves up to fight for money. For them, AirSea Battle isn't about China or protecting the US, its about the defense budget." Odierno's next move was even less subtle. With the Navy and Air Force bragging about their newfound belief in "interoperability," Odierno pressed the Navy to adopt a series of exercises that would have Army helicopters land on amphibious ships, including aircraft carriers. The landings were touted by the Army as proof that their service has a role to play in "a littoral combat environment"—combat operations in the Pacific.[25]

Odierno's fight over ASB lasted well beyond the 2012 announcement of a new strategic tilt. In October 2013, when a House subcommittee on seapower held a hearing on the ASB issue, Odierno's staff worked overtime to make sure that the Army was invited. What an Army officer was doing at a seapower subcommittee hearing was so puzzling, it even confused the officer Odierno assigned to the task. "I confess I'm a little surprised myself to be here," Army major general Gary Cheek told the subcommittee, "but I would frankly tell you that, for the Army, we look forward to any and every opportunity to partner with our joint brothers and sisters. This is really what makes our military unique, is the fact that we can bring our pieces together." But Odierno wasn't the only Army officer upset about ASB. While the 2012 DSG was directed by Obama and supported by Defense Secretary Panetta, Dempsey had been cool toward the new doctrine in his first months as JCS chairman. But he'd been brought around by Panetta, and by the realization that his new position required him to take a less parochial, less Army-centric approach. Then too, Dempsey concluded, the Air Force and Navy had it right: the emerging threats to US interests lay in the Pacific and Persian Gulf. Dempsey, who appeared beside the president on January 5, 2012, knew that members of the press were aware of his hesitations, so after Panetta finished his remarks, he addressed them head-on. "This is a real strategy," he said. "It represents real choices. And I'm here today to assure you that it has real buy-in among our senior military and civilian leadership."[26]

Dempsey's statement was a broad hint at the criticism he'd faced, particularly from the Army, in the weeks leading up to the release of the defense guidance. The Army's intransigence had left Dempsey exasperated, but in the weeks before Obama's Pentagon appearance, Dempsey had laid out the bottom line for Odierno. Both were West Point graduates and shared the same wars, and neither were Petraeus partisans or coindinista apostles. Dempsey allowed Odierno to lead the anti-ASB fight for a time, but then pulled him back. Prior to the January 2012 announcement, the two had had a short talk, in which Dempsey told Odierno that ASB could not be stopped. "I think it's pretty clear," a senior Army officer says, "that Dempsey worked to bring Odierno around. This was a done deal, so his message was simple: 'Ray, it's time to get on board.'"[27]

Odierno was on board, but just barely. The Army's initial response to the January 2012 announcement was to meld what it had learned from counterinsurgency operations with its traditional commitment to large units, heavy tanks, and massed artillery. The new concept was called "hybrid war," but it sounded more like a half pivot aimed at placating the service's armored warfare power center. Hybrid war gave a desultory nod to Panetta's requirement that the Army create swift-moving expeditionary forces, highly trained special operations units, and airborne infantry. A more pointed response was the Army's announcement that its Special Operations Command would team up with the Marines, the core group of ASB critics, to conduct a study (the "Strategic Landpower Task Force Research Report") on how to meld the lessons learned from Iraq and Afghanistan into a more overarching strategy. The report's conclusion would claim that no military strategy can be successful without "a human component," a phrase that purposely slapped at ASB's tech-heavy requirements. There was a maritime domain, an air domain, and a cyber domain, but that left out the "human domain," the study said. And that became the Army's mantra: war was all about the human domain. The primary thinker behind the study, Dr. Steven Metz, the leading Army intellectual at the Army War College, argued that while ASB "provides a strong case for service integration," it was incomplete. "You can't have a national military strategy that includes just two of the four services," he said. "What we need is a multi-service component; that's the only way that any doctrine can be truly joint." For Air Force and Navy thinkers, the Metz statement brought knowing half smiles: he wasn't providing an argument for why the new doctrine shouldn't be accepted, he was making a plea that the Army be included.[28]

Barack Obama's Asia pivot would make the next one hundred years, as he said, "America's Pacific Century," with the US solidifying its alliances with Japan, Thailand, South Korea, the Philippines, and Australia, while deepening its economic ties to the region. From New Delhi to San

Francisco, the Indo-Pacific's commercial highways would be patrolled by US Navy ships, protected by an umbrella of US Air Force fighter-bombers. America, Hillary Clinton predicted, would be "right at the center of the action." Yet, over the next years, and stretching into the final months of Barack Obama's second term, the Asia pivot seemed stillborn, with the president forced to refocus his attention on the Middle East. The pull had the same effect as quicksand: the more America struggled to extract itself from the region, the more deeply mired it became.

IN DECEMBER 2010, Mohamed Bouazizi, a Tunisian fruit seller, set himself afire in protest of his mistreatment by government officials. The incident sparked demonstrations that led to the ouster of Tunisian strongman Zine el-Abidine Ben Ali and seeded antigovernment demonstrations in Egypt, Yemen, Syria, Bahrain, and Libya—the Arab Spring. The United States intervened in Libya, but was more deliberate elsewhere, and particularly in Egypt, where close US-Egyptian ties allowed senior US military officers to counsel their Egyptian counterparts to keep their troops on the sidelines during the protests that engulfed Cairo. But Syria presented a special problem.[29]

The Syria crisis began in March 2011 when demonstrations erupted in Deraa, in southern Syria. The protests escalated, devolving into a bloody civil war, with secular activists and then jihadists taking up arms against the government of Bashar al-Assad. By July, tens of thousands of Syrians were in the streets and by the end of the year the Free Syrian Army was fighting the government in the suburbs of Damascus. By early the next summer, sixteen thousand Syrians were dead and tens of thousands were refugees. The Obama administration was slow to respond, the result of the controversies set off by its Libya intervention. In fact, Libya looked like a repeat of what the United States had faced in Afghanistan and Iraq, with a persistent conflict fueled by sectarian violence. But the unintended result of Odyssey Dawn had its greatest impact on the president, who told Bob Gates just before Gates's retirement that he'd been right: Libya was a mistake.

By the late spring of 2012, Obama was facing increasing pressure from his national security staff to provide arms to anti-Assad rebels, an initiative authored by Hillary Clinton and David Petraeus. But Obama wasn't convinced. It wasn't simply that the president feared that some of the weapons the United States supplied to the rebels would end up in the hands of extremists, it was that the program's authors weren't clear on how the arms would help end the conflict, or who exactly they were intended to strengthen. For Republican senator John McCain, who'd urged the administration to open a bombing campaign targeting the Assad government, Obama's nonresponse symbolized all that was wrong with the president's foreign policy. Obama, he said, was weak and indecisive, his Syria policy an embarrassment. In Libya, he'd argued, the US was "leading from behind," while now, in Syria, it wasn't leading at all.[30]

At first, both Dempsey and Panetta supported the Clinton-Petraeus initiative, but in time the JCS chairman shifted into the Obama camp. The reason was rooted in Dempsey's experiences during the Iraq war. When Dempsey arrived in Baghdad in 2003, he'd had an important discussion with John Abizaid, whom he viewed as a mentor, about the "now what" question. Both were convinced they had only a short time to get Iraq back on its feet. "How long do you think we have?" Abizaid had asked. "Three years," Dempsey said. Abizaid agreed. But as Dempsey soon learned, he had far less than that. Within days, Dempsey's 1st Armored Division was fighting armed gangs that Saddam had let loose on the city, while the next year his division was battling the Sadrists in Najaf. It was a bitter experience, and Dempsey kept cards with the names of those killed under his command in a special box marked "Make it matter" on his desk.[31]

Perhaps more than any other JCS chairman who'd preceded him, including Colin Powell, Dempsey had a sophisticated and carefully articulated strategic viewpoint, which he detailed in a series of interviews during his tenure. His convictions were the result of his forty years in uniform, and his command assignment in Iraq. State-on-state wars demanded a large number of troops, he said, while fighting nonstate actors demanded innovation—and willing local partners. The coindinistas' focus on tactics, he implied, missed the larger question of whether local populations would take responsibility for their own future. It was up to them to "own it from the beginning." The United States could not do for countries what the countries were unwilling to do for themselves. US soldiers shouldn't be expected to be nation builders. That conclusion was reflected in his opinion of the surge, which Dempsey claimed he'd supported, but with this caveat: he believed in a surge of Iraqi troops. His experience solidified his view that what the US was fighting in the region was not terrorism, but "despair, lack of hope, lack of inclusive governance, and grotesque economic disparity." Deploying soldiers wouldn't solve those problems.[32]

Dempsey's views reflected those of the JCS, but his most important ally was his vice chairman, Sandy Winnefeld, whose impeccable credentials as a graduate of the Navy Fighter Weapons School ("Top Gun") gave him cachet inside the military. The Dempsey-Winnefeld relationship contrasted with that of Mullen and Cartwright, whose fierce competition undermined the military's standing with the White House. Dempsey and Winnefeld, on the other hand, worked as a team: while the JCS chairman focused on the White House, Winnefeld focused on the military, defending the 2012 strategic guidance and pushing the services to shift their thinking. His message reflected Dempsey's strategy and the new budget realities. And Winnefeld stood with Dempsey on Syria: the era of the long wars was over, he said, not least because those wars were bankrupting the nation. Congress's 2011 passage of the budget control act, sequestration (congressionally mandated cuts in the federal budget), was simply a recognition that serial military interventions were costly, and not just in terms of lives. Winnefeld, and the military, opposed the act in public, but in private the vice chairman acknowledged that sequestration imposed as much discipline on Obama's critics as it did on the president: if Congress wanted the United States to intervene in Syria, then it would have to figure out a way to pay for it. And Winnefeld stood with Dempsey on the question of arming Syria's opposition, where care had to be taken that US arms did not fall into the wrong hands. Winnefeld now regularly cited influential World War I general Fox Conner's celebrated rules for going to war to military audiences: "never fight unless you have to, never fight alone, and never fight for long." Do we really have to fight in Syria? Winnefeld would ask. And who exactly are "the opposition"?[33]

By the spring of 2012, Dempsey and Petraeus were on opposite sides of the Syria question, with Dempsey asking pointed questions during the administration's debate on whether to arm the Syrian opposition: What did Assad's opponents believe? What was their vision for Syria? Who were they? No one seemed to know. Dempsey's questions signaled his anti-interventionist stance, but without making it explicit. Obama kept pushing Dempsey to speak out in public, but Dempsey was reticent. Obama had been exasperated by Mullen, who always had something to

say, but was now equally exasperated by Dempsey, who rarely said anything. At key points in the debate over Syria, Obama turned to Dempsey,
soliciting his political views. "That is not a military question," Dempsey
would say. "I am here to give military advice." Obama would nod, half
expecting the answer. "I know that, Marty," he'd answer, patiently, "but
I want your views anyway." Dempsey's style offered a deep contrast to
that of presidential adviser Samantha Power, who remained among the
most outspoken advocates for a Syria intervention. Power, whose book on
genocide was still touted inside the White House, could be shrill. Obama
had once interrupted her, rudely. "Samantha, enough," he said, "I've read
your book."[34]

By the early summer, Dempsey had told Obama that while he still favored arming Syrian opposition forces, he also favored a "whole of government" approach to the conflict. Roughly translated, Dempsey's support
for a military intervention was contingent on a deeper diplomatic initiative, which included enlisting the help of America's allies while pressuring Russia, Assad's ally, to take steps against the Damascus government.
The JCS chairman's views on Syria aligned the military with a president
whose intuitions told him that an intervention would lead the US down a
Libya-like slippery slope of deepening military involvement. But Obama's
position left him vulnerable to Mitt Romney, the 2012 Republican nominee for president. Romney piled into Obama for failing to openly support
anti-Assad rebels. Obama, he said, was following "a policy of paralysis"
and that he'd "failed to lead in Syria." The Romney critique was part of
an emerging anti-Obama argument that painted the president as a feckless appeaser unwilling to use military power. Even so, Obama was on
solid ground, at least with the American public, which polls showed was
overwhelmingly opposed to another military intervention.[35]

By the end of 2012, the administration was deeply divided over the
Syria question, with Power, UN ambassador Susan Rice, and Hillary
Clinton (the "cruise missile liberals") and CIA director Petraeus favoring
intervention, while Obama adviser Tom Donilon, Panetta, and Dempsey
took a more cautious approach. Officially, Dempsey still favored some
support for the Assad opposition, so long as the flow of arms and other
aid could be sent to "properly vetted" groups—those not associated with
al-Qaeda or other Islamic extremists. The divisions were noticeable in
Washington, with a national security establishment so severely divided
that political pundits regularly described the White House foreign policy

process as "dysfunctional." In reality, however, the administration's internal debates had little public impact, with the 2012 election focused on the economy, taxes, and the deficit. On November 6, Obama's political calculation—that the public (and the military) had little appetite for another foreign adventure—was redeemed by the surprising ease of his reelection victory over Romney. Even so, Obama knew that the worsening situation in Syria and the Middle East and, increasingly, the debate over what to do about Iran's nuclear program, would likely consume his second term.

ON NOVEMBER 8, two days after the election, FBI officials told Obama that his CIA director had been having an extramarital affair with author Paula Broadwell. The liaison came to light as the result of a complaint filed with the agency by Jill Kelley, a Tampa socialite, that she'd been receiving "anonymous threatening emails" from a user identified as "kelleypatrol." Kelleypatrol, the agency determined, was Broadwell. The next day, when the scandal made headlines, Petraeus submitted his resignation to the president. But the affair was only a part of Petraeus's problem. The FBI's investigation had peeled back the sometimes tawdry relationships of senior commanders stationed at CENTCOM's MacDill Air Force Base with its local web of nonuniformed supporters, a kind of fan club that feted Petraeus and other commanders in a whirlwind of receptions and high-profile dinners. Rumors of indiscretion spread, Cartwright-like, through Tampa and the Pentagon.[36]

Worse yet, the FBI suspected that Petraeus had mishandled classified information: it seized notebooks that Petraeus had given Broadwell containing code words for secret intelligence programs, the identities of covert intelligence officers, and information about war strategy and White House discussions on international events. The scandal hit the Obama administration like a bombshell, but set off subdued celebrations among the anti-Petraeus cohort inside the Army, which included long-time Petraeus competitors. "There were officers who just couldn't wait for Dave to be taken down a notch," an Army officer said. Included in this number, though not surprisingly, was Ray Odierno. "Ray lived for the day that Petraeus was busted to private," an Odierno colleague said at the time. The Broadwell scandal removed a powerful voice from White House foreign policy deliberations, though Petraeus wasn't the only one no longer at the table. After Obama's reelection, Hillary Clinton also departed, replaced as secretary of state by Democratic senator John Kerry, as did Leon Panetta, replaced by Republican senator Chuck Hagel. The changes did little to shift the Syria debate, but it transformed the Pentagon's command calculus. Marty Dempsey was now the administration's most influential military voice.[37]

"Dempsey was simply not an influential player in his first two years as chairman," a senior Army officer says. "But after Petraeus left the CIA he hit his stride. He became more outspoken. It was the fact that Petraeus wasn't there, but it was also Syria. The Syria fight defined him." Martin Dempsey's "Syria fight" took place after he was nominated, in June 2013, for a second two-year term by the president, when the JCS chairman faced off against John McCain. The Republican was the Obama administration's most prominent foreign policy critic, and the most outspoken advocate for US intervention in Syria. And until the previous March, he believed he could count on Dempsey's support. But by July 2013, Dempsey's private hesitations were public, and McCain was livid. On July 18, McCain lit into Dempsey during the JCS chairman's renomination hearing before the Senate Armed Services Committee, where Dempsey appeared alongside Admiral Sandy Winnefeld, who'd also been nominated for a second term.[38]

Nearly shaking in anger, McCain bore in on Dempsey, implying he'd shifted his views on Syria to satisfy Obama. "I must tell both the witnesses at the onset, I'm very concerned about the role you have played over the last two years," McCain said. "General Dempsey and Admiral Winnefeld, do you believe the continued cost and risk of our inaction in Syria are now worse for our national security interest than the cost and risk associated with limited military action?" Dempsey started to answer, but McCain cut him off. "I'd like to know an answer rather than a filibuster," he said. "I have six minutes and 10 seconds." Dempsey remained unfazed, saying that the emergence of radical groups in Syria was putting the United States at risk. "You're not answering my question, General," McCain sputtered. In fact, McCain added, the administration had done nothing on the issue, implying that Dempsey was the reason why. "With all due respect, Senator, you're asking me to agree that we've been inactive, and we have not been inactive," Dempsey responded. McCain glared at Dempsey and asked the question a third time: was inaction on Syria putting the nation at risk? This time Dempsey said he was in favor of building a moderate opposition, and then supporting it. "We've given [President Obama] options," Dempsey said. "The members of this committee have been briefed on them in a classified setting. We've articulated the risk. The decision on whether to use force is the decision of our elected officials." McCain wasn't satisfied, telling Dempsey that he might take action to hold up his confirmation.[39]

Dempsey had seen this before: during Chuck Hagel's confirmation hearings, McCain had angrily confronted his former colleague on his opposition to the 2007 Iraq troop surge. Hagel had called it "the worst military blunder since Vietnam." During his confirmation hearings, McCain reminded Hagel of this. "I want to know if you were right or wrong?" he asked. "That's a direct question." Hagel answered that he would allow history to judge. McCain wasn't satisfied: "You're on the wrong side of it," he said, "and your refusal to answer whether you were right or wrong on it is going to have an impact on my judgment on whether to vote for your confirmation."[40] During the Dempsey hearings, McCain again revisited the surge issue. "Actually, General Dempsey, you and I went through this in 2006," he said, "when I said that it wasn't succeeding and that we had to have a surge and that only a surge could succeed in reversing the tide of battle, and you disagreed with me then. Way back then. And I think history shows that those of us who supported the surge were right, and people like you, who didn't think we need a surge were wrong."[41]

In fact, senior military officers concluded, McCain's surge reference actually had little to do with Iraq (or Syria), and everything to do with McCain's war—in Vietnam. That war could have been won, McCain apparently believed, if only the nation's civilian leaders had been as committed to winning in Vietnam as Bush and Petraeus were to winning in Iraq. Which is why, for some officers on the Joint Staff, McCain's anti-Dempsey outburst seemed "almost unbalanced." McCain had been refighting his war for years, and still was. Dempsey, for his part, spent the night following the hearing at the Pentagon drafting a response to McCain that would be given to the committee's chairman, Senator Carl Levin. The memo, in the form of a letter, detailed five military options for dealing with Syria: training the Syrian opposition, conducting limited air strikes against key Assad assets, implementing a no-fly zone, creating a buffer zone along Syria's border, and securing the regime's chemical weapons. But uniquely, the Dempsey letter included estimated costs for each of the options. A training mission, Dempsey noted, would cost $500 million, while a full intervention would cost $1 billion a month. The response was, in fact, a restatement of what Dempsey and Winnefeld had been saying for months: that if Congress wanted the US military to conduct an interventionist foreign policy, it could vote the money to pay for it. Which meant breaking the sequester, voting the money, and telling American taxpayers that their country was engaged in yet another Middle East adventure.[42]

The depth of the Obama administration's opposition to intervening in Syria was underscored the following month, in August 2013, when the president announced that the Syrian government had used chemical weapons in attacks near Damascus. The use of the weapons, Obama announced, crossed a "red line" he'd laid out the previous summer. "We have been very clear to the Assad regime," he'd said in the summer of 2012, "that a red line for us is we start seeing a whole bunch of chemical weapons moving around or being utilized. That would change my calculus." But then, the next year, after asking Dempsey for a plan to destroy Assad's chemical stockpiles (which included a sustained bombing campaign to destroy the regime's air defense system), Obama changed his mind. The shift in Obama's thinking was abrupt, unexpected. On August 30, 2013, following a celebrated walk with Chief of Staff Denis McDonough on the south lawn of the White House, Obama decided to call off the attacks. He announced his decision the next day. "After careful deliberation," he told the American people, "I have decided that the United States should take military action against Syrian regime targets. I'm also mindful that I'm the president of the world's oldest constitutional democracy . . . and that's why I've made a second decision: I will seek authorization for the use of force from the American people's representatives in Congress."[43]

The announcement surprised everyone, including Marty Dempsey, who later told reporters that the military was "ready to pull the trigger." Now, Obama had kicked that decision into Congress. In the end, while Obama's controversial about-face sparked widespread criticism of his conduct of foreign policy, Secretary of State John Kerry negotiated the removal of Assad's chemical weapons stockpiles by Russia. In the years that followed, it became increasingly apparent that Obama's unexpected decision was consistent with the policies he'd followed from his first days in office: while he might be repeatedly pulled back into the Middle East, he was determined to carry out his pivot—and to end America's costly

Middle East interventions. As crucially, Obama and his key advisers calculated, a Syria intervention might well have sparked a confrontation with Iran, Assad's ally, and endangered the multilateral negotiations the United States was leading on Iran's nuclear program. In fact, as military officers later speculated, Obama had two red lines: while he would not tolerate Assad's use of chemical weapons, he would do nothing to endanger the talks on Iran's nuclear program, which had begun in March 2013 and involved the US, China, France, Russia, the United Kingdom, and Germany. Obama's critics weighed in on the president, linking Syria and the Iran talks. The president, they said, wasn't thinking about Syria, he was thinking about Iran. Obama's critics inside the military had a different take: the president was sacrificing the Syrian people in the name of appeasing Iran, which was pursuing a nuclear program that would make it the paramount power in the region—and an existential threat to Israel.[44]

Obama paid a heavy political price for his commitment to the Iran talks, but so too did the military and, in particular, Marine general James Mattis. Mattis, whom Obama had appointed to head CENTCOM in the summer of 2010, had always been an Obama skeptic, but no more so than on Iran. In part, Mattis's skepticism was the result of his close ties with the Israeli military and in particular with Israel's military attaché, Major General Gadi Shamni, whom he often visited during his trips to Washington. The two "would have eyeball-to-eyeball Saturday night dinners," where they would compare notes on the region, a senior Pentagon official says. The White House knew of the meetings but could hardly bar Mattis from having them—though Israel was not in CENTCOM's region. Mattis admired the Israeli Defense Forces, and found their views on Iran convincing. But Mattis didn't need the Israelis to convince him of Iran's "malign intentions" (a phrase he used every time he testified on the issue in Washington)—he'd seen them firsthand in Iraq. The Obama White House, Mattis told one aide, was being "gulled by the mullahs" in Tehran, who were supporting Assad, running Shia death squads in Iraq, funding the Hezbollah terrorist group in Lebanon, shipping missiles to Hamas in Gaza, taking sides in the Yemeni civil war—and undermining US interests throughout the region. Within months of taking over at CENTCOM, Mattis was pushing hard on Obama's people to send him more naval units to interdict Iranian vessels, which, he said, were shipping arms to radical groups throughout the region. He was turned down.[45]

Then, in January 2012, Mattis requested the Obama administration dispatch an additional carrier group to meet what Mattis called "the increased Iranian threat." Once again, Mattis's request was denied. The carrier was needed in the Pacific, he was told. Through all of this, Mattis carefully kept his disagreements with Obama out of public view, though his aides often leaked the details of his military requests, and their denials, to the press. Nor did the White House publicize its disagreements with the CENTCOM commander. "General Mattis is a key player in administration debates and a vital implementer of the administration's policies," Denis McDonough told one reporter. Which was only technically true: Mattis's disagreements with Obama's policies were circulated inside the White House, causing tensions among the president's foreign policy advisers, and particularly with Tom Donilon.[46]

It seemed inevitable that the two would clash, as they did in December 2012, when the White House noticed that Mattis had moved one of his carrier groups closer to Iranian national waters. It seemed to Obama that Mattis was testing him, or perhaps attempting to pick a fight with Tehran. Donilon got on a secure line with the CENTCOM commander. "Pull it back," Donilon told Mattis. Mattis, who'd disliked Donilon from the moment he'd heard that he was responsible for pushing James Jones out of the administration, snapped back, angrily. "I don't take orders from you," he said. "You're not in the chain of command." Donilon told Mattis that the order came from the president himself. "Then he can call me," Mattis said, and he hung up the telephone. Obama didn't call Mattis—he didn't need to, as Mattis pulled back the carrier group on his own. But Mattis's move was the final straw. The next month, on January 25, 2013, the Marine general was handed a note from an aide telling him that, in March, he would be replaced as the head of CENTCOM. Mattis's allies in the Marine Corps were enraged: the president had dismissed a warfighter who'd spent his life serving his country, without even bothering to speak to him.[47]

Writing in the *Weekly Standard*, the neoconservative voice in Washington, Naval War College professor Mackubin Thomas Owens slammed the Obama decision. "By pushing Mattis overboard," he said, "the administration is sending a message that it doesn't want smart, independently minded generals who speak candidly to their civilian leaders." That was the view of most of the military, who'd admired not only Mattis's plain-speaking honesty, but his undeniable talents on the battlefield. But there were also, here and there, some dissenting voices, including in the Marine Corps. "Jim Mattis was a great general," a fellow Marine Corps officer said after Mattis's forced retirement, "but he never had a sophisticated grasp of diplomacy. He was a warfighter, it was in his DNA. He was a fine, fine officer, and a patriot. But if anyone deserved to be fired, it was Jim Mattis."[48]

ON THE EVENING of August 6, 2014, Marty Dempsey joined the president in his limousine at the State Department, where the president had been attending a session of the US-Africa leaders summit. It was the first time in several weeks that Dempsey had had a chance to talk with the president, who normally saw the JCS chairman at regularly scheduled Thursday afternoon meetings in the Oval Office. But now the two were face-to-face as the limo headed to the White House. "We have a crisis in Iraq, Mr. President," Dempsey said. "ISIS is a real threat." Dempsey leaned into Obama, his voice devoid of the studied informality he reserved for their exchanges. But this was different: this meeting was official. "This demands your immediate attention, Mr. President," Dempsey said.[49]

Dempsey's warning was underscored by reports he'd been receiving from US military intelligence sources in Baghdad. ISIS had overrun the northern Iraqi city of Mosul, seized stockpiles of heavy weapons from the hapless Iraqi military (including US heavy weapons, left behind in the care of the Iraqi government), and was attacking thousands of ethnic Yazidis fleeing the conflict. Obama listened carefully as Dempsey outlined the militants' recent gains. The ISIS fighters were coming in waves, overwhelming the Iraqi military. Baghdad could be overrun. "It's that bad?" Obama asked. Dempsey nodded: "Yes, it is, Mr. President," he said.

Obama wasn't surprised by what Dempsey told him, because he'd been receiving reports on the ISIS military offensive from Secretary of State John Kerry. Kerry's briefings had recently been supplemented by a report on ISIS's military gains given to the president two weeks previously during an informal basketball game by his friend Martin Nesbitt, who'd received the information by way of a businessman who owned a large US company doing business in the Iraqi city of Basra. The report made it into Obama's hands when the business executive gave it to a close friend and Obama campaign funder from Chicago, who then passed it to Nesbitt. The report, read by Obama as he stood under a basketball hoop, was a one-page summary of what the businessman had observed during a visit to Erbil, where Kurdish Peshmerga fighting units were facing off against an ISIS militia on the western edge of the city. "We're going to be overrun, slaughtered," the Peshmerga commander had told the businessman. Dempsey's report confirmed the businessman's back channel communication. The JCS chairman was worried.[50]

After Dempsey's intervention, Obama convened a meeting of his top foreign policy team that included Dempsey, national security adviser Susan Rice (who'd recently replaced Tom Donilon in that role), chief of staff Denis McDonough, and others. Obama then conducted two lengthy discussions on the crisis the next day, August 7. Of all of those advising Obama, Dempsey's voice was now the most important. The JCS chairman provided a plan for helping the Iraqis fight ISIS, which included an air interdiction campaign that would roll back the ISIS threat. Inevitably, over the next two years, that plan would include American advisers on the ground, training the Iraqi Army for battle. Obama adopted the Dempsey plan and that same night, a Thursday, he appeared on national television to announce that he had authorized US air strikes on ISIS positions. Over the next weeks, Obama's anti-ISIS strategy was deepened to include a diplomatic offensive to build support for the embattled Iraqi government. On September 10, Obama told a national television audience that the US strategy was to "degrade, and ultimately destroy" the Islamist group, and on September 11 he appointed retired Marine general John Allen to oversee the effort. The Allen appointment irritated the Pentagon, and particularly General Lloyd Austin, the head of CENTCOM, who'd once led Buff Blount's soldiers into Baghdad. "Why do we need Allen around?" Austin asked his aides. But Austin, too, fell in line, though not until he'd signaled his displeasure: when Allen requested the Pentagon provide an aircraft to fly him to Baghdad, Austin turned him down. "Get one from the State Department," the Army chief sniffed.[51]

The ISIS offensive provided the final, if ironic, commentary on Martin Dempsey's tenure as JCS chairman. Like Obama, Dempsey was committed to America's pivot to Asia, had understood the need for the austerity that the war on terror exacted on the Pentagon budget, and had regularly defended the president to his military detractors. Most importantly, Dempsey agreed with Obama's most fundamental belief: that the continued deployment of soldiers, sailors, and airmen to fight the war on terror had exacted a too-costly burden, killing and wounding thousands of Americans and nearly bankrupting the country. But the nation could not un-ring the bell. The nation's ill-conceived fights in Afghanistan and Iraq could not be set aright, no matter how committed the nation became to defeating ISIS. And yet, as Dempsey must have reflected, the US re-pivot to Iraq might have been avoided—if only America had made different decisions, found the visionary military commanders to implement them, or more carefully thought through what would and wouldn't work in the wake of 9/11. If it had only asked the question—"and then what?" It hadn't.

Over the previous twenty-eight years—from the fall of the Berlin Wall in 1989 until Donald Trump was inaugurated as president in 2017—the United States had been involved in eleven armed conflicts on four continents. It had thrown the Taliban out of Kabul, sent al-Qaeda scampering into the mountains, defeated the Iraqi army, chased Saddam Hussein into hiding, surged troops into Baghdad, removed Muammar Qaddafi in Libya, subdued the Mahdi Army in Iraq, awakened Anbar, killed Osama bin Laden, deployed drones to kill terrorists in Yemen, sent advisers to Iraq to help in the fight against ISIS—and failed. The war on terror was not won, it simply continued.

ON SEPTEMBER 25, 2015, Marty Dempsey retired from the US military. He'd served for forty-five years. Predictably, during his retirement ceremony at Fort Myer (and in the midst of a persistent drizzle), Dempsey serenaded his friends, family, and colleagues (including Barack Obama) with a rendition of "Parting Glass," a seventeenth-century Scottish "air" popular in Ireland—and a Dempsey favorite:

> *Oh all the comrades that e'er I've had*
> *Are sorry for my going away*
> *And all the sweethearts that e'er I've had*
> *Would wish me one more day to stay*
> *But since it falls unto my lot*
> *That I should rise and you should not*
> *I'll gently rise and I'll softly call*
> *Good night and joy be with you all* [52]

Marine general Joseph Dunford became the nineteenth chairman of the Joint Chiefs of Staff on the day that Dempsey retired, and paid tribute to Dempsey during his retirement ceremony. Dunford had an almost typical Marine Corps officer background, coupled with a celebrated military pedigree. Like Dempsey, he was Irish and Catholic, but unlike him had not attended any of the nation's military academies. A graduate of Boston College, he became a Marine in 1977, rising swiftly if surely through the officer ranks through three wars—in Iraq twice, and in Afghanistan. He'd served in the Corps in its most influential senior officer positions and was named by Barack Obama as JCS chairman after serving as the US Marine Corps commandant. More crucially, as Obama no doubt knew, Dunford was a part of a service that senior military officers viewed as a model for what the US military, and especially the US Army, was fast becoming: light, mobile, tough, and armed with the weapons made possible by the revolution in military affairs. It could go anywhere, quickly, and win. "If you want to know where the military is going," Merrill McPeak said soon after Dunford's appointment, "just study the Marines."[53] Dunford was a symbol of this. In Operation Iraqi Freedom, he'd served as Jim Mattis's chief of staff, as the 1st Marine Division battled its way through the boiling, fedayeen-infested Shia cities of Iraq's south.

More crucially, Dunford and Obama got along well and saw eye to eye on the country's national security issues. The two had cooperated closely on setting out the plan for US troop withdrawal from Afghanistan, where Dunford had been meticulous, tirelessly boring into the withdrawal plan's details. "I know Joe. I trust him," Obama had told the press. "He's already proven his ability to give me his unvarnished military advice based on his experience on the ground." Obama had finally gotten his general.[54]

EPILOGUE

Original Sin

"Our job was to protect the
innocent. We didn't do it."

F IVE MONTHS AFTER Martin Dempsey's retirement and twenty-five
years after the end of Operation Desert Storm, in early March 2016,
a group of retired senior US Air Force commanders who'd reached prominence during that conflict met in Washington, DC, to review their victory. But the conference was not a celebration. On the day of the Desert
Storm reunion, American soldiers were fighting in more wars in more
countries, and with less success, than at any time since the end of World
War II. The conflicts had led to thousands of American deaths, strained
the nation's resources, divided American society, escalated interservice
sniping, undermined civilian-military cooperation, and spurred a questioning of American power.

Among those attending the Washington conference was retired
Air Force general Albert "Chuck" Horner, the celebrated officer who'd
flown combat missions in Vietnam before commanding his service's
most elite fighter units, then leading them in Desert Storm. He'd envisioned Saddam's tanks rolling through downtown Riyadh, fought with
John Warden, enlisted Dave Deptula as his assistant, empowered Buster

Glosson to coordinate his air assets, then shaped the world's greatest and most successful air campaign. Many thought Horner, and not Norman Schwarzkopf, should have led the Desert Storm victory parade in Washington.

But Horner's reputation had not changed his views on his own service. While he remained his service's greatest living air commander, he quietly disdained those who extolled the Air Force's claim to strategic dominance, retaining his distaste for "airpower airheads." Proud of the role he'd played during the Iraq war, Horner was subdued during the conference, even as his former colleagues, including Warden, gathered to greet him. Inevitably, their discussion turned to the controversies of the previous decades—and the question of what had happened to their country in the years since their victory. Why was it that a military whose power was unmatched in 1991 found itself straining under the leadership of a president their senior officers mistrusted, while plagued by questions over its prowess? How was it that the United States, the sole superpower at the end of the Cold War, squandered its promise to provide a more stable international order? What had happened? Horner was asked.

With those around him falling expectantly silent, Horner searched for a single and simple answer. But he couldn't find it. "It's complicated," he said, finally. "It's really complicated."[1]

HORNER WAS RIGHT: it is complicated. The history of America's foreign policy from the end of the Cold War to the rise of ISIS will consume American historians for years to come, though it is likely their focus will be on the same question asked of America's former Desert Storm air commander: How was it that the United States squandered its promise to provide a more stable international order? What had happened? For many military officers, the answer to those questions reprised the warnings given by the late admiral William Crowe to a reporter just years after the fall of the Berlin Wall.

For some, the United States has been guilty of "overreach," to use Crowe's word. "Military power and good judgment are not the same thing," retired lieutenant general Dave Deptula says. "We can win wars, but winning the peace is something entirely different. It's a lesson that we had to learn, over and over again, over the last thirty years. I'm not sure we've learned it yet." Deptula remains proud of his service and the expertise shown by Air Force officers. John Warden had rewritten history, confirming Norman Schwarzkopf's conclusion: airpower was what made America a superpower. Nothing in the past thirty years, Deptula notes, has changed that.[2]

But for others, the history of America's post–Cold War military adventures is the result of what Crowe described as "bending a culture" to America's will. Nation building, he'd said, "was fated to fail." America's leaders believed that just as the US military could defeat any enemy it could also shape societies according to American ideals. But in each case, and particularly in Afghanistan and Iraq, that program had failed. The application of American force over a period of three decades was controversial, but the idea of nation building was even more so. By 2016, that conclusion animated nearly every debate over American power—it was why, ultimately, US military leaders opposed a military intervention in Syria, just as they'd once opposed an intervention in Libya. The conclusion undergirded the military's most fundamental belief in what it could do, and what it couldn't.

"You know, a lot of people in this country think that in every Iraqi or Syrian or whoever, there's a little American desperately trying to get out," retired Army colonel David Johnson says. "We think that all that needs to be done is to write a constitution and have a vote, and presto—the problem is solved. Well, it's not true. The hatreds are very deep, they go back a long ways, and they're not going to be solved just because we want them solved."[3]

But it wasn't simply nation building that led to the military crisis of the last three decades. Over the last years of the Obama administration, senior military officers attempted to identify the precise moment when America started to get it wrong. They called it "the original sin" of the war on terrorism. For Johnson, but also for many others, the United States underestimated the impact of Saddam's oppression of Iraq's Shias following the victory of Desert Storm. The original sin was the White House decision to stand aside as Saddam's military slaughtered the people of southern Iraq, a misjudgment so dark, so cynical that it haunted America's leaders for a generation. All it would have taken was a telephone call to the Iraqi military high command that relayed a simple message, one senior Army officer says: "If you use your helicopters, we'll shoot them down." But the call was never made. "Why are we stopping?" a soldier had asked at 73 Easting.[4]

But the decision is defended by President George H. W. Bush, the man who made it. He argues that had the US military gone north to Baghdad, the coalition it had shaped would have unraveled. "We set the goal, formed the coalition, did the diplomacy, gave peace a chance, had the fight, defined the mission of the battle, fought and won," Bush said.[5] More simply, the United States had gained international support for expelling Saddam's legions from Kuwait, and no more. That is true, but it also implies a choice—and the choice was to maintain a coalition while tens of thousands were slaughtered. So we stopped that war, saved the coalition, maintained the trust of the international community—and failed the innocent and the oppressed, the thousands of men and women who heeded our call to rise up and overthrow a monster. Yet, inexplicably, we somehow assumed that years later these same people would strew flowers in our path as we rode our tanks through their towns. "Our job was to protect the innocent," a Marine Corps officer said, "and we didn't do it."[6]

ON NOVEMBER 8, 2016, the American people elected Donald Trump president of the United States. Trump came into office on the thinnest of margins, losing the popular vote, but winning the electoral college. But if only members of the US military had voted, Trump would have won in a landslide. Hillary Clinton lost the military vote, overwhelmingly. It was a repudiation not only of Clinton's candidacy, but of her service as Barack Obama's secretary of state. The views of the military rank-and-file, the polls showed, were also starkly different than those of a number of high-profile officers who supported the former secretary of state, including Marine general John Allen, who endorsed Clinton in a speech at the Democratic National Convention. His endorsement made no difference to those he'd once commanded. He liked Clinton; they didn't.

Allen's convention speech was controversial with senior military officers, who criticized his public involvement in politics. The most outspoken criticism was authored by retired JCS chairman Martin Dempsey. "The military is not a political prize," Dempsey wrote in a highly publicized letter to the *Washington Post*. "Politicians should take the advice of senior military leaders, but keep them off the stage."[7] In fact, both Clinton and Trump put the military front and center during their campaigns—and the military noticed. As it turned out, Trump's views on the military accorded with what the military believed about itself.

In the wake of Trump's election, a public poll of serving military personnel showed that Trump's military support was tied directly to the nation's military failures. "After 15 Years of War," the *Military Times* headlined, "the Military Has About Had It with Nation Building."[8]

As crucially, while Clinton touted her popularity among some senior officers, her reputation as a liberal interventionist undercut her credibility. She paid the price for her role in the Libya intervention, and for being a "cruise missile liberal," while Trump skated through a series of verbal gaffes that included criticizing war hero John McCain and questioning the patriotism of the parents of a soldier killed in Afghanistan. Neither of those missteps outweighed the military's judgment that Clinton would lead it into more foreign interventions. For those reporters who spent their careers focused on the Pentagon, Clinton seemed shockingly tone deaf, trotting out former secretary of state Madeleine Albright, the author of the Kosovo War and "assertive multilateralism," as an ally.

The military's support for Trump in the 2016 election was strengthened in its aftermath when the president-elect nominated Marine general James Mattis as secretary of defense. The Mattis appointment was nearly universally praised, as was Trump's appointment of Marine general John Kelly to lead the Department of Homeland Security. Both men breezed through their confirmation hearings. In fact, the nation's national security establishment now had three Marine generals in its most powerful positions: Mattis was secretary of defense, Kelly was secretary of homeland security, and Joe Dunford was JCS chairman. All three had served together, in the unit that Mattis had commanded, during Operation Iraqi Freedom. Kelly had been one of his regimental commanders, while Dunford was his chief of staff. The appointments of Mattis and Kelly were followed by the naming of Army lieutenant general H. R. McMaster, one of the heroes of 73 Easting, as the president's national security adviser. Tough, articulate, and celebrated for his political sophistication, McMaster's appointment (he was not retired, but remained in the military) was nearly universally acclaimed. The new president, it was thought, had surrounded himself with a group of competent, careful, and battle-tested military officers who were familiar with the terrible costs of war—and so would be unlikely to support the military interventions that had marred the terms of the four previous presidents.[9]

Or so it was believed. In reality, each of these four officers believed deeply in American military power—and in its ability to shape the

international environment. While supporting Barack Obama's Iran negotiations, newly confirmed secretary of defense James Mattis continued to
warn of Iran's malign influence; retired Marine John Kelly, on the other
hand, was given his job as secretary of homeland security after warning
the new president of the rise of powerful drug lords in Central America
(the result of his experience heading up SOUTHCOM in the wake of
his Iraq service). JCS chairman Joe Dunford named Russia as America's greatest challenge, and favored matching their invasion of Ukraine
with a buildup of US forces in Europe, while H. R. McMaster pointedly
endorsed a policy of "forward deterrence"—of deploying troops to face
down America's adversaries on potential battlegrounds overseas.

Senior military commanders who knew and had served with Mattis,
Kelly, Dunford, and McMaster now regularly reassured the press that
the election of Trump would not lead to an upending of America's traditional role as the enforcer of global stability. The war on terrorism would
continue, the defense budget would be increased, the US military would
be strengthened, and, as Donald Trump reassured the public, the United
States "would start winning wars again."[10]

Would it?

THE SIMPLE TRUTH is that America has been lucky. Whenever our nation
has needed great military leadership, we have found it. George Washington was matched perfectly to the Continental Army. He ached to defeat
the British, but recoiled from deploying his regiments in a winner-take-
all battle. To win, his army simply needed to survive. He knew this, and
triumphed.

When, during our Civil War, Abraham Lincoln needed to find a
commander who understood the conflict's calculus, he found the relentless Ulysses S. Grant, who defined the American way of war. He remains
our greatest battlefield commander: better than Lee, better than Eisenhower, better than anyone.

In World War I, General John Pershing rejected the advice of French
and British officers who insisted that US troops come under their command, setting a precedent for national military pride that has lasted to
this day. And in World War II, Eisenhower, Marshall, Arnold, Nimitz,
and MacArthur (a military pantheon) won the most decisive and selfless
victory in world history.

Finally, during the Cold War—in spite of some notable setbacks—the nation's military was led by officers who understood the stakes, and what a single misstep would cost: Admiral Arleigh Burke, generals Matthew Ridgway and Creighton Abrams, Air Force general David Jones, and JCS chairman William Crowe led the military capably, even brilliantly.

We have not been so lucky since. The Revolution in Military Affairs transformed the US military, and Goldwater-Nichols ended decades of interservice rivalry, but neither could ensure the promotion of visionary leaders. It is true that we have the best trained and best equipped military in the world, but that is not enough. So much depends on leadership. But in our era, military leadership is tested not only on the battlefield, but in Washington, where others, elected by the people, choose which wars to fight and when. Civilian control of the military is a hallmark of our democracy. But the laws and customs that dictate that elected officials must command those in uniform does not also require military silence. Being in uniform is not a disqualification for freedom of speech.

Over the last twenty-eight years, the brilliance of our battlefield leadership has not been matched by those in Washington who are responsible for making certain that our soldiers, sailors, and airmen (and women) not only have what they need to win, but are backed by strong leaders who speak their minds. In all of those twenty-eight years, no single senior military officer of any service has ever told a president "no"—or even "yes sir, but." Except for one: Colin Powell told Bill Clinton "no"—and that was on the issue of gays in the military, hardly as momentous as sending men and women to their deaths. On the issue of war and peace, no senior military officer ever insisted that our civilian leaders question their assumptions or rethink their options. No one even raised their voice. Not once. Not ever.

Those in uniform deserve better. And so do we.

Acknowledgments

I AM ONCE again indebted to Lara Heimert, the publisher at Basic Books, for her continued support of my work; to Roger Labrie for editing this manuscript; and to Gail Ross, my unfailingly patient agent. This book would not have been possible without the attention given to it by four readers who reviewed parts of the manuscript. Included among these was Marc Schanz, the director of publications at the Mitchell Institute for Aerospace Studies; the other three read the manuscript and provided needed corrections as well as their own observations, but preferred that their names remain confidential. I am indebted to Army colonel David Johnson for his observations on the US Army and Marine fight for Iraq prior to and during the surge and for his insights on the US military. I am, as always, indebted to my wife, Nina Perry; my son, Cal; and my daughter, Madeleine Ellis, for their patience during the writing of this narrative. I have dedicated the book to my grandchildren, Amaya, Nayel, and Wilder.

A Note on Sources

In the autumn of 1985, I interviewed General Bruce Palmer Jr., the former acting chief of staff of the Army, for *The Veteran*, a newspaper I was editing at the time. Palmer was a legend among Vietnam veterans because of his command of I Corps in northern South Vietnam. He was also widely admired by veterans as an advocate for their rights and for his criticisms of the nation's civilian leaders during the Vietnam conflict. And so it was that, from time to time, our interview was interrupted by someone who would appear at the door, anxious to meet the officer who symbolized their service. Palmer was gracious, greeting each of those who wanted to talk with him by asking where they'd served and what they were doing now, before returning to answer my questions.

At the end of our interview, Palmer suggested that I write a book about the Joint Chiefs of Staff and their role in that conflict, saying he would help me by arranging interviews with the JCS's key players as well as with influential senior battlefield commanders and military thinkers of his era. Palmer subsequently arranged interviews with senior military officers whom he knew and had served with, then talked through parts of the manuscript that would become *Four Stars*, my first book on the US military.

Palmer's help set me on a career of reporting and writing on the US military. More than thirty years later, *The Pentagon's Wars* takes up where

Four Stars left off. *Four Stars* was a history of the nation's senior military commanders and their relationship with the nation's civilian leaders from World War II to the end of the Cold War. *The Pentagon's Wars* is an account of America's senior commanders and their relationship with the nation's civilian leaders from the end of the Cold War to the last days of the Obama administration. As *Four Stars* ends with the eleventh JCS chairman, the late admiral William Crowe, so this book—a three-decade narrative history of the divide between those who command our men and women in uniform, and those who send them to battle—begins with Crowe.

My relationship with Palmer placed me in a unique position. I not only interviewed the senior commanders whom he suggested, I extended this network over the next decades to include those they commanded who took their places in senior military positions. My military reporting comprises information from informal discussions over coffee, lunch, or dinner, as well as more formal interviews conducted by telephone, in person, or via e-mail. This book, then, is a result of those discussions and detailed and lengthy interviews with dozens of senior US military officers conducted over the last three decades but, for purposes of this narrative, particularly over the last two years. I have conducted eighty-two separate formal interviews with more than fifty senior military officers for this work, as well as dozens of other interviews that have been more informal.

Not surprisingly, at the insistence of those with whom I've spoken, a number of the interviews have been off the record, the information gleaned from them the result of my pledge that those interviewed will not be named. I have kept that pledge, but diligently checked what I was told during those interviews with other military officers and with senior civilian leaders at the Pentagon who have direct knowledge of the events I've described. Those who have agreed to be named have been identified in the book and in the endnotes.

Finally, I have benefited greatly from the reporting of others, and most especially from those who have provided voluminous and detailed accounts of US military operations, from Operation Desert Shield and Desert Storm to Operation Iraqi Freedom. I have supplemented those accounts with reporting of my own, much of which has appeared in national magazines or in online articles. These articles have appeared under my byline in *Al Jazeera America*, *Al Jazeera* (English), *Asia Times*, *The Beirut Daily Star*, *The Daily Beast*, *Foreign Affairs*, *Foreign Policy*, *The Nation*, *Politico*, *Politico Magazine*, *Slate*, *The Strategy Bridge*, and *War in Context*.

Notes

Prologue: Bill Crowe's Warning

1. "Your mind is like a parachute": "Selected Works of William J. Crowe, Jr." Joint History Office, Office of the Chairman of the Joint Chiefs of Staff, Washington, DC, 2013. "He saved my sleep": Arthur T. Hadley, "In Command," *New York Times*, August 7, 1988.

2. "That's the ultimate": author interview with Adm. William Crowe.

3. William J. Crowe Jr., *Line of Fire* (New York: Simon and Schuster, 1993), 61.

4. Nicholas M. Horrock, "Reagan Pick for Joint Chiefs an About-face," *Chicago Tribune*, July 14, 1985.

5. "Crowe's appointment is unprecedented": author interview with Adm. Eugene Carroll (1985); "so we don't have to": author interview with Caspar Weinberger (1985).

6. Andrew Krepinevich and Barry Watts, *The Last Warrior* (New York: Basic Books, 2015).

7. James R. Locher III, *Victory on the Potomac* (College Station: Texas A&M Press, 2002).

8. Linton Weeks, "The Admiral Charts an Unknown Course," *Washington Post*, November 22, 2006.

Chapter One: John Warden's War

1. "National Victory Celebration," C-Span, June 8, 1991, https://www.c-span.org/video/?18328–1/national-victory-celebration-parade.

2. Michael R. Gordon and General Bernard E. Trainor, *The Generals' War* (Boston: Little, Brown, 1995), 300–1; see also Rick Atkinson, *Crusade: The Untold Story of the Persian Gulf War* (Boston: Houghton Mifflin, 1993), 67–69.

3. Atkinson, *Crusade*, 198.

4. Interview with Lieutenant General Calvin Waller, "The Gulf War," *Frontline*, PBS, n.d., http://www.pbs.org/wgbh/pages/frontline/gulf/oral/waller/1.html.

5. Ibid.

6. Author interview with senior US Army CENTCOM staff planner, June 1996. See also Atkinson, *Crusade*, 105.

7. John Andreas Olsen, *Strategic Air Power and Desert Storm* (London: Routledge, 2003), 92.

8. "Freeing American Hostages in the First Gulf War," Moments in US Diplomatic History, Association for Diplomatic Studies and Training, n.d., http://adst.org/2015/07/freeing-american-hostages-in-the-first-gulf-war/; see also http://www.pbs.org/wgbh/pages/frontline/gulf/oral/schwarzkopf/1.html.

9. Author discussion with Gen. John M. "Mike" Loh (USAF, ret.). Gen. Loh refused to be formally interviewed for this book, but informally shared his recollections with me during a May 2016 conference held to commemorate the 25th Anniversary of Operation Desert Storm. The conference was organized by the Arlington, VA–based Mitchell Institute for Aerospace Studies.

10. Ibid.; see also Gordon and Trainor, *The Generals' War*, 76, and "Desert Storm: 25 Years Later, Lessons from the 1991 Air Campaign in the Persian Gulf War," Mitchell Institute for Aerospace Studies, Air Force Association, Arlington, VA, March 2017, at http://www.mitchellaerospacepower.org/mitchell-studies.

11. A. J. Plunkett, "High Profile: John Michael Loh," *Daily Press*, July 12, 1993.

12. The nickname "Right Turn Warden" competed with others given to Warden: "Mad John" and "Saint John" were two others.

13. Author discussion with Gen. Loh, supplemented by a discussion of his own experiences in the Persian Gulf War with Gen. David Deptula (USAF, ret.).

14. There are disagreements with the description of Warden's views and influence that I have presented here. After the conclusion of the Gulf War, Gen. Wilbur Creech, the former head of the US Air Force Tactical Air Command, wrote that Warden's role had been exaggerated. He circulated a notice among air force officers that they correct the record, by some well-aimed "counterbattery fire." Creech's views gained widespread currency, with Warden's role officially downgraded, his papers taken off required air force reading lists, and his views dampened in air force professional schools.

15. Gary M. Jackson, USAF major, "Warden's Five-Ring System Theory," dissertation, Maxwell Air Force Base, Alabama, April 2000.

16. I discussed the importance of Clausewitz on the US military's thinking in an essay I wrote for the online military publication *The Strategy Bridge* in 2015: see https://medium.com/the-bridge/what-would-clausewitz-do-66e22466422c#.5lzr7bwik.

17. Olsen, *Strategic Air Power and Desert Storm*, 281.

18. Atkinson, *Crusade*, 60.

19. Paul F. and Allison J. Crickmore, *F-117 Nighthawk* (Minneapolis, MN: Zenith Press, 2003), 100.

20. Diane T. Putney, *Airpower Advantage: Planning the Gulf War Air Campaign, 1989–1991* (Washington, DC: Air Force History and Museums Program, United States Air Force, 2004), 72.

21. Ibid., 93

22. Olsen, *Strategic Air Power and Desert Storm*, 102.

23. John Andreas Olsen, *John Warden and the Renaissance of American Air Power* (Lincoln: University of Nebraska Press, 2007), 164. Olsen's work on the obstacles faced by Warden in promoting and gaining approval for Instant Thunder is authoritative; that work has been supplemented here by my own interviews with the principal players.

24. Gordon and Trainor, *The Generals' War*, 83–84.

25. William M. Arkin, "Fog of War," *Washington Post*, July 30, 1998.

26. Author interview with senior US Air Force officer.

27. *War In The Persian Gulf, Operations Desert Shield and Desert Storm* (Washington, DC: Center of Military History, 2010), 32.

28. Atkinson, *Crusade,* 67–71.

29. Olsen, *John Warden and the Renaissance of American Air Power*, 171.

30. Ibid., 173.

31. Ibid., 151.

32. Ibid., 196.

33. Robert H. Gregory, *Clean Bombs and Dirty Wars: Air Power in Kosovo and Libya* (Lincoln: University of Nebraska Press, 2015), 9.

34. Frederick Kagan, *Finding the Target: The Transformation of American Military Policy* (New York: Encounter Books, 2007), 134.

35. Author interview with senior US Air Force officer.

36. Interview with General Buster Glosson, "The Gulf War," *Frontline*, PBS, n.d., http://www.pbs.org/wgbh/pages/frontline/gulf/oral/glosson/1.html.

37. Author discussion with Gen. Loh.

38. Gordon and Trainor, *The Generals' War*, 96–98.

39. "US Disavows 'Decapitation' War Strategy," *Los Angeles Times*, Sept. 17, 1991.

40. Gordon and Trainor, *The Generals' War*, 135.

41. Ibid., 137–41. See also Atkinson, *Crusade*, 110.

42. Atkinson, *Crusade*, 111–12.

43. Frank N. Schubert and Theresa L. Krause, eds., *The Whirlwind War: The United States Army in Operation Desert Shield and Desert Storm* (Washington, DC: Center of Military History, 1995), 201.

44. Mark Perry, "The Pentagon's Fight Over Fighting China," *Politico Magazine*, July/August 2015.

45. "Schwarzkopf," *Newsweek*, September 27, 1992.

46. Christopher M. Gacek, *The Logic of Force: The Dilemma of Limited War in American Foreign Policy* (New York: Columbia University Press, 1994), 283.

47. Douglas Macgregor, *Margin of Victory* (Annapolis, MD: Naval Institute Press, 2016), 147.

48. Ibid., 144; and author interview with Col. Douglas Macgregor (US Army, ret).

49. Atkinson, *Crusade*, 406.

50. Gordon and Trainor, *The Generals' War*, 416.

51. Ibid., 418.

52. Author discussion with Gen. Charles A. "Chuck" Horner. Gen. Horner shared his recollections of the Desert Storm air campaign during a May 2016 conference held to commemorate the 25th anniversary of Operation Desert Storm. The conference was organized by the Arlington, VA–based Mitchell Institute for Aerospace Studies.

53. "Desert Storm: 25 Years Later, Lessons from the 1991 Air Campaign in the Persian Gulf War," Mitchell Institute for Aerospace Studies, Air Force Association, Arlington, VA, March 2017, http://www.mitchellaerospacepower.org/mitchell -studies; and author discussion with Gen. Loh.

Chapter Two: Colin Powell's Other Doctrine

1. Jim Dresbach, "Vibrant Atmosphere of Myer Was Fine for Colin Powell," Pentagram, March 8, 2013.

2. Eric Schmitt, "Colin Powell, Who Led US Military Into a New Era, Resigns," *New York Times*, October 1, 1993.

3. Author interview with former assistant secretary of defense Lawrence Korb.

4. General Colin Powell, "Go, Gunfighter, Go," *Chicken Soup for the Soul*, website, http://www.chickensoup.com/book-story/49808/go-gunfighter-go.

5. Joe Klein, "Can Colin Powell Save America?," *Newsweek*, October 9, 1994.

6. Michael Takiff, *A Complicated Man, The Life of Bill Clinton as Told by Those Who Know Him* (New Haven, CT: Yale University Press, 2003), 32.

7. Quoted in Behzad Yaghmaian, "Refugees Are an Overlooked Casualty of Iraq War," *USA Today*, February 6, 2007.

8. As reported by Randall Richard in the *Providence Journal*; see Joyce Chediak, "The 1991 Iraq Gulf War, America Bombs the 'Highway of Death,'" Global Research, April 4, 2016.

9. "A Soldier of Conscience," *Newsweek*, March 10, 1991.

10. "A Mountain of a Man," *Newsweek*, February 28, 1991.

11. Governor Bill Clinton, "Veterans Day Remarks," C-Span, November 11, 1992, http://www.c-span.org/video/?34469-1/veterans-day-remarks.

12. Art Pine, "General to Retire Over Clinton Flap," *Los Angeles Times*, June 19, 1993.

13. Author interview with senior US Army officer.

14. Author interview with senior retired Marine Corps officer.

15. Author interview with Gen. Merrill McPeak (USAF, ret.).

16. Eric Schmitt, "The Transition," *New York Times*, November 12, 1992.

17. Author interview with senior US Army officer.

18. Colin Powell (with Joseph E. Persico), *My American Journey* (New York: Ballantine, 2003), 564.

19. As related to me by a JCS staff officer whom I interviewed at the time.

20. Laurie Goodstein, "Gay-Rights Group Reels Off a Reply to Critics," *Washington Post*, February 18, 1993.

21. Melissa Healy, "Powell Confirms He Is Considering Leaving Office Early," *Los Angeles Times*, February 11, 1993.

22. According to a senior civilian official and colleague of Aspin.

23. Michael Lee Lanning, *The African-American Soldier: From Crispus Attucks to Colin Powell* (South Carolina: Citadel, 1997), 282.

24. Nathaniel Frank, *Unfriendly Fire: How the Gay Ban Undermines the Military and Weakens America* (New York: Thomas Dunne, 2009), 72–75.

25. David Evans, "Nunn Urges Clinton, Senate to Stay Cool," *Chicago Tribune*, January 28, 1993; see also Thomas L. Friedman, "Compromise Near on Military's Ban on Homosexuals," *New York Times*, January 29, 1993.

26. Author interview with Gen. McPeak.

27. "Pat Schroeder vs. Colin Powell: The Congresswoman Taunts, the General Replies," *Crisis Magazine*, July 1, 1992.

28. Author interview with Gen. McPeak.

29. Adam Clymer, "Lawmakers Revolt on Lifting Gay Ban in Military Service," *New York Times*, January 27, 1993.

30. Aaron Belkin et al., "How to Repeal 'Don't Ask, Don't Tell,'" *Palm Center*, University of California, Santa Barbara, May 2009.

31. Thomas L. Friedman, "Compromise Near on Military's Ban on Homosexuals," *New York Times*, January 29 1993.

32. Eric Schmitt, "Pentagon Speeds Plan to Lift Gay Ban," *New York Times*, April 16, 1993.

33. "Clinton was apoplectic": "Anecdotes," *Frontline*, PBS, n.d., http://www.pbs.org/wgbh/pages/frontline/shows/clinton/anecdotes/2.html; "You can get the joint chiefs off my ass": author interview with Gen. David Jones (USAF, ret.), and Robert O. Muller. Muller was then the president of the Vietnam Veterans of America Foundation and founder of the International Campaign to Ban Landmines. The exchange took place between Jones, Muller, Gen. Robert Gard, and President Clinton during a dinner at the White House.

34. Carl M. Cannon, "Clinton Jogs with General Insulted at White House," *Baltimore Sun*, April 5, 1993; the mix-up in intentions on what the Clinton staffer meant was relayed to me by an aide to Gen. McCaffrey at the time of the incident.

35. Author interview with William Crowe.

36. Author interview with Gen. McPeak.

37. Barton Gellman, "Warship Gives Clinton a Not-So-Hail to the Chief," *Washington Post*, March 13, 1993.

38. Author interview with Prof. Richard Kohn, University of North Carolina.

39. Michael R. Gordon, "General Ousted for Derisive Remarks About President," *New York Times*, June 19, 1993; as also, author interview with senior Joint Staff officer.

40. Eric Schmitt with Thomas L. Friedman, "Clinton and Powell Discover That They Need Each Other," *New York Times*, June 4, 1993.

41. Edwin Ferebee Williamson, "A Comparison of the Post-Cold War Defense Budget Reduction to Prior Post-Conflict Reductions after World War II, Korea and Vietnam," thesis, Naval Post Graduate School, Monterey, CA, September 1993;

see also Barton Gellman, "Aspin Moves to Ensure Fighting Readiness of Armed Forces," *Washington Post*, May 20, 1993.

42. John T. Correll, "The Legacy of the Bottom Up Review," *Air Force Magazine*, October 2003.

43. Author interview with a senior Joint Staff officer.

44. Melissa Healy, "Pentagon Blasts Tailhook Probe, Two Admirals Resign," *Los Angeles Times*, September 25, 1992.

45. Ellen Goodman, "The Navy Does the Right Thing," *Baltimore Sun*, September 29, 1992.

46. Author interview with senior US Navy officer.

47. Ibid.

48. Ibid.

49. Author interview with senior US Army officer.

50. Author interview with senior Joint Staff officer.

51. Author interview with Gen. McPeak.

52. Colin L. Powell, "Challenges Ahead," *Foreign Affairs*, Washington, DC, Winter 1992.

53. Stephen S. Rosenfeld, "Colin Powell's Somalia Operation," *Washington Post*, December 11, 1992.

54. "Reluctant Warrior," *The Guardian*, September 29, 2001, https://www.theguardian.com/world/2001/sep/30/usa.afghanistan.

55. Author interview with Gen. McPeak.

56. Ibid.

Chapter Three: Wes Clark: Water Walker

1. Douglas Jehl, "Clinton Doubling US Force in Somalia, Vowing Troops Will Be Home in Six Months," *Washington Post*, October 8, 1993; see also Mark Bowden, *Black Hawk Down* (New York: Grove Press, 2010); and Thomas Friedman, "The Somalia Mission," *New York Times*, October 7, 1993.

2. Don Oberdorfer, "The Path To Intervention," *Washington Post*, December 6, 1992; see also Walter S. Poole, "The Effort to Save Somalia" (monograph), Joint History Office, Office of the Joint Chiefs of Staff, August 2005.

3. Thomas Cutler, ed., *The US Naval Institute on Vietnam: A Retrospective* (Annapolis, MD: Naval Institute Press, 2016), 119.

4. David Evans, "Clinton Dines with 15 Candidates for Joint Chiefs Helm," *Chicago Tribune*, August 11, 1993.

5. Author interview with Gen. Joseph Hoar (USMC, ret.).

6. David Halberstam, *War in a Time of Peace* (New York: Scribner, 2002), 321.

7. Quoted in Wesley Clark, *Waging Modern War* (New York: Public Affairs, 2002), 31.

8. Ibid., 31–35.

9. Peter J. Boyer, "General Clark's Battles," *New Yorker*, November 17, 2003.

10. Author interview with senior US Army officer. Also see Anton Myrer, *Once An Eagle* (New York: Harper Collins, 2002).

11. Michael Karnish, "An Arkansas Alliance, and High-Ranking Foes," *Boston Globe*, November 17, 2003.

12. "From Cow Pasture to Kosovo," March 22, 2011, http://fromcow pasturestokosovo.blogspot.com/2011/03/remembering-heroes-of-green-ramp-23 .html.

13. Halberstam, *War in a Time of Peace*, 229.

14. Wesley K. Clark, *Don't Wait for the Next War: A Strategy for American Growth and Global Leadership* (New York: Public Affairs, 2014), 19–21.

15. "humanitarian led foreign policy": James D. Boys, "A Lost Opportunity: The Flawed Implementation of Assertive Multilateralism (1991–1993)," *European Journal of American Studies*, Spring 2012; "assert them": author interview with senior US Navy officer.

16. P. Girard, *Clinton In Haiti: The 1994 Invasion of Haiti* (New York: Palgrave MacMillan, 2004), 118.

17. General Hugh Shelton (with Ronald Levinson and Malcolm McConnell), *Without Hesitation* (New York: St. Martin's Press, 2010), 52–53.

18. Steven J. Mrozek, *82nd Airborne Division* (Nashville: Turner, 2000), 79.

19. Ibid., 233–34.

20. Girard, *Clinton In Haiti, The 1994 Invasion of Haiti*, 118

21. Quoted in Halberstam, *War in a Time of Peace*, 273.

22. Jenine Davidson, *Lifting the Fog of Peace: How Americans Learned to Fight Modern War* (Ann Arbor: University of Michigan Press, 2010), 92; see also Halberstam, *War in a Time of Peace*, 273.

23. *War in a Time of Peace*, 317.

24. Author interview with senior US Army officer.

25. quoted in Halberstam, *War in a Time of Peace*, 273

26. Ibid., 326–27.

27. Ibid., 328.

28. Author interview with Gen. Wesley Clark (US Army, ret.).

29. Elaine Sciolino, "The Clinton Record: Bosnia Policy Shaped by US Military Role," *New York Times*, July 29, 1996.

30. Author interview with senior Joint Staff officer.

31. "Admiral Leighton W. 'Snuffy' Smith, Interview," *Frontline*, PBS, n.d., http://www.pbs.org/wgbh/pages/frontline/shows/military/guys/smith.html.

32. Halberstam, *War in a Time of Peace*, 346.

33. Ibid.

34. Author interview with Gen. Clark. Clark confirmed the gist of the conversation, adding that he felt "chagrined" by Smith's reminder.

35. Clark, *Waging Modern War*, 62.

36. Ibid., 73.

37. Peter J. Boyer, "General Clark's Battles," *New Yorker*, November 7, 2003.

38. Paul F. J. Aranas, *Smokescreen: The US, NATO and the Illegitimate Use of Force* (New York: Algora, 2012), 116; see also Clark, *Waging Modern War*, 67.

39. "I have more pull than Denny": author interview with senior US Navy officer; "I've seen it a dozen times": author interview with Gen. George Joulwan (US Army, ret.).

40. Author interview with senior US Army officer; see also Michael E. Ruane, "Why Did Admiral Take His Own Life?," *Seattle Times*, May 17, 1996.

41. As James Webb, when he was secretary of the Navy, accused the author of being.

42. Author interview with senior US Army officer.

43. Author interview with Gen. Joulwan.

44. Ibid.

Chapter Four: Hugh Shelton: Clinton's General

1. Clinton named Berger's White House predecessor, Tony Lake, as CIA director, but Lake eventually withdrew his name after his appointment met with a tepid response on Capitol Hill.

2. David Halberstam, *War in a Time of Peace* (New York: Scribner, 2002), 370.

3. Bradley Graham, "Cohen Plays Skeptic Role on Bosnia," *Washington Post*, November 30, 1997.

4. Robert Kagan, "Clinton and Cohen in Bosnia," *Weekly Standard*, May 5, 1997.

5. "Admiral Leighton W. 'Snuffy' Smith, Interview," PBS, *Frontline*, n.d., http://www.pbs.org/wgbh/pages/frontline/shows/military/guys/smith.html.

6. Ibid.

7. "New Nato Head for Bosnia," *Irish Times*, June 7, 1996.

8. George Joulwan was the next to go: http://www.presidency.ucsb.edu/ws/?pid=52365; in the dinner's wake: http://www.presidency.ucsb.edu/ws/?pid=52365; and, "Shalikashvili retires soon; successor talks start," Associated Press, January 30, 1997.

9. Author interview with senior Joint Staff officer at the time

10. Mary Dejevsky, "Female B-52 Pilot Quits over Charges of Adultery," *The Independent*, May 18, 1997; see also Elaine Sciolino, "From a Love Affair to a Court Martial," *Washington Post*, May 11, 1997.

11. Elaine Sciolino, "From a Love Affair to a Court Martial," *Washington Post*, May 11, 1997.

12. John Barry, "A Rebels in the Ranks," *Newsweek*, July 13, 1997.

13. Author interview with Gen. George Joulwan (US Army, ret.).

14. Eric Schmitt, "New Leader of Military Will Need Right Answer," *New York Times*, June 30, 1997.

15. General Hugh Shelton, *Without Hesitation* (New York: St. Martin's Press, 2010), 299.

16. Randall Mikkelsen, "Shalikashvili Retires Amid High Praise," *Pittsburgh Post-Gazette*, October 1, 1997.

17. Author interview with senior Joint Staff officer.

18. Shelton, *Without Hesitation*, 319.

19. Jim Garamone, "Dempsey Describes Chairman's Job as Being 'The Dash,'" *DoD News*, July 7, 2015.

20. "UN Security Council Resolution 1160," http://www.nato.int/kosovo/docu/u980331a.htm

21. Wesley Clark, *Waging Modern War* (New York: Public Affairs, 2002), 117.

22. "as big as a football field": author interview with senior State Department official.

23. Author interview with retired diplomat Daniel Serwer.

24. "Milosevic will pretend to negotiate": Clark, *Waging Modern War*, 117.

25. Ibid.

26. "we are seeing the emergence": Stefan Troebst, *The Kosovo Conflict, 1998*, Stockholm International Peace Research Institute (draft) (Oxford: Oxford University Press, 1998), see http://www.reteccp.org/kossovo/attivita/1998/antologia/conflict.html.

27. Halberstam, *War in a Time of Peace*, 399.

28. "Kosovo and Serbia: Trading Blows," *The Economist*, August 5, 2011.

29. "How It Was Fought," *Frontline*, PBS, n.d., http://www.pbs.org/wgbh/pages/frontline/shows/kosovo/fighting/fighting.html.

30. Author interview with Lt. Gen. Robert Gard Jr. (US Army, ret.), and author interview with Gen. Joulwan.

31. Peter J. Boyer, "General Clark's Battles," *New Yorker*, November 17, 2003.

32. The Kosovo bombing: Michael W. Lamb Sr., "Operation Allied Force Golden Nuggets for Future Campaigns," Lt. Col. USAF, Air War College Maxwell Paper No. 27, Maxwell Air Force Base, Alabama, August 2002; "The boss will take care of this": author interview with senior US Army officer at the time.

33. Robert Dudney, "Verbatim Special, The Balkan War," *Air Force Magazine*, June 1999.

34. Boyer, "General Clark's Battles."

35. Benjamin S. Lambeth, *NATO's Air War for Kosovo: A Strategic and Operational Assessment* (Washington, DC: Rand Corporation, 2002), 38.

36. "We hit what we targeted": Author interview with senior US Air Force officer. The judgment was agreed to by Gen. Alexander Haig (US Army, ret.) in an author interview at the time. Haig was proud of the strike: "It was an example of the superb use of precision munitions," Haig told me. Haig confronted the Chinese ambassador on the incident: "You Chinamen have to get used to the idea that we're a superpower."

37. Tom Peck, "How James Blunt Saved Us from World War 3," *Independent*, November 15, 2010, http://www.independent.co.uk/news/people/news/how-james-blunt-saved-us-from-world-war-3-2134203.html.

38. "Oh, well, Jackson was overwrought": the details of the Clark-Jackson confrontation were the subject of a wide-ranging author interview of Gen. Wesley Clark. See also Mark Tran, "I'm Not Going to Start . . . ," *The Guardian*, August 2, 1999; and Peck, "How James Blunt Saved Us from World War 3."

39. Author interview with Gen. Joulwan.

40. "General Michael C. Short," *Frontline*, PBS, n.d., http://www.pbs.org/wgbh/pages/frontline/shows/kosovo/interviews/short.html.

41. Walter Isaacson, "Madeleine's War," *Time*, May 9, 1999.

42. "He was weak": author interview with senior retired US Army officer; and William Saletan, "Hugh Shelton Smears Wes Clark," *Slate*, September 29, 2003.

43. David Von Drehle and R. Jeffrey Smith, "US Strikes Iraq for Plot to Kill Bush," *Washington Post*, June 27, 1993.

44. "You know, it would scare the shit": Shelton, *Without Hesitation*, p. 122.

45. Author interview with senior US Army officer.

46. "Sanctions and Childhood Mortality in Iraq," *Lancet*, May 27, 2000, http://thelancet.com/journals/lancet/article/PIIS0140-6736(00)02289-3/fulltext.

47. "Standoff with Iraq: War of Words," *New York Times*, February 19, 1998.

48. Author interview with senior Marine Corps officer.

49. Author interview with Gen. Anthony Zinni (USMC, ret.); see also, "Post-Saddam Iraq: The War Game Desert Crossing," National Security Electronic Briefing Book, No. 207, http://nsarchive.gwu.edu/NSAEBB/NSAEBB207/.

50. Shelton, *Without Hesitation*, 398–99.

Chapter Five: Tommy Franks: Rumsfeld's General

1. "Presidential Debate at Winston-Salem," American Presidency Project, October 11, 2000, http://www.presidency.ucsb.edu/ws/?pid=29419.

2. "We have a well-funded military": Michael R. Gordon, "The 2000 Campaign: The Military; Bush Would Stop U.S. Peacekeeping In Balkan Fights," *New York Times*, October 21, 2000; "This comes down to function": Christopher Lane, "Bush-Rice Plan Identifies US Interests," *Los Angeles Times*, October 24, 2000.

3. "Clinton: I Warned Bush About Bin Laden Threat," *WND*, October 16, 2003.

4. The story was first told to me by General David Jones (USAF, ret.) and later widely repeated at the senior levels of the JCS.

5. Frank Bruniaug, "Bush Said to Pick Air Force General as Military Head," *New York Times*, Aug. 23, 2001.

6. James Daoaug, "Man in the News; A Low-Key Space Buff," *New York Times*, August 25, 2001.

7. "Madeleine K. Albright Oral History," Miller Center, University of Virginia, August 17, 2006.

8. "Much Ado About QDR," William Matthews, *Armed Forces Journal*, January 2006; it didn't make sense: author interview with senior USAF officer.

9. Author interview with senior Department of Defense civilian official who served at the time. Prior to his death, the author interviewed Martin Hoffman, a former secretary of the Army and close Rumsfeld protégé. Hoffman confirmed details of Rumsfeld's personality quirks, which he attempted to dampen.

10. Author interview with Martin Hoffman.

11. Author interview with senior US Army officer.

12. Author interview with senior USAF officer.

13. See, Douglas J. Feith, "The Donald Rumsfeld I Know," *Washington Post*, November 12, 2006; "How the fuck": author interview with senior retired USAF officer who served at the time.

14. Hugh Shelton, *Without Hesitation* (New York: St. Martin's Press, 2010), 430–31.

15. History Commons, "Profile: Julian H. Burns," February 5, 2002, http://www.historycommons.org/entity.jsp?entity=julian_h__burns_1; see also Center for US Military History, "History: 9/11 Attacks," summary, n.d., http://www.history.com/topics/9-11-attacks.

16. Ibid.

17. Rachel Quigley, "'I Wanted to Project a Sense of Calm,'" *Daily Mail*, London, July 29, 2011, http://www.dailymail.co.uk/news/article-2020215/President-Bush-explains-blank-face-told-9-11-attacks.html.

18. History Commons, "Profile: Ralph Eberhart," October 16, 2001, http://www.historycommons.org/entity.jsp?entity=ralph_eberhart.

19. Shelton, *Without Hesitation*, 142.

20. Robert L. Grenier, *88 Days to Kandahar* (New York: Simon and Schuster, 2015), 3–7; and author interview with Robert L. Grenier.

21. "The War in Afghanistan," *Frontline*, PBS, n.d., http://www.pbs.org/wgbh/pages/frontline/darkside/themes/afghanistan.html.

22. Author interview with senior civilian Pentagon official.

23. Author interview with aide to General Tommy Franks; see also, Michael DeLong, *Inside Centcom* (Washington, DC: Regnery, 2004), 33–35.

24. "I'm fighting this war, you're not": ibid., 27–28. "Tommy took the bait": Author interview with senior retired US Army general at the time.

25. "a mob of Title X motherfuckers": Hugh Shelton, "Inside the War Room, the Final Days," October 12, 2010, http://www.thehistoryreader.com/military-history/inside-war-room-final-days/; "You're my general": author interview with senior retired US Army general at the time. NB: There are two accounts of the Franks meeting. In *Cobra II*, Franks is reported to have used this phrase in the late fall of 2001; see Michael R. Gordon and General Bernard E. Trainor, *Cobra II: The Inside Story of the Invasion and Occupation of Iraq* (New York: Pantheon, 2006), 47. In *Plan of Attack*, the phrase is used by Franks in a full meeting in the tank the next March (of 2002); see Bob Woodward, *Plan of Attack* (New York: Simon and Schuster, 2004), 117, Subsequent reporting from a participant who knows of both incidents reports that both stories are correct—"Franks was proud of what he said," this participant told me.

26. "It was almost useless bombing" and "our guys were listening": "CIA Agent I Was Sent to Get Bin Laden's Head," CBS News, October 7, 2011, http://www.cbsnews.com/news/cia-agent-i-was-sent-to-get-bin-ladens-head/.

27. "Interview: Gary Schroen," *Frontline*, PBS, n.d., http://www.pbs.org/wgbh/pages/frontline/darkside/interviews/schroen.html.

28. Author interview with former CIA officer; author interview with senior US Army officer.

29. "Interview: Tom Ricks," *Frontline*, PBS, n.d., http://www.pbs.org/wgbh/pages/frontline/shows/pentagon/interviews/ricks.html; see also Michael R. Gordon, "A Prewar Slide Show Cast Iraq in Rosy Hues," *New York Times*, February 15, 2007.

30. James Risen, *State of War: The Secret History of the CIA and the Bush Administration* (New York: Free Press, 2006), 61; and author interview with Martin Hoffman.

31. Author interview with former CIA officer.

32. "Find them": DeLong, *Inside Centcom*, 26.

33. Peter J. Boyer, "The New War Machine," *New Yorker*, June 30, 2003.

34. William Hamilton, "Bush Began to Plan War Three Months After 9/11," *Washington Post*, April 17, 2004.

35. DeLong, *Inside Centcom*, 64.

36. Ibid., 67.

37. "The Iraq War: Part I," National Security Archive, Washington, DC, September 22, 2010, http://nsarchive.gwu.edu/NSAEBB/NSAEBB326/print.htm.

38. George W. Bush, "An Axis of Evil," State of the Union Address, Washington, DC, January 29, 2002, http://www.pbs.org/wgbh/pages/frontline/shows/tehran/etc/evil.html.

39. The "Top Secret Polo Step," National Security Archive, Washington, DC, February 14, 2007, http://nsarchive.gwu.edu/NSAEBB/NSAEBB214/.

40. Michael R. Gordon, "A Prewar Slide Show Cast Iraq in Rosy Hues," *New York Times*, February 15, 2007.

41. Douglas Jehl, "The Struggle for Iraq; Strategy; U.S. Says It Will Move Gingerly Against Sadr," *New York Times*, April 17, 2004; see also Woodward, *Plan Of Attack*, 145.

42. "Interview: Richard Armitage," *Frontline*, PBS, n.d., http://www.pbs.org/wgbh/pages/frontline/bushswar/interviews/armitage.html.

43. "Real men don't do MOOTWA": The phrase is attributed to JCS chairman John Shalikashvili, who first used it during his tenure. See also Dr. Bert Frandsen, "The Insurgents," review, Air Force Research Institute, Maxwell Air Force Base, n.d., http://www.au.af.mil/au/afri/review_full.asp?id=580.

Chapter Six: Richard Myers: The Invisible Chairman

1. Geoffrey Aronson, "Echo of History: Victor, Beware," *Los Angeles Times*, March 3, 2003.

2. Andrew Syke, ed., "The Military Papers of Lieutenant-General Frederick Stanley Maude, 1914–1917," Army Records Society, London, http://www.h-net.org/reviews/showrev.php?id=37773.

3. "a catchy notion": Bob Woodward, *Plan of Attack* (New York: Simon and Schuster, 2004), 145.

4. Department of Defense, *21st Century Military Documents: Shock and Awe, Achieving Rapid Dominance-Momentous Defense Paper on New Strategies*, Progressive Management, Washington, DC, 2005; see also Harlan Ullman and James Wade Jr., *Shock & Awe: Achieving Rapid Dominance* (Washington, DC: National Defense University, 1996).

5. Author interview with senior retired US Army officer.

6. Ullman and Wade, "Shock and Awe: Achieving Rapid Dominance."

7. Gregory Fontenot, E. J. Degen, and David Tohn, *On Point: United States Army in Operation Iraqi Freedom* (Annapolis, MD: Naval Institute Press, 2005), 47.

8. Author interview with senior CIA officer.

9. Ibid.

10. Author interview with senior US Army officer.

11. Author interview with senior CIA officer.

12. Chris Suellentrop, "Ahmad Chalabi," *Slate*, April 9, 2003.

13. Author interview with senior CIA officer.

14. Author interview with USAF officer; Author interview with Gen. Merrill McPeak. McPeak withheld comment on the views of other USAF officers he was in contact with during this period. "I won't comment on what others thought," he told me.

15. Author interview with senior CIA officer.

16. Thomas Ricks, *Fiasco: The American Military Adventure in Iraq* (New York: Penguin Books, 2007), 66.

17. Author interview with senior retired US Navy officer.

18. Author interview with senior retired US Army officer.

19. "keep your mouth shut order": author interview with senior US Army officer.

20. Ibid.; see also, David Margolick, "The Night of the Generals," *Vanity Fair*, April 2007.

21. Richard Holloran, "Shinseki's Not a Quitter," *Politico Magazine*, May 29, 2014.

22. Author interview with senior retired USAF officer.

23. Bradley Graham, *By His Own Rules* (New York: Public Affairs, 2010), 532; see also, Scott Harrup, "Admiral Vern Clark: Looking to the Future with Time Tested Values," *Pentecostal Evangel*, October 22, 2000.

24. H. R. McMaster, *Dereliction of Duty* (New York: Harper Row, 2004).

25. Author interview with Gen. Bruce Palmer Jr. (1986).

26. Mark Perry, *Four Stars* (Boston: Houghton Mifflin, 1989), 163–65.

27. "If you don't like change": James Dao and Thom Shanker, "No Longer a Soldier, Shinseki Has a New Mission," *New York Times*, November 10, 2009.

28. Author interview with Col. Douglas Macgregor (US Army, ret.).

29. "thanks for coming": author interview with senior retired US Army officer; see also Douglas Macgregor, *Breaking the Phalanx* (New York: Praeger, 1997).

30. Author interview with Col. Macgregor.

31. Author interview with senior retired US Army officer.

32. Graham, *By His Own Rules*, 522; author interview with Martin Hoffman.

33. Author interview with senior retired USAF officer.

34. "He didn't understand artillery": Author interview with Gen. Paul Van Riper.

35. Scott Shuger, "Outgunned; What the Crusader Cancellation Really Means to the Army," *Slate*, May 23, 2002.

36. Ibid.

37. James Daomay, "Army Liaison Who Lobbied Congress for Weapon Resigns," *New York Times*, May 11, 2002.

38. "a firing squad": author interview with senior USAF officer.

39. Peter J. Boyer, "The New War Machine," *New Yorker*, June 30, 2003.

40. Author interview with senior US Marine Corps officer; see also David Ignatius, "Rumsfeld and the Generals," *Washington Post*, March 30, 2005.

41. Woodward, *Plan of Attack*, 208.

42. Author interview with Gen. Paul Van Riper. The interview was conducted within weeks of the end of the war game.

43. Author interview with Gen. Van Riper.

44. Jason Vest, "Losing the Peace," *Village Voice*, March 27, 2003.

45. Gregory Fontenot, E.J. Degen, and David Tohn, *On Point, The U.S. Army in Operation Iraqi Freedom*, CreateSpace Independent Publishing, Seattle, 2012, pp. 162–164, at: http://www.globalsecurity.org/military/library/report/2004/onpoint /ch-2.htm

46. "Even at this late stage": author interview with senior retired US Army officer.

47. Ibid.

48. Bernard E. Trainor and Michael R. Gordon, *Cobra II: The Inside Story of the Invasion and Occupation of Iraq* (New York: Pantheon, 2006), 148–49; and author interview with senior US Marine Corps officer.

49. "A unit showing up at the airfield": Dr. Donald Wright and Col. Timothy R. Reese, *On Point II* (Fort Leavenworth, KS: Combat Studies Institute Press, 2008), 453–57; "because I've been doing this": author interview with senior retired US Air Force officer.

50. "Amateurs talk about tactics": Andrew de Grandpre, "Task Force Violent," *Military Times*, March 12, 2015; author interview with senior US Army officer.

51. D. Reveron and Judith Hicks Stiehm, *Inside Defense: Understanding the U.S. Military in the 21st Century* (New York: Palgrave Macmillan, 2008), 63.

52. James Fallows, "Karmic Justice: Gen. Eric Shinseki," *The Atlantic*, December 7, 2008.

53. Paul Krugman, "March of Folly," *New York Times*, July 17, 2006; see also David Corn, "Remember When Paul Wolfowitz . . . ," *Mother Jones*, June 17, 2014.

54. Pete Ogden, "Who is Stephen Cambone?," Center for American Progress, July 20, 2004.

55. Author interview with Gen. Raad al-Hamdani; see also "Interview: Lt. Gen. Raad Al-Hamdani," *Frontline,* PBS, n.d.

56. Author interview with al-Hamdani.

57. Ibid.

Chapter Seven: "Mad Dog" Mattis and the Fight for Iraq

1. Jack Kelly, "How the Bold Run to Baghdad Paid Off," *Pittsburgh Post-Gazette*, April 13, 2003.

2. Stephen T. Hosme, *Why the Iraqi Resistance to the Coalition Invasion Was So Weak* (Washington, DC: Rand Corporation, 2007), 63–65; author interview with Gen. Raad Hamdani.

3. "Interview: General Raad Al-Hamdani," *Frontline*, PBS, see: http://www .pbs.org/wgbh/pages/frontline/shows/invasion/interviews/raad.html

4. "We crossed the Euphrates, we had about seven different crossings": "Conversations with Gen. Buford 'Buff' Blount," March 23, 2013, https://thereseapel .wordpress.com/tag/3rd-infantry-division/.

5. "the reason we're fighting today": author interview with senior US Marine Corps officer; "I was always under the impression": author interview with senior US Marine Corps officer; see also Evan Wright, "The Killer Elite," *Rolling Stone*, June 26, 2003.

6. "one of the boys": author interview with senior US Marine Corps officer; "bronchitis": author discussion with former *Washington Post* reporter who covered the events.

7. Christopher Cooper, "How a Marine Lost His Command In Race to Baghdad," *Wall Street Journal*, April 5, 2004, 16–22.

8. Author interview with Gen. Anthony Zinni (USMC, ret.); see also Cooper, "How a Marine Lost His Command In Race to Baghdad."

9. Oliver Poole, "Fanatics Forced into Hopeless Fight," *The Telegraph*, London, March 31, 2003.

10. Tim Pritchard, *Ambush Alley* (New York: Presidio Press, 2006); "what had happened in Mogadishu": author interview with senior US Marine Corps officer.

11. "McKiernan threw it in the trash": author interview with senior US Army officer.

12. "Interview with Lt. Gen. William Scott Wallace," *Frontline*, PBS, n.d., http://www.pbs.org/wgbh/pages/frontline/shows/invasion/interviews/wallace.html; see also Jean Edward Smith, *Bush* (New York: Simon and Schuster, 2016), 359.

13. "The enemy we're fighting": Jim Dwyer, "A Nation At War: In The Field . . ." *New York Times*, March 28, 2003; "Shit flows downhill": author interview with senior US Army officer; "Who the hell gave him permission": author interview with senior US Army officer.

14. Thom Shanker and John Tierney, "Top General Denounces Internal Dissent on Iraq," *New York Times*, April 2, 2003.

15. "Austin was the brains": author interview with senior US Army officer.

16. David Zucchino, "The Thunder Run," *Los Angeles Times*, December 7, 2003; see also Peter J. Boyer, "Downfall," *New Yorker*, November 20, 2006; and PBS "Frontline" interview with Lt. Gen. Wallace.

17. Author interview with senior US Marine Corps officer.

18. Kathleen T. Rehm, "Bush Appoints State Department Official to Administer Iraq," American Forces Press Service, Washington, DC, May 6, 2003.

19. "We'd sit there in a meeting": author interview with senior CIA official; "I'm going to give you a new set": Stuart W. Bowen, ed., *Hard Lessons: the Iraq Reconstruction Experience* (CreateSpace Independent Publishing, 2009), 63.

20. Author interview with James Clad, former assistant secretary of defense for Asian and Pacific security affairs. The author conducted dozens of interviews with military officers and senior Pentagon officials on the Garner-Bremer reconstruction controversy in Iraq for *Talking to Terrorists* (Basic Books, New York, 2010), my book on the Iraq War and the Anbar Awakening.

21. Author interview with senior CIA official; see also "Opposition Meeting Set Tuesday in Iraq," CNN, April 11, 2003.

22. Jane Perlez, "Iraqis Divided as Talks Open," *International Herald Tribune*, April 16, 2003.

23. Ibid.

24. "Hey, I'm calling just to tell you": Mark Perry, *Talking to Terrorists* (New York: Basic Books, 2010), 36; see also Patrick E. Tyler, "New Overseer Arrives in Iraq in U.S. Shuffle," *New York Times*, May 13, 2003; "Who the fuck is": author interview with senior CIA officer.

25. Author interview with senior Pentagon official.

26. Author interview with Col. Paul Hughes (US Army, ret.).

27. Perry, *Talking to Terrorists*, 41.

28. Author interview with Jaber Awad.

29. Author interview with Col. Hughes.

30. Author interview with senior Pentagon official.

31. Sydney J. Freedberg, "Abizaid of Arabia," *The Atlantic*, December 2003; see also David Cloud and Greg Jaffe, *The Fourth Star* (New York: Crown Publishing, 2009), 32–34.

32. "Let me repeat to you": Cloud and Jaffe, *The Fourth Star*, 114; "he just thought the whole thing was nuts": author interview with senior US Army officer.

33. Author interview with senior US Army officer.

34. "Bring it on!": Cloud and Jaffe, *The Fourth Star*, 126. "Keane reluctantly agreed": author interview with senior US Army officer.

35. Peter J. Boyer, "Downfall," *New Yorker*, November 20, 2006.

36. Ed O'Loughlin, "It's Guerilla War, New Commander Admits," *Sydney Morning Herald*, July 18, 2003.

37. Author interview with senior US Army officer.

38. "He's flailing": author interview with senior US Army officer; "There are corpses in the streets": author interview with senior US Army officer.

39. Robert Fisk, "Bremer Closes Hardline Newspaper and Iraqis Ask: Is This Democracy US Style?," *The Independent*, March 29, 2004.

40. Seymour M. Hersh, "The General's Report," *New Yorker*, June 25, 2007.

41. Peter Baker, *Days of Fire* (New York: Random House, 2013), 332–33. "Myers said he would take care of it": author interview with senior US Army officer.

42. "On Ronald Burgess": Perry, *Talking to Terrorists*, 10; "They are Nazis": Ibid., 10.

43. Author interview with Jerry Jones. Information on this aspect of the Anbar Awakening is based on author interviews with senior Pentagon officials, including Jones, Martin Hoffman, James Clad, as well as senior US Marine Corps officers including Col. John Walker, Maj. Patrick Maloy, Lt. Col. David Harlan, and Iraqi nongovernmental officials (former) Gen. Raad Hamdani and Talal al-Gaood.

44. Interview with Col. Mike Walker (USMC, ret.); author also had access to e-mail traffic from Walker to his commander, Gen. James Conway.

45. Author interview with James Clad.

46. Ibid.

47. The claim, made primarily by those inside the US Marine Corps who participated in it, is controversial inside the Army, which says the awakening took place in Tal Afar and was begun by the US Army. The claims are the constant subject of interservice rivalry.

48. George Packer, "The Lesson of Tal Afar," *New Yorker*, April 10, 2006.

49. Russell Crandall, *America's Dirty Wars: Irregular Warfare from 1776 to the War on Terror* (Cambridge: Cambridge University Press, 201), 386.

50. Author interview with senior US Army officer; see also Perry, *Talking to Terrorists*, 69.

Chapter Eight: Jack Keane's Coup

1. Paul D. Eaton, "A Top-Down Review for the Pentagon," *New York Times*, March 19, 2007.

2. "Meet The Press Transcript for April 2," *NBC News*, April 2, 2006, http://www.nbcnews.com/id/12067487/print/1/displaymode/1098/.

3. Lt. Gen. Gregory Newbold, "Why Iraq Was a Mistake," *Time*, April 9, 2006.

4. David S. Cloud and Eric Schmitt, "More Retired Generals Call for Rumsfeld's Resignation," *New York Times*, April 14, 2006.

5. Author interview with senior US Marine Corps officer.

6. "Stay in your lane, John": author interview with Col. John Coleman; "We had every opportunity": "Retired General Calls for New Leadership at the Pentagon," *PBS NewsHour*, PBS, April 13, 2006, http://www.pbs.org/newshour/bb/military-jan-june06-iraq_4-13/.

7. David S. Cloud, Eric Schmitt, and Thom Shanker, "Rumsfeld Faces Growing Revolt by Retired Generals," *New York Times*, April 13, 2006.

8. David Barstow, "Behind TV Analysts, Pentagon's Hidden Hand," *New York Times*, April 20, 2008.

9. "This is the ultimate irony": author interview with Gen. Joseph Hoar (USMC, ret.); Lt. Gen. William E. Odom, "Cut and Run? Why Not," *Los Angeles Times*, October 31, 2006.

10. Lionel Beehner, "The Baker-Hamilton Commission," Council on Foreign Relations, December 6, 2006, http://www.cfr.org/iraq/baker-hamilton-commission-aka-iraq-study-group/p12010.

11. "He worked his staff to death": author interview with senior US Army officer.

12. "recommendations for the way ahead": author interview with senior US Army officer.

13. "goat rope": Mark Perry, *Talking to Terrorists* (New York: Basic Books, 2010), 90.

14. Author interview with senior US Army officer.

15. Author interview with senior Pentagon official.

16. Author interview with former US senator Charles "Chuck" Robb. My discussion with Robb came during an overseas trip on which we were part of a larger delegation that included several former members of the ISG.

17. Bing West, "Streetwise," *The Atlantic*, January 1, 2007.

18. "Jesus Christ, Bill, we're not winning": author interview with senior US Marine Corps officer; "Without being overly dramatic": Michael R. Gordon, *The Endgame: The Inside Story of the Struggle for Iraq* (New York: Pantheon, 2012), 276.

19. Ibid., 281.

20. Bob Woodward, *The War Within: A Secret White House History 2006–2008* (New York: Simon and Schuster, 2008), 130.

21. Author interview with senior US Army officer; see also Steve Coll, "The General's Dilemma," *New Yorker*, September 8, 2008; and "Losing Iraq," *Frontline*, PBS, n.d., http://www.pbs.org/wgbh/frontline/film/losing-iraq/transcript/.

22. Author interview with Gen. Hoar.

23. Author interview with senior Joint Staff officer.

24. Author interview with Col. Peter R. Mansoor (US Army, ret.).

25. Peter R. Mansoor, *Surge* (Hartford, CT: Yale University Press, 2013), 41–45.

26. Author interview with senior Pentagon official.

27. Author interview with Mansoor.

28. Author interview with senior US Air Force officer.

29. Gordon, *Endgame*, 286.

30. Author interview with Jerry Jones.

31. Author interview with senior Pentagon official.

32. "General and Surge Architect Discusses War," NPR, September 18, 2007, http://www.npr.org/templates/transcript/transcript.php?storyId=14501222; see also Kimberly Kagan, *The Surge* (New York: Encounter Books, 2009), 27–29.

33. Woodward, *The War Within*, 280–82; see also Peter Feaver, "The Right to Be Right," *International Security* 35, no. 4 (2011).

34. "Since when does AEI": author interview with senior US Army officer.

35. Author interview with senior Joint Staff officer.

36. "I'm having a hard time getting a hearing": author interview with senior US Army officer.

37. Woodward, *The War Within*, 288–90. In an interview with the author, a senior army aide to Gen. Schoomaker adds: "There are different views of whether Gen. Schoomaker was expressing his dissatisfaction that Bush was president. My view is that it was clear that he was. It was the most uncomfortable meeting in the Pentagon that I've ever witnessed."

38. Author interview with Dr. Peter D. Feaver.

39. Ibid.

40. Ibid.

41. "lame duck": ibid.

42. Author interview with senior Joint Staff officer.

43. Mark Perry, "How Iraq's Army Could Defeat ISIS in Mosul," *Politico Magazine*, December 15, 2016.

44. Mark Thompson, "Beneath Glowing Public Image, Petraeus Had His Critics," *Time*, November 13, 2012.

45. "How many miles did Napoleon run": author interview with senior US Army officer.

46. Author interview with senior US Army officer.

47. "Can This Man Save Iraq?" *Newsweek*, June 27, 2004, http://www.prnews wire.com/news-releases/newsweek-cover-can-this-man-save-iraq-75166612.html.

48. Fred Kaplan, *The Insurgents* (New York: Simon and Schuster, 2013), 137–59.

49. Author interview with Dr. Feaver.

50. Mansoor, *Surge*, 108–12.

51. "results coming slowly": author interview with Mansoor; see also "Operation Phantom Thunder," Institute for the Study of War, June 15, 2007, http://www.understandingwar.org/operation/operation-phantom-thunder.

52. "General Betray Us": The Fact Checker, "General Betray Us?" *Washington Post*, September 20, 2007; "our assessments underscore": Report to the US House of Representatives: General David Petraeus," US State Department, Washington, DC, September 10, 2007, https://2001-2009.state.gov/p/nea/rls/rm/2007/91966.htm.

53. "Because he outranks me.": Mansoor, *Surge*, 102–5; author interview with senior US Army officer. See also Kaplan, *The Insurgents*, 263–64.

54. Author interview with Mansoor.

55. "an overall decline": DoD News Briefing with Secretary Gates from the Pentagon, Presenter: Secretary of Defense Robert M. Gates, June 5, 2008; "This won't take long": author interview with senior Pentagon official; see also Julian E. Barnes and Peter Spiegel, "Air Force's Top Leaders Are Ousted," *Los Angeles Times*, June 6, 2008.

56. Amanda Terkel, "Gates Forced Pace to Resign to Avoid Congressional Oversight of Iraq War," *ThinkProgress*, June 8, 2007, https://thinkprogress.org/gates-forced-pace-to-resign-to-avoid-congressional-oversight-of-iraq-war-fe62bfb833bd.

Chapter Nine: Mike Mullen: The Navy's George Marshall

1. Fred W. Baker III, "Success in Iraq, Afghanistan Critical to Military Way Ahead: Mullen," Armed Forces Press Service, December 17, 2007, http://archive.defense.gov/news/newsarticle.aspx?id=48436.

2. Author interview with senior Joint Staff officer.

3. "Gates Joint Chiefs Appointment a Neighborly Gesture," *Washington Examiner*, July 16, 2007.

4. Steve Proffitt, "Joint Chiefs Nominee Had Hollywood Upbringing," NPR, July 30, 2007, http://www.npr.org/templates/story/story.php?storyId=12350070.

5. "There's no group that's quicker": Ellen Galinsky, "Admiral Michael Mullen—A Leadership Style We Can Believe In," *Huffington Post*, May 25, 2011; "George Marshall": author interview with Capt. John Kirby, US Navy. Kirby thereafter went on to become the high-profile spokesperson at the US State Department.

6. "Are the ground forces broken?": "First Public Address by Mike Mullen," Center for a New American Security, Washington, DC, October 25, 2007, at https://www.youtube.com/watch?v=ZmHUDxottA4; "No more adventures": author interview with senior US Army officer.

7. Joshua Partlow, "Iran's Elite Force Is Said to Use Hezbollah as 'Proxy' in Iraq," *Washington Post*, July 3, 2007.

8. Peter Baker, *Days of Fire* (New York: Random House, 2013), 572.

9. Alex Spillius, "George Bush Warns Putin over World War III," *The Telegraph*, October 18, 2007.

10. Author interview with senior US Marine Corps officer.

11. The author was present during this exchange at an NDU seminar.

12. "Nuclear Intelligence Estimate, Iran–Nuclear Intentions and Capability," Council on Foreign Relations, Washington, DC, November 2007, http://www.cfr.org /iran/national-intelligence-estimate-iran-nuclear-intentions-capabilities/p14937.

13. Robert Gates, *Duty* (New York: Knopf, 2014), 183–84.

14. Spencer Ackerman, "New CENTCOM Chief: Stop All This War Talk," *Talking Points Memo*, February 14, 2007.

15. John Barry, "The Cost of Fallon's Candor," *Newsweek*, March 11, 2008.

16. Ibid.

17. "What is it with these admirals?": Gates, *Duty*, 187.

18. Author interview with senior US Marine Corps officer.

19. Thomas P. M. Barnett, "The Man Between War and Peace," *Esquire*, June 23, 2010.

20. Gates, *Duty*, 187–88.

21. Brandon Friedman, "Election Data: Military Communities Shift Democratic in 2008," *Huffington Post*, December 14, 2008.

22. "Obama's Remarks on Afghanistan and Iraq," *New York Times*, July 15, 2008.

23. Author interview with senior Pentagon official.

24. Bob Woodward, *Obama's Wars* (New York: Simon and Schuster, 2011), 105–7.

25. "The future of Afghanistan": "Transcript: Obama Announces New Afghanistan, Pakistan Strategy," *Washington Post*, March 27, 2009; "to integrate our civilian and military efforts": Author interview with senior CIA official.

26. "The two couldn't be in the same room": author interview with senior US Army officer.

27. Author interview with senior US diplomat.

28. "David Petraeus would be number two": author interview with senior US Army officer.

29. Author interview with senior US Army officer.

30. "There are those who": Rajiv Chandrasekaran, "Pentagon Worries Led to Command Change," *Washington Post*, August 17, 2009; "What's this?": author interview with senior US Army officer.

31. Author interview with senior US diplomat.

32. Michael Yon, "New Boss for Afghan Fight," *Michael Yon Online Magazine*, May 12, 2009, https://www.michaelyon-online.com/new-boss-for-afghan-fight .htm.

33. Mark Perry, "The Day the General Made a Misstep," *Asia Times*, December 10, 2009.

34. "We were going around in circles": Mark Perry, "A Salvo at the White House," *Asia Times*, January 23, 2008.

35. Author interview with senior US diplomat.

36. Gates, *Duty*, 351–52.

37. "Even in Iraq": David Ignatius, "Roll the Dice on Afghanistan," *Washington Post*, September 2, 2009; "The Ignatius piece": author interview with aide to Gen. David Petraeus.

38. Michael Gerson, "U.S. Has Reasons to Hope for Afghanistan," *Washington Post*, September 4, 2009; "This was the Keane and Kagan crowd": author interview with senior White House official.

39. C. Christine Fair, "False Choices in Afghanistan," *Foreign Policy*, January 11, 2011; see also Ross Douthat, "One Way Out," *New York Times*, June 27, 2010.

40. Woodward, *Obama's Wars*, 167.

41. Author interview with senior Joint Staff officer.

42. Bob Woodward, "McChrystal: More Forces or Mission Failure," *Washington Post*, September 21, 2009; "they may crush me": Woodward, *Obama's Wars*, 194; see also Michael Hastings, *The Operators* (New York: Blue Rider Press, 2012), 91–92.

43. "act as a kind of translator": author interview with senior Joint Staff officer; "We would never do that": Woodward, *Obama's Wars*, 197.

44. Joe Klein, "Admiral Mike Mullen," *Time*, April 29, 2010.

45. Elizabeth Bumiller, "Top Defense Officials Seek to End 'Don't Ask, Don't Tell,'" *New York Times*, February 2, 2010.

46. "This is going to happen": author interview with senior Joint Staff officer.

47. Author interview with Harlan Ullman.

48. George E. Gordon Jr., "Obama Reveals New Details on Bin Laden Raid," *The Atlantic*, May 2, 2012.

49. Srdja Trifkovic, "Obama's Svengali," *Chronicles*, April 11, 2016, https://www.chroniclesmagazine.org/obamas-svengali/.

50. Charles R. Kubic, "Hillary's Huge Libya Disaster," *The National Interest*, June 15, 2016.

51. Author interview with senior Joint Staff officer; "the three harpies": Andrew Bacevich, "Obama Still Hammering Away," *TomDispatch*, April 12, 2011.

52. Rick Moran, "Tests Ahead for New Joint Chiefs of Staff Chair," *Frontpage Magazine*, June 1, 2011. See also Mark Perry, "Obama's Perfect Chairman," *Politico Magazine*, May 7, 2015; and Craig Whitlock, "Gen. Cartwright, Poised to Lead Joint Chiefs, Had His Shot Derailed by Critics," *Washington Post*, May 28, 2011.

53. Woodward, *Obama's Wars*, 259; author interview with senior US Army officer.

54. "Don't get caught up in nation building": author interview with senior US Marine Corps officer; "I am concerned": Lloyd Gardner, *Killing Machine: The American Presidency in the Age of Drone Warfare* (New York: New Press, 2013), 58.

55. Author interview with senior State Department official: see also Perry, "The Day the General Made a Misstep," *Asia Times*, December 10, 2009.

56. "Obama Afghanistan strategy: More Troops in Quickly, Drawdown in 2011," CNN, December 1, 2009.

57. Author interview with senior US Marine Corps officer.

58. Author interview with senior US Army officer; see also Mark Perry, "The Petraeus Briefing," *Foreign Policy*, March 14, 2010.

59. "Does it help if folks": e-mail communication between David Petraeus and Max Boot, in the possession of the author; "I'm a big boy": author interview with senior US Army officer.

60. Michael Hastings, "The Runaway General," *Rolling Stone*, June 22, 2010.

61. Author interview with senior CIA officer.

62. "government in a box": Noah Shachtman, "Marjah's 'Government in a Box' Flops as McChrystal Fumes," *Wired*, May 25, 2010.

63. Dexter Filkins, "Marja Offensive Is a New Model War," *New York Times*, June 22, 2010.

64. Author interview with senior US Army officer.

65. Mark Landler, "The Afghan War and the Evolution of Obama," *New York Times*, January 1, 2017.

66. Tom Bowman, "The Name Game: Who Will Be the Next Chairman of the Joint Chiefs of Staff?" NPR, May 17, 2011.

67. Author interview with senior US Army officer.

Chapter Ten: The Rise of Martin Dempsey

1. Author interview with senior US Marine Corps officer. See also Bob Woodward, *Obama's Wars* (New York: Simon and Schuster, 2011), 335–37.

2. Author interview with senior US Army officer.

3. Craig Whitlock, "Obama Taps Army General to Lead Joint Chiefs, Top Military Leaders Are Reshuffled," *Washington Post*, May 31, 2011.

4. "Powell problem": author interview with senior US Army officer.

5. Author interview with senior US Marine Corps officer.

6. "Gen. Dempsey Sings Anthem at Ballpark," *NBC News*, July 4, 2013, http://www.nbcnews.com/video/nightly-news/52396655#52396655.

7. Author interview with senior US Marine Corps officer.

8. Lt. Col. Paul Yingling, "A Failure of Generalship," *Armed Forces Journal*, May 1, 2007.

9. Author interview with Col. Gian Gentile (US Army, ret.); see also Gian Gentile, "Beneficial War: The Conceit of American Counterinsurgency," *Small Wars Journal*, December 25, 2011.

10. "coindinista cult": Colonel Gian Gentile, *Wrong Turn: America's Deadly Embrace of Counterinsurgency* (New York: The New Press, 2013), 139–40; "the sprawling Baghdad district": author interview with Col. David Johnson, (US Army, ret.).

11. Author interview with senior US Army officer.

12. Thomas E. Ricks, *The Gamble: General Petraeus and the American Military Adventure in Iraq* (New York: The Penguin Press, 2009), 303.

13. Author interview with Col. David Johnson (US Army, ret.); see also Col. David Johnson, *The 2008 Battle of Sadr City* (Washington, DC: Rand Corporation, 2013).

14. Thomas Ricks, "Cage Match in a Cornfield," *Foreign Policy*, May 30, 2013; see also "Cage Match in a Cornfield: G. Gentile Wrestles J. Nagl on Counterinsurgency," Grinnell College, September 30, 2013, http://www.grinnell.edu/news/external/cage-match-cornfield-g-gentile-wrestles-j-nagl-counterinsurgency.

15. "defense strategic guidance": Catherine Dale and Pat Towell, "In Brief: Assessing the January 2012 Defense Strategic Guidance," Homeland Security Digital Library, September 13, 2013, https://www.hsdl.org/?abstract&did=743281; "Asia

pivot": Secretary of State Hillary Clinton, "America's Pacific Century," *Foreign Policy*, October 11, 2011.

16. Mark Perry, "The Pentagon's Fight over Fighting China," *Politico Magazine*, July/August 2015.

17. "Sustaining US Global Leadership, Priorities for 21st Century Defense," Council on Foreign Relations, Washington, DC, January 5, 2012, http://www.cfr.org /defense-strategy/sustaining-us-global-leadership-priorities-21st-century-defense /p26976.

18. Perry, "Pentagon's Fight over Fighting China."

19. Ibid.

20. Gen. David G. Perkins, "Multi-Domain Battle," Army Capabilities Integration Center, Association of the United States Army, Washington, DC, November 14, 2016.

21. "sent Odierno into a tizzy": author interview with senior US Marine Corps officer.

22. "There was always tension": author interview with senior US Army officer; "The memorandum was classified": Perry, "Pentagon's Fight over Fighting China."

23. "He stiffed us": author interview with senior US Air Force officer. See also Mark Thompson, "A New Leader for a New Air Force," *Time*, June 9, 2008.

24. Andrew F. Krepinevich, "Why AirSea Battle?," Center for Strategic and Budgetary Analysis, February 19, 2010.

25. "The Army has no business": author interview with Lt. Gen. David Deptula (USAF, ret.).

26. "I confess": Sydney J. Freedberg Jr. "Army Shows Cheek . . . ," *Defense One*, October 11, 2013; "This is a real strategy": Perry, "Pentagon's Fight over Fighting China."

27. Author interview with senior US Army officer.

28. Dr. Steven Metz, "Strategic Landpower Task Force Research Report," Strategic Studies Institute, October 3, 2013; see: http://ssi.armywarcollege.edu/index .cfm/articles//STRATEGIC-LANDPOWER-TASK-FORCE/2013/10/3 and author interview with Dr. Steven Metz.

29. Rania Abouzeid, "Bouazizi: The Man Who Set Himself and Tunisia on Fire," *Time*, January 21, 2011.

30. Michael Boyle, "Obama: Leading from Behind on Libya," *The Guardian*, August 27, 2011.

31. Author interview with senior US Army officer.

32. R. D. Hooker Jr. and Joseph J. Collins, "From the Chairman: An Interview with Martin E. Dempsey," *Joint Forces Quarterly*, July 2, 2015.

33. Author interview with senior Joint Staff officer.

34. "I am here to give military advice": author interview with senior US Army officer; "Samantha, enough": Jeffrey Goldberg, "The Obama Doctrine," *The Atlantic*, April 2016.

35. "President Obama Defends His Foreign-Policy Record . . . " Associated Press, September 23, 2012.

36. Amy Davidson, "Shirtless Agent in Bottomless Scandal," *New Yorker*, November 16, 2012.

37. "There were officers who": author interview with senior US Army officer; "Ray lived for the day": author interview with senior US Marine Corps officer.

38. "Dempsey was simply not an influential player": author interview with senior Joint Staff officer.

39. Thom Shanker and Jeremy W. Peters, "McCain to Block New Term for Joint Chiefs Chairman," *New York Times*, July 18, 2013.

40. "Chuck Hagel Defends Record at Confirmation Hearing," *PBS NewsHour*, PBS, January 30, 2013, https://www.pbs.org/newshour/amp/bb/chuck -hagel-defends-record-at-confirmation-hearing.

41. Mark Perry, "General Dempsey to the Rescue," *Politico Magazine*, October 23, 2014.

42. "almost unbalanced": author interview with senior Joint Staff officer.

43. Barack Obama, "Statement by the President on Syria," The White House, Washington, DC, August 31, 2013, https://obamawhitehouse.archives.gov/the-press -office/2013/08/31/statement-president-syria.

44. "ready to pull the trigger": Patrice Taddonio, "The President Blinked," *Frontline*, PBS, May 25, 2015.

45. "eyeball to eyeball": author interview with senior Joint Staff officer.

46. Eli Lake, "As Obama Preaches Patience, Mattis Prepares for War with Iran," *Daily Beast*, May 21, 2012.

47. "You're not in the chain of command": author interview with senior US Marine Corps officer; see also Tom Ricks, "The Obama Administration's Inexplicable Mishandling of Marine Gen. James Mattis," *Foreign Policy*, January 18, 2013.

48. "By pushing Mattis overboard": Mackubin Thomas Owens, "America's Kinder, Gentler Department of Defense," *Wall Street Journal*, February 22, 2013; "If anyone deserved": author interview with senior US Marine Corps officer.

49. Perry, "General Dempsey to the Rescue."

50. Author interview with US businessman; author interview with senior Anbar Province government official; see also Mark Perry, "Fighting Saddam All Over Again," *Politico Magazine*, April 28, 2015.

51. Mark Perry, "Is Gen. John Allen in over His Head?" *Foreign Policy*, October 30, 2014.

52. "The Parting Glass performed at General E. Dempsey's Retirement Ceremony 2015," September 25, 2015, at https://www.youtube.com/watch?v=sgJ1Ma4b _Q0.

53. Author interview with Gen. McPeak.

54. Mark Perry, "Obama's Perfect Chairman," *Politico Magazine*, May 7, 2015.

Epilogue: Original Sin

1. Discussion with Gen. Charles Horner (USAF, ret.).

2. Author interview with Lt. Gen. David Deptula (USAF, ret.).

3. Author interview with Col. David Johnson (US Army, ret.).

4. "Why are we stopping?": author interview with Col. Douglas Macgregor (US Army, ret.).

5. "We set the goal": Mark Perry, "Why Americans Don't Win Wars Anymore," *Politico Magazine*, February 28, 2017.

6. Author interview with senior US Marine Corps officer.

7. Gen. Martin Dempsey, letter to the editor, "Military Leaders Do Not Belong at Political Conventions," *Washington Post*, August 1, 2016.

8. "has about had it": Andrew Tilghman, "After 15 Years of War, America's Military Has About Had It with 'Nation Building,'" *Military Times*, September 22, 2016.

9. Mark Perry, "James Mattis' 33-Year Grudge Against Iran," *Politico Magazine*, December 4, 2016.

10. Perry, "Why Americans Don't Win Wars Anymore."

Index

MARK PERRY IS a military and foreign affairs analyst whose articles have appeared in *The Nation*, *Foreign Policy*, *Washington Post*, and *Politico Magazine*. Perry lives in Arlington, Virginia.